D0849542

# STRUCTURED LEARNING THERAPY

# STRUCTURED LEARNING THERAPY

## THERAPY

## Toward a Psychotherapy for the Poor

*ARNOLD P. GOLDSTEIN*

*Department of Psychology*
*Syracuse University*
*Syracuse, New York*

**ACADEMIC PRESS**     1973
New York   San Francisco   London

*A Subsidiary of Harcourt Brace Jovanovich, Publishers*

ACADEMIC PRESS, INC.
111 Fifth Avenue, New York, New York 10003

*United Kingdom Edition published by*
ACADEMIC PRESS, INC. (LONDON) LTD.
24/28 Oval Road, London NW1

Library of Congress Cataloging in Publication Data

Goldstein, Arnold P
    Structured learning therapy.

    Bibliography: p.
    1.   Psychotherapy.    2.   Poverty–Psychological
aspects.    3.   Schizophrenia.   I.   Title.
[DNLM:   1.  Behavior therapy.   2.   Poverty.
3.   Psychotherapy. WM420 G624s 1973]
RC454.4.G64         616.8′914         72-12197
ISBN 0−12−288750−6

*To My Own Important Models . . .*

*Benjamin Balinsky*

*William U. Snyder*

*Jerome D. Frank*

# CONTENTS

vii

## Part 2 Structured Learning Therapy

## Part 3 Paraprofessional Training

## Part 4  **Conclusion**

### *Chapter* 9  FUTURE DIRECTIONS

### Appendix  **Modeling Scripts**

#### PATIENT SKILL-ENHANCEMENT INVESTIGATIONS

PARAPROFESSIONAL SKILL-ENHANCEMENT INVESTIGATIONS

# PREFACE

Perhaps the most significant failure in contemporary psychotherapy has been the marked absence of treatment approaches of demonstrated or even apparent usefulness for lower- and working-class patients. The wide array of attempts to employ traditional outpatient psychotherapies with such patients has yielded an overwhelmingly dismal pattern of treatment outcomes. In fact, "outcome" may even be somewhat of a misnomer in this context, since in a very significant proportion of such treatment attempts psychotherapy never really gets started in any meaningful sense. The fact that inpatients from these social class levels continue to accumulate, i.e., to become an ever greater proportion of the chronic mental hospital population—especially during a decade when the rate of mental hospital discharges has increased significantly—stands as perhaps even grimmer testimony to the gross inadequacy of contemporary psychotherapies for such patients. The data and dilemmas relevant to this state of affairs will be examined in detail in Chapter 1.

Other investigators exploring this domain have often pointed to several major disparities between the typically middle-class psychotherapist and the lower- or working-class patient as a means of partially explaining the brief duration, poor therapeutic relationship, negative therapeutic outcome, or chronicity common to such patients. Yet the sources of these disparities provide more than just explanation for why current procedures so frequently fail. I propose that they also provide the raw material for building new and more appropriate treatment techniques—social class-relevant techniques. Concretely, I refer here to incongruent expectations regarding psychotherapy; differing language "codes"; contrasting life styles; personality differences in such realms as authoritarianism, dependency, and conformity; and such diverse areas of difference as time perspective, the nature of gratification, educational attainment and the importance attached thereto, and so forth. Stated otherwise, just as I would propose that traditional, verbal, insight-oriented psychotherapy is fully congruent with most major dimensions of middle-class life style and personality, dimensions of lower- and working-class status such as those men-

tioned above simultaneously explain the inappropriateness of such traditional psychotherapy and suggest the paths along which to search for
treatment procedures which form an optimal "fit" for *these* patients. Thus,
we will explore several of these dimensions rather fully in this book,
seeking as we do to comprehend in depth the meaning and quality of
lower- and working class life, and building, along with such comprehension,
the beginnings of what appears to be a more optimal, targeted or lower-
class-relevant psychotherapy.

Research on child rearing, parental behavior, and personality development as it relates to social class is examined in Chapter 2. In my view,
the "basic training" which later helps determine the goodness of fit for
any subsequent psychotherapy which may be necessary takes place in
these areas. Chapter 3 draws upon research on language development
and usage for similar purposes of both explanation and therapy construction. The final chapter in Part 1, Psychopathology and Sociopathology, is
given considerable emphasis. It is all too characteristic of modern psychotherapy that diagnosis, whether elaborately or simply determined,
is irrelevant to the treatment instituted. Building on the previous chapters,
this chapter seeks to provide a comprehensive picture of the manifold
interaction of social class and psychopathology, particularly schizophrenia.
Much of its substance combines with the preceding materials in Part 1
to yield an explicit rationale for the purpose of beginning to construct
what may be an optimal treatment approach for lower- or working-class
patients.

Research examining the therapeutic usefulness of what I thus propose
as a potentially optimal treatment for the lower- or working-class patient
is presented in Part 2. This set of treatment procedures, which we have
termed *Structured Learning Therapy*, consists primarily of a combination
of modeling, role playing, and social reinforcement. Chapter 5, which provides the necessary background, presents research conducted by other
investigators, examining the nature and impact of these procedures in
clinical contexts involving primarily middle-class patients. Chapters 6 and
7 are a presentation of the research program, providing initial tests of the
efficiency of Structured Learning Therapy and its components with lower-
and working-class inpatients and outpatients. Here, as well as in the
chapter that follows, I have also sought to describe the initial attempt to
implement transfer training procedures as vehicles for maximizing the likelihood of transfer to real-life contexts of skills learned via structured learning procedures.

The encouraging results of these patient research programs led to the
development and execution of a companion research series, one examining

the usefulness of the modeling–role-playing–social reinforcement combination for the training of working-class change agents. The increasing use of nurses, attendants, housewives, college students, prison guards, ministers, and related persons to fill paraprofessional therapist roles has led to increased concern with their preparation and training. Research oriented toward examining the efficacy of our procedures for these training purposes is presented in Part 3 (Chapter 8). Part 4 (Chapter 9) seeks to summarize this book's major themes and findings, and point out directions which may aid the further growth and development of lower-class-linked psychotherapies in general, and Structured Learning Therapy in particular.

# ACKNOWLEDGMENTS

The research reported in this book was supported in part by PHS Grant No. MH 16426 from the National Institute of Mental Health and by the Netherlands Organization for the Advancement of Pure Research.

The research programs presented reflect the sustained efforts of many persons. Martin Gutride, Haverford State Hospital, Haverford, Pennsylvania, and Arnold Goodhart of the Free University, Amsterdam, Holland have been particularly important collaborators. Their contributions to both the design and execution of a number of our investigations are especially appreciated.

An active and stimulating group of graduate students developed around our research program. Beyond their individual investigations, they brought with them the questions and concerns which provided much of the steam to keep our series of studies moving and, hopefully, improving in quality as we proceeded. Special thanks, therefore, are offered to Dorothy Ben, William Friedenberg, Rosanne Godwin, Dorothea Lack, Bernard Liberman, Martha Perry, Karen Sutton, and William Walsh.

Many institutional and clinic doors were opened for us in our several searches for appropriate research samples. After stepping through these doors, we not only found our samples but, much more often than not, a source of wise counsel and specific aid regarding a wide array of research-relevant and treatment-relevant concerns. We most certainly wish to express our sincere gratitude to these several persons—Bernard Rashap, Utica State Hospital, Utica, New York; Mary Helmle and Mary Sklorolski, Marcy State Hospital, Marcy, New York; Henk Wijngaarden, Free University, Amsterdam, Holland; Alexander Paslofky, Wm. Arntz Hoeve, Den Dolder, Holland; L. H. D. Van der Muelen and A. M. de Waard, Provincial Ziekenhius, Santpoort, Holland; and F. C. Stam, J. U. Postma and A. P. Cassee of the Valarius Klinick, Amsterdam, Holland.

Harriet Aronson, Len Krasner, Bernard Liberman, Murray Miron, Lee Sechrest, and Len Ullmann have been kind enough to read drafts of parts or all of this book, and respond with incisive comments, questions, and reactions for which I heartily thank them.

Corrine Intaglietta, Vera Richardson, and Mary Schaefer have done the real work, typing manuscript drafts 1 through $n$, and always removing more errors than they added. Thank you ladies.

Finally, my wife, Lenore, and my daughters, Susan and Cindy, have made a major contribution to this book by offering moral support, concrete assistance, and keeping the dog out of the den.

## Quotation Credits

The author gratefully acknowledges permission to reprint excerpts from the following works:

Pages 6 and 7      McMahon, J. T. The working class psychiatric patient: A clinical view. In F. Riessman, J. Cohen, & A. Pearls (Eds.), *Mental health of the poor.* New York: The Free Press. Pp. 283–302. © 1964 by The Free Press.

Page 10            Lee, S. D. & Temerlin, M. K. Social class, diagnosis and prognosis for psychotherapy. *Psychotherapy: Theory, Research, and Practice,* 1970, **7**, 181–185.

Page 19            Riessman, F. & Goldfarb, J. Role playing and the poor. In F. Riessman, J. Cohen, & A. Pearl (Eds.), *Mental health of the poor.* New York: The Free Press, 1964. Pp. 336–347. © 1964 by The Free Press.

Pages 20 and 21    Shaffer, J. B. Paradigmatic therapy and the low income patient. In M. C. Nelson, B. Nelson, M. H. Sherman, & H. S. Strean (Eds.), *Roles and paradigms in therapy.* New York: Grune & Stratton, 1967. Pp. 259–263.

Pages 25 and 26    Hoehn-Saric, R., Frank, J. D., Imber, S. D., Nash, E. H., Stone, A. R., & Battle, C. C. Systematic Preparation of patients for psychotherapy. I. Effects on therapy behavior and outcome. *Journal of Psychiatric Research,* 1964, **2**, 267–281.

Pages 28 and 29    Magaro, P. A. A prescriptive treatment model based upon social class and premorbid adjustment. *Psychotherapy: Theory, Research, and Practice,* 1969, **6**, 57–70.

Page 30            Kohn, M. L. Social class and parent–child relationships: An interpretation *American Journal of Sociology,* 1963, **68**, 471–480. © 1963 by the University of Chicago Press.

Page 30            Davis, S. & Havighurst, R. J. Social class and color differences in child rearing. In C. Kluckholn, H. A. Murray, & D. M. Schneider (Eds.), *Personality in nature, society and culture.* New York: Knopf, 1954. Pp. 308–320. Reprinted from *American Sociological Review,* 1946, **2,** 699.

Page 33            Kohn, M. L. Social class and parental values. *American Journal of Sociology,* 1959, **44,** 337–350. © 1959 by the University of Chicago Press.

Page 34            Kohn, M. L. Social class and the exercise of parental authority. *American Sociological Review,* 1959, **24,** 352–366.

Page 36            Kohn, M. L. *Class and conformity.* Homewood, Ill.: Dorsey Press, 1969.

Page 37            Shaffer, J. B. Paradigmatic therapy and the low income patient. In M. C. Nelson, B. Nelson, M. H. Sherman, & H. S. Strean (Eds.), *Roles and paradigms in therapy.* New York: Grune & Stratton, 1967. Pp. 259–263.

Pages 41–42        Bernstein, B. Social structure, language and learning. *Educational Research,* 1961, **3,** 163–176.

Pages 44 and 45    Schatzman, L. & Strauss, A. Social class and modes of communication. *American Journal of Sociology,* 1955, **60,** 329–338. © 1955 by the University of Chicago Press.

Page 48            Bernstein, B. Social class, speech systems, and psychotherapy. *British Journal of Sociology,* 1964, **15,** 54–64.

Page 49            Whorf, B. L. Science and linguistics. In J. B. Carroll (Ed.), *Language, thought, and the school.* Cambridge, Mass.: M. I. T. Press, 1956. Pp. 207–219.

Page 67            Kohn, M. L. *Class and conformity.* Homewood, Ill.: Dorsey Press, 1969.

Page 67–68         Roman, P. M. & Trice, H. M. *Schizophrenia and the poor.* Ithaca, N. Y.: Cornell Univ. Press, 1967.

Pages 82–83        Bandura, A., Blanchard, E. B., & Ritter, B. The relative efficacy of desensitization and modeling approaches for inducing behavioral, affective, and attitudinal changes. *Journal of personality and social psychology,* 1969, **13,** 173–199.

Pages 93–94        Lazarus, A. A. Behavior rehearsal vs. non-directive
                   therapy vs. advice in effecting behavior change. *Be-
                   havior Research and Therapy*, 1966, 4, 209–212.

Page 98            Sarason, I. G. & Ganzer, V. J. Social influence tech-
                   niques in clinical and community psychology. In
                   C. D. Spielberger (Ed.), *Current topics in clinical
                   and community psychology*, vol. 1. New York: Aca-
                   demic Press, 1969. Pp. 1–66.

*Part 1*

**SOCIAL CLASS**

# Chapter 1

## PSYCHOTHERAPY: INCOME AND OUTCOME

The implications of a patient's social class for his psychotherapeutic treatment destiny are numerous, pervasive, and enduring. If the patient is lower class, all such implications are decidedly and uniformly negative.* In comparison with patients at higher social class levels, the lower-class patient or patient-candidate seeking psychotherapeutic assistance in an outpatient setting is significantly more likely to: (1) be found unacceptable for treatment, (2) spend considerable time on the clinic's waiting list, (3) drop out (or be dropped out) after initial screening, (4) receive a socially less desirable formal diagnosis, (5) be assigned to the least experienced staff members, (6) hold prognostic and role expectations incongruent with those held by his therapist, (7) form a poor-quality relationship with his psychotherapist, (8) terminate or be terminated earlier, and (9) improve significantly less from either his own or his therapist's perspective.

Analogous dimensions relevant to mental hospital settings yield an even grimmer pattern for the lower-class inpatient. Let us concretize and elaborate several of these phenomena more fully.

---

* Throughout this book we will focus primarily upon the lower-class patient, but essentially take the position supported by our research (see Chapters 6–8), that our recommendations for a more optimal, class-linked psychotherapy are appropriate for *both* lower- and working-class patients. This is not to say that there are not major differences between lower- and working-class persons. While such differences obviously do exist, we would propose that they are not in the main relevant to the overriding issue of the effectiveness of the therapeutic procedures we have investigated.

**3**

## Psychotherapy and the Middle-Class Ethic

In an important and provocative article written in 1938, Davis called attention to what he viewed as the underlying cultural and philosophical basis for the mental hygiene movement.

> . . . mental hygiene, being a social movement and a source of advice concerning personal conduct, has inevitably taken over the Protestant ethic inherent in our society, not simply as the basis for conscious preachment but also as the unconscious system of premises upon which its "scientific" analysis and its conception of mental health itself are based [p. 55].

Noting that those persons prominently associated with this movement were almost all middle-class professionals whose own achievement followed from sustained effort and delay of gratification, Davis further characterized the Protestant ethic as consisting of belief in vertical mobility, competition, ambition, self-discipline, "wholesome" fun, prudence, rationality, and foresight. This ethic or world view essentially constitutes "middle classness" and Davis observed, underlies the most widely held conceptions of mental hygiene, mental health, and mental disorder. These observations are far more than historically interesting speculations. As research evidence provided by Gursslin, Hunt, and Roach (1960) indicates, it is a contemporary finding of demonstrated reliability. These investigators gathered and content-analyzed 27 widely disseminated mental health pamphlets, from such sources as the National Association for Mental Health, the New York State Department of Mental Hygiene, and several large mental health clinics. Approximately 60% of the text of these pamphlets promoted essentially middle-class themes—the value of work, control of emotions, planning ahead, problem solving, striving, adjustment, and community participation. Gursslin *et al.* comment:

> The basic conclusion to be drawn from a sizable portion of the content under investigation is that the middle-class prototype and the mentally healthy prototype are in many respects equivalent. . . . Like Davis, we must also conclude that the mental health movement is unwittingly propagating a middle-class ethic under the guise of science. If anything, this conclusion has even greater import today than it had 20 years ago. . . . To the extent that the mental health movement is successful in advancing this mental health prototype as a desirable model to emulate, it may have a considerable personally disorganizing effect upon those lower-class persons who accept the mental health prototype. For example, the "message" sets forth a way of life which is most unrealistic for lower-class people, who must make some adjustment to the conditions and culture of the lower-class [p. 410].

Cole, Branch, and Allison (1962) and Schermerhorn (1956) have offered similar observations, as has Schneiderman (1965), who also comments upon the prejudicial effects of conceptualizing and conducting the diagnostic and therapeutic endeavor with lower-class patients in a manner consistent with the middle-class ethic. Furthermore, he describes a "lower-class ethic," one from which more congruent diagnostic and therapeutic procedures might grow. This ethic includes an inclination to subject oneself to, or live harmoniously with, what is viewed as given or natural in life, in contrast to the middle-class value of mastery over the physical and social environment; an inclination toward relatively free expressiveness, spontaneity, and a nondevelopmental conception of activity, in comparison to the "doing," accomplishing, go-getting, middle-class value; and a tendency toward greater orientation to the present rather than the past or future, in contrast to the typical middle-class concern with future planning. In accord with Gursslin et al. (1960) and Schermerhorn (1956), Scheiderman (1965) stresses the appropriateness and adaptiveness of this ethic and its consequent life style for the realities of functioning adequately in the lower-class environment.

We wish to summarize this brief presentation rather strongly, urging a position we will seek to defend in subsequent sections, by asserting that almost all forms of traditional psychotherapy are singularly middle class in nature—in their underlying philosophies of man, their elaborated theoretical rationales, and their broad arrays of specific techniques.

## YAVIS and NON-YAVIS Patients

In a thorough and penetrating analysis of the sociology of contemporary psychotherapy in the United States, Schofield (1964) has called our attention to the YAVIS patient—young, attractive, verbal, intelligent, and successful. Mr. YAVIS is, for the vast majority of present-day psychotherapists, the preferred type of patient. His social status is middle or upper class. As Williams (1956) notes, Mr. YAVIS typically seeks psychotherapy in reaction to a threat which is not apparent in his current situation but, instead, is intimately related to past events and future goals. He seeks psychotherapy typically with volition, and for purposes of gaining an understanding of the causes of his disturbance and learning methods for both eliminating their presence and preventing further difficulties. He is in major accord with his psychotherapist, for verbal, insight-oriented, introspective psychotherapy is Mr. YAVIS' treatment of choice also, and drug or physical therapies are viewed as less desirable, palliative interventions. He enters treatment with a participation expectation, anticipating he will play an active and often stressful role over the course of psychotherapy. The pattern of defense mechanisms he typically displays is likely to be some combination of isolation, rationalization, and reaction formation. He tends to establish a favorable psychotherapeutic relationship with his psychotherapist, remain in psychotherapy for an extended series of sessions, and more often than not derive apparent therapeutic benefit therefrom. The pattern thus described, while somewhat overstated, does indeed portray in general terms, the therapy-relevant flavor of the YAVIS patient.*

Our ultimate interest lies more with a contrasting type of patient, whom we will call Mr. NON-YAVIS. He is typically lower or working class. We have described him elsewhere (Goldstein, 1971) as often middle-aged or elderly, physically ordinary or unattractive, verbally reticent, intellectually unexceptional or dull, and vocationally unsuccessful or marginal. As Williams (1956) observes, the stress precipitating his seeking psychotherapy is likely to be an immediate and concrete problem, often pertaining to an environmental crisis he finds himself unable to resolve. He comes to psychotherapy, often with the considerable urging of significant others, seeking immediate relief from the stress or disability he is experiencing. His set toward treatment may be described as a guidance expectation, in which he anticipates stating his problem and then assuming a largely passive role. He anticipates his therapist will offer advice and actively guide him toward problem solution. Since Mr. NON-YAVIS often views his problem as physical, he is also likely to anticipate receiving medication. Displacement, denial, and repression are the commonly present defense mechanisms. His therapeutic relationship tends to develop poorly, duration tends to be brief, and the therapeutic outcome unsatisfactory—or at least clearly less so than is typically true for the YAVIS patient. In the sections which follow, we will examine more fully a number of pretherapy and in-therapy aspects of the NON-YAVIS patient's treatment destiny.

---

* McMahon (1964) has further described the YAVIS patient or good therapy candidate as someone who evidences:

logical thinking rather than magical expectations; internalization of problems and the tendency to self-blame rather than acting out and projection; a wish to actively change one's environment instead of a passive, fatalistic stance toward reality; self-control; a need to relate to people; and a desire to talk with others about personal problems [p. 236].

### Patient–Therapist Expectancies

McMahon's (1964) observations are representative of the clinical lore which has developed regarding the therapy-relevant expectations of the lower-class patient, and the incongruity of these expectations with those held by the typical middle-class psychotherapist. He comments:

> The consensus is that the working class person expects his therapist to be more active, medically oriented, and immediately helpful in relieving his symptomatic distress. The patient is inclined to expect that the therapist will act "on" him, and "do" something for him. . . . This working class expectation of immediate help has at times been viewed as incongruous with the value, behavior, and treatment orientation of many middle class therapists. A therapist often becomes irritated at being put into the role of the medical . . . man who works instantaneous magic. . . . The kind of symptom formation that appears more syntonic with the middle-class therapist's wishes and skills are: the introspective schizoid, the inwardly depressed, the symbolic neurotic, and the intelligent paranoid [p. 286].

A number of independent investigations confirm this expectational pattern—the lower-class patient typically anticipates active, problem-oriented, concrete, and at times directive, psychotherapeutic assistance from his psychotherapist—that is, his expectations are fully consistent with all he has probably experienced whenever he previously sought medical assistance. Such expectations will often find behavioral expression in advice-seeking requests; in requests that the therapist "speak to," "do something about," or otherwise intervene directly with a spouse or other relative; in the question, in a variety of forms, "Am I mentally ill?"; and in pleas for direct symptomatic relief (Borghi, 1965; Freedman, Englehardt, & Hankoff, 1958; Heine & Trosman, 1960; Overall & Aronson, 1963; Sobel & Ingalls, 1964). But such expectations stand in very marked contrast to those preferred by most middle-class, YAVIS-preferring psychotherapists. Heine and Trosman's (1960) investigation led them to describe these typical psychotherapist expectations regarding the optimal role to be played by the patient as: someone who desires an interpersonal relationship in which he is free to talk openly about himself and his problems, who views the relationship as instrumental for discomfort relief rather than expecting such relief to follow from more impersonal manipulation (e.g., drugs, directive advice, environmental intervention), and, thus, as someone who perceives himself as partially responsible for the quality of the eventual therapeutic outcome. The therapists in this study explicitly did *not* anticipate assuming an active or directive role, even in response to marked patient passivity. Others have reported similar findings. Therapists typically anticipate being, in contrast to what their lower-class patients appear to expect, not active but reflective, not problem-oriented but personality-oriented, not primarily concrete but largely abstract, not directive but catalytic or interpretive (Goldstein, 1962; Riessman, Cohen, & Pearl, 1964).

It is not only patient–therapist *role* expectations—anticipations of their own and the other's in-therapy behavior—which may be discrepant. We have elsewhere examined the implications for therapeutic outcome of patient and therapist *prognostic* expectations, i.e., the amount of patient change anticipated by patient and therapist. In these investigations we demonstrated that high levels of (lower-class) patient change were associated with moderate patient prognostic expectancy and high therapist prognostic expectancy (Goldstein, 1962). Yet, if clinical observations are correct, in the typical pairing of a lower-class patient and a middle-class therapist, the patient enters treatment with excessively high prognostic expectancies (Borghi, 1965; McMahon, 1964) and the therapist characteristically anticipates minimal patient change (Goldstein, 1971; Overall & Aronson, 1963).

Such discrepant role and prognostic expectancies have been demonstrated to lead to very rapid termination of therapy (by the therapist, the patient, or both), a poor quality relationship characterized by considerable strain or disequilibrium, persistent therapist–patient communication difficulties, and low levels of patient change (Chance, 1959; Goldstein, 1962; Heine & Trosman, 1960; Lennard & Bernstein, 1960; Overall & Aronson, 1963). For a lower-class patient to terminate his psychotherapy rapidly in the face of a major expectational mismatch seems appropriate and adaptive. He simply does not anticipate that his pressing needs, as he defines them, will be met. For the psychotherapist to view such a patient as "unsuitable," or "resistant" is also, it seems to us, technically correct and appropriate, though such terms are often used in a pejorative manner in this context; i.e., the locus of the "difficulty" is viewed as the patient, rather than more appropriately as the patient–therapist-treatment combination. In this sense, the patient is no more nor less "unsuitable" than the therapist, or the techniques he proffers.

### Diagnosis

Both clinical lore and experimental findings concur in reporting major diagnostic biases often inherent in the act of diagnosing the lower-class applicant for psychotherapy. Kadushin (1969), in a review of the clinical literature in this domain, notes that diagnosticians are frequently observed to be "tougher" on lower-class than on middle-class patients; that is, a given degree of psychopathology, when displayed by a lower-class patient, is more likely to lead to a psychotic diagnosis than when it is displayed by a middle-class patient. Harrison, McDermott, Wilson, and Schrager (1944), Siegel, Kahn, Pollack, and Fink (1962), and Simon (1967) report observational data which concur with this impression. The latter also notes that the diagnostic bias may in part be a reaction to the clinical literature itself. That is, the sheer frequency of reports indicating highest incidence and prevalence of schizophrenia among lower-class patients may itself augment the likelihood of such a diagnosis being made. Perhaps this rather macabre self-fulfilling prophecy also underlies the finding that, in spite of apparently similar drinking behavior and related symptomatology, the diagnoses of acute or chronic alcoholism are significantly more likely to be assigned to lower-class than middle-class problem drinkers (Schmidt, Smart, & Moss, 1968; Wolf, Chafetz, Blane, & Hill, 1965). It is not just summary diagnostic labels such as "schizophrenic" and "chronic alcoholic," however, which have been observed to reflect class-related biases, but also the substance of diagnostic reports. In Schmidt et al. (1968), in which alcoholic symptomatology did *not* appear to vary with social class, middle-class patients were described more frequently than lower-class patients in terms of activity, discontent, guilt, self-dissatisfaction, and an array of neurotic behaviors; whereas the terms most frequent for the lower-class patients were low motivation, low insight, retiringness, loneliness, and the like. Raines and Rehrer (1955) have referred to "projective elements in diagnosis," a notion utilized by Schmidt et al. (1968) to explain tentatively the emphasis on *feelings* in diagnostic statements about middle-class patients, in contrast to the heavy reliance on *behavioral* terms in reports about similarly disturbed lower-class patients. They note:

> Because, in general, feelings are verbally communicated and behaviors are observed, these differences may be understood as reflecting degrees of intimacy in the relationship between therapists and patients; observation is possible even when the relationship is a distant one [p. 85].

Experimental data exist in direct support of these clinical observations of class-linked diagnostic bias. Lee and Temerlin (1970) structured 40 psychiatric residents to believe that the patient they were about to observe being interviewed was either upper-, middle-, or lower-class. The residents then viewed the identical interview, one in which the patient (actor) presented a picture of psychological health, and no apparent information relevant to his social class. Control Ss, also psychiatric residents, observed the same interview, but received no prior structuring. All Ss then rated the "interviewee's" mental health and prognosis. The upper-class, middle-class, and control structuring each resulted in ratings of significantly higher mental health and better prognoses than did lower-class structuring. The investigators' second study similarly demonstrated a reciprocal diagnostic bias effect: Prior information regarding level of mental disturbances will lead to predictable ratings of social class. Their essential paradigm paralleled the foregoing investigation. Prior to viewing the standard interview, Ss were told that "two boarded psychiatrists and a psychoanalyst" had diagnosed the patient as "normal," "neurotic," or "psychotic." As predicted, results indicated that the residents' postinterview ratings of the patient's social class were highest when he was labeled "normal," significantly lower when "neurotic," and significantly lower again if "psychotic" prestructuring had been provided. Lee and Temerlin (1970) observe, in response to these findings, that:

> Both mental health and high social status have positive value for psychiatric residents. In a competitive, status-oriented society, it is not surprising that residents would expect one who had achieved high social status to be "healthier" than one who had not. This bias may be inherent in training programs in which the resident has high social and economic aspirations and socializes with other professional people, but does clinical work primarily with patients who cannot afford psychotherapy with private practitioners [p. 184].

A related investigation conducted by Haase (1964) makes clear that diagnostic bias is not unique to one professional group. Subjects were 75 psychologists who were asked to respond to two Rorschach protocols, each of which was paired with information indicating that the testee was middle- or lower-class. The middle-class information depicted the testee as a college graduate, with $10,000 yearly income, living in an attractive home in a desirable neighborhood, and whose father was a CPA. In contrast, lower-class structuring described the testee as someone with a high school education, who lived in a walk-up tenement in a poor neighborhood, and whose father was a $45 per week fruit and vegetable dealer. Results demonstrated that both diagnostic and prognostic ratings were significantly more favorable when middle-class structuring had been provided.

Essentially identical results have been reported by Garfield and Weiss (1971) in their study of social class bias in public school counselors. A randomly selected half of the counselor sample were given information about a 9-year-old boy that described an array of behavior problems in school, and explicitly placed the boy at an upper middle-class level. The other counselors were provided identical information regarding the boy's school behavior, but were clearly informed he was of lower social class standing. The counselors provided with the middle-class structuring, results indicated, were more likely than those to whom the boy was described as lower-class to: (1) agree to meet with the boy for counseling, (2) schedule a teacher conference to explore alternative classroom management strategies, (3) schedule a home visit, and (4) consult with their supervisors regarding the boy. Once again, therefore, social class bias appears to be a significant influence upon a broad array of change agent diagnostic and helping behaviors. This broad conclusion has recently received still further support in findings reported by Levy and Kahn (1970) and Trachtman (1971).

It is not just the presence of a lower social class or a specific diagnostic *label*, however, that can lead to diagnostic bias, but also descriptions of therapy-relevant, patient characteristics often purported to be associated with lower-class life style. An investigation conducted by Beal (1969) is illustrative. Her subjects, 114 clinical psychology graduate students from 14 universities, were constituted into 9 experimental conditions. Each group of Ss was provided an intake report about a patient whom they were to later view being interviewed in a movie of a psychotherapy session. The content of the report was systematically varied in terms of the movie patient's purported level of motivation for treatment (high, low, or not stated) and diagnosis (neurotic, psychopathic, or not stated). All Ss then viewed the *identical* movie. Beal's procedures were such that what may be termed both diagnostic and therapeutic biases could be discerned. Measurement for the former was obtained by postviewing ratings by the Ss regarding their attraction toward the movie patient, their willingness to treat him, and his prognosis. Regular pauses in the movie permitted Ss to indicate what they would say to the patient at various points in the session if they were treating him. These responses were subsequently content-analyzed for empathy and warmth, thus providing the opportunity to examine the effects of purported patient motivation and diagnosis on overt "therapist behavior." As Beal had predicted, the high motivation information, as compared to low motivation, pulled significantly more favorable prognostic estimates and significantly greater willingness to treat the patient. In a manner consistent with the investigations described earlier, the neurotic label elicited significantly greater attraction, empathy, and warmth than did the psychopathic diagnosis.

A final investigation in this domain (Thain, 1968) has similarly substantiated the occurrence of class-linked diagnostic bias. Of special interest in this study was the use of both middle- and lower-class diagnosticians as subjects. The former offered diagnostic ratings which were consistently more in agreement with the purported psychiatric diagnoses of the stimulus-patients. The middle-class diagnosticians also consistently rated the "patients' " antisocial behavior as significantly more pathological than did lower-class diagnosticians. The tendency to recommend the stimulus-patient for psychotherapy was also significantly greater for middle-class diagnosticians, and significantly greater for *all* diagnosticians when the stimulus-patient himself was described as middle-class as opposed to lower-class. This last finding raises a rather important issue. Investigations described earlier point to the operation of class-linked diagnostic biases in professional, middle-class diagnosticians. Thain's finding suggests that lower-class individuals themselves may share this biased perspective. Yet, one of the foundation stones for the very rapidly growing usage of paraprofessional therapists holds that working-class and lower-class individuals can function as effective psychotherapists precisely because they and their patients share the same social class standing—and thus life style, language, meanings, etc. Therefore, in a highly pragmatic sense, the presence or absence of diagnostic (and therapeutic) bias in such paraprofessional therapists is a question of some moment. We have begun to address this issue in some of our own research, and thus will return in this topic in Chapter 8, in which we focus upon the training of paraprofessional psychotherapists.

In addition to diagnostic bias whose general source is the cognitive and emotional disposition of the examiner, brief mention should also be made of diagnostic bias inherent in either test materials themselves, or in the interaction of these materials with the types of test-taking behavior often characteristic of the lower-class respondent. Investigators concerned with intelligence testing of lower-class children were the first to raise questions about possibly biased test materials. A number of studies had reported significantly higher IQs for middle-class, as opposed to lower-class children—a finding characteristically explained either in terms of social selection or enhanced stimulation (Anastasi, 1958; Bereiter & Engelmann, 1966; Eells, Davis, Havighurst, Herman, & Tyler, 1951; Gray & Klaus, 1965; Havighurst & Janke, 1944; Lesser, Fifer, & Clark, 1965; Pasamanick & Knoblock, 1950). Numerous other investigators responded to this consistent finding by raising and examining possible cultural and class-linked biases in the testing process itself as a more parsimonious explanation of such between-class IQ differences. Perhaps, as Stodolsky and Lesser (1967) posited, the decrement in IQ scores for lower-class children was largely a function of the rapport, speed, motivation, and reward conditions of the examining procedure. Or, as Fishman, Deutsch, Kogan,

North, and Whiteman, (1964) observe, the lower-class child's test performance:

> . . . may be affected by poor skills in test-taking, a disruptive level of anxiety, lowered motivation to perform well on tests, less concern with speed, poorer understanding of test instructions, unfamiliarity with format, and poorer rapport with the examiner [p. 160].

These several components of test bias led first to (unsuccessful) attempts to develop "culture-free" measures of intelligence and then, more recently, to efforts at constructing "culture-fair" intelligence tests and testing procedures, in which test items are based upon a pool of experience common to the (lower-class) respondent population and in which the conditions of test administration are arranged to minimize negative or spurious effects of rapport, motivation, and the like. In short, attempts to reduce or eliminate diagnostic bias in intelligence tests and testing have led investigators to seek to develop materials and procedures that are responsive to the congnitive, affective, and motivational characteristics of the target population. The spirit and, to some extent, the substance of these efforts parallel quite directly the attempt represented by the present volume to develop therapeutic materials and procedures that fit or are responsive to the needs and life style of lower-class populations.

Many of the same or similar sources of bias have been identified or posited as operating in personality tests and testing, though far fewer corrective, bias-removing attempts have been made. Hoffman and Albizu-Miranda (1955) provide evidence indicating that neuroticism scores on the Bernreuter Personality Inventory are inflated for lower-class respondents by items which appear to reflect realistic conditions of the lower-class environment, rather than psychopathology per se; e.g., "Do you worry over possible misfortunes?" Similar conclusions may be inferred from the research of Brown (1936), Hoffeditz (1934), Riessman and Miller (1958), and Springer (1938). More generally, Chilman (1970) has commented regarding the use of questionnaires with lower-class respondents.

> Among the difficulties are the following: a low-level of literacy frequently obtains; words and concepts often have different culturally affected meanings; there is a strong tendency in low-income subjects to respond in the affirmative in order to ingratiate themselves with the researcher; the testing situation may be far from ideal, with lack of privacy, etc. [p. 9].

Radin and Glasser (1965) observed and sought to alter several of these test-taking behaviors in their study of the Parental Attitudes Research Instrument with lower-class mothers. Possible respondent illiteracy was dealt with by administering each instrument individually and orally. Concern with interclass differences in word meaning was responded to by developing a standard set of substitute terms and phrases to be used when the respondent seemed puzzled or confused. An attempt was made to deal with difficulties associated with the test-administration setting by administering all tests in the respondents' homes—at a quiet time with minimal distraction. An effort was made to minimize difficulties of rapport and related matters associated with tester–testee social class differences by using testers who were either middle-class but had much experience working with lower-class respondents, or by using testers who themselves shared social class or ethnic background with the respondents. Radin and Glasser's (1965) attempt is a pioneering effort, but a rare one. Beyond their report, and such studies as Minuchin and Montalvo's (1966) creative use of behavioral tasks with lower-class respondents, and Riessman and Miller's (1958) suggestions for dealing with social class bias in projective testing, little has been forthcoming from the psychological community that seeks to deal effectively with response contamination or distortion due to test, or test-taking, social class bias. Considerable and sophisticated psychometric effort has been devoted to concern with validity, reliability, item analysis, and a wide array of response sets held to operate in personality measures, but very little attention has been paid to the implications of social class biases.

## Process and Outcome

In a manner similar to our consideration of diagnosis and expectancies, in the materials which follow we will examine several aspects of the therapeutic process and outcome as they relate to the lower-class patient. In the investigation by Schmidt et al. (1968), the social class levels of 412 alcoholic outpatients were determined. Controlling for patient age, sex, marital status, and ethnicity, they report that upper-class patients were eight times more likely than lower-class patients to be physician-referred; the higher the social class, the greater the likelihood that individual psychotherapy would be recommended; and the lower the social class, the greater the likelihood of recommendation for drug therapy. In a sample of 322 outpatients, Cole et al. (1962) found that lower-class patients are less likely to be accepted for treatment, stay in treatment for fewer sessions if accepted, and are less likely to be rated improved after ten sessions. Schaffer and Myers (1954) report similar relationships between patient social class and both recommended disposition and duration of treatment. Using the five-category social class system developed by Hollingshead and Redlich (1958), they report that 64% of Class II, and 55% of Class III patients were accepted by the treatment clinic for psychotherapy, while 66% of Class IV, and 97% of Class V patients were rejected. This wide, class-linked disparity in purported acceptability for psychotherapy held for the entire sample, as well as for their neutrotic ($N = 148$) and psychotic ($N = 47$) subsamples separately. Schaffer and Myers also report a clear relationship, for those patients accepted into treatment, between patient social class and the status or experience level of the treating therapist. Class II and III patients were seen by senior staff, Class IV patients by psychiatric residents, and the lower-class (Class V) patients were most typically assigned to medical students. Finally, a significant relationship between social class and duration of therapy was also obtained. Findings on acceptability for treatment, therapist assignment, and duration of therapy were each independent of patient age, sex, referral source, diagnosis, or type of intake interviewer. Controlling for these effects, of course, increases the probability that the findings obtained were in fact reliably a function of patient social class. Other investigations are clearly consistent with this outpatient picture. Brill and Storrow (1960) found a significant difference favoring upper- and middle-class outpatients in acceptability for psychotherapy. Imber, Nash, and Stone (1955) report significantly briefer therapy duration for lower-class patients, and a significantly greater likelihood for these patients not to return after initial screening. Grey's (1969) results independently confirm these unacceptability and duration findings, and also confirm the finding of significantly lower rated improvement for lower-class outpatients. Rosenthal and Frank (1958), Schneiderman (1965), Stieper and Wiener (1965), Strotzka (1969), and Winder (1955) have each reported concurring results. In terms of acceptance into treatment, type of treatment recommended, experience level of therapist assigned, duration, and rated outcome, the lower-class outpatient fares significantly more poorly than his middle- or upper-class counterparts.

The typical middle-class therapist's contribution to these phenomena is real and—most often—negative. McMahon and Shore (1968) speak of

> . . . cultural differences [which] often involve matters of great emotional significance to the middle-class professional. Free impulse expression, dependence, deprivation, squalor, dirt, and disease arouse strong feelings as they collide with long-standing defenses [p. 562].

Redlich, Hollingshead, and Bellis (1955) explain their research finding that therapists liked their middle-class patients significantly more than their lower-class patients by noting,

> Therapists disliked the Class V patient's lack of responsibility and discipline, their dependency and ineptness at facing and correcting their emotional problems. Many of the therapists became discouraged in treating Class V patients, especially when extremely difficult reality situations were added to other difficulties [p. 67].

In a similar manner, Brody's (1968) study led him to note a strong tendency for the therapists studied ". . . to feel pessimistic, annoyed, bored, remote, or anxious with the least priviledged patients, and to like, to feel liked by, and to become more interested in the more priviledged one [p. 274]." Feelings and reactions such as these often lead to rapid termination via rejection-like processes that have been variously described as "the chuck out" (Baum, Felzer, D'zmura, & Shumaker, 1966); the mechanical, acting-out, or noncommunicative therapist (Baum *et al.*, 1966); the punitive–rejecting, overidentifying, or apathetic therapist (McMahon & Shore, 1968); or by "cooling out," a process described by Adams and McDonald (1968) in which the lower-class patient is ". . . confused, consoled and condemned in such a manner that termination becomes very probable."

By noting these observations, we seek not to condemn the contemporary psychotherapist but, instead, to simply offer a perspective which must be acknowledged if effective therapies for lower-class patients are to be developed. As the author (1971) has commented elsewhere:

> A therapist's humanness may mean warmth, interpersonal sensitivity, patience, perceptiveness, depth of understanding and a broad array of other pro-therapeutic virtues. This same humanness, however, is also likely to mean a preference for others who share our values, an ability to communicate best with others who "speak our language," ability to empathize most fully with those who share our basic assumptions about mental disturbance and its treatment, and discomfort in the presence of those whose life style overlaps little with one's own. Thus, to note that psychotherapists hold biases, engage in stereotyping behavior or are in some ways xenophobic, is simply to comment upon their humanness [pp. 60–61].

Much of the foregoing material derives from clinical lore or observation, but experimental confirmation is not lacking. Byrne, Clore, and Worchel (1966) note that tests of social comparisons theory have demonstrated that individuals are attracted to one another on the basis of similarity in opinions, abilities, and emotional state. They predicted that interpersonal attraction would also be a function of perceived economic similarity. The economic status of 84 Ss was determined, and then each S was asked to evaluate a stranger described as either similar or dissimilar to S in economic status. Independent of the absolute economic level involved, similarity of economic level led to significantly greater interpersonal attraction than did dissimilarity. Carkhuff and Pierce (1967) conducted an investigation in which four therapists who themselves represented four possible combinations of social class (middle or lower) and race (white or black) each interviewed four different schizophrenic pateints—one in each of the four class–race combinations. Six 4-min excerpts were randomly selected from each of the 64 interviews and content-analyzed for depth of patient self-exploration. Significant main effects were obtained for both social class and race such that patient self-exploration was greater when therapist and patient were similar in either or both of these regards. Therapist social class is, of course, rarely varied, and thus there is little additional systematic research similar to Carkhuff and Pierce's. Mitchell and Namenek (1970) have, however, plausibly suggested that the findings of studies comparing the relative success of "A versus B" type therapists (Carson, 1967; McNair, Callahan, & Lorr, 1962; Whitehorn & Betz, 1960) may be reinterpreted as offering additional evidence of the crucial role for therapeutic outcome played by therapist and patient social class.

## Attempted Solutions

Contemporary psychotherapy's failure to assist the lower-class patient effectively is clearly not a failure in problem recognition, for the bulk of the observations and findings described above derives from the efforts of practicing psychotherapists or active psychotherapy researchers. Yet attempts to develop more optimal, class-linked psychotherapeutic approaches are largely a recent development. It is these efforts we now wish to examine.

### *Directed Activity*

A few creative psychotherapists have sought to assist the lower-class patient more adequately by modifying traditional approaches to psychotherapy. They have done so largely by utilizing techniques responsive to such generalizations about lower-class patients as desire for authority and direction; preference for activity, rather than introspection; desire for structure and organization; and preference for concrete and objectively demonstrable explanations, rather than engagement in more symbolic activities. Perhaps equally important, certain of these modifications are responsive not only to the cognitive and emotional life style of the lower-class patient, but also to a number of the harsh environmental realities of lower-class living.

Gould (1967), working in a union-supported outpatient clinic, describes procedures by which assistance was immediately available; was offered in places other than a "professional" office; was varied in length; relied heavily on education and guidance; was maximally informal; and was actively supported by trusted union officials. Blane and Meyers (1964) similarly champion the value of reducing or eliminating waiting-list time and of more "doing for" the patient, or what they term, "communication through action." Yamamoto and Goin (1965) sought to conduct their therapy with lower-class patients "as if each session were probably the last." They actively provided directive counseling oriented toward the relief of specific problems or symptoms. Their treatment staff also made considerable use of group psychotherapy of variable length and frequency. In addition, they describe the use of volunteers, refreshments, and a variety of "social" activities as an attempt to bring the therapeutic community concept to an outpatient setting. Short-term therapy flexibly administered has also been described by Koegler and Brill (1967) under the term "brief contact therapy." They, as well as Jones and Kahn (1964), Shader, Binstock, and Scott (1968), and Schmidt *et al.* (1968) sought to provide evidence for the value of meeting the lower-class patient's definition of emotional disturbance as physical in nature by providing him with medication or other somatic treatment. These brief descriptions of short-term, directive, and often somatically oriented procedures represent but a sample of the many offered in the literature. While such reports are clearly more valuable than the even more frequent type of article which seeks to demonstrate that traditional* therapeutic ap-

---

* Especially in the context of this discussion, it appears appropriate to elaborate upon the term "traditional." While traditional psychotherapy in the United States today may mean verbal, introspective, insight-oriented psychotherapy, we may benefit from being reminded that traditional in the United States is not equivalent to universal. Ziferstein (1968) describes the behavior of Soviet psychiatrists as follows:

They were all very active in giving their patients emotional support and reassurance, advice and guidance. They vigorously engaged in reeducating their patients and presenting to them values and standards of behavior. . . . When they considered it necessary, they manipulated the patient's environment, his job, occupation, place of work, or residence [p. 262].

Kiev (1964) and Prince (1969) have similarly espoused the value of concrete thera-

proaches "don't work" with lower-class patients and adds that "someone ought to do something" about this fact, most of the reports briefly described above are quasi-experimental at best. Their "findings" tend to be decidedly impressionistic and, thus, while helpfully pointing us in certain directions, their conclusions must be considered quite tentative.

## Role Playing

Role playing and related actional procedures, while enjoying a long psychotherapeutic history, have only recently been viewed as particularly appropriate for lower-class patient populations. Reissman and Goldfarb (1964) assert:

> Miller and Swanson, on the basis of a number of different investigations, arrive at the conclusion that an outstanding characteristic of the low income person's style is its emphasis on the physical, in particular the motoric. . . . It is not simply that the poor *are* physical; that their labor is characterized by working with things; that their child-rearing typically utilizes physical punishment; that their religious expression very often includes physical manifestations of emotion . . . that when they become mentally ill they are likely to develop motoric symptoms such as conversion hysteria and catatonia . . . that they are especially responsive to extra-verbal communication such as gesture. The significant factor is that low income people work through mental problems best when they can do things physically. . . . [Miller & Swanson's] results indicate the desirability of exploring a variety of new psychotherapeutic techniques, particularly those in which words and concepts are subordinated to non-verbal and even motoric activities. . . . Role-playing appears admirably suited to this physical, action-centered motoric style [p. 340].

It is not an uncommon observation of those concerned with the relationship of therapeutic theory to practice that psychotherapists holding very different theoretical views may behave in very similar ways when actually meeting with patients. Such seems to be the case with regard to the four major attempts to use role-playing techniques with NON-YAVIS patients. Working from a psychoanalytic perspective, Nelson (1962) has

---

peutic procedures based upon authoritarian suggestion, acting out, directive advice, etc., in a large number of "primitive" cultures. Prince comments

> . . . there is a growing awareness that psychotherapeutic practices aimed at independence and insight are not appropriate for a large and important segment of our western population, the chronically poor; on the other hand, it is becoming clear that the vast majority of the emotionally disturbed of the non-western world can be successfully treated (and are being successfully treated) by techniques that foster dependency and unreasoned belief [p.20].

presented an approach he describes as "paradigmatic psychotherapy."
Paradigmatic psychotherapy, he states, "means the systematic setting
forth of examples by the analyst to enable the patient to understand the
significant intrapsychic processes or interpersonal situations of his life,
past and present [p. 123]." Considerable use is made in this approach of
role playing, imitation, and interpretation. Though Nelson clearly offered
an important departure for psychoanalysis with his introduction of the
paradigmatic approach, we would take exception to his original statement
in two respects. As is so characteristic of most psychoanalytic innovations, the simple is too rapidly denigrated and the complex too often preferred. In the complete absence of anything even approaching experimental scrutiny of either the paradigmatic approach as a whole or any of its
major components, Nelson argues strongly against "anything so crude as
[the analyst] deliberately acting as a model for the patient." We will later offer evidence that procedures analogous to those criticized by Nelson
do indeed appear to be effective forces for change. We would take even
stronger exception, as we have elsewhere (Goldstein, Heller, & Sechrest,
1966), to the common psychoanalytic stance that holds "basic" psychoanalytic procedures are inviolable—innovations are to be treated as
mere "additions," or "trimmings" that may augment the basic procedures, or "ready" the patient for classical treatment. Nelson creatively
describes the use of role playing, mirroring, duplicating reported experiences in vivo, and a host of related procedures—but all such procedures, he holds, are to be used "until the patient is able to profit
by classical interpretation." In contrast to this viewpoint, we will present evidence that suggests the possibility that modeling, role playing,
and social reinforcement may well be the necessary and sufficient therapeutic conditions for the lower-class patient, not mere additions, or priming techniques. This viewpoint has been anticipated in part by Shaffer's
(1967) use of paradigmatic psychotherapy with lower-class patients.
He comments:

> The paradigmatic model offers more than a means of holding the patient in
> treatment during its initial stages; it offers the strategy rationale that is
> geared to the entire treatment, a rationale that seems particularly suited to
> . . . the typical socialization experiences of the low income urban culture
> [p. 254].

Shaffer describes this typical socialization experience* as follows:

---

* Class-linked socialization experiences and related materials are examined in detail in Chapter 2.

> Several writers have pointed out the emphasis placed by working class parents on the child's obedience to external norms. This is not to say that middle-class parents do not also require conformity but that theirs is often in the direction of conformity to internalized standards that have been related to either the parent's feelings . . . or to the consequences of the act for the child's feelings. Either approach . . . makes *empathy* a basis for role behavior. The child rearing behavior of the working class families observed by Gans . . . would seem to offer a fairly typical contrast: these parents tend to raise the child impulsively, de-emphasize a recognition of the child's unique needs and thereby discourage the child's sensitivity to his own needs. Because the parents neither articulate their feelings about themselves to the child nor attempt to take his own point of view, the child grows up without models for adopting other people's perspectives [pp. 251–252].

Thus, Shaffer holds, such persons are ill-prepared for the introspective, self-reflective demands of traditional psychotherapy, but may well benefit greatly from procedures which enhance their ability to more fully experience and recognize their own feelings, to view themselves as others may see them, and to develop more adequate role flexibility and a broader array of roles.

Very similar procedures, growing from a markedly different theoretical viewpoint, have been suggested by A. A. Lazarus (1966) under the term *behavioral rehearsal*. Here the emphasis is not upon the patient's intrapsychic functioning, nor is the orientation one of role playing for purposes of the cathartic expression of past traumas. As the term implies, behavior rehearsal involves procedures designed overtly to prepare a patient to deal effectively with a present or anticipated difficulty. Most of its application thus far has been to assist patients to learn to behave more independently or appropriately assertive. Behavioral rehearsal corresponds in major ways with the type of psychotherapy we ourselves will recommend as optimal for lower-class patients, and thus we will return to Lazarus' work in considerable detail in a later chapter.

Psychodrama is the third psychotherapeutic approach which makes major use of role-play techniques, often oriented to the NON-YAVIS patient (Goldman & Goldman, 1968; Levit & Jennings, 1960; Riessman, 1964a; Young & Rosenberg, 1945). This has been a popular approach for almost 60 years. Moreno and his co-workers have developed role play and related procedures in an extensive, detailed, and imaginative manner. Yet, their creativity not withstanding, the psychodramatic movement rests upon a foundation particularly lacking in experimental support. Their "documentation" consists almost singularly of claims, counter-claims, and intuitive speculation.

A final approach to the use of role playing with lower-class patients is "instrumented role playing," developed by Rothaus and his colleagues (Rothaus & Morton, 1962; Rothaus, 1964). In its application thus far, psychiatric inpatients are paired with naive (nonpatient) raters. Each patient enacts a variety of affective roles, and receives feedback regarding his enactment from his paired raters. Major use is also made in this approach of patient group decision making and evaluation, particularly as part of the feedback process.

Thus, there currently exist four diverse theoretical approaches to the use of role playing and related techniques with NON-YAVIS patients. We feel these clinical attempts are creative, provocative, and heuristic. Yet, with the partial exception of Lazarus' and Rothaus' efforts, they are markedly lacking in either systematization or experimental verification of clinical utility. This generalization is of course equally applicable to most psychotherapeutic techniques of whatever type and, it should be noted, also applies to the related attempts to use role-play techniques as a major therapeutic approach with middle-class YAVIS patients.*

### Relationship Enhancement

The quality of the therapist–patient relationship has historically been viewed as a crucial therapeutic ingredient by almost all schools of psychotherapy, and as such it is understandable that relationship variables have received considerable attention as they concern therapy with the lower-class patient. Most such attention has led to the position described earlier, recommending a more directive, authoritarian, and giving orientation by the therapist. Miller and Mishler (1964) perhaps reflect this viewpoint most strongly. They propose that the lower-class patient

> . . . rather than asking for "less" than he is offered . . . may actually be asking for "more" in the sense that he wants a fuller, more extensive, and more permanent relationship than is possible either within the traditional definition of the therapeutic relationship or in terms of what the therapist is willing to enter into [p. 33].

In contrast, Gendlin (1961a) appears to be offering an opposing position with his comment:

---

* Kelley's (1955) fixed role therapy, Otto's (1967) strength-role therapy, O'Connell's (1963) Adlerian psychodrama, and Strean's (1961) use of role playing with children. It should also be noted in this context that almost all of the great many studies demonstrating the successful use of role playing for purposes of attitude change in the social-psychological laboratory made use of college student, YAVIS subjects.

> The patient whose socio-economic background gives him no familiarity with psychotherapy, and whose emotional difficulties involve many experiences of hurtful interpersonal relationships, is not likely to welcome the pressureful and puzzling advances of a psychotherapist [p. 135].

Gendlin operationalized this position by arranging to have a number of therapists available on an inpatient ward to meet with patients as often or as seldom as each given patient wished. Therapists rarely initiated patient contacts. Initially, therapist–patient interactions on this ward were infrequent and brief. Over time, however, closer relationships and regular sessions occurred for a large proportion of the patients. Coleman and Hewett (1962) have similarly provided descriptive evidence for a type of "therapy on demand" in their work using what they describe as "open-door therapy" with adolescents.

Enhancing the quality of the lower-class patient's relationship with his therapist has also been the focus of an extensive research program conducted by the author (Goldstein, 1971). The theoretical rationale for this program held that there exists a basic unity across seemingly diverse areas of psychological inquiry. Change processes developed in one context may operate similarly in a very different domain. Thus, we proposed, findings available on the teacher–pupil, physician–patient, or experimenter–subject relationship could yield general principles of use in clinical contexts. Our research program was, therefore, extrapolatory in nature, testing procedures from other contexts for their usefulness with psychotherapy patients. Social psychologists have focused a great deal of research attention upon procedures predicted to increase *interpersonal attraction*—the degree to which one member of a dyad likes, or is attracted to, the other. Working in laboratory settings, usually with college student Ss, such research has yielded several different procedures for reliably enhancing interpersonal attraction. It was from this research that we extrapolated in our own investigation. Each procedure was examined for its utility in increasing liking of, or attraction to, the psychotherapist for both YAVIS patients (at a university counseling center) and NON-YAVIS patients (at outpatient community clinics, state and Veterans Administration hospitals, a penitentiary, etc.). The procedures included:

1. Direct structuring: the patient is directly led to believe he will like his therapist.
2. Trait structuring: the patient is provided with information about his therapist, such as his "warmth" or "experience."
3. Status: both verbal and physical information is used to lead the patient to believe his therapist is of high status.

4. Effort: the therapeutic interaction itself is deliberately made more effortful for the patient.
5. Modeling: the patient is provided with the opportunity to view a model who is highly attracted to his psychotherapist.
6. Matching: therapist and patient are paired based upon test results concerning their interpersonal needs or therapy-relevant attitudes.
7. Conformity pressure: both attractive and unattractive therapists were rated as attractive by experimental cohorts.

The results of this research program were remarkably consistent. Almost every procedure worked successfully to increase the attraction of YAVIS patients to their therapist; almost every procedure failed to do so with NON-YAVIS patients. Modeling and trait structuring were of partial value with NON-YAVIS patients, but, essentially, our research program may be viewed as but one more example of the manner in which the technology of contemporary psychotherapy is a middle-class technology. Since each of the laboratory procedures designed to increase interpersonal attraction were originally developed on YAVIS persons (college student Ss), it is perhaps not surprising that the limit of their extrapolatability proved to be the YAVIS patient. Thus, we may note in summary of this research program that one additional and rather extensive attempt to fit the NON-YAVIS patient to a major aspect of traditional psychotherapy—the intensive and "intimate" therapist–patient relationship—was unsuccessful. The alternative strategy, of seeking to develop treatment procedures to fit the patient, thus became to us a strategy of considerable appeal.

### Role Induction

We have proposed elsewhere (Goldstein, 1971) that the lower-class psychotherapy patient will ultimately benefit from both evolutionary and revolutionary changes in the nature of contemporary psychotherapeutic procedures. Revolutionary changes would be interpreted by us to mean relatively new and different procedures, or combinations thereof, previously used rarely or not at all. By evolutionary changes we mean minor or moderate alterations in traditional techniques, or techniques that "make a patient" out of the lower-class patient-candidate by priming, indoctrinating, or somehow motivating him to participate in traditional psychotherapy in a manner more akin to that of the typical YAVIS patient. We are no longer especially hopeful regarding the ultimate utility of evolutionary departures in a traditional psychotherapeutic context. The long series of injunctions in the literature suggesting that the middle-class ther-

apist be more directive, more concrete, more giving, or that he try harder
to enter the patient's frame of reference, or try to "speak his language"
appear to have yielded rather little therapeutic benefit. Also, as described
above, our own evolutionary attempt at relationship enhancement was of
little success for our lower-class patient samples. Yet, as happens all too
seldom in the promulgation and evaluation of psychotherapeutic positions, one must avoid assuming a too categorical, all-or-none stance. Research reported by the Phipps Clinic psychotherapy research group
(Hoehn-Saric, Frank, Imber, Nash, Stone, & Battle, 1964) rather convincingly demonstrates the therapeutic value of at least one such evolutionary approach. We refer here to their development and examination of
the *Role Induction Interview* as a means of successfully realigning discrepant patient–therapist role expectations. Their efforts were in response to
the literature, reviewed above, demonstrating a large array of negative
therapeutic consequences when major incongruities exist in the anticipations held by a patient and his therapist.

Forty NON-YAVIS psychiatric outpatients participated in this investigation. All underwent an initial evaluation interview, after which a
randomly selected half of the patients participated in a Role Induction Interview (RII). Based upon Orne and Wender's* (1968) socialization interview, the RII dealt with the general nature of (traditional) psychotherapy;
the types of in-therapy behaviors expected of a patient and a therapist; preparation for certain typical psychotherapeutic events, such as resistance; and induction of realistic prognostic expectancies. Furthermore,
the patient was informed

> . . . that the therapist would not give the type of advice which he might ex-
> pect from other physicians, that the therapist would talk very little but
> would listen carefully and try to understand and clarify his problems and
> feelings. It would be up to the patient, however, to find his own way to han-
> dle problems and make decisions. The interviewer also briefly explained the
> meaning of the "unconscious" and the importance of childhood experiences
> and their consequences for current behavior. The patient was urged to talk
> freely to the therapist and cautioned that at first this would be quite diffi-
> cult. He was encouraged to describe his fantasies and daydreams and to ex-
> press his feelings, including especially those toward the therapist [Hoehn-
> Saric *et al.*, 1964, pp. 270–271].

Following the RII, the 20 experimental patients and the 20 control patients not provided this interview experience were assigned to psychother-

---

* Baum and Felzer (1964), Jacobs, Charles, Jacobs, Weinstein, and Mann (1972)
and Meyer, Spiro, Slaughter, Pollack, Weingartner, and Novey (1967) have described
related techniques, but in a much less complete and systematic manner.

apists who were unaware of each patient's experimental condition. Individual psychotherapy sessions were held weekly for a 4-month period. Results indicated that, in comparison to the control patients, those undergoing the RII were rated as exhibiting more adequate in-therapy behavior, attended therapy more regularly, were more favorably rated by their therapists with respect to establishing and maintaining a therapeutic relationship, and were rated as significantly more improved by both the therapists and the patients themselves. The investigators acknowledge that these favorable results reflect upon their procedures as a composite, but which components of the RII were most responsible is not discernable from their investigative procedures. We wish, however, to cite one of their speculations, since it accords so well with the general theme of our own presentation:

> The work of Wallach and Strupp and Parloff has shown that therapists tend to respond more favorably to patients who approach their criteria of "good" patients. It was predicted that the RII would help the patient present himself as a more favorable psychotherapeutic candidate than he would be able to do otherwise, and that he would therefore be capable of evoking a more positive response from the therapist which would in turn result in a more favorable outcome. The finding that experimental patients were rated by residents as having a greater ability to form a positive relationship than control patients supports this view [p. 277].

This investigation, therefore, quite directly manipulated patient pretherapy expectancies in order to bring such expectancies more in line with those held by the participating therapists. Positive benefit for both the therapy process and outcome ensued. These results have been largely confirmed by Sloane, Cristol, Pepernik, and Staples (1970) and Strupp and Bloxom (1971). We join the investigators in urging further experimental examination and development of not only the RII, but also such related expectancy-clarifying procedures as Rotter's (1954) successive structuring; Truax, Wargo, Carkhuff, Kodman, and Noles's, (1966) vicarious therapy pretraining; and Bordin's (1955a) and Yalom, Houts, Newell, and Rand's (1967) recommended techniques for ambiguity reduction in psychotherapy.

### Prescriptive Psychotherapy

At several earlier points in this chapter we have briefly spoken to the need for more optimal, better fitting, or class-linked psychotherapeutic approaches for the lower-class patient. The tendency for psychotherapists to hold that any given approach is equally applicable to all or most types of psychotherapy patients seems to be rapidly passing. Instead, we find Kiesler (1966) writing of the need to correct the "patient uniformity myth," Heller's (1963) urging that we develop "precision rifles" in lieu of "therapeutic shotguns," and a growing number of psychotherapists writing of the need to develop treatment approaches which are contingent upon, and not irrelevant to, diagnostic or related information about the patient. Stated otherwise, there is a growing recognition of the need for prescriptive psychotherapies. Directed activity, role playing, relationship enhancement, and role induction, to the extent that their utilization is appropriate *because of* specifiable patient characteristics, may be correctly viewed as prescriptive techniques. The use of therapists who themselves are from lower or working class backgrounds, an innovation examined in Chapter 8, has also been introduced in response to specific patient considerations and may thus also be considered prescriptive. In the present section we wish to examine one additional and particularly creative prescriptive approach to the lower-class patient, that developed by Magaro (1969).

Magaro observes that, in general terms, the mental hospital may be viewed as promoting two types of treatment goals. The first is to permit and encourage previously learned adaptive behaviors that were dominant prior to the onset of psychotic behavior to reemerge. The second is to teach new skills, to add new behaviors to the patient's repertoire—those particularly adaptive for his environment and life circumstances. The milieu therapy approach, for example, appears to emphasize the utilization of social skills that often are part of the middle-class patient's prepsychotic repertoire. The custodial approach, with its emphasis on order, minimal social interaction, passivity, and an authoritative ward and hospital structure, is likely detrimental for the middle-class patient in that these emphases are likely to inhibit the reemergence of social skills. In fact, Magaro holds, a custodial hospital orientation very likely serves to encourage or reinforce psychotic, withdrawn patterns of behavior in the middle-class patient. The lower-class patient, however, appears to be in precisely the opposite position. The passivity, directiveness, structure, and minimal focus on examination of interpersonal behavior characteristic of the custodial approach appears to be fully consistent with *this* patient's prepsychotic life style and, as such, may serve to encourage the reemergence of prepsychotic adaptive behaviors. A milieu therapy approach would require of the lower-class patient that he exhibit interpersonal social behaviors that are contrary to his prior experience and that are, therefore, minimally practiced. Magaro speculates that such a pairing of patient and treatment might well cause the competing psychotic behavior to remain dominant over the desired social behavior, thus eventuating in long-term hospitalization. Speaking directly to the issue of class-determined prescriptive treatment, Magaro comments:

> If the hospital is viewed as having a treatment model which inherently defines certain types of behavior to be correct, the defining and rewarding of the correct behavior by the hospital may increase nonpsychotic behavior of one social class, i.e., treatment, and increase the psychotic behavior of another social class, i.e., institutionalization. What would be considered treatment, therefore, would depend upon the matching of the hospital-defined healthy behavior and social class group [1969, p. 66].

The notion of prescriptive psychotherapies is, in certain senses, relatively new, and vast amounts of empirical work lie ahead. Not only is there much to do, but there is also much to avoid doing. One such pitfall is the common occurrence of placing great importance on a single variable or dimension, to the exclusion of others and in the absence of evidence. This Magaro avoids, by his recognition that patient social class appears to interact with patient premorbid personality in determining the most appropriate prescription. Both his own evidence and that accumulated by others seems to indicate that the psychotic patient with good premorbid personality tends to be discharged rather quickly regardless of the nature of his hospital treatment. Since descriptions of the good premorbid personality are of individuals who have developed behaviors appropriate for adequate functioning in their given social class environment, perhaps the most appropriate role for the hospital is to create conditions which allow the previously dominant adjustive behavior to reemerge. Thus a nonintervening but social class-linked hospital environment would appear optimal for the good premorbid patient. Magaro terms this treatment approach "recovery" and concretely proposes it be operationalized by having all good premorbid patients treated on entering wards. The middle-class, good premorbid patient would be placed on a milieu therapy ward, i.e., one which expects prepsychotic social interaction patterns to reemerge by emphasis on social activities and simple decision making. He views social workers as perhaps the most appropriate treatment personnel on such a ward. The lower-class, good premorbid patient would enter a more authoritarian ward, one with considerable structure and relatively little emphasis on social activities. Occupational and industrial therapy would be emphasized, using as primary therapists persons trained in these particular areas.* As Magaro comments with regard to both classes of good pre-morbid patients:

> In effect, the entering wards would attempt to re-create the past life experiences of the patient without the environmental stresses. The goal of the program would not be to teach, but to practice former pre-morbid behavior and increase its dominance. Living conditions, entertainment, recreational facilities, etc. should simulate the specific social class as much as possible [1969, p. 68].

The poor premorbid patients, according to Magaro's schema, would be placed on "teaching" wards, consistent with the second potential type of treatment goal, that of teaching new adaptive behaviors. A further goal for these noncustodially oriented wards would be to combat chronicity or "colonization" by attention to not making hospital living too comfortable vis-à-vis the patient's extrahospital environment. Operationally, the prescribed treatment for the middle-class, poor premorbid patient would emphasize procedures which teach an array of interpersonal skills, such as group or family therapy. The lower-class, poor premorbid patient, viewed as deficient in an array of behavioral skills and best treated by use of concrete, action-oriented procedures would be treated ("taught") via use of behavior modification techniques. Once basic adaptive behavioral patterns were mastered, such patients would also be taught occupational skills.

Magaro has thus provided us with a provocative prescriptive model for the treatment of hospitalized psychotic patients. It remains, of course, a largely speculative model that calls for considerable experimental validation. Our own research relates closely to one aspect of this model, as our efforts sought to apply a combination of behavior modification techniques to patients who were primarily lower class and of poor premorbid personality. Further bases for our prescription, and its value with such patients will be examined in the following chapters.

---

* A potential added benefit of such a program, one which serves to reestablish and perhaps further develop the lower-class patient's work-relevant skills is minimization of the likelihood of subsequent downward "social drift" (see Chapter 4).

## Chapter 2

# PERSONALITY DEVELOPMENT
# AND PREPARATION FOR PATIENTHOOD

The materials to be considered in this and the two following chapters are intended to serve two purposes simultaneously. They will illustrate in considerable detail *why* traditional psychotherapy is so consistently inappropriate for the lower-class patient, and at the same time provide the beginnings of a prescriptive basis for a therapeutic approach that may well be appropriate. The materials thus utilized in the present chapter consist of sociological and psychological research on social class-relevant aspects of child-rearing, socialization, parental behavior, and, more generally, personality development.

Social class and its manifold implications have long been of major concern to American sociology. At a most general level, Kohn (1963) observes:

> . . . social class has proved to be so useful a concept because it refers to more than simply educational level, or occupation, or any of the large number of correlated variables. It is so useful because it captures the reality [of] different basic conditions of life at different levels of the social order. Members of different social classes, by virtue of enjoying (or suffering) different conditions of life, come to see the world differently, to develop different conceptions of reality, different aspirations and hopes and fears, different conceptions of the desirable [p. 471].

From a more developmental perspective, Davis and Havighurst (1954) comment:

> . . . the social class of the child determines not only the neighborhood in which he lives and the play groups he will have, but also the basic cultural acts and goals toward which he will be trained. The social class system maintains cultural, economic and social barriers which prevent intimate so-

cial inter-mixture between the slums, the Gold Coast, and the middle class. We know that human beings can learn their culture only from other human beings, who already know and exhibit that culture. Therefore, by setting up barriers to social participation, the American social class system actually prevents the vast majority of children of the working class, or the slums, from learning any culture but that of their own groups. Thus the pivotal meaning of social class . . . is that it defines and systematizes different learning environments for children of different classes [p. 309].

Most early research responsive to these sentiments was concerned with class-linked differences in child-rearing and socialization patterns. The bulk of this "culture and personality" research is descriptive in nature and based primarily on interview data. Though often somewhat weak methodologically, perhaps such research ought not be criticized too harshly. The domain of inquiry was largely new and uncharted. Further, fallible studies whose weaknesses are not additive can yield, as a group, meaningful conclusions.

### Permissiveness, Self-Direction, and Conformity

The major ground-breaking investigation in this area was conducted by Davis and Havighurst (1954). Their data consisted of interviews concerned with an array of child-rearing behaviors, obtained from 100 middle-class and 100 lower-class families, half of which were white and half black. Their major finding was the consistently greater permissiveness of lower-class mothers. They, in contrast to middle-class mothers, were less likely to follow a strict nursing schedule or to restrict the child's sucking period, more likely to wean later and gradually, to begin toilet training later, and were more likely to breastfeed. Furthermore, the middle-class mothers generally followed stricter regimes in other areas of behavior also (naps, bedtime, free play, etc.), and expected their children to take responsibility for themselves earlier. In a second early report, similarly descriptive in nature, Davis and Dollard (1948) described childhood in the lower class in terms of greater physical and social freedom, minimal restraints in expressing aggression and sexuality, and an emphasis on immediate rather than delayed gratification of needs. Ericson (1946), based on interviews with 50 middle-class and 50 lower-class mothers, similarly concluded that lower-class mothers were more permissive. Middle-class children, she observed, experienced greater social pressure, more frustration and were forced to assume greater responsibility at an earlier age.

In spite of the consistency of these early findings, an equally consistent set of quite opposite results began to emerge. Sears, Maccoby, and Levin (1957), based upon interviews with 379 middle- and lower-class mothers, reported more severity in toilet-training practices in lower-class homes, less permissiveness in sexual matters, more restrictiveness of aggression toward either parent or peers, more physical punishment, more demands placed upon the child—all in the lower-class sample. Such findings led Sears *et al.* to conclude that research such as Davis and Havighurst's was indicative not of greater permissiveness in lower-class homes, but of greater rejection of the child. The major findings of Sears *et al.* were independently reported by others. Using data collection and sampling procedures very similar to Davis and Havighurst's (1954), White (1957) reported that middle-class mothers were as permissive or more so than their lower-class counterparts. Bayley and Schaefer (1960), in a longitudinal investigation of a sample of children at age 3 years and later at ages 9–14, found a tendency for middle-class mothers to be more warm, understanding, and accepting; and for lower-class mothers to be more controlling, irritable, and punitive. Klatskin (1952) and Miller and Swanson (1958) reported similar findings. The latter also distinguished between the lower-class tendency toward use of physical punishment in contrast to the middle-class tendency toward "psychological discipline" which relied on the manipulation of inner dynamics—the child's fear of loss of love, arousal of guilt, and related techniques.

Bronfenbrenner (1958), in an evaluative review of the foregoing literature, suggests a basis for resolving the major discrepancy between the early and later results. He proposes that over the last two decades middle-class child-rearing practices have indeed become more permissive and equalitarian than that provided in lower-class homes. This changing orientation parallels rather directly identical changes in the content of the most widely read and most influential lay publications offering child-rearing advice and recommendations during this period (Wolfenstein, 1953). Boek, Sussman, and Yankauer (1958), Stendler (1950), and others provide evidence that the middle-class mother is much more likely to be exposed to and responsive to such literature.

The general theme of permissiveness versus conformity to more authoritarian discipline has been a focus of considerable additional research. Studies conducted by Dolger and Ginanes (1946), Pearlin and Kohn (1969), and Tuma and Livson (1960) have each demonstrated the major emphasis in lower-class child rearing on conformity to externally imposed authority or proscriptions. Duvall's (1946) research led him to describe lower-class and working-class parental values as "traditional." They want their children to be neat and clean, to obey and respect adults, to conform to externally imposed standards. In contrast to this behavioral emphasis, Duvall characterizes middle-class parental values as "developmental." They want their children to be eager to learn, to share and cooperate, to confide in their parents and, in general, they are much more concerned with inner dynamics than are the "traditionally" oriented parents. Kohn's (1959a) investigation led him to identical conclusions. Working-class parents valued obedience, cleanliness, and neatness more highly than did middle-class parents. The latter, in turn, contrasted with working-class parents in their greater emphasis on curiosity, happiness, and especially self-control. Kohn comments,

> To working-class parents it is the overt act that matters; the child should not transgress externally imposed rules; to middle-class parents, it is the child's motives and feelings that matter; the child should govern himself [p. 475].

Thus, both Duvall and Kohn suggest that class-linked parental values quite early in life orient the middle-class child to his own inner dynamics and evaluative standards, the lower- or working-class child to his overt behavior and its relation to externally imposed standards. This is a distinction of some importance for our current theme, and one that has received further experimental attention, especially by Kohn. Just as we, in the present book, are seeking to develop a rationale for a therapeutic approach which fits, or is congruent with, a lower-class life style, Kohn's writings are distinguished by his efforts to demonstrate that parental values and behavior in the working-class are appropriate to, or logically consistent with, the realities of their life circumstances. In response to the findings of his first investigation, noted above, Kohn (1959a) comments:

> There appears to be a close fit between the actual working-class situation and the values of the working-class parents; between the actual middle-class situation and the values of middle-class parents. In either situation the values that seem important [in the sense that failure to achieve them would adversely affect the child's future] but problematic [in the sense that they are difficult to achieve] are the ones most likely to be accorded high priority. For the working-class the "important but problematic" centers around qualities that assure respectability; for the middle-class it centers around internalized standards of conduct [p. 337].

Kohn (1959b) next pursued the same theme, i.e., the correspondence of parental values and behaviors to class-linked realities, around the issue of parental punishment. Representative samples of 200 white middle-class and 200 white working-class families, each with a fifth grade child, were selected. All 400 mothers were interviewed as well as every fourth father and child. Findings indicated that there were indeed class-linked differences in the circumstances under which middle- and working-class parents resorted to physical punishment of their child. Middle-class parents, for example, were much more likely than working-class parents to respond with physical punishment to outbursts of temper, but not to wild play. Working-class parents, in contrast, responded most aggressively when the child engaged in wild play, or fought with a sibling. Disobedience was more severely punished in the working-class home, but not if it was likely to provoke a disturbance more serious than the one already underway. More generally, *both* types of parents appear to be responsive not to the absolute level of disturbance per se, but to their respective views of the meaning and consequences of the child's behavior. Kohn suggests that middle-class parents appear to punish or refrain from doing so on the basis of their interpretation of the child's *intent*.

Concretely, he holds that such parents are responding to

> . . . the fundamental importance they attach to internal standards for governing one's relationship with other people and, in the final analysis, with one's self. . . . An outburst of temper . . . may signal serious difficulty in the child's efforts at self-mastery; it is the type of behavior most likely to distress the parent who has tried to inculcate in his child the virtue of maintaining self-control [p. 362].

Working-class parents, Kohn continues, are much more likely to respond in terms of the immediate *consequences* of the child's behavior. For them, the criteria of relevance are *behavioral transgressions.* As Kohn (1959b) notes, ". . . the measure of disreputability is the degree to which the act transgresses rules of propriety. Fighting and wild play are disobedient, disreputable behavior only when sufficiently extreme to be seen as transgressions of rules [p. 362]." For reasons made especially clear in Kohn's next investigation, he views this differential concern with intentions versus consequences, with inner dynamics versus overt behavior, as fully appropriate to the respective realities of the middle and working class.

The fulcrum of Kohn's (1963, 1969) later work is father's occupation as a summarizing constellation which determines many aspects of parental values, behaviors and goals relevant to child rearing and personality development. Beyond such obviously relevant occupational characteristics as security, stability of income, and prestige\*, Kohn points to three ways of concern to our theme in which middle-class and working-class occupations differ. Middle-class occupations tend to involve the manipulation of interpersonal relations, ideas, and symbols; working-class occupations are generally oriented toward the manipulation of objects. Middle-class occupations tend to involve self-direction; working-class positions are usually more subject to direct supervision and standardization. One must conform to rules and procedures established by external authority. Finally, upward mobility in middle-class work environments is characteristically a function of one's own activities and accomplishments; the working-class worker is more dependent on collective activity (particularly union) for advancement. All three considerations rather clearly make it more appropriate and adaptive for the middle-class worker to be concerned with inner dynamics, intentions, motivation, interpersonal functioning, etc.; and for his working-class counterpart to focus instead on overt behavior, the consequences of one's actions, and so forth. These discrepant concerns are relevant not only to one's own adaptation but, similarly, may well be highly relevant to what one anticipates for one's child.

Kohn's (1969) tests of these notions yielded clearly supportive results. First, in two large samples in the United States and one in Italy, middle-class fathers, in contrast to those of working-class status, valued self-direction, curiosity, and responsibility more highly for both themselves and their children. Also in all three samples, there was greater valuing in the working-class groups of conformity to externally imposed standards. Kohn related these dispositional findings to characteristics of the fathers' occupations. The degree to which the father valued conformity in his children was significantly associated with (1) the closeness with which he is supervised in his own job, (2) the extent to which his job requires working with things rather than data, and (3) the extent to which his job is routine and structured. Fathers with occupations requiring diverse, complex work, self-reliance, and little supervision, value self-direction much more highly in their children. Kohn's (1969) broad conclusion to this research series is of interest:

---

\* Kohn comments:

That middle-class parents still have somewhat higher levels of income and much greater stability of income makes them able to take for granted the respectability that is still problematic for working-class parents. They can afford to concentrate instead on motives and feelings . . .[1969,p. 164]

> Our thesis, the central conclusion of our studies, is that social class is signif-
> icant for human behavior because it embodies systematically differentiated
> conditions of life that profoundly affect men's views of social reality. The
> essence of higher class position is the expectation that one's decisions and
> actions can be consequential; the essence of the lower-class position is the
> belief that one is at the mercy of forces and people beyond one's control,
> often, beyond one's understanding. Self-direction—acting on the basis of
> one's own judgment, attending to internal dynamics as well as to external
> consequences, being open-minded, being trustful of others, holding personal-
> ly responsible moral standards—this is possible only if the actual conditions
> of life allow some freedom of action, some reason to feel in control of fate.
> Conformity—following the dictates of authority, focusing on external con-
> sequences to the exclusion of internal processes, being intolerant of non-
> conformity and dissent, being distrustful of others, having moral standards
> that strongly emphasize obedience to the letter of the law—this is the inevi-
> table result of conditions of life that allow little freedom of action, little
> reason to feel in control of fate [p. 189].

Kohn's contribution to our understanding of social class is considerable, as is the relevance of his findings to psychotherapy. Clearly, training
in self-reliance; concern with inner dynamics, feelings, intentions, and
motivations; interpersonal skills; the manipulation of ideas and symbols;
and role complexity constitute excellent "basic training" for subsequent
traditional, introspective, verbal psychotherapy. To be trained to be responsive to externally imposed standards, to conform, to learn that others
will determine much of one's destiny, to learn that the consequences of one's
actions are much more important than one's intentions all constitute singularly inappropriate preparation for the type of assistance most contemporary
psychotherapists are prepared to offer. Such lower- and working-class socialization, however, does accord well with a treatment approach which is
primarily behavioral, demands conformity to concrete example, and
whose procedures are authoritatively determined and administered.

### Role-Taking Experience

Contemporary psychotherapeutic theory places considerable emphasis
upon interpersonal dimensions, both in the development and modification
of psychopathology. A measure of interpersonal skill appears necessary
for successful participation in traditional psychotherapy, particularly that
type of skill which enables one to assume to some degree the role of another. Such a level of at least moderate role-taking skill is requisite to an
adequate relationship with one's therapist, to an ability to take the
perspective of significant others in one's life, and to reflect upon one's

own feelings and history. In this domain also, the working- or lower-class patient is purported to receive inadequate early preparation. Compared to middle-class socialization experiences, a hallmark of the interpersonal world of lower- and working-class people is held to be a restrictiveness in both breadth and depth of role-taking experience. The working- and lower-class person, in comparison to the middle-class, associated and dated primarily members of his own social class in adolescence (Hill, 1955; Stendler, 1949); associates primarily with relatives and neighborhood friends of his own social class in adulthood (Cohen & Hodges, 1962; Pavenstedt, 1963; Wright & Hyman, 1958); has fewer social relationships (Langner & Michael, 1963; Schmidt et al., 1968); and belongs to significantly fewer voluntary organizations (Dotson, 1951; Scott, 1958). Again, it seems likely that such between-class differences are largely adaptive reflections of differing environmental realities. Such a relatively restricted range of interpersonal experience follows, and perhaps follows logically, from both the types of interclass barriers noted by Davis and Havighurst (1954) and certain consequences of lower-class child rearing. Shaffer (1967) comments:

> A consequence of these [lower-class] child-rearing techniques is that the child, since he has not been provided with the opportunity to observe people taking other people's point of view—particularly his own point of view—does not learn to see himself as others see him; as a result, he fails to develop the conceptualization of the "generalized other" that Mead declared essential to a stable, well differentiated self-image. Gans refers to the diffuse self concept of the working-class child as "monistic" in that it fails to distinguish clearly between its own view of itself and the view toward it that others seem to adopt. . . . Analytically oriented psychotherapy, with its profound emphasis on the "self" as a distinct aspect of cognitive experience, and of a reflective turning back upon the self, would necessarily be a very difficult and somewhat threatening task for anyone lacking this kind of self-awareness [pp. 252–253].

Kerckhoff (1969) has offered similar observations, and adds that the purportedly greater middle-class parental emphasis on nurturance, internal control, and the provision of general principles as a means of explaining (particularly interpersonal) behavior to the child serves to increase the child's skill and motivation in both role taking and role playing. Such nurturance, internal control, and provision of meaningful interpersonal and personal generalizations is, he proposes, considerably diminished in lower-class child rearing.

To the extent that these observations are valid, it would appear that treatment approaches for lower-class patients need incorporate role-taking training and practice in empathy-building activities—rather than assume such skills as given to build upon.

## Delay of Gratification

A course of traditional psychotherapy, as typically conceived and implemented, lasts a considerable length of time. During the customary year or two of such treatment, the patient is required to engage in lengthy processes of exploring historical and contemporary material to derive patterns of current and future usefulness, and scrutinize in detail and often with considerable repetition his inner life, interpersonal world, and environmental circumstances. All such activities fairly demand considerable patience under pressure, and a high level of ability to pursue distant and ambiguous goals in the absence of appreciable reward for much of the time one is doing so, especially in the early months of treatment. Yet there are many observations in the sociological and psychological literature of a purported tendency among lower-class populations to find it difficult to delay or defer gratification. Schneider and Lysgaard (1953), for example, examined delay of gratification as a function of social class in a sample of 2500 high school students. They report lessened ability or desire to defer gratification as one descends the social class ladder in such areas as aggression, education, and level of aspiration. LeShan (1952), working with a sample of 8- to 11-year-old children, analyzed the stories he had them write in terms of the time perspective portrayed and related dimensions. The stories written by upper- and middle-class children, as compared to those by lower-class children, included significantly more future planning and regularity of activity. Lower-class children produced significantly more themes involving shorter time spans and quick sequences of tension and relief. Rosen (1956), in a study of social class and achievement motivation, reported his lower-class adolescent subjects were significantly more present oriented, more passive and more family oriented than were middle-class subjects. The latter, in turn, were highly future and activity oriented. Lipset (1966), Pollack, Ochberg, and Meyer (1969), Prince (1969), and others have offered similar observations.

As Kohn was noted to observe earlier regarding parental values and use of punishment, and as we have noted earlier regarding other characteristics of lower-class persons, the lower-class tendency not to defer gratification appears to be fully and appropriately consistent with the realities of the total lower-class environment. Delay of gratification, a major component of the middle-class ethic, is generally appropriate and adaptive in a middle-class context. Delay is frequently rewarded. In a lower-class context such pursuit of distant goals, of putting off receiving today to receive more at a later date, is simply often maladaptive. Such enhanced reward is rarely forthcoming. Thus, there is often little reason why the lower-class person *should* defer seeking immediate gratification. We are fully in accord with Miller and Riessman (1969) who comment:

> The nature of the conditions of working-class lives (jobs, opportunities, family structure) affects behavior more than has been frequently realized; similarly, modes of understanding the environment can be more important than deep-seated personality factors in behavioral patterns. For example, worker's low estimates of opportunities and high expectation of risk and loss may be more crucial in the unwillingness to undertake certain long-term actions than personality inadequacies involved in a presumed inability to defer gratification [p. 87].

We would derive from the foregoing the suggestion that, in addition to the features suggested by earlier sections, an optimal, class-linked psychotherapy for lower-class patients would be brief and would provide early, continuing, and frequent reinforcement of desired patient behavior.

In summary, we have examined in this chapter a number of observational reports and investigations comparing dimensions of middle-class vs. lower-class personality development. As our particular emphasis we focused upon those dimensions of greatest apparent relevance to the search for a prescriptive psychotherapy for lower-class patients. Findings in such domains as self-direction, conformity, role-taking experience, and delay of gratification combine to simultaneously support the appropriateness of traditional psychotherapies for middle-class patient populations, and suggest the gross inappropriateness of traditional approaches for lower-class patients. Instead, from these data, we infer that a potentially more appropriate and more successful psychotherapy for such patients, one also more congruent with the character of the lower-class environment, would be brief; authoritatively administered; have a behavioral emphasis; and involve conformity to concrete example; role-taking training; and early, continuing, and frequent reinforcement.

# *Chapter 3*

# LANGUAGE AND MALCOMMUNICATION

Communication between the middle-class therapist and the lower-class patient has been described as having ". . . the aura of a Kafka scene: two persons ostensibly playing the same game but actually adhering to rules that are private [Mayer & Timms, 1969, p. 37]." Haas (1965) portrays such verbal interaction as one in which ". . . the patient listens with faint heart and half an ear to the psychiatric intonations, and the psychiatrist hears with cynical and paternal indulgence the recital of the lower class patient [p. 408]." There is indeed considerable reason to believe that such communication is largely pseudocommunication; that much of what is said across this particular social class gulf goes unheard; that in several major and highly consequential ways, therapist and patient are literally not talking the same language.

## Elaborate versus Restricted Codes

Sapir (1931) has maintained that the smaller an interpersonal circle, and the more complex is the level of understanding already arrived at by its members, the more economical can the intercommunication within it become. Thus, he proposes, a single word passed between members of an intimate group, in spite of its apparent vagueness and ambiguity, may constitute a far more precise communication than volumes of carefully prepared correspondence interchanged between two governments. Vygotsky (1962) has similarly held that the more a subject of dialogue is held in common, the more likely it is that the dialogue will consist of condensed and abbreviated speech. Bernstein (1961b), a major contributor to the issues we wish to examine here, has taken a similar position. He observes that a child's language when interacting with other children differs in both structure and content from that used when speaking to an adult; that the spoken language within combat units differs in an analogous manner from that typically used in civilian life; and that similarly condensed speech patterns may be observed in married couples, between old friends, and the like. In such relationships, Bernstein observes, meaning does not have to be made fully explicit; a slight shift in pitch or stress, or a small gesture, can convey complex meanings. He notes that under these circumstances

> Communication goes forward against a backcloth of closely shared identifications and affective empathy which removes the need for elaborate verbal expression. This . . . form of communication may render what is actually said gravely misleading to an observer who does not share the history of the relationship [p. 167].

Of major relevance to our own theme, Bernstein (1961b) comments:

> It is suggested that this is the situation in which many children of the lower working-class grow up. Their society is *limited* to a form of spoken language in which complex verbal procedures are made irrelevant by the system of non-verbal, closely shared identifications which serve as a backcloth to the speech. The form of the social relationship acts selectively on language potential. Verbalization is limited and organized by means of a narrow range of formal possibilities. These restricted formal strategies, for the sustained organization of verbal meaning, are capable of solving a comparatively small number of linguistic problems, yet, for this social group they are the *only* means of solving all and every verbal problem requiring a sustained response. It is not a question of vocabulary, it is a matter of the means available for the organization of meaning. . . . The linguistic relationship between the lower working-class mother and her child is such that little pressure is placed upon the child to verbalize in a way which signals and symbolizes his unique experience. . . . Spoken language is *not* perceived as a major vehicle for presenting to others inner states of the speaker. . . . The shift of emphasis from non-verbal to verbal signals in the middle-class mother-child relationship occurs earlier and the pattern of verbal signals is far more elaborate. Inherent in the middle-class linguistic relationship is a pressure to verbalize feeling in a relatively individual manner and this process is guided by a speech model which regularly and consistently makes available to the child the formal means whereby the process is facilitated. It can be said that for the middle-class child there is a progressive development towards verbalizing and making explicit, subjective intent, while this is not the case for the working-class child [p. 167].

> The experience of children from these gross strata follows different paths from the very beginnings of speech. The type of learning, the conditions of learning and the dimensions of relevance initiated and sustained by the spoken language are completely different. In fact, it would not be too much

> to say that in strategic respects they are antithetical. . . . They have learned
> two different forms of spoken language; the only thing they have in common
> is that the words are English [p. 168].

These two language forms or emphases, characteristic of middle-class and working-class children respectively, Bernstein has termed elaborate and restricted codes. The elaborate code is distinguished by a sensitivity to *structure,* defined as a learned ability to respond to an object perceived, and defined in terms of a matrix of relationships. This verbal code, more fully, is characterized by:

1. Accurate grammatical order and syntax which regulate what is said
2. Logical modifications and stress which are mediated through a grammatically complex sentence construction, especially through the use of a range of conjunctions and subordinate clauses
3. Frequent use of prepositions which indicate logical relationships, as well as prepositions which indicate temporal and spatial continuity
4. Frequent use of personal pronouns, e.g., I, one, it
5. A discriminative selection from a range of adjectives and adverbs
6. Individual qualification which is verbally mediated through the structure and relationships within and between sentences
7. Excessive symbolism which discriminates between meanings within speech sequences, rather than reinforcing dominant words or phrases, or accompanying the sequence in a diffuse, generalized manner
8. It is a language use which points to the possibilities inherent in a complex conceptual hierarchy for the organizing of experience.

A restricted verbal code, held by Bernstein to characterize working-class persons, is distinguished by a sensitivity to *content,* defined as a learned ability to respond to the boundaries of an object, rather than to the matrix of relationships in which it stands with other objects. It is marked by a rigidity of syntax, a restricted range of verbal organizations, and a relatively condensed pattern of speech in which certain meanings (*not* the quantity of speech) are restricted. It is further characterized by:

1. Short, grammatically simple, often unfinished sentences with a poor syntactical form often stressing the active voice
2. Simple and repetitive use of conjunctions, e.g., so, then, because
3. Little use of subordinate clauses to break down the initial categories of the dominant subject.
4. Infrequent holding of a formal subject through a speech sequence, thus presenting a dislocated informational content
5. Rigid and limited use of adjectives and verbs

6. Infrequent use of personal pronouns as subject of conditional clauses
7. Frequent use of categorical statements in which the reason and conclusion are confounded
8. A large number of phrases which seek to support the previous speech sequence, e.g., "You see?"; "Wouldn't it."; "You know."— a process known as sympathetic circularity
9. Individual qualification is implicit in the sentence organization. It is, Bernstein holds, a language of implicit meanings.

Bernstein's further description of a restricted code is of interest. He views such language as essentially a vehicle for expressing and receiving concrete, global, and descriptive relationships organized at a low level of conceptualization. Word sequences strongly tend to refer to broad classes of contents rather than progressive differentiation within a class. Or, alternatively, a range of items within a class may be specified without apparent awareness of the concept which summarizes the class. The categories referred to tend not to be broken down systematically and this, Bernstein holds, has critical implications if the reference to be designated is the subjective state of the speaker. Furthermore, he adds, the characteristic focus on implicit meanings makes it progressively more difficult to make explicit, and verbally elaborate, subjective intent. The code is generated in social relationships in which the intent of others may be largely taken for granted. There is a sharing or expectation of common intent which simplifies the structure of speech and increases its predictability. Such shared interests, identifications, and cultural perspectives greatly reduce the need for verbal elaboration of unique experiences. Thus, for example, the number of qualifiers of various types used in speech is markedly reduced. The speech, Bernstein observes, is relatively impersonal and serves primarily to transmit similarities rather than differences in personal experience. The restricted code functions mostly to permit the signaling of social rather than personal identity. When aspects of personal identity are communicated, such communication occurs largely through nonverbal means, rather than verbal elaboration. The code emphasizes and makes relevant concrete, here-and-now actions, rather than reflective, abstract relationships. Interest in motivational processes are minimal. The self is rarely the subject of verbal investigation. The restricted code, Bernstein feels, serves the purpose of strengthening within-group solidarity by minimizing the signaling of personal differences. Such differences may be signaled, but they are rarely explored systematically.

That the elaborate versus restricted code dichotomy in fact exists, and does so along social class lines, may rather convincingly be concluded not only from Bernstein's highly creative but descriptive efforts, but also from a series of rigorous investigations conducted by Bernstein (1959, 1961b, 1962, 1965), Brandis and Henderson (1970), and Lawton (1968). These studies, involving large samples of middle- and working-class children, and controlling for age and nonverbal intelligence, do in fact demonstrate significant between-class differences in most of the specific characteristics of elaborate and restricted codes presented above. Yet it must be noted that Bernstein's and Lawton's investigations were conducted in Great Britain, using British school children as subjects. In the absence of evidence, the external validity of their findings for American adults is indeterminate. Fortunately, at least some evidence of such cross-cultural verification does exist. Though not addressed explicitly to the examination of elaborate and restricted verbal codes per se, a number of investigations in the United States have identified between-class linguistic differences whose nature corresponds very closely to what Bernstein has identified as characteristics of the two verbal codes.

Schatzman and Strauss (1955), following the occurrence of a tornado in the southern United States, interviewed residents of a stricken community regarding their reactions to the disaster. One of their explicit purposes in doing so was to compare the verbal styles and behaviors of middle- and lower-class respondents under stressful circumstances. The investigators and their research team interviewed 340 middle-class (one or two years of college minimum plus family income of $4000 or more) and lower-class (grammar school education plus family income less than $2000) respondents. Schatzman and Strauss (1955), based upon their interview data, observe:

> The difference [between middle- and lower-class respondents] is not simply the failure or success, of lower and upper groups respectively, in communicating clearly and in sufficient detail for the interviewer's purposes. Nor does the difference merely involve correctness or elaborateness of grammar or use of a more precise or colorful vocabulary. The difference is a considerable disparity in (a) the numbers and kinds of perspectives utilized in communication, (b) the ability to take the listener's role, (c) the handling of classifications, and (d) the frameworks and stylistic devices which order and implement the communication [p. 337].

In greater detail, the following, major between-class differences in communication patterns were observed:

1. *Perspective or Centering*. Almost all lower-class respondents offered descriptions of events as seen through their own eyes only. Their "best" response, as judged by the investigators, was a straight, direct nar-

rative of events as they saw and experienced them. Such Ss, in a manner consistent with our earlier consideration of lower-class role-taking deficiencies, only very rarely assumed the role of another toward still others. The responses of middle-class subjects typically reflected a much broader perspective, with frequent and varied descriptions offered as they imagined other people or groups of persons might have experienced the event.

2. *Correspondences of Imagery between Speaker and Listener.* Lower-class respondents appeared to display a relative lack of sensitivity to disparities in perspective between themselves and their interviewer. The narratives provided by their Ss contained little elaboration, qualification, depth, or use of examples. Summary statements were virtually absent. In contrast, middle-class respondents seemed to much more fully recognize that imagery may be diverse and that context must be provided. Hence their statements contained many contextual and other clarifications and qualifications. As the investigators comment,

> He sets the stage with rich introductory material, expands themes, frequently illustrates, anticipates disbelief, meticulously locates and identifies places and persons. . . . The middle-class person—by virtue, we would presume, of his great sensitivity to his listener—stands more outside his experience [p. 332].

3. *Classification and Classificatory Relations.* Lower-class Ss make reference primarily to the acts and persons of particular individuals, rarely referring to classes of persons or to entire organizations. Their verbalizations tend to be particularistic and concrete. A much fuller use of classificatory terms and concepts were offered by middle-class respondents, who similarly offered frequent generalizations and abstractions.

And, of apparent relevance for understanding the communicative implications when a lower-class patient is paired with a middle-class psychotherapist, the investigators conclude:

> The lower-class person in these Arkansas towns infrequently meets a middle-class person in anything like [this] interview. Here he must talk at great length to a stranger about personal experiences, as well as recall for his listener a tremendous number of details. Presumably he is accustomed to talking about such matters and in such detail only to listeners with whom he shares a great deal of experience and symbolism, so that he need not be very self-conscious about communicative technique. He can, as a rule, assume that words, phrases and gestures are assigned approximately similar meanings by his listeners. But this is not so in the interview or, indeed, in any situation where class converses with class in nontraditional modes [p. 337].

Other components of elaborate and restricted codes have been demonstrated to vary across social classes in American samples. Day (1932), Davis (1932), and McCarthy (1930) each demonstrated that middle-class children used longer and more complex sentences at an earlier age than lower-class children, a difference which increased as the children got older. Templin (1957), working with preschool children, demonstrated that lower-class children, in comparison to those from middle- or upper-class homes, used less adequate sentence structure and had significantly poorer sound discrimination and vocabulary scores. John (1963) has shown that lower-class children, in comparison to their middle-class peers, used shorter, less abstract, and less integrated sentences, and drew upon a narrower range of vocabulary in doing so. Deutsch's (1963) findings, in a manner very similar to Bernstein's, led him to conclude that lower-class school children use an informal language structure, and do so mainly to convey concrete needs and immediate consequences, while middle-class language usage tends to be more formal, abstract, and emphasize the interrelation of concepts. Deutsch's data are based on the intensive study of family interactions in 292 lower- and middle-class homes. He suggests that while the elaborate versus restricted code dichotomy may fit the American social class system somewhat less well than is true in Great Britain, it nevertheless appears to be largely applicable. In lower-class socialization, he holds,

> . . . language is used in a convergent or restrictive fashion, rather than adivergent elaborative fashion . . . an imperative or a partial sentence frequently replaces a complete sentence or an explanation: if a child asks for something, the response is too frequently "yes," "no," "go away," "later" or simply a nod. The feedback is not such that it gives the child the articulated verbal parameters that allow him to start and fully develop normative labeling and identification of the environment [p. 80].

As other investigators in this domain have reported, Deutsch indicates that the foregoing language deficits increase with increasing age. Jenson (1964, 1967) similarly reports that the language of the lower-class individual consists largely of a small repertoire of stereotyped phrases and expressions which are used rather loosely and with little effort to achieve subtle correspondence between perception and verbal expression. In contrast, he holds, middle-class language is more detailed, abstract, flexible, and descriptively subtle. Hess and Shipman (1965) report that, as was true of the middle-class mothers in Bernstein's research, the middle-class mothers in their investigation consistently used more words than lower-class mothers, provided their children more opportunities for labeling, for identifying feelings, and for dealing with interpersonal interaction. Even when total verbal output was controlled, middle-class mothers' sentences were much more complex, gramatically subtle, and contained more abstraction. Heider (1971) has reported consistent social class differences in encoding style, with middle-class Ss proving to be superior or more descriptive encoders. When the encoding products (responses) of her middle- and lower-class Ss were then presented as stimuli to be decoded by other such Ss, it was demonstrated that Ss most successfully decode material originated by same social class Ss—a finding certainly consistent with the interclass communication issues at the heart of the present chapter.

These several investigations, conducted primarily by psychologists and reporting interclass discrepancies in syntax, vocabulary, abstraction, etc., have been interpreted as support for the *deficit* viewpoint in what is currently described as the "deficit-difference controversy" (Williams, 1970). The deficit viewpoint is essentially an environmentalist position which proposes that the lower-class child's language behavior is *inferior* to that of his middle-class counterpart because of an inferior language environment, e.g., lack of adequate parental speech models at home, insufficient or inappropriate language stimulation, insufficient corrective feedback, etc. The *difference* position, promulgated primarily by linguists (Baratz, 1970; Labov, 1970; Shuy, 1970; Stewart, 1970), holds that:

> . . . no natural language or dialect can really be considered more primitive, rudimentary, or underdeveloped than another. In brief, as applied to the deficit position on the language of the poor, this group of linguists is arguing [instead] that what we are observing are often language differences, and if there is a discrepancy between the demands of the school, for example, and the performance of the child, we are seeing the consequences of forcing a child to perform in a linguistic system other than his primary one. Nonstandard English, the linguists hold, is a well-ordered, highly structured, highly developed language system which, in many respects, is different from standard English [Williams, 1970, p. 5].

The deficit position has led to recommendations for language remediation based upon the lower-class child's purported unreadiness for school, e.g., Head Start or other compensatory education programs. The difference viewpoint, in contrast, has placed the burden of unreadiness upon the schools themselves, upon methodological inadequacies in teaching procedures. These conflicting viewpoints are strikingly parallel to the central theme of the present book. Shall we continue to view the lower-class psychotherapy patient as "unready," and expend our therapeutic efforts toward indoctrinating him, toward teaching him our therapeutic language? Or shall we, instead, more fully acknowledge our own unreadiness, our own paucity of skills for assisting such patients, and thus seek to develop techniques responsive to "the difference"?

If it is thus indeed the case that the contemporary, American, middle-class psychotherapist communicates (speaks and, in a sense, listens) via an elaborate verbal code, and the typical lower-class patient utilizes a restricted code to both send and receive his verbal messages, their psychotherapeutic interaction would appear to be almost destined to fail—as material reviewed earlier in fact frequently demonstrates. Bernstein (1964) concludes in this regard:

> The therapy relationship is based upon the belief that the conditions which brought the patient into the relationship may be ameliorated by communication in a context which involves the suspension of the patient's social identity, and where the referent for the communication is the discrete experience of the patient. . . . From the therapist's point of view the lower working class patient's communication will seem to be inadequate, there will be a low level of insight, the patient may seem to be negative and passive, so forcing the therapist into taking a more dominant role than he would wish, above all the therapist will meet an unwillingness on the part of the patient to transform his personal feelings into unique verbal meanings . . . these difficulties . . . originate in the speech system the child learns in his culture . . . this speech system creates for the developing child dimensions of relevance and learning usually appropriate for his natural environment but inappropriate for orienting the individual in special relationships like therapy [p. 55].

> It is a code which does not facilitate the verbal elaboration of meaning; it is a code which does not help the user put into words his intent, his unique purposes, beliefs, and motivations. It also does not help him to receive such communications from others. It is a code which sensitizes the user to a particular form of social relationship, which is unambiguous, where the authority is clearcut and serves as a guide to action. . . . From this perspective the psychotherapy relationship involves, for a member of the lower working class, a radical change in his normal coding process. What requires to be made relevant for this relationship is almost the antithesis of what is made relevant by the coding process the individual normally uses in his cultural environment [p. 158].

## Linguistic Relativity

Beyond the specification and partial demonstration of between-class verbal code differences, there is a second basis for questioning the nature of communication between the middle-class therapist and lower-class patient. We suggested above, in effect, that therapist and patient experienced major difficulties in communication because they were in fact using different languages in their efforts to discuss, describe, and alter given symptoms, feeling states, and behaviors. Now we wish to examine the proposition that *because* their languages are different, their very thinking about or conceptualization of these phenomena may themselves differ. This proposition reflects what has come to be known as linguistic relativity, a formulation originally developed by Whorf (1956). Whorf observes:

> According to natural logic . . . talking, or the use of language, is supposed only to "express" what is essentially already formulated non-linguistically. Formulation is an independent process, called thought or thinking, and is supposed to be largely indifferent to the nature of particular languages. Languages have grammers, which are assumed to be merely norms of conventional social correctness, but the use of language is supposed to be guided not so much by them as by correct, rational, or intelligent thinking. Thought, in this view, does not depend on grammar but on the laws of logic or reason which are supposed to be the same for all observers of the universe . . . whether they speak Chinese or Choctaw. Natural logic holds that different languages are essentially parallel methods for expressing this one-and-the-same rationale of thought and, hence, differ really in but minor ways which may seem important only because they are seen at close range [pp. 68–69].

> When linguists became able to examine critically and scientifically a large number of languages of widely different patterns, their base of reference was expanded; they experienced an interruption of phenomena hitherto held universal. . . . It was found that the background linguistic system (in other words, the grammar) of each language is not merely a reproducing instrument for voicing ideas but rather is itself the shaper of ideas, the program and guide for the individual's mental activity, for his analysis of impressions, for his synthesis of his mental stock in trade. . . . We dissect nature along lines laid down by our native languages. . . . We cut nature up, organize it into concepts and ascribe significance as we do, largely because we are parties to an agreement to organize it in this way—an agreement that holds throughout our speech community—and is codified in our language. . . . We are thus introduced to a new principle of relativity, which holds that all observers are not led by the same physical evidence to the same picture of the universe, unless their linguistic backgrounds are similar . . . [p. 71].

There are, as Lawton (1968) notes, varying degrees of attachment to this linguistic relativity hypothesis. Von Humboldt (Lawton, 1968) observes that, "Man lives with the world about him exclusively as language presents it." Sapir (1931) comments that,

> The real world is to a large extent unconsciously built upon the language habits of the group. . . . We see and hear and otherwise experience very

largely as we do because the language habits of our community predispose certain choices of interpretation [p. 80].

Vygotsky (1962) notes that,

> . . . the speech structures mastered by the child become the basic structures of his thinking . . . thought development is determined by language. . . . Thought is not merely expressed in words, it comes into existence through them [p. 74].

And Miller (1951) has proposed that ". . . thinking is never more precise than the language it uses." Similarly, Brown (1958) observes that,

> Children acquiring their first language learn more than a set of vocal skills, they take on the world view of their group. . . . The language of the world, like the professional vocabularies within one language, are so many different windows on reality [p. 31].

The linguistic relativity position has similarly been promulgated by Olmstead (1950) in his work on "ethnolinguistics," and by Hymes (1964) in a domain he describes as "anthropological linguistics." Yet, in spite of its apparent popularity, relevant research has yielded an equivocal outcome. While Diebold's (1965) review of some of this research led him to a position in support of the interdependence of language and thought (a position itself somewhat more conservative than the original Whorfian formulation), Carroll's (1964) extensive examination of relevant investigations led him to offer that, ". . . the linguistic relativity hypothesis has thus far received very little support. Our best guess at present is that the effects of language structure will be found to be limited and localized." Our own consideration of this literature leads us to a more intermediate position, one in agreement with that offered by Hoijer (1951) and Lawton (1968). Hoijer states:

> Far from being simply a technique of communication (language) provides . . . habitual modes of analyzing experience into significant categories. And to the extent that languages differ markedly from each other, so should we expect to find significant and formidable barriers to cross-cultural communication and understanding. . . . It is, however, easy to exaggerate linguistic differences of this nature and the consequent barriers to intercultural understanding. . . . There are important resemblances between all known cultures that stem in part from diffusion and in part from the fact that all cultures are built around biological, psychological, and social characteristics common to all mankind. The language of human beings do not so much determine the perceptual and other faculties of their speakers vis a vis experience

as they influence and direct these faculties along prescribed channels
[Lawton, 1968, pp. 68–69].

Based upon the child-rearing and socialization research presented in
the previous chapter, and the investigations of divergent verbal codes presented above, we would propose that it is not too great an exaggeration to
claim that the American middle- and lower-classes are in many real and
important respects *different* cultures, and that as such much of the foregoing material dealing with intercultural linguistic differences and their
consequences for thinking may be directly relevant to interclass communication in the United States. Both Davis (1967) and Jensen (1967)
have taken similar positions. While we are clearly not proposing that
middle- and lower-class are analogous in degree to Chinese and Choctaw,
we would speculate nevertheless that the important interclass linguistic
differences which do exist may yield significant, if often subtle, differences in meaning and thought. To be very concrete, we would propose
that when using terms such as the following, the middle-class therapist
and the lower-class patient may often not mean the same thing, may often not be seeking to communicate the same meanings, and at times may
in fact be conceptualizing *very* different phenomena or experiences: security, frustration, satisfaction, dependency, fear, manliness, responsibility, sex, marriage, fun, crazy, motherhood, discipline, psychotherapy, doctor, boss, feelings, happiness, etc.*
It thus seems quite possible that the middle-class psychotherapist and
the lower-class patient are often literally not speaking the same language
in their therapeutic pseudo-conversation and, when they do in a sense ut-
ter the same words, their meanings and thought processes may often be
subtly or even grossly different. Three possible solutions to these class-
linked language barriers seem possible. Bernstein (1961b) has reported
that while lower-class persons are limited to a restricted verbal code,†
middle-class persons appear able to shift codes, and thus converse in either elaborate or restricted systems. Several psychotherapists have urged
their middle-class colleagues to seek to actively enter the linguistic world
of their lower-class patients (Baum & Felzer, 1964; Bernard, 1953;
Gould, 1967; Koegler & Brill, 1967; Lerner, 1972). The evidence in support of such efforts thus far is rather modest, however, and at this point

* For a very complete illustration of the manner in which words may vary in
meaning according to social class, see Landy (1971).

† Lawton (1968) and Williams and Naremore (1969) however, report data indicating that their samples of restricted code users could, when sufficiently pressed, make
considerably greater use of an elaborate linguistic code.

we would wonder if a sufficient number of middle-class psychotherapists are sufficiently skilled and motivated for this particular linguistic solution to be considered a viable one in any important sense.

A second potential means for breaching these class-linked linguistic barriers would seem to involve the utilization as psychotherapists of persons whose own social class background and consequent life style has resulted in the characteristic use of a restricted verbal code as their prepotent linguistic system. By this suggestion, we refer to the use of paraprofessional or nonprofessional psychotherapists of lower- or working-class background. We are indeed hopeful about this growing movement, and will explore its nature and ramifications in greater depth in Chapter 8.

Finally, in lieu of either linguistic training or seeking out therapists who are already facile in the use of a restricted code because of their own social class background, there is the possibility of employing therapeutic methods which are much less dependent upon complex or abstract verbalization, methods which would suffer rather little if therapist and patient operated on largely different linguistic wavelengths. We refer here to the type of action-oriented psychotherapeutic approach we have begun to describe in earlier chapters, one whose major components are modeling, role playing, and social reinforcement, that is, *Structured Learning Therapy*. These emphases on concrete prosocial examples, behavioral rehearsal, and social reward require considerably less therapeutic conversation of traditional types and, as such, appear to pose a correspondingly reduced linguistic problem. Furthermore, the concrete and action-oriented nature of these techniques appears to be highly congruent with a restricted code disposition.

# Chapter 4

# PSYCHOPATHOLOGY AND SOCIOPATHOLOGY

## Introduction

Perhaps one of the most often replicated and enduring findings in the history of psychiatry and psychology is the disproportionately high concentration of schizophrenia in the lowest social class. In separate reports covering public, or public and private, mental hospital facilities in Ohio; New York State; New York City; Kansas City; Milwaukee; Omaha; Worcester; Baltimore; St. Louis; Peoria; Chicago; Detroit; Rochester, Minnesota; Rochester, New York; Nova Scotia; Nigeria; Taiwan; Norway and Great Britain; in separate publications reflecting the years 1856, 1889, 1909, 1925, 1929, 1935, 1939, 1941, 1942, 1944, 1948, 1949, 1951, 1952, 1954, 1955, 1958, 1960, 1963, 1965, 1966 and 1967; and whether social class was defined in terms of income, type of occupation, educational level, quality of housing or some combination thereof, the same general finding has almost always appeared—by far the greatest number of hospitalized schizophrenic patients are lower social class (Bodian, 1963; Clark, 1948b; Clausen & Kohn, 1959; Dunham, 1965; Frumkin, 1955; Fuson, 1943; Gardner & Babigian, 1966; Gerard & Houston, 1953; Hare, 1956; Hollingshead & Redlich, 1958; Hyde & Kingsley, 1944; Jaco, 1960; Jaffe & Shanas, 1939; Klee, 1966; Leighton, 1963; Leighton & Lambo, 1963; Lin, 1966; Locke, 1958; Malzberg, 1940, 1956; Nolan, 1917; Odegaard, 1932; Schroeder, 1942; Turner & Wagenfeld, 1967; Wanklin, Flemming, Buck, & Hobbs, 1955). The sheer number and diversity of settings, procedures, social class criteria, investigators, and dates of investigation add to the strength of this finding. Yet, its strength, or durability, and replicability notwithstanding, this same diversity of investigative characteristics also masks a welter of methodological problems and at least a few plausible rival hypotheses.

**53**

The concentration of schizophrenia among lower-class persons and in lower-class urban centers may largely represent, according to Mishler and Scotch (1963), an artifact of measurement. Many of the investigations cited above made use of *only* state mental hospital admissions as their source of data. There is reason to believe that such institutions are used disproportionately by lower- and working-class populations in the United States, with patients of higher social classes relying proportionately more upon private psychiatric hospitals, psychiatric units in general hospitals, and a variety of outpatient facilities. In response to such likely measurement bias, several studies have included private psychiatric hospitals in their sources of data collection. When such has been the case, the disproportion of lower-class schizophrenic patients was *still* obtained. However, Mishler and Scotch note that biases, albeit more subtle ones, may be operative even here, and thus the basic findings may still in large measure be artifactual. They note, for example, that private hospitals, those disproportionately populated by middle- and upper-class patients, may for reasons of avoidance of social stigma and in response to greater sensitivity to feelings of relatives, actually use the diagnostic category "schizophrenia" much less often. Yet the basic finding has also emerged in those investigations which sought to avoid hospitals and hospital statistics altogether by studying undiagnosed psychopathology in the general community (Pasamanick, Roberts, Lemkau, & Krueger, 1959; Srole & Langner, 1962).

The majority of the investigations noted above rely on *incidence* data (number of new admissions per unit of time) rather than *prevalence* data (number of cases in existence per unit of time). Mishler and Scotch note that middle- and upper-class patients are relatively more likely to have had their emotional difficulties detected early and, if hospitalized, to have been released after a considerably shorter period than is true for the typical lower-class schizophrenic patient. In successive age categories, an increasingly higher proportion of middle- and upper-class patient's admissions would be *readmissions*—thus reducing in studies based upon incidence the apparent incidence of schizophrenia in these higher social class groups. It may also be the case, they note, ". . . that admissions to hospitals do not constitute a representative sample of persons becoming schizophrenic, but are a sample of those who did not recover quickly [p. 334]." The families of higher social class patients are more familiar with, and more likely to have the resources to use, the types of private and outpatient treatment facilities which may decrease the likelihood of hospitalization for the developing schizophrenic patient. A wide array of biases in the diagnostic process, examined in Chapter 1, may similarly lead to overuse or underuse of the label "schizophrenia" as an artifactual function of patient social class.

The placement of patients in social class categories presents analogous measurement problems. In addition to the several types of measurement issues relevant to social class which have been raised in contemporary sociology and epidemiology (Gordon, 1950; Grey, 1969; Hodge, 1964; Kahl, 1957; Pfautz, 1952; Tumin, 1967), there are certain mensurational concerns especially relevant to the schizophrenia–social class relationship. Mishler and Scotch (1963) correctly observe that reliable coding of even the single social class criterion of occupation requires several items of information as well as detailed coding instructions. In most of the studies cited above, information as to patient social class was obtained from hospital admitting office records, which likely contain large numbers of errors. Occupational coding is likely particularly difficult at the lower-class level, and for persons with a history of employment instability. For example, how long a period without work equals "unemployed"? Is one's most recent occupation coded, or one's usual occupation? And, however reliably occupation is coded, what of the occupational code or standard itself? Murphy (1969) observes that an individual may be allocated to a given social status based, in a sense, upon national norms (e.g., *Dictionary of Occupational Titles*), but the same occupation may mean very different social class standing within his own ethnic subcommunity. Gordon (1958) holds a similar view and has sought to fuse social class and ethnic conceptualizations in his notion of "ethclass." He comments that ". . . attempts to stratify members of urban subcommunities in terms of criterion levels derived from the analysis of non-ethnic groups are apt to be in serious error."

We have presented above essentially but a sampling of the measurement concerns associated with the schizophrenia-social class relationship and the allocation of patients to schizophrenic versus nonschizophrenic and to social class categories.* We have done so to provide some perspective on the overwhelmingly consistent pattern of findings presented at the beginning of this chapter. Our position remains, in spite of these quite legitimate concerns regarding measurement artifacts, that the evidence very substantially points to a real and disproportionate concentration of schizophrenia in the lower class. This conclusion is further sup-

---

* For a fuller consideration of the methodological issues particularly relevant to this research domain, see Dohrenwend and Dohrenwend (1965), Kohn (1969) and Mishler and Scotch (1963).

ported by Mishler and Scotch (1963) who examined in particular detail those few studies in this domain which were largely free of the artifactual possibilities described above. They comment:

> The most consistent finding, which emerges in light of the nine studies, is that the highest incidence [of schizophrenia] is associated with the lowest social class groupings used in each study. In six studies it is the unskilled or laborers category, in the seventh it is the unemployed, and in the eighth, it is the lowest of four social classes—defined by an index of occupation, education and residence—that produces the highest rate [p. 326].

If the concentration of schizophrenia in the lower class is thus not largely artifactual, the major task remains of explaining on psychological, sociological, or other bases the sources of such psychopathology-social class association.

## The Social Selection Hypothesis

This broad hypothesis, and its variants, may be stated most generally from a causal viewpoint as the position that a patient's psychological or psychopathological condition largely *determines* his social class position. The developing psychological disturbance is held to antedate and lead to lower-class status. Faris and Dunham (1939), Gardner and Babigian (1966), Gerard and Houston (1953), Klee (1966), Schroder (1942), and several other investigators have each found that schizophrenics are disproportionately concentrated in the lower socioeconomic areas of (especially large) American cities. The social selection hypothesis, and in particular its "social drift" variant, holds that it is not the case that more schizophrenics are *produced* in these areas, but that schizophrenics whose disturbance developed in other, often higher-status areas, are unable to maintain their level of functioning in these original areas and drift to the bottom of the ecological-occupational heap. At the time of hospitalization they are counted as having come from these latter areas and occupations. Evidence bearing upon this hypothesis is equivocal. The essential question addressed to the data of relevant studies concerns the presence or absence of evidence of downward mobility in either quality and location of residence or in occupation prior to hospitalization for schizophrenia. Gerard and Houston (1953), for example, calculated the incidence of schizophrenia by ecological area in Worcester, Massachusetts, and indeed found that the large majority of their subjects had lived in the economically poorer areas only a short period of time. Hare (1956) reports similar findings. Lapouse, Monk, and Terris (1956), however, obtained contrary evidence in their study of ecological movement in Buffalo. The ecological distribution of their sample of lower-class schizophrenic patients at the time of first admission to a hospital was not significantly different from (1) their distribution at an earlier point in time, or (2) the ecological distribution of a group of nonschizophrenic matched controls. Hollingshead and Redlich (1958) have obtained similar results. In their study, most Class I and II patients had *always* lived in the best ecological areas; most Class V patients had *always* lived in the worst areas.

Equally conflicting results are apparent when one considers occupational mobility or drift. Goldberg and Morrison (1963) report that at the time of the patients' births in their sample, the social class distribution of patients' fathers was very similar to the population as a whole. The patients' own occupational history, however, showed a major decline in occupational status from both father to son and within the patients' own occupational histories. Lystad (1957) and Schwartz (1946) report concurring findings. Yet, Hollingshead and Redlich (1958) found that only 1% of Class V patients in their sample were downwardly mobile from the occupational level of their family of orientation, 87% of the Class V schizophrenics came from Class V families of orientation. Clausen and Kohn (1959), in a similar test of the drift hypothesis via use of intergenerational mobility data, compared father's occupational level against S's occupational level in both schizophrenic and normal samples. No significant differences emerged between the two samples in the percentage of Ss who rose, fell, or remained at the same occupational level as their fathers'. Dunham (1964) and Srole and Langner (1962) were similarly unable to find support for the social (occupational) drift hypothesis.

Turner and Wagonfeld (1967), in one of the best controlled studies in this domain, report a somewhat different investigative outcome. They compared the occupational histories of a schizophrenic sample to that of a representative sample of normals. Compared to their fathers, more schizophrenics than normals were indeed downwardly mobile. But this downward mobility (from father's social class level) was not a matter of decline from a higher level already achieved by the patient. It reflected instead a failure to ever have achieved as high an occupational level as might be expected based upon father's occupation. Kohn (1970) observes in response to these findings:

> This argues strongly against a simple drift hypothesis—it is *not*, as some have argued, that we have erroneously rated men at lower than their usual class status because we have classified them according to their occupations

at time of hospitalization, after they have suffered a decline in occupational position. It is more likely that a more sophisticated drift hypothesis applies —that some people genetically or constitutionally or otherwise predisposed to schizophrenia show some effects of developing illness at least as early as the time of their first jobs, for they are never able to achieve the occupational levels that might be expected of them. If so, the possibilities of some interaction between genetic predisposition and early social circumstances are very real indeed [p. 119].

Schizophrenia, in light of our knowledge to date, is an exceedingly complex disorder or set of disorders, involving possible genetic, constitutional, environmental, and social learning determinants. As such, it appears appropriate to conclude from the studies examined above that social selection may be among the factors responsible for the lower-class concentration of schizophrenia. It is clearly not the only factor, and the extent of its contribution is presently indeterminate.

## The Social Causation Hypothesis

The social causation hypothesis may be stated most generally from a causal viewpoint as the position that a patient's social class standing largely *determines* his psychological or psychopathological condition. *Stress* is the fulcrum of this hypothesis. Most broadly, it is held that the conditions of lower-class life antedate and lead to the development of the high concentration of schizophrenia. Many investigators have championed this social causation position in one of its several forms, focusing on a specific stress or combinations thereof which are particularly characteristic of lower-class living. It is a position, as will be seen below, which we too have largely embraced.

A stress-induced theory of causation as a means of relating social class to schizophrenia is a notion of very long standing. Dain (1964), examining psychiatric thought during the early nineteenth century, notes there was considerable emphasis during this period upon:

> . . . the effect of socioeconomic forces on the emotional and physical condition of the individual. The growth of industry and rise in business speculation, the influx of immigrants, the struggle over Negro slavery, and the attempts to care for the mentally ill of the lower classes brought socioeconomic conditions to greater prominence in psychiatric thought. . . . They believed that insanity usually occurred when frustrations were greatest, and in an affluent society those who failed to achieve their highest ambitions were subject to keen disappointment and possible mental illness [p. 89].

Other early proponents of a stress-induced, social causation view of severe emotional disturbances include Miller (1924), who wrote of "oppression psychosis"; Mayo (1937), who sought to relate the effects of urban, industrial environments to the development of individual psychopathology; Faris (1932), who observed the effects of urban overcrowding upon emotional disorders in children; and such others as Elliot (1914), Frank (1939), and Hallowell (1934).

There is all manner of evidence—in professional literature, social commentaries, everyday publications, and so forth—that lower-class living is indeed often very stressful, and clearly more so than in higher social classes. In perhaps all areas of personal, interpersonal, familial, social, and economic functioning; in housing, medical care, education, employment, and a full array of other areas of functioning, lower-class living can and very often does involve intense and persistent frustration, anxiety, stress, and perhaps most damaging, little hope for change.

For example, a very partial sample of the stress-relevant, interclass, comparative professional literature reveals that lower-class persons, in comparison to those of higher social class standing, experience as children greater anxiety (Sewell & Haller, 1959), feelings of rejection (Mitchell, 1957), psychosomatic complaints (Mitchell, 1957), and maladjustment (Burchinal, Gardner, & Hawkes, 1958; Coleman, 1940). They are significantly more likely as children to lose one of their parents, to experience moderate to severe emotional disturbance associated with this loss, and to experience considerable interpersonal difficulty with step-parents (Langner & Michael, 1963). They are more likely to feel academically and socially inadequate in school (Bertrand, 1962), perform significantly less well, and dropout significantly earlier (Bertrand, 1962; Brooke, Buri, Byrne, & Hudson, 1962; Davis, 1954; Mussen, Conger, & Kagen, 1963; Toby, 1957). During their school years they will often be treated with hostility or rejection by their typically middle-class teachers (Becker, 1952a & b; Davis, 1954; Mussen et al., 1963; Neugarten, 1956) who will frequently discipline them more harshly and rate them as more maladjusted than their middle-class peers (Dolger & Ginandes, 1946; Groff, 1963; Wallin & Waldo, 1964). The school years also will contain significantly fewer social and extracurricular activities for the lower-class child (Bertrand, 1962; Cook, 1945; Coster, 1958). The lower-class pupil will receive a disproportionately low share of high grades, prizes, awards, and student government positions (Abrahamson, 1952). On a wide variety of criteria, the physical and material quality of the school attended by the lower-class child is likely to be inferior to the middle-class child's school

(Sexton, 1961). In addition, the teachers are likely to be less qualified, the curriculum less varied, and remedial services less available (Sexton, 1961). The "psychological climate" of the school with predominantly lower-class pupils will very often be oriented toward discipline or "management," rather than fostering growth, achievement, aspiration, or hope (Herriott & St. John, 1966; Michaels, 1961; Turner, 1964; Wilson, 1959). While it is indeterminate whether he will engage in more "delinquent" behavior than persons of other class levels, he is significantly more likely to be detected, charged and convicted for such behavior (McDonald, 1969).

As a child and continuing into his adult years, his physical health and the treatment he receives when physically ill will be significantly poorer (French, 1963; Lee & Schneider, 1958; Nortensen, 1959; Pell & D'Alonzo, 1961). In comparison to middle-class persons, he will have a significantly higher rate of arthritis, heart disease, high blood pressure (U.S. National Health Center, 1964); cancer (Buell, Dunn, & Breslow, 1960; Dorn & Cutler, 1959); serious personal injuries (U.S. public Health Survey, 1964); visual disorders, diabetes, and pneumonia (James, 1965); premature births (Rider, Taback, & Knoblock, 1955); and a wide array of dental problems (Stadt, 1967; Szwejda, 1960, 1962). He has significantly less correct information about physical health and disease (Rosenblatt & Suchmen, 1964; Rosenstock, 1966; Lazarsfield & Kendall, 1966), will visit a physician significantly less frequently, and will tend to do so for diagnosis or treatment rather than preventive purposes (Ross, 1962).

He will report to be generally feeling more anxious (Bradburn & Caplovitz, 1965; Gurin, Gurin, Lao, & Beattie, 1969); more powerless (Dean, 1961; Lefcourt, 1966; Mechanic, 1965); to be subjectively less happy (Bradburn & Caplovitz, 1965; Inkeles, 1960); and be having more marital difficulty (Blood & Wolfe, 1960; Roth & Peck, 1951). He is also more likely to be divorced (Chilman & Sussman, 1964; Goode, 1956; Miller, 1959). His housing will be of much poorer quality, more crowded in terms of "use crowding" (rooms designated for one function are used for two or more functions, e.g., a living room doubles as a bedroom), and often will cost more in a relative sense for less in several senses (Chapin, 1961; Schorr, 1964, 1970; Wilner, Walkley, Pinkerton, & Tayback, 1962). In the world of work, compared to those in middle-class positions, he will experience less gratification, security, compensation and status; he will probably work much harder physically, with more physical risk to his person, and with much less hope for advancement along financial, security or status dimensions; and will more frequently be unemployed or underemployed (Bell, 1956; Garbin & Bates, 1966; Hodge, 1964; Jacobs, 1965; Miller & Riessman, 1969; Reiss, 1961; Shostak, 1969). He is less likely to have savings, life insurance, or pension plan coverage; more likely, as a consumer, to be subjected to high-pressure selling, "bait" advertisements, "switch" sales, misrepresentation of price and quality, and the sale of used merchandise as new; more likely to have his wages garnished, and find himself unemployed (and often unemployable) because of his garnishment record (Caplovitz, 1970).

Thus the environmental, interpersonal, physical, and intrapsychic stresses associated with lower-class standing are significantly more widespread and severe than those associated with higher social class standing. That such high levels of stress exit is rather clearly beyond debate. However, what of the position that such stress is largely responsible for the concentration of schizophrenia in the lower class? A number of investigations have been addressed to precisely this question. Langner and Michael (1963) provided indirect evidence in their study of the epidemiology of mental illness in New York City. They found a strong positive correlation between the level of stress (broadly defined) reported by their respondents and their judged levels of emotional disturbance. Their results also indicated that, at the same level of stress, lower-class respondents were more likely than those of middle-class standing to be mentally disturbed.

Also defining stress on rather broad and diverse criteria, Rogler and Hollingshead (1965) conducted an intensive, case-study investigation involving 40 lower-class families in Puerto Rico. Half of the families had one spouse who was schizophrenic, half did not. No major differences were apparent in level of stress experienced by the schizophrenic as compared to the normal respondents during either childhood or adolescence. Physically, interpersonally, and in other domains, the two groups were similar until after the time of marriage. At this point the two groups rather clearly diverged in terms of stress experienced. On several dimensions of personal and social adjustment the schizophrenic respondents, but not the normals, began to experience what Kohn (1970) has described as ". . . an unbearable onslaught of stress." The stressors, which typically commenced approximately one year before the appearance of schizophrenic symptoms, included physical deprivation or illness; major interpersonal difficulties with spouse, extended family and/or neighbors; and severe economic problems. Concurring evidence regarding the disproportionate occurrence of major life stress in the period of time preceding the onset of severe emotion disorders has been reported by Adamson and Schmale (1965), Brown and Birley (1969), Casey, Masuda, and

Holmes (1967), and Clayton, Desmaris, and Winokur (1968). It is perhaps not irrelevant to note in companion to these investigations that both Meyer and Haggerty (1962) and Rahe, Meyer, Smith, Kjaer, and Holmes (1964) have independently demonstrated significant differences between physically healthy controls and samples of patients suffering from such disorders as tuberculosis, cardiac disease, and certain skin diseases in that the latter, but not the former, experienced severe stress or what Rahe et al. (1964) term a "psychosocial life crisis" approximately 1–2 years prior to disease onset. Further relevant evidence is provided by the work of Dohrenwend (1967) who has reported several findings illustrating the manner in which psychological stress of a variety of types can increase the incidence of symptoms of emotional disturbance. The evidence he marshals indicates this stress–symptomatology relationship to hold not only for lower-class individuals in response to the several types of stressors noted above, but for all individuals of whatever social class to such stressors as combat, disaster, fatigue, life events signifying downward occupational mobility, etc. He notes that, with the frequent exception of the lower-class environment (in which stress often persists at high levels), further evidence of the stress–symptomatology relationship is provided by those investigations demonstrating the disappearance or amelioration of symptoms following removal of the stressor.

In response to evidence such as the foregoing, Lapouse et al. (1956) have put forth a stress-induced view of the concentration of schizophrenia in the lower class. They comment:

> . . . the higher rates of schizophrenia in poor neighborhoods may well be due to the psychologic strain imposed by low income with the constant struggle to obtain the necessities of living, fear of unemployment, the lack of job satisfaction, the over-crowded and inadequate housing, the restricted educational and recreational opportunities, and the low social status [p. 985].

In addition to these few supportive studies, in all of which stress was operationalized multidimensionally, there exists considerable research on the stress–schizophrenia relationship in which stress has been defined along a single dimension, a dimension predicted by the given investigator to be particularly potent in the etiology of schizophrenia. It is these investigations we now wish to consider.

### Social Isolation

Faris and Dunham (1939) examined a number of variables characteristic of persons living in the areas of Chicago marked by high rates of schizophrenia. Social class was not among their major concerns. They found that schizophrenia rather strongly tended to concentrate in the center city area, and decline in all directions toward the periphery. This finding has subsequently been replicated in other urban areas on several occasions (Green, 1939; Hadley, 1944; Mowrer, 1939; Queen, 1940; Schroeder, 1942). Aside from the possible implications of this finding for a social drift formulation, which we have considered above, Faris and Dunham suggested its critical, etiological implication for schizophrenia was the manner in which this ecological distribution indicated high levels of social isolation antedating the development of schizophrenia.

Jaco (1954) conducted a somewhat more direct test of the social isolation hypothesis. He defined social isolation generally as the ". . . cutting off or minimizing of contact and communication with others." Based upon mental hospital admissions during 1940–1952, he chose two high and two low concentration census tracts (of schizophrenia) in Austin, Texas, and interviewed samples of individuals residing in each area. His results indicated significantly more social isolation in the high concentration areas, as compared to the tracts from which few schizophrenics came, on the following specific social isolation criteria:

1. Knowing the names of fewer neighbors
2. Fewer personal friends
3. Fewer acquaintences
4. More renting than owing homes
5. Less membership in lodges or fraternal organizations
6. Greater unemployment
7. More job turnover
8. Fewer visits to the central business district
9. Fewer visits to other areas of the city
10. Fewer visits with friends
11. Fewer trips out of town
12. Less intercity migration
13. Fewer friends in remote areas

Kohn and Clausen (1955), in contrast, found no evidence to support the social isolation rationale. They set their adult Ss a somewhat difficult task, by asking them to recall and recount aspects of their social interaction and participation at ages 13–14. No schizophrenic–nonschizophrenic social isolation differences were obtained on the dimensions used, i.e., relationships in parental family, adolescent friendships, and adolescent activity patterns.

In somewhat altered form, however, there exists still further support for the social isolation position. In relation to what may be termed the "ethnic isolate" hypothesis, Schwartz and Mintz (1963) demonstrated that Italian-Americans living in predominately non-Italian neighborhoods in Boston had very high rates of schizophrenia, while those residing in predominately Italian neighborhoods did not. Halmos (1952); Lemert (1948); and Wechsler and Pugh (1967) independently report very similar findings with other ethnic groups for schizophrenia, as well as other mental disorders. Several of these investigations are correlational in nature, and therefore do not speak to a causal relationship between social isolation and schizophrenia. Nevertheless, the weight of the studies examined in this section maintain the viability of the hypothesis that social isolation—which we have translated to represent but one dimension of interpersonal and personal stress—is etiologically related to schizophrenia. Furthermore, the literature examined earlier in our consideration of role taking deficiencies among lower-class persons suggests the possibility that social isolation may be disproportionately characteristic of such individuals.

### Goal-Striving Stress

The general focus of research and speculation relevant to goal-striving stress concerns the discrepancy between an individual's achievement and aspiration, between the real and the hoped for. While most of the work in this domain has examined the psychopathological implications of achievement–aspiration discrepancies in occupation, other dimensions of discrepancy have also been explored.

In an early investigation in this area, Gould (1941) worked with a sample of 81 college students and demonstrated that those from lower-class backgrounds had, relative to those from middle-class origins, higher discrepancies between actual and aspired performance on a series of experimental tasks. Empey (1956) analogously reported, based on study of a high school pupil sample, that while the absolute occupational aspirations of lower-class seniors were lower than those held by their middle- or upper-class peers, their relative occupational aspirations (defined as the distance between their father's actual and their own aspired occupations) were higher than either of the two other groups. These findings combine with similar results reported by Centers and Cantril (1946), as well as Merton's (1957) speculations regarding the "status-frustration hypothesis" to suggest the possibility that highly discrepant achievement–aspiration status may be particularly characteristic of lower-class individuals. Such discrepancies, the goal-striving stress hypothesis holds, may lead to the development of major psychopathology. Merton's formulation of this position has been summarized by Roach and Gursslin (1964) as follows:

> Success goals, a central feature of American culture, are highly esteemed by
> all members of society. Herein lies the root of much social pathology in the
> lower-class. Motivated to attain success . . . lower-class persons are blocked
> in their ambitions by socially structured barriers. They perceive that legiti-
> mate access to high status positions is restricted by external forces beyond
> their control. The combination of frustration due to thwarted ambition and
> a sense of injustice leads to deviant adaptation [p. 503].*

Early research evidence bearing upon this hypothesis was supportive
but somewhat post hoc. Hollingshead, Ellis, and Kirby (1954) reported
major achievement–aspiration discrepancies in both occupation and education among samples of lower-class schizophrenics and psychoneurotics.
Kleiner and Parker (1959) examined first hospital admissions for a
group of black patients in Philadelphia and found that Southern black
migrants were underrepresented in the patient population, while both native and Northern migrants were overrepresented. Both the Northern migrant and native subsamples had the same occupational distribution as
the Southern migrant subsamples, but the former had considerably greater education, and thus presumably a greater achievement–aspiration discrepancy. The investigators speculated that these data may indicate ". . .
that the discrepancy between level of aspiration and goal attainment for
native Negroes is larger than that for the (Southern) migrants, leading to
greater stress among the former [p. 690]." Tucker and Kleiner (1962)
then proceeded to directly test this speculation. Controlling for race and
religious affiliation, they collected occupational (their index of achievement) and educational (their index of aspiration) information on 1360
consecutive male first admissions to a large, urban, mental hospital. Their
data revealed

> . . . with no exceptions . . . more schizophrenia among those above the me-
> dian education of their respective occupational group than among those be-
> low. A more refined analysis also showed that the relative incidence of schizo-

---

* Roach and Gursslin (1964) take strong exception to this position. They hold
that, while such a formulation may indeed apply to members of the working-class,
lower-class persons in contrast

> . . . have limited interest in educational or occupational achievements.
> Their primary concerns are with subsistence rather than status. . . . Ideas
> of what the outside world is like are garbled and hazy. There is inadequate
> comprehension of the implications or possible alternatives in critical life
> choices [p. 504].

phrenia increased as the discrepancy between aspiration and achievement increased [p. 445].

In yet another investigation, this research group (Parker & Kleiner, 1966) provided evidence that goal-striving stress was significantly greater in schizophrenic persons than in a sample of normal individuals residing in the same community. Analogously, Sewell and Haller (1959) reported a significant relationship between "achievement frustration" and symptoms of emotional disturbance in a large sample of school children. And, further, Hinkle and Wolfe (1957) demonstrated in a sample of working-class individuals that the highest incidence of mood and behavioral disturbance, as well as physical illness, occurred in those individuals who reported most frustration of their occupational aspirations and most disappointment in their occupational achievements.

It would seem appropriate to conclude tentatively from these several findings, in a manner perhaps even more definitive than was the case for the social isolation hypothesis, that goal-striving stress may be a significant contributor to the etiological complex which antedates the development of schizophrenia, and a possibly important contributor to the concentration of schizophrenia in the lower class.

## Stress and Structured Learning Therapy

It thus appears appropriate to tentatively implicate stress—in many or singular forms—as a major factor responsible for the high concentration of schizophrenia in the lower class. One may speculatively go beyond this position and suggest that for the lower-class patient it is not only the high, diverse, and enduring levels of stress which contribute to severe emotional disturbances, but also lifelong inadequate preparation in how to adequately cope with stress. In earlier chapters we proposed that child-rearing, language code usage, concreteness of thought, reliance on authority, and a host of related developmental characteristics ill prepares the lower-class patient for what might fairly be called "middle-class psychotherapy." We would now tentatively extend this point and suggest that all of these dimensions of rearing, socialization, and personality development, which seem quite appropriate for adequate adjustment to a lower-class environment, also ill prepares the individual for adequate coping and development in an essentially middle-class society—and especially for adequate coping with the stresses of this society. Others have suggested similar notions. Langner and Michael (1963), in response to their finding that lower-class respondents exhibited greater emotional disturbance than middle-class respondents even when the level of stress experienced was held constant, proposed that lower-class living may result in diminished resistance to stress, or less resiliency. Elaborating on this notion, Kohn (1969) observes:

> . . . what is there about the conditions of life of the lowest social strata that might make it more difficult for their members to cope with stress? . . . Their occupational conditions and their limited education gear their thinking processes to the concrete and the habitual; their inexperience in dealing with the abstract may ill-equip them to cope with ambiguity, uncertainty, and unpredictability; their mental processes are apt to be too gross and rigid when flexibility and subtlety are most required. Or, a related hypothesis, the lower and working class valuation of conformity to external authority, the disvaluation of self-direction, might cripple a man faced with the necessity of suddenly having to rely on himself in an uncertain situation where other cannot be relied on for guidance [p. 126].

Similarly, Roman and Trice (1967) comment:

> We assert that an explanation [of the etiology of schizophrenia] based on social psychological variables requires the consideration of . . . the development of individual abilities to "function adequately" in social reality [and] the social psychological character of life in the lowest stratum. . . . The basic premise of the explanation is that the concentration of schizophrenia in the lowest stratum is in the main a result of the interplay of the . . . two sets of phenomena . . . the process of acting upon reality occurs over and over in everyday life, and *if there is consistency in the feedback that one receives from acting upon reality,* a set of behaviors or orientations emerge which are used by the individual in reacting to various situations in the services of his needs or goals. . . . Secondly, the effectiveness with which one is able to interact with his environment is partly determined by his ability to adapt to new and complex situations, to deal with the unexpected and the previously unknown. This adaptability is partly determined by the scope of the orientations to reality that he learns. . . . Research data on lower class family life indicate a high degree of family disorganization which may lead to cognitive inadequacies in children and narrowness of cognitive development. . . . There is also evidence to indicate that the child from the lowest stratum is placed at a further disadvantage by the school system. . . . Thus . . . many children from the lowest stratum do not receive the socialization necessary to cope adequately with reality. . . . Life in the lowest stratum is typified by the lack of social organization . . . lack of security [and] all forms of deviance . . . it appears that the combination of basic cognitive deficiencies in the perception of, and adaptation to, a reality which is confusing, unstructured, and inconsistent sets the stage for schizophrenic behavior in two ways. First, schizophrenic behavior may simply be the picture of a cognitively deficient individual attempting to deal with a confusing reality. In other words, in certain cases schizophrenia may be the behavioral outcome of socialization in and adaptation to a stressful

environment, rather than a breakdown in psychological functioning. Secondly, the combination of poor cognitive ability and a stressful environment may lead to a withdrawal from this reality as a mechanism for reducing frustration [pp. 61–62].

We have titled this chapter "Psychopathology and Sociopathology." The literature we have examined converges to suggest that the high concentration of schizophrenia in the lower class is etiologically in part both a psychological and a social phenomenon. The lower-class schizophrenic appears to be an individual whose psychological resources by dint of both early socialization and later experience may be inadequate to deal with the severe social stresses which are constantly placed upon him. We are interested in this book in *prescriptive* therapy, in increasing the degree to which treatment follows cause, and is not irrelevant to it. As such it is important that we urge further development of *both* social and psychological treatment.

Frank (1936) and Chilman (1968) are quite correct in their observation that to a very major extent, *society is the patient.* Increased social legislation in the United States, enacted at an increased rate and implemented in a manner consistent with the optimal spirit of such legislation, would clearly serve as an exceedingly major force in dealing adequately with the sociopathological component of lower-class mental disorder.

Regarding the psychopathological component, we have presented above an immense amount of evidence indicating that our traditional psychotherapeutic techniques are simply and grossly both inadequate and inappropriate for the lower-class patient. Perhaps our most adequate professional contribution to the lives of lower-class patients, or at least a very major one to which we have given grossly insufficient attention, may be in adding to their repertoire of specific social, interpersonal, and personal skills. This coping or skill-enhancement viewpoint is fully consistent with recent interest in what has been termed crisis theory (Jacobson, Strickler, & Morley, 1968; Kalis, 1970; Klein, 1960; Miller & Iscoe, 1963; Rapaport, 1962; Sifneos, 1960). Miller and Iscoe (1963) observe:

> Currently there is great concern about the finding that an average of two-thirds of the individuals utilizing the services of child guidance and mental health clinics do so only for a total of four or less sessions. It would seem that if one were to employ the crisis model as an explanatory device, these "defectors" could be better understood. Namely, a crisis motivates them to seek help and the abatement of the crisis lowers the motivation. Most clinics, however, fail to consider their clients in this light. They adhere rigidly to the notion of extended treatment and there is great concern about the withdrawal from treatment [p. 199].

Others subscribing to a crisis theory model have responded to such traditional, psychotherapeutic inflexibility by urging that treatment for the lower-class patient emphasize "rehearsal for reality" (Rapaport, 1962) and, as Schmidt *et al.* (1968) observe:

> The therapeutic goal for lower-class persons should be self-determination first and, possibly, self-actualization later; the focus must shift from how they are *reacting* to how they are *acting*, from defensive styles to coping styles, from changing their reactions to teaching them more successful actions [p. 85].

We are urging here, therefore, increased utilization of treatment approaches which ares less a function of our own life styles and professional preferences, and more responsive to the needs, life styles and environmental realities of the lower-class patient. One such approach appears to be what we have termed *Structured Learning Therapy*, in which explicit focus can be placed upon skill training—via the use of modeling, role playing, and social reinforcement—to enhance patient autonomy, assertiveness, internal control, role taking ability, sense of mastery, social interaction skills, accuracy of affective perception and communication, tolerance for frustration and ambiguity, and a host of other useful behaviors in which he may be deficient.

*Part 2*

# STRUCTURED LEARNING THERAPY

*Chapter 5*

# STRUCTURED LEARNING
# AND THE MIDDLE-CLASS PATIENT

In previous chapters we have proposed that class-linked research on child rearing, personality development, language use, and psychopathology each lead to the conclusion that *Structured Learning Therapy* may well be an optimal prescriptive psychotherapy for the lower-class patient. The major components of Structured Learning Therapy are modeling, role playing, and social reinforcement. As such, we wish in the present chapter to review and examine existing research using these procedures with clinical populations.* It will be noted as we present this research literature that, to date, when modeling or role playing has been utilized toward psychotherapeutic ends, the patients involved have most often been middle-class patients. In some of these research reports, patient social class is not clearly specified. In general, it is to be noted that to the present time, modeling and role playing have been used exceedingly little with lower-class psychotherapy outpatients or inpatients.

**Modeling: General Considerations**

Imitative behavior, described by such related terms as matched-dependent behavior, copying, and same-behavior (Miller & Dollard, 1941); empathetic learning (Mowrer, 1966); observational learning (Berger, 1961); identification (Maccoby & Wilson, 1957); vicarious learning (DeCharms & Rosenbaum, 1960); and, most frequently, modeling (Ban-

---

* Our primary focus will be upon modeling and role playing, singly and in combination. We will deal only briefly with social reinforcement since, as will be noted, its nature and influence has recently been examined in considerable depth elsewhere, by the author and by others.

dura, 1969), has long been an important focus of psychological research. Early instinctual theories (McDougall, 1908; Morgan, 1896; Tarde, 1903) eventually yielded to simple reinforcement formulations (Miller & Dollard, 1941) and then to more complex reinforcement paradigms (Aronfreed, 1970; Gerwitz & Stingle, 1968; Rosenbaum & Arenson, 1968) as an adequate theoretical attempt to account for imitative behavior. Bandura's (1969) contiguity-mediational theory of imitation learning is perhaps the most sophisticated effort to date to comprehensively explain and integrate the now very substantial modeling research literature. We do not intend here to examine in depth either these theoretical positions or the very extensive laboratory research that has been conducted dealing with imitative processes. Both have been reviewed and evaluated very adequately and quite recently by others (Bandura, 1969; Flanders, 1968; Kanfer & Phillips, 1970). We do wish to highlight certain of the major replicated findings that derive from laboratory modeling studies and have apparent relevance for clinical contexts.

In most general terms, it may be noted that modeling has been demonstrated to be an effective, reliable and, relative to other learning procedures, rapid technique for both the development of new responses and the strengthening or weakening of previously acquired responses. Bandura (1969) has suggested three broad types of behavior change that may follow from observer exposure to modeling procedures:

1. *Observational Learning Effects.* The acquisition of new responses or response patterns that previously did not exist in the behavioral repertoire of the observer.

2. *Inhibitory and Disinhibitory Effects.* The strengthening or weakening of responses or response patterns that previously did exist in the behavioral repertoire of the observer, but that had a low probability of occurrence due to social disapproval or other potential negative consequences.

3. *Response Facilitation Effects.* The performance of previously acquired responses or response patterns that are neither novel nor previously a source of potential negative consequences. The model's behavior serves as a "releasor," or discriminative stimulus for the observer.

Laboratory investigations have demonstrated the successful use of modeling procedures for the acquisition, inhibition, disinhibition, or facilitation of aggression (Bandura, 1969); altruism (Bryan & Test, 1967); moral judgments (Bandura & McDonald, 1963); speech patterns (Hingtgen, Coulter, & Churchill, 1967); career planning (Krumboltz & Schroeder, 1965); emotional arousal (Schwartz & Hawkins, 1965); dependency (Bandura, 1969); sexual anxiety (Bandura, 1969); sexual assertiveness (Walters, Bowen, & Parke, 1963); self reward and self-punishment

(Bandura & Kupers, 1964); and a host of other, disparate behaviors. Thus, it is clear from findings such as the foregoing that learning by modeling can be a powerful and enduring procedure for the modification of behavior. Yet, most individuals observe dozens and perhaps hundreds of behaviors by others each day which they do not imitate. Many persons are exposed daily, via television and the popular press, to highly sophisticated modeling displays of purchasing behavior, but do not model the enacted behaviors. And many persons, on occasion, are exposed to expensively produced, expertly acted, and seemingly persuasive instructional films, yet remain uninstructed. There are several possible reasons for these "failures" of modeling or, stated more appropriately, for the fact that individuals model under some circumstances, but not others. Laboratory investigations of modeling have provided a wealth of information identifying and elaborating what may be termed "modeling-enhancers," that is, characteristics of the model, the observer, the display, or the displaying procedures that augment the probable level of modeling by the observer. It will assist our understanding of the functioning of modeling enhancers if we note that modeling involves certain major phases or components. Different enhancers are relevant to different components. Bandura (1969) has described the modeling process as involving:

1. *Attentional Components.* The observer must attend to the modeling display, often in a context involving other extraneous stimuli. For successful modeling to occur, procedures are necessary that maximize discriminative observation by the observer; that is, that maximize the likelihood of sensory registration of the modeled stimuli. A number of modeling enhancers are relevant at this stage of the modeling process. It has been demonstrated that laboratory subjects will evidence significantly more modeling behavior, presumably in part because of fuller and more accurate discriminative attention to the intended modeling stimuli, when the modeling display itself is vivid, novel, and contains several heterogeneous models; when the model is of high status, competent, powerful, of the same age and sex as the observer and, in particular, when the model is rewarded for engaging in the depicted behavior; when the observer has received prior instructions, set or expectancy to model; when competing stimuli are minimized; and especially when the observer is provided reward for modeling.

2. *Retentional Components.* In order to reproduce the behavior he has observed, the observer must cognitively retain it. Symbolic coding of the modeling stimuli is an important aid in the retention process. Such coding or classifying may assist the observer to reorganize elements of the modeling display into familiar and more easily retained patterns. Ban-

dura (1969) also stresses, as we too have via the role playing component of Structured Learning Therapy, the significant role of both covert and overt rehearsal of the modeled behaviors by the observer. As was true of the attentional stage, reward to the model and/or the observer appear to be important stimuli to the rehearsal process and consequent enhanced retention.

3. *Motor Reproduction Components.* This phase of the modeling process involves the use by the observer of symbolic representations (imaginal and verbal) of the modeling display to guide his overt performance. Bandura (1969) observes that such "representational guidance" is quite similar to learning by following a series of instructions or an externally depicted pattern, except that here performance is monitored not by external cues, but by symbolic counterparts of absent stimuli that were displayed earlier.

4. *Incentive and Motivational Components.* An individual may attend to and retain, i.e., learn, how to perform modeled behaviors, but his overt performance of such learned behavior will be largely contingent upon his anticipation of reward for doing so. Such anticipation of reward has been demonstrated to be enhanced by the strength, consistency, recency, and frequency of reward he observes being provided the model. The importance as a modeling enhancer of reward consequences to both the model and the observer, at all stages of the modeling process, deserves special emphasis. Bandura (1969) comments:

> Incentive variables not only regulate the overt expression of matching behavior, but they also affect observational learning by exerting selective control over the modeling cues to which a person is most likely to be attentive. Further, they facilitate selective retention by activating deliberate coding and rehearsal of modeled responses that have high utilitarian value [p. 142].

Several characteristics of the model which depict him as a receiver of reward, such as power, competence, and status, as well as observer attraction to the model, and real or apparent (to the observer) attitude or background similarity to the model may all directly or indirectly serve as additional incentives to the observer to perform the behaviors he has imitatively acquired.

As the operationalization of modeling procedures in our own investigations is described in later chapters, we will have occasion to return in very concrete form to the issue of modeling enhancers and their implementation.

## Modeling-Clinical Studies with
## Middle-Class Observers

### Therapist as Model: Suggestive Reports

While the clinical literature dealing with patient modeling of his psychotherapist is far from extensive, one may speculate that such modeling may well be a frequent and at times consequential psychotherapeutic event. The literature which does exist accords well with this speculation, though it often remains unclear in such writings as to how incidental or central to therapeutic outcome such modeling may be, and whether or not the therapist's behavior as model was unintentional or to some extent purposeful. A portion of this body of literature consists of case reports. For example, Levy (1939) reports enhanced ability to engage in finger paint activity by a previously reluctant patient who first viewed her therapist finger painting with enthusiasm. Slavson (1950) observes that highly aggressive members of his activity therapy groups often display decrements in this type of behavior following observation of "constructive" task activity by the therapist. Alexander (1967) reports that an unplanned display of anger by the therapist appeared to at least temporarily disinhibit a patient who had previously experienced considerable difficulty in expressing anger. Sturm (1965) describes several examples of therapist-as-model behavior enacted by directors of psychodrama groups during the warm-up, problem presentation, and role-playing segments of such group sessions. Similarly suggestive of therapist-as-model effects are those investigations that demonstrate a convergence of therapist and patient values, attitudes, or behaviors over the course of psychotherapy. Rosenthal (1955) found that patients judged as improved after individual psychotherapy had revised their pretherapy values in the areas of sex, aggression, and authority in the direction of those held by their therapist; while these values held by patients judged as unimproved tended to become less like their therapists. Pentony (1966) and Pepinsky and Karst (1964) report similar therapist–patient value convergence. Analagous behavioral convergence has been demonstrated by Heller, Davis, and Meyers (1966), Matarazzo and Wiens (1967), and Matarazzo, Wiens, and Saslow (1965). These investigations in part demonstrate that increases or decreases in therapist verbal activity lead to parallel rate alterations by the patient. This sampling of relevant case reports and investigations of therapist–patient convergence, while clearly supportive of a present purposes, for they do not necessarily point to *modeling* as the therapist *influence* process, must be considered as only suggestive for our

sole or even major influence process involved. When a therapist responds in a consistently calm manner to highly anxious material presented by a patient, and the patient subsequently displays marked anxiety reduction, is the responsible change process *modeling,* i.e., vicarious extinction, or something best described as *unsystematic desensitization?* When a patient increasingly adopts and displays his therapist's explicit therapeutic rationale and beliefs, his very choice of language, gestures, or other behaviors —apparently not uncommon occurrences—the responsible mechanisms remain indeterminate. Modeling may well be the major mediational process, but so too may other learning or social influence processes. Nevertheless, findings such as these do appropriately lead to speculation as to the therapeutic role of the therapist-as-model. Mowrer (1966), Parloff, Iflund, and Goldstein (1960) and Pentony (1966) are among those who have suggested that the therapist is indeed an important imitative source for his patients. Mowrer, in particular, has noted that therapists traditionally display a very limited range of social behaviors during treatment and, furthermore, that those they do display have rather little utility for the patient. He urges that therapists purposefully and overtly enact a fuller range of prosocial behaviors and emphasizes, in particular, the likely enhancing effect on patient self-disclosure of marked openness about himself by the therapist. Kanfer and Phillips (1970) have even more broadly urged therapists to use their own behaviors as intentional modeling displays as part of what they term "replication therapy." Similar viewpoints have been put forth in the context of vocational counseling (Warman, 1964), family therapy (R. Liberman, 1970), milieu therapy (Daniels & Kuldau, 1967), and what has been termed "identification therapy" (Albert, 1968). Furthermore, as will be made concrete below, in our examination of behavior modification studies, Bandura (1969) and his colleagues have provided substantial evidence for the value of the therapist-as-model in their studies of modeling combined with guided participation.

### Analogue Investigations

Laboratory analogue studies constitute a small, but important, body of experimental evidence pointing to the usefulness of modeling procedures for clinically relevant purposes with middle-class observers. These are investigations which have rather carefully examined the efficiency of modeling as a means of altering, in a laboratory context, behaviors of apparent significance for psychotherapeutic settings.

Marlatt, Jacobson, Johnson, and Morrice (1970) examined the effects of exposure to a tape-recorded, high problem-revealing model on the level of observer problem disclosure. In addition, they studied the influence on the observer of the type of feedback the model received for such disclosure—positive, negative, or neutral. The Ss were 32 university undergraduates, assigned to any one of three model-plus-feedback conditions, or to a no-model, control condition. All Ss first participated in an initial base-rate interview, followed by modeling or control procedures in accord with the experimental condition to which they had been assigned, and then a postexposure, second interview. The study's major dependent variable was the increase in subject problem statements from the first to the second interview. The several significant results may be summarized as indicating that exposure to a model indeed augments observer problem disclosure, and that such disclosure is heightened even further when the model receives either positive or neutral (as opposed to negative) feedback for his disclosure behavior. These findings have been replicated by Duke, Frankel, Sipes, and Stewart (1965) in a study in which the modeling display was presented in script form, rather than by audiotape.

Marlatt (1968a) next sought to test the prediction that modeling of problem disclosure behavior would be enhanced if the information provided the observer about the interview task and the behavior expected of him therein was ambiguous. Under such conditions, he held, the model's behavior would serve as a more powerful orienting or discriminative one than was true under low ambiguity conditions—as the latter were defined in the investigation. The 32 university student Ss were assigned to model—no-model and high ambiguity—low ambiguity experimental conditions. Results indicated both significant modeling and ambiguity effects such that Ss exposed to a model and provided highly ambiguous information displayed (as predicted) greater problem disclosure. In contrast to the Marlatt (1970) "feedback" study described above, significant modeling effects emerged in the present investigation in the absence of reinforcement to either model or observer. Yet, the evidence in laboratory contexts regarding the modeling-enhancing power of such reinforcement is very considerable. In response to such evidence, the role of reinforcement, both vicarious (to model) and direct (to observer), became the focus of Marlatt's (1968b) third analogue investigation. The Ss again were university students, and his criterion was problem disclosure. Subjects were first exposed to no model (control), or to a problem-disclosing, taped model who received either positive ("Mmm-hmm," "Yes," etc.), negative ("Uh-uh," "No," etc.), or neutral ("I see," "Go on," etc.) vicarious verbal reinforcement. Immediately following exposure to the model or the control condition wait period, each observer participated in an individual interview in which his own problem disclosure behavior was responded to by positive, negative, or neutral direct reinforcement analogously operationalized. One week later, as a test for generalization effects, a second interview with no reinforcement provided was conducted with each observer. Again, findings indicated that exposure to a model, independent of type of reinforcement, led to significantly greater problem disclosure than was true for control Ss. Both vicarious and direct reinforcement proved to yield significant modeling-enhancement effects in the predicted order (positive $\geq$ neutral $\geq$ negative), as measured at the first interview. The effects of vicarious, but not direct, reinforcement still obtained at the time of the generalization interview. Marlatt's investigations, therefore, provide consistent evidence in the therapy-relevant domain of problem disclosure for the utility of modeling procedures. Furthermore, his careful examination of the role of task ambiguity and both vicarious and direct reinforcement in this context provides us with information whereby greater clinical usefulness of such modeling procedures is possible.

Two clinical analogue-modeling studies have been reported in an area closely related to problem disclosure. Blackburn (1970) sought to increase self-disclosure by university student observers via use of high disclosing taped models. Such imitation failed to occur, a finding Blackburn explained as due to insufficient procedural concern with enhancing the likelihood that Ss would attend to the self-disclosure behavior depicted by the model. Whalen's (1969) study compensated in large measure for this design weakness. She too sought to increase self-disclosure behavior by modeling in student observers, and succeeded in doing so, but only when such modeling was combined with detailed instructions to observers regarding the value and explicit nature of self-disclosure. Closely related studies reported by Brody (1968), Wilder (1968), and Spiritas and Holmes (1971) each demonstrate significant increases in self-referent verbal behavior as a function of exposure to a relevant model.

A final analogue study, conducted by Godwin (1970), examined the effects of modeling procedures upon a central aspect of the therapeutic relationship—patient attraction to the therapist. She also examined the role of subject self-esteem upon the degree of modeling, since laboratory studies have demonstrated that low self-esteem Ss tend to model more than high self-esteem Ss. The Ss were 40 high and 40 low self-esteem Ss. Half of each group were played a tape depicting a therapy session in which the patient displayed high levels of attraction for his therapist; the other half heard the same patient-model display low attraction to (the same) therapist. As predicted, there emerged a highly significant modeling effect for attraction; observers hearing the high attraction model were themselves significantly more attracted to the taped therapist. Though low self-esteem Ss were significantly more open to therapist influence than were their high self-esteem counterparts, no self-esteem by modeling effect emerged for attraction.

These analogue investigations, as a group, clearly provide added confidence for the utilization of modeling procedures in therapeutic contexts. They also provide valuable beginning information on the possible strengths and weaknesses for clinical purposes of certain selected modeling enhancers. These studies, however, are a prime example of the manner in which the research considered in the present chapter speaks primarily to the value of modeling and role playing for middle-class patients. In each of the studies examined above, the observers were university students; that is, primarily middle-class YAVIS individuals. Furthermore, the dependent variable targets in these investigations (increased problem disclosure, self-disclosure, or attraction to the therapist) are clearly "middle-class therapy" targets. Each seeks to increase the type of skills that would make an individual a "better" patient in verbal, insight-oriented, relationship-based psychotherapy. In no instance is it the case that the study conceives of or is designed to test modeling as a means of directly altering maladaptive patient behaviors. In the section that follows we will examine a series of investigations whose intent is more consistent with that of Structured Learning Therapy, in that the modeling procedures employed were oriented directly toward problem resolution, not the enhancement of the patient's verbal, insight-oriented therapy skills.

### Behavior Modification Investigations

Kleinsasser (1968) reported an investigation in which 40 university student Ss, each with major anxiety associated with public speaking, were assigned to four treatment conditions: (1) systematic desensitization, (2) modeling, (3) modeling plus systematic desensitization, (4) control. The desensitization Ss (Group 1) participated in seven, hour-long sessions of systematic desensitization oriented toward the reduction of public speaking anxiety. Modeling Ss (Group 2) viewed videotapes of seven, hour-long sessions of systematic desensitization oriented toward the same goal. The experimenter served as therapist on these tapes, and an actor served as the patient. Subjects assigned to participate in both modeling and desensitization (Group 3) viewed two such videotapes constructed by abstracting scenes from the seven tapes discussed above, and participated in seven sessions of desensitization. Control Ss were given relaxation training and were provided a rationale for the relationship of such training to possible reduction in their public speaking anxiety. These Ss then spent a period of time equivalent to that employed with experimental Ss (seven, one-hour sessions), listening to music while relaxed, and engaging in certain task activities designed to augment the credibility of the control procedures as "treatment." Results indicated that, in comparison to these control Ss, systematic desensitization led to a significant decrease in public speaking anxiety on both self-report and objectively rated measures of such anxiety. While this effect was not augmented by the addition of modeling (Group 3), modeling only Ss (Group 2) also reported significantly greater anxiety reduction than did control Ss. Kleinsasser's findings, therefore, suggest that at least on one level of measurement (self-report) viewing systematic desensitization treatment for public speaking anxiety is as effective as actually participating in it.

Bandura, Blanchard, and Ritter (1969) conducted a related investigation. The Ss were 48 snake-phobic individuals, who had responded affirmatively to a newspaper advertisement requesting volunteers to participate in an experiment designed to eliminate fear of snakes. The research report does not provide information by which Ss' social class might be ascertained. Subjects were matched on pretreatment avoidance behavior and then randomly assigned to four conditions: (1) systematic desensitization two times per week until either (fear reduction) criteria had been met, or 5¼ hours total had been reached; (2) symbolic modeling, also to criteria or time limit; (3) live modeling with guided participation; or (4) no-treatment control. The symbolic modeling Ss observed a film depicting children, adolescents, and adults engaging in progressively more threatening interactions with a snake. The film began with scenes showing the fearless models handling plastic snakes and graduated to displays in which they touched and held a large king snake, draped it around their necks, and let it crawl freely over their bodies. The investigator's description of their third treatment condition, live modeling with guided participation, is as follows:

> In the initial procedure subjects observed through a one-way mirror the experimenter perform a series of threatening activities with the king snake that provided striking demonstrations that close interaction with the snake does not have harmful consequences. During this period . . . the experimenter held the snake close to his face, allowed it to crawl over his body at will, and let it loose to slither about the room. After returning the snake to its glass cage, the experimenter invited the subjects to join him in the room and to be seated in one of four chairs placed at varying distances from the experimenter's chair. The experimenter then removed the snake from the cage and commenced the treatment, beginning with relatively non-threatening performance tasks and proceeding through increasingly fear-provoking

activities. . . . At each step the experimenter himself performed fearless behavior and gradually led subjects into touching, stroking, and then holding
the mid-section of the snake's body with gloved and then with bare hands
while the experimenter held the snake securely by the head and tail. Whenever a subject was unable to perform the behavior upon demonstration
alone she was asked to place her hand on the experimenter's and to move
her hand down gradually until it touched the snake's body. After subjects
no longer felt any apprehension about touching the snake under these se-
cure conditions, anxieties about contact with the snake's head area and en-
twining tail were extinguished . . . as subjects became less fearful the experimenter gradually reduced his participation and control over the snake until
eventually subjects were able to hold the snake in their laps without assistance, to let the snake crawl freely over their bodies. Progress through the
graded approach tasks was paced according to the subject's apprehensive-
ness. . . . Treatment was terminated when subjects were able to execute all
the snake interaction tasks independently [p. 180].

Results of the investigation indicated that, in comparison with control
Ss, all three treatment approaches produced significantly greater generalized and enduring reductions in fear arousal and avoidance behavior. Of
the three approaches, modeling with guided participation was most
powerful, achieving essentially complete extinction of phobic behavior in
every S. Furthermore, when Ss provided desensitization or symbolic
modeling achieved only partial improvement, and were then exposed to
live modeling with guided participation, they too achieved virtually complete extinction of their snake phobia. Thus we are provided with a
second rather powerful demonstration of the efficiency of modeling procedures for the direct reduction of maladaptive avoidance behaviors. More-
over, it should be noted that in an independent investigation, conducted
by Rimm and Mahoney (1969), comparison was also made of modeling
with guided participation, against no treatment for the reduction of snake
phobia. As above, a significant difference emerged favoring the modeling
with guided participation group.

Other investigations add strength to the conclusion emerging here regarding the power of modeling to reduce avoidance behavior. Geer and
Turteltaub (1967) exposed their college student Ss to a live model who
either closely approached and handled a live snake (low-fear model condition), a live model who avoided approaching the snake and who verbalized considerable discomfort (high-fear model condition), or to no
model (control condition). In comparison to both the high-fear model
and control condition Ss, those exposed to a low-fear model approached
the snake significantly closer and significantly more frequently crossed
the barrier in which the snake was enclosed. Fryrear and Werner
(1970), Litvak (1969), Mann (1972), Rimm and Madeiros (1970),

and Ritter (1965, 1969a&b) have each provided similar results illustrating the value of modeling procedures as a means of significantly reducing diverse types of avoidance behavior.

These investigations, which combine to provide an impressive demonstration of the usefulness of modeling procedures to alter specific maladaptive avoidance behaviors, involve primarily middle-class, relatively intact individuals. There is, however, at least some evidence that modeling procedures are similarly effective for behavior change purposes with lower-class, severely disturbed individuals. Sherman (1965) has reported an intensive case study in which modeling procedures were successfully utilized to reinstate verbal behavior in a mute psychotic patient. Staples (1963) worked with a sample of near-mute schizophrenic patients, and sought to increase their level of verbal behavior by use of modeling or reinforcement techniques. Patients in three experimental conditions were shown a set of slides depicting landscapes, animals, and other stimuli, and were asked to discuss and describe these slides as freely as they could. Following the slides, one group of patients (modeling condition) was exposed to a talkative model who openly and in detail discussed the several slides as requested. A second group of patients (reinforcement condition) heard no model, but were reinforced with cigarettes for whatever verbalizations they did offer. The third patient group (control condition) spent an equivalent time period listening to music. All Ss were then exposed to a second series of slides, instructions to verbalize were repeated, and measurement of patient verbal behavior conducted. Those patients exposed to the talkative model verbalized significantly more than either reinforcement or control condition patients. Consistent with our earlier discussion of modeling enhancers, Wilson and Walters (1966) conducted an extension of this investigation, which sought to examine whether reward for imitation would further augment verbal behavior with this type of patient sample. Such indeed proved to be the case. Patients exposed to a talkative model and rewarded for imitating his behavior verbalized significantly more than those exposed to a model but receiving no reward for modeling, or those receiving no reward or exposure to a model. Thus, evidence is provided that modeling procedures can heighten the level of verbal activity in chronic schizophrenic patients.

While rate of verbal activity may appropriately be considered a complex behavior in an absolute sense, it may also be viewed as rather simple behavior relative to the fuller range of social and interpersonal behaviors that are often inadequately or maladaptively performed by schizophrenic patients. Can modeling procedures, for example, be employed effectively to teach schizophrenic patients to function more adequately in "handling anger, taking responsibility, personal appearance, not sleeping too much, dealing with domineering relatives, avoiding 'crazy talks,' avoiding fighting, social conversation, and handling money." These more complex behaviors were the target of alteration by modeling in a study conducted on chronic schizophrenic patients by Burrs and Kapche (1969). The Ss were 51 such hospitalized patients, who participated in groups of 3 to 8, in 11, 45-min modeling sessions. Each session consisted of presentation of two 3–5 min videotapes depicting the themes described above, followed by group discussion of the themes depicted and, on occasion, a further presentation of the modeling display. Dependent variable measurement took form in a series of questionnaires completed by the patient, and by ward and other hospital personnel. On none of the several measures thus obtained were there significant effects demonstrable for the modeling procedures.

It is indeed the case that in the course of experimental research, one can learn much from investigative failures. Burrs and Kapche failed to confirm their experimental predictions, but what they did not find has much to teach us. We would hold that much more than the complexity per se of the behaviors they were seeking to alter accounts for their absence of results. Attempts to alter complex behaviors demand complex, or at least powerful, manipulations. We would speculate that Burrs and Kapche's use of modeling failed because its implementation was too weak. Modeling alone, with little attention to modeling enhancers or to supplementary techniques, may be sufficient to alter disclosure behavior or avoidance behavior in normal or neurotic persons, and may be sufficient to alter "simple" behaviors (e.g., verbal rate) in schizophrenic individuals, but are inadequate to the task of altering complex behaviors in "complexly disturbed" persons. Schizophrenia is in part a disorder of attention, of symbolic behavior, and probably of motivation. It appears to us that modeling attempts to alter complex behaviors in schizophrenics must attend in detail to modeling enhancement at each phase of the modeling process, i.e., to increase attention to the modeling display, to aid in symbolic coding, to provide opportunity for overt or covert rehearsal, and to provide motivation for performance. Burrs and Kapche's investigation was insufficiently responsive to these necessities and, we would speculate, these failures primarily account for their absence of results. A strategy that focused patient attention on one, not several behavioral themes; aided the translation of the display into terms most familiar for the patient; provided extensive opportunity, encouragement, and guidelines for role playing or related forms of rehearsal; and offered reward to both model and patient for adequate performance, is a strategy we feel to be more consistent with laboratory research on modeling and the nature of schizophrenia. In essence, as will be seen in the chapter which follows, we have sought to give expression to this strategy in our own studies of Structured Learning Therapy and its components.

### Group Psychotherapy Investigations

A few investigations have examined the usefulness of modeling procedures employed in the context of group psychotherapy. Truax *et al.* (1966) examined the psychotherapeutic influence of what they termed *vicarious therapy pretraining*. Eight psychotherapy groups of 10 patients each were the sample. Half the groups were hospitalized mental patients, the remaining 40 patients were institutionalized juvenile delinquents. Prior to the first of a series of 24 group psychotherapy sessions, two groups of each type were exposed to a tape recording that constituted the therapy pretraining. The tape consisted of a series of actual excerpts of group therapy interactions in which the patients were engaged in relatively deep exploration of their problems and feelings. The investigators report significantly greater intrapersonal exploration and significantly greater change on a series of self-report measures for patients provided such vicarious therapy pretraining, as compared to those not exposed to the pretraining tape.

Fikso (1970) worked with a sample of 30 male undergraduate students. Half had neurotic diagnoses; half were classified as academic underachievers. Within each subgroup of 15, 5 persons were randomly selected to participate in group psychotherapy. Each group of 5 members met for 12 sessions. The other members of each subsample, in groups of 5, observed all 12 sessions, live, through one-way mirror arrangements. No observer–participant difference emerged on change criteria derived from pre- and post-TAT administrations. However, vicarious therapy members improved significantly more than did those actually participating in group therapy in terms of academic achievement (grade point average).

Yet another type of modeling display was used in less formal studies reported by Schwartz and Hawkins (1965) and Goldstein, Gassner, Greenberg, Gustin, Land, Liberman, and Streiner (1967). Schwartz and Hawkins (1965) used actual patients to serve as models in increasing the number of affective statements from other group members. Goldstein *et al.* (1967) planted cohorts who acted as patients into two patient groups in order to increase level of self-disclosure and within-group cohesiveness. Both studies report descriptive evidence suggesting the success of the modeling procedures thus employed. We note therefore, in a manner consistent with the investigations described earlier, that the few attempts to put modeling procedures to therapeutic advantage in a group context appear to have been successful.

## Child and Adolescent Observers

A substantial number of investigations have examined the utility of modeling procedures for altering maladaptive behavior in (again, primarily middle-class) children and adolescents. Jack (1934) and Page (1935), in early efforts of this type, made successful use of modeling techniques to alter inhibited behavior in young children. Chittenden (1942) worked with highly aggressive children and had them observe a series of plays in which dolls representing preschool children reacted non-aggressively to frustrating situations. On both experimental test criteria and within-school behavioral measures, these children behaved with significantly less aggression than did nonobserving control children. Gittelman (1965) reports concurring results. Risley and Wolf (1967); Sloane, Johnston, and Harris (1968); and especially Lovaas, Berberick, Perloff, and Schaeffer (1966), Lovaas (1967), and Lovaas, Freitag, Nelson, and Whalen (1967) have made major and successful use of modeling procedures to develop communicative speech and an array of nonverbal behaviors in autistic children.

On yet another behavioral dimension, O'Connor (1969) assigned nursery school children who displayed marked social withdrawal to one of two experimental conditions. One group observed a film depicting increasingly more active social interactions between children, plus reward to the models for such interaction. Control group children observed a film containing no social interaction nor, for that matter, human characters. A highly significant difference on posttest social interaction emerged with children who had viewed the social interaction film obtaining clearly higher scores. Marshall and Hahn (1967) and O'Connor (1972) have reported similar findings. Clements, Roberts, and Lantz (1970) however, failed to obtain a significant modeling effect in their study with shy, withdrawn children. They speculate, quite correctly it appears to us, that the difference in result between theirs and O'Connor's (1969) study may be attributable to the way in which O'Connor, but not Clements et al., accompanied his modeling display with a narrative indicating appropriate model behaviors and, furthermore, presented these behaviors in a gradually more socially interactive sequence. Clements et al., stated otherwise, appear to have given insufficient methodological substance to the attentional phase of the modeling process by failing, respectively, to operationalize adequate model–observer similarity (all models were completely free of any social isolate behavior) or adequate assistance to the observer in identifying which model behaviors in particular were to be modeled.

Modeling as a means of reducing a different type of avoidance behavior was the focus of an investigation reported by Hill *et al.* (1968). Children with marked fear of dogs were assigned to modeling or no-modeling conditions. The former viewed a film in which a child, without apparent fear, approached and interacted with a large dog. The no-modeling children were not exposed to this film. As was the case for the studies described earlier, modeling exposure led to a significant reduction in avoidance behavior. Spiegler, Liebert, McMains, and Fernandez (1968) have provided yet another similar demonstration of this general finding.

Bandura and his co-investigators, clearly the most active contributors to modeling research in general, have also investigated the utility of modeling as a means of altering avoidance behavior in children. Bandura, Grusec, and Menlove (1967) worked with 48 nursery school children who had evidenced marked fear of dogs. The children were assigned to one of four experimental conditions. In the *modeling-positive context* condition, Ss participated in eight 10-min long parties during which a peer model unknown to the children entered with a cocker spaniel (age unknown) and in a prearranged, graduated manner played with the dog for a 3-min period during each session (party). Children assigned to the *modeling-neutral context* observed the same sequence of approach responses performed by the same peer model. The parties were omitted and, in each of the eight sessions, the children simply sat at a table and observed the modeled performances. The third experimental condition, *exposure-positive context,* was similar to the first in the occurrence of parties and the presence of the dog, but no model interacted with the dog, which was simply brought into the party room and left in a pen for 3 min during each party. Finally, in the *positive context* condition, both model and dog were absent. The children assigned to either modeling condition (positive or neutral context), in comparison to both conditions providing no model, evidenced significantly greater reduction in avoidance behavior, both on immediate posttesting and on testing for generalization one month later. These findings have been replicated by Hill *et al.* (1968), using filmed rather than live models.

In our earlier discussion of modeling enhancers, it was noted that laboratory evidence indicated that exposure to multiple models results in greater imitative learning than does exposure to a single model, even when the total frequencies of exposure are the same. In a second investigation, Bandura and Menlove (1968) examined the generality of this finding for the reduction of avoidance behavior. Children similar in fearfulness of dogs to those participating in the previous study (1) observed a graduated series of films in which a model displayed progressively more intimate interactions with a single dog, or (2) observed a similar set of films in which a variety of models interacted nonanxiously with several dogs varying in size and fearsomeness, or (3) observed a movie containing no animals. Compared to these latter, control group children, those exposed to either the single- or multiple-model films evidenced significantly greater reduction in avoidance behavior. Of the two modeling conditions, only that involving multiple models reduced fear sufficiently to enable the children to perform potentially threatening interaction with dogs.

In sum, the evidence is consistent and positive: particularly with reference to reduction of avoidance behavior, but on other dimensions as well, modeling appears to be an effective and efficient behavior modification approach. Much the same conclusion may be drawn regarding the effectiveness of modeling procedures with adolescent Ss. Warner and Hansen (1970) successfully reduced what they described as feelings of alienation among a sample of high school students by use of modeling techniques. Mann and Rosenthal (1969) report similar results for the reduction of test anxiety; Myrick (1969) for increasing the number of self-references during counseling; Krumboltz and Schroeder (1965), Krumboltz, Varenhorst, and Thorensen (1967), and LaFleur and Johnson (1972) for increasing information-seeking behavior by high school counselees; and Whalen and Henker (1971) have made effective use of modeling techniques to improve the quality of social behavior in retarded adolescents. In general terms, just as Bandura (1969) has concluded regarding laboratory investigations of modeling, we too may state, with reference to clinical applications of modeling techniques, that such techniques appear to be a rapid, efficient, and reliable approach to behavior modification. In later chapters we will consider whether this conclusion may be applied with equal appropriateness to clinical applications of modeling involving lower-class and working-class patient populations.

### Role Playing: General Considerations

Role playing has been defined by Mann (1956) as ". . . a situation in which an individual is explicitly asked to take a role not normally his own, or if his own, in a setting not normal for the enactment of the role [p. 227]." As we noted was the case for modeling procedures, role playing has been the focus of a long and fruitful series of laboratory investigations. We will not detail these studies here, as we and others have done so elsewhere (Goldstein et al., 1966; Goldstein & Simonson, 1971; Krasner, 1959; Mann, 1956), but will seek instead to briefly communicate the major outcomes of this investigative series. Much of this laboratory research has sought to determine the consequences for attitude change of participation in role playing. In the typical experimental paradigm in this domain, a sample of Ss are premeasured on one or more salient attitude dimensions. Subjects are then randomly assigned to either a role-play condition, some type of exposure condition, or a control group. The role-play Ss are requested to make a speech or other public statement championing a position *counter* to their initial attitude. Exposure condition Ss passively listen to such statements, and control group Ss neither present nor hear the counterattitudinal communication. Postmeasurement on the relevant attitude dimension is then obtained. This design, or a variant of it, has repeatedly yielded results indicating significantly greater attitude change in the direction of the counterattitudinal position in role play, versus both exposure and control Ss (Culbertson, 1957; Elms & Janis, 1965; Harvey & Beverly, 1961; Janis & King, 1954; King & Janis, 1956; Rosenberg, 1952). Investigations such as these have, furthermore, identified what may be termed *role-play enhancers*, i.e., characteristics of the role-play procedures whose presence function to augment the degree of role-play-determined attitude change. Attitude change will be greater, the greater S's:

1. Degree of perceived *choice* regarding whether to participate in role playing
2. *Commitment* to the counterattitudinal position in the sense that his enactment is public rather than private, or otherwise difficult to undo or disown
3. Degree of *improvisation* in enacting the counterattitudinal position
4. *Reward*, approval, reinforcement, or other means of stabilizing the role-played position

### Role Playing: Clinical Investigations

In our presentation in Chapter 1 of attempted solutions to the inadequacy of traditional psychotherapies for lower-class patients, we briefly described the uses of role playing with such patients as operationalized by

Nelson (1962), Riessman and Goldfarb (1964), and Shaffer (1967). We also briefly alluded to fixed role therapy (Kelley, 1955) and the work of O'Connell (1963), Otto (1967), and Strean (1961); that is, attempts to make use of role playing with primarily middle-class patients. With the partial exception of behavioral rehearsal, which we will examine in the section that follows, experimental support for the clinical application of role playing is rather sparse. Corsini (1966) has published a book on role playing in psychotherapy but it, accurately reflecting the existing literature in this domain, is almost exclusively descriptive and impressionistic. A series of investigations exists suggesting the successful use of role playing to alter an array of disordered behaviors in school children, e.g., social withdrawal (Hubbel, 1954), intergroup conflict (Nichols, 1954), family conflicts (Brunelle, 1954), interpersonal insensitivity (Chesler & Fox, 1966), lack of spontaneity (Lang, 1959), and acting-out behavior (Harth, 1966; Schaeffer & Von Nessen, 1968). Yet all these investigations lack adequate experimental controls and, as a group, must be considered as simply suggestive. Though the early research literature on role playing with adult patients is similarly suggestive at best (e.g., Harrow, 1951; Jones & Peters, 1952), a small amount of more recent work does adequately provide experimental tests of the usefulness of role playing with adult samples. Janis and Mann (1965) designed an investigation of the effects of role playing on the reduction of smoking. All Ss (all females and smokers) were asked to assume they were medical patients who had just undergone a series of diagnostic tests and were awaiting the results. The experimenter enacted the part of physician. Half of the 26 participating Ss were asked to play the role of patient (role play condition); the other 13 "patients" listened to recordings of these role enactments (exposure condition). All Ss were premeasured on attitudes toward smoking, cancer, and on future plans regarding smoking behavior. The role-play Ss then enacted five scenes with the experimenter-"physician"—all of which were designed to be fear arousing. The scenes included an apprehensive soliloquy in the waiting room in expectation of the diagnostic results; a conversation with the physician during which the patient was told she had lung cancer and that surgery was necessary; enactment of intense concern about the diagnosis and the moderate probability of a favorable outcome; making hospital arrangements; and a conversation with the physician about the relationship between smoking and lung cancer. Immediately following the role-play (and exposure) sessions, Ss' attitudes on the dimensions noted above were reassessed. This measure, as well as information on number of cigarettes smoked per day, were also obtained after two weeks. In each instance, the role-play Ss were significantly more negative toward smoking and smoked significantly fewer cigarettes, than did exposure Ss. This decrease in smoking behavior favoring the role-play Ss was still in effect 18 months later, which indeed is impressive evidence of the power of the role-play participation. Results consistent with these findings, though not as enduring, have emerged in investigations conducted by Lichtenstein, Keutzer, and Himes (1969); Mann (1967); Platt, Krassen, and Mausner (1969), and Streltzer and Koch (1968). In addition to their primary findings regarding changes in smoking behavior, these studies are of interest for their demonstration of enhanced effectiveness of role playing when one is enacting with a high status coactor (Streltzer & Koch, 1968), and when the role player is high in internality on Rotter's (1966) scale for internal–external control (Platt et al., 1969).

As we noted in our earlier discussion of the Burrs and Kapche (1969) investigation, much can be learned for future research from investigations that fail to obtain significant results, especially if such investigations are reasonably well designed and executed. Just such an investigation in the area of role playing was conducted by Hollander (1970). The Ss were 45 male psychiatric inpatients in a small, rural, Veterans Administration Hospital. All were lower- or working-class persons, with a diagnosis of alcoholism or some type of character disorder. The goal of the investigation was to increase patient attraction to psychotherapy and the psychotherapeutic staff at the hospital. Following premeasurement on these dimensions, the subjects were randomly assigned to role play, exposure, and control conditions. Role-play Ss were given a *choice* regarding participation in the study, at least a moderate level of *commitment* was established in that he knew another patient would hear his enactment, and an intermediate level of *improvisation* was required for each role-play enactment. Thus, in terms of attention to role-play enhancers, this investigation appears to have been implemented in a quite satisfactory procedural manner. Yet its results not only failed to yield any significant between-condition differences, they also raised serious questions about whether there had been, in effect, any actual experimental manipulation! It had been planned that each role-play condition patient would role play for 10 min. In fact, in spite of the presence of both the role-play enhancers described above, plus considerable encouragement and cajoling from E, the average length of role-play enactments was 1–2 min! Our major position in this book is that for patients such as those in the Hollander study, patients whose repertoire of social skills is broadly deficient in a variety of respects, modeling must accompany role-play enactments in order that the very substance of what is to be role played originally be provided the patient. If this is not done, the skill deficit combines with the type of role-taking deficiencies described in Chapter 2 to result in patients' inability to perform the role-play task. We would propose that this is precisely what occurred with Hollander's patients. Prior to enactment, each patient was told:

> Hello, I'm Mrs. Helberg. I guess you know we have been trying to learn how you feel about psychiatrists and psychologists. Well, right now we have a patient who is very worried about going to a psychologist, and we wonder if you could tell this man why going to a psychologist is a good thing to do. You can tell him how much psychologists know about mental and nervous problems, how friendly and understanding psychologists are, how psychologists can be trusted, how much better he is going to feel after he has talked with a psychologist, and anything else you can think of. Now, you don't *have* to do this for us, but we'd really appreciate it if you would. OK? Remember, this patient is going to listen to what you've said, so really try to convince him.

These instructions, we feel, simply fail to provide patients deficient in the cognitive arguments in favor of "seeing the psychologist" with sufficient material for a satisfactory role enactment. A more positive result, we would hold, would likely have emerged if prior to role enactment each patient was exposed to a vivid, detailed, rewarded, repetitive modeling display that depicted a patient-model overtly expressing attraction to a psychologist, and if such displaying was accompanied—in addition to the role playing—by procedures that assisted the viewer in paying attention to, and coding, the major themes, and that rewarded both model and viewer for the behaviors depicted. The investigations we shall examine in the section that follows provide direct empirical tests of the therapeutic usefulness of such modeling–role-playing combinations.

## Modeling and Role Playing Combined

A. A. Lazarus has been an important contributor to efforts seeking to alter maladaptive behavior by a combination of modeling and role playing. Using the term "behavioral rehearsal" for this combination of procedures, Lazarus initially sought to increase patient assertive behavior. He has described (Lazarus, 1966) the procedures as follows:

> In this method patient and therapist role-played various scenes which posed assertive problems for the patient . . . expressing disagreement with a friend's social arrangements, asking a favour, upbraiding a subordinate at work, contradicting a fellow-employee, refusing to accede to an unreasonable request, complaining to his employer about the inferior office fixtures,

requesting an increment in salary, criticizing his father's attire, questioning his father's values, and so forth. Commencing with the less demanding situations, each scene was systematically rehearsed until the most troublesome encounters had been enacted to the satisfaction of patient and therapist. The therapist usually roleplayed the significant persons in the patient's life according to descriptions provided by the latter. The patient's behavior was shaped by means of constructive criticism as well as modeling procedures in which the therapist assumed the patient's role and demonstrated the desirable responses. A situation was regarded as "satisfactorily covered" when (1) the patient was able to enact it without feeling anxious . . . ; (2) when his general demeanor, posture, facial expression, inflection in tone, and the like, lent substance to his words . . . and (3) when agreement was reached that his words and actions would seem fair and fitting to an objective onlooker. In order to expedite the transfer from consulting room to actual life, the patient was initially encouraged to apply his newly acquired assertive behavior only when negative consequences were highly improbable. . . . He soon grew proficient at handling most situations that called for uninhibited and forthright behavior. . . [pp. 209–210].

Other case reports demonstrating the apparent value of behavioral rehearsal for assertiveness training purposes subsequently appeared (Gittelman, 1965; Lazarus, 1966; Piaget & Lazarus, 1969). A. A. Lazarus (1966) has also reported a quasi-experimental evaluation of the efficacy of behavioral rehearsal. Seventy-five patients experiencing some type of interpersonal difficulty were briefly and individually treated by behavioral rehearsal, direct advice, or by reflective-interpretive therapy. Lazarus reports that 23 of the 25 patients receiving behavioral rehearsal showed improvement; 11 of 25 who had received advice; and 8 of 25 who had received reflective-interpretive treatment. While the significance of these findings is attenuated by the fact that Lazarus, obviously theoretically biased in favor of behavioral rehearsal, served as therapist for all 75 patients, and by the fact that judgments of patient improvement were not made independently, these results nevertheless contribute to incremental evidence regarding the efficacy of behavioral rehearsal.

A considerably more systematic and objective examination of behavioral rehearsal has been provided by McFall and Marston (1970). Forty-two university students who viewed themselves as too unassertive and who volunteered to participate in an experiment on assertive training served as Ss. Four experimental conditions were constituted: (1) behavioral rehearsal with performance feedback, (2) behavioral rehearsal with no performance feedback, (3) placebo therapy control, and (4) waiting-list, no-treatment control. A series of assertiveness-relevant, stimulus situations were developed for use in the two behavioral rehearsal conditions. For example, in one situation S would hear an audiotape description as follows:

*Narrator:*    Imagine that this morning you took your car to a local Standard station, and you explicitly told the mechanic to give you a simple tune-up. The bill should have been about $20. It is now later in the afternoon and you're at the station to pick up your car. The mechanic is walking over to you.

*Mechanic:*    Okay, let me make out a ticket for you. The tune-up was $12 for parts and $8 for labor. Uh, grease and oil job was $6. Antifreeze was $5. Uh, $4 for a new oil filter, and uh, $5 for rotating the tires. That's $40 in all. Will this be cash or charge?

At the end of each such stimulus situation presentation, S was required to offer a response. In the performance feedback condition, S then heard a recorded playback of his own response. No performance feedback Ss were asked to spend an equivalent amount of time recalling and reflecting upon their response. Both types of behavioral rehearsal Ss were asked to verbally evaluate their responses—was it direct enough?; how was the tone of voice?; inflection? communication of affect? etc.—stating how it might be improved in subsequent rehearsal trials. Each of 24, gradually escalated assertiveness situations were presented, and each was responded to four times (four rehearsals) before the next situation was heard. Thus, it is clear that a considerable amount of role playing was incorporated into the study procedures. The degree to which modeling procedures were present is a bit more obscure. The provision of general rules about directness and voice quality may, perhaps, be viewed as a type of quasi-modeling—by rule not by example—though "instructions" seems a more appropriate description. Of course, in addition, Ss receiving performance feedback might be said to be engaged in a self-modeling process,* one that might have contributed to increased assertiveness as the S's overt performance itself became more assertive. However, in either event, it is clear that the role play or rehearsal component is likely the more important component of the procedures utilized.

Subjects assigned to the placebo therapy control group engaged in four sessions in which S and E discussed assertiveness and instances of assertive behavior naturalistically performed by S in the past, or between ses-

---

* Creer and Miklich ( 1970) report the successful use of very similar procedures, under the term "self-modeling" in a single case experiment designed to increase self-care behavior.

sions. In essence, the procedures associated with this condition were intended as an attention-relationship control. No treatment Ss were placed on a waiting list and participated only in the study's pretesting and posttesting.

Though behavioral rehearsal with performance feedback tended to result in greater assertiveness than rehearsal without feedback, no significant differences on the study dependent measures emerged between the two behavioral rehearsal conditions. When these two conditions were combined, however, and compared against the two control conditions, significant results were obtained. Behavioral rehearsal Ss increased in assertiveness, measured in terms of pre- and post-behavioral test scores, significantly more than control Ss. They also reported significantly less anxiety associated with assertiveness behavior. Two weeks following completion of posttesting, each S was telephoned by an E posing as a magazine salesman. Working from a prepared script, the "salesman" delivered a hard sell pitch seeking to sell magazine subscriptions. The call was terminated only after (1) S agreed to buy, (2) after 5 min had elapsed without a "sale," (3) after all sales gambits had been exhausted without success, or (4) after S had hung up on the "salesman." In this important behavioral test for generalization of assertiveness training effects, behavioral rehearsal Ss exhibited resistance to the "salesman" at a significantly earlier point in the telephone interaction. McFall and Marston have thus provided a rigorous and substantial demonstration of the efficacy of behavioral rehearsal. In a subsequent investigation, McFall and Lillesand (1971) provided further evidence for the value of behavioral rehearsal, this time more explicitly combined with modeling procedures, for increasing assertive behavior in nonassertive Ss.

A third such demonstration, also with increased assertiveness as the target, has been provided by Friedman (1968). Subjects were 100 college students evidencing low scores on both self-report and behavioral measures of assertiveness. Following pretreatment behavioral assessment of S assertiveness, six experimental conditions were constituted. In the *directed role playing condition*, Ss rehearsed aloud four times a prepared script to an accomplice of E. The scene in the script was a reading room in a college library. One student was quietly reading a book when a second student started irritating and insulting him. The first student, whose role was played by S, then verbally asserted himself in a number of ways, such as demanding that the second student stop talking so loud. In the *improvised role playing condition*, Ss were given the same script as was used in directed role playing except that the lines for the student being irritated and insulted were omitted, and had to be supplied by S. During this enactment, which took place four times, *E*'s accomplice played the role of the insulting student. In the *modeling condition,* Ss observed two accomplices of *E* rehearse the script used for directed role playing four times; *modeling plus role playing condition* Ss also observed four enactments of this script, after which one accomplice left the room and S and the remaining accomplice enacted the script two times with S in the role of the insulted student. The directed role-playing script was simply read four times by Ss assigned to the *assertive script condition* and, finally, *nonassertive script condition* Ss read, also four times, a script of neutral conversation between two college students in a college library.

On this investigation's major dependent variable measure of increased assertiveness, modeling plus role-playing Ss scored significantly higher than all other conditions except improvised role playing. The modeling, directed role playing, improvised role playing, and assertive script groups did not differ significantly from each other, but did differ significantly from the nonassertive script control group. Friedman (1968) comments:

> The major variable assumed to mediate behavioral changes in the modeling plus role playing condition was overt response repetition (overt rehearsal) plus exposure to a variety of cues (visual, gestural and auditory) to assertive material. Separately, overt response repetition (directed role playing) and a variety of sensory inputs (modeling) did not suffice to establish differences between these two conditions and the assertive script condition . . . when both modeling and directed role playing are combined the S has available to him assertive information, a variety of symbolic cues for assertiveness, and a repertoire of overtly rehearsed assertive responses to emit in the presence of these cues. Thus it is likely that the combination of these mediating variables produces the greatest increase in assertive behavior [pp. 91–92].

Other research, completed or in progress, accords with these findings. Rosenhan and White (1967) successfully demonstrated the superiority of modeling plus rehearsal over either procedure alone as a means of increasing altruistic behavior in children. Higgings, Ivey, and Uhlemann (1969) utilized a combination of modeling, role playing, and feedback procedures, which they termed *media therapy,* to successfully enhance client communication skills. Sarason and Ganzer (1969) have used modeling combined with role playing to alter a variety of behaviors among institutionalized juvenile delinquents. Behaviors dealt with were coping with authority, control of impulsive behavior, importance of planning ahead, dealing with negative peer pressure, and making a good impression. Sarason and Ganzer (1969) describe their modeling plus role playing procedure as follows:

Each session is attended by six persons, two models and four boys. One complete scene is used for each meeting. An orientation to our procedures and a short example scene is presented, modeled, and role played during a new group's initial session. All sessions are either audio or video taped. Each subsequent meeting follows a sequence from: (a) one model introduces and describes the scene for the day, (b) the models role-play the scripts while the boys observe, (c) one boy is called upon to summarize and explain the content and outcome of the situation, (d) models comment on and discuss the scene, then replay the recording, (e) pairs of boys imitate and rehearse the roles and behaviors, (f) a short "break" is taken, while soft drinks are served and one of the two role-playing imitations is replayed, (g) the remaining boys act out the scene, (h) one of these two performances is replayed, and finally, (i) summaries and comments concerning the scene, and aspects of its importance and general applicability are emphasized [pp. 35–36].

On several of the behavioral dimensions noted above, this combined procedure proved clearly superior to either role playing alone or no participation in either modeling or role playing.

### Social Reinforcement

Structured Learning Therapy, as we currently conceptualize and operationalize it, has one other component—social reinforcement. In the present book, we will not review and examine social reinforcement research in great depth, for such reviews have recently been provided elsewhere by the author (Sorcher & Goldstein, in press) and by other investigators (Bandura, 1969; Franks, 1969; Glaser, 1971; Kanfer & Phillips, 1970). Nevertheless, we would be remiss if we did not describe at least briefly its implementation in Structured Learning Therapy. Having viewed a modeling display of optimal skill behavior of a given type, the patient (observer) in our procedures commences as part of a group of such patients to role play the displayed behaviors under the guidance of two group role-play leaders. As the patients' enactments increasingly approximate that of the model, he is provided social reinforcement in the form of the usual array of verbal approval statements (e.g., "fine," "good," "you did that just like the tape," etc.). Similar evaluative feedback rather rapidly also begins to be provided by other group members. Perhaps it is sufficient for our present purposes to indicate that the systematic inclusion of such social reinforcement delivery follows from the singularly powerful demonstration in the research literature regarding the significant influence of social reinforcement upon verbal behavior (Cohen, Kalish, Thurston, & Cohen, 1954; Hildum & Brown, 1956; Krasner, 1958; Miller & Drennen,

1970; Verplank, 1955); group behavior (Oakes, 1962; Oakes, Droge, & August, 1960, 1961; Zdep & Oakes, 1967); expression of feeling (Salzinger & Pisoni, 1957); evaluations of other people (Gelfand & Singer, 1968); acceptance of self (Nuthman, 1957); hostility (Binder, McConnell, & Sjoholm, 1957; Phillips, 1968); social interaction (Milby, 1970), and a host of other behaviors relevant to the targets for which we have already begun to use Structured Learning Therapy. Further details regarding the utilization of social reinforcement will be provided in subsequent chapters, as we describe our specific experimental procedures.

We have in this chapter examined a large number of investigations of modeling, role playing, and the combined use of these two procedures. The large majority of these studies has yielded positive results. In most instances, Ss were middle class, and thus the external validity of such findings for lower-class persons remains to be determined. We are hopeful in this regard, and in the chapters that follow, in which we present our own investigative findings, it will become clear that such feelings of optimism appear well placed.

*Chapter 6*

## STRUCTURED LEARNING AND
## THE LOWER-CLASS INPATIENT

Our investigations of Structured Learning Therapy with psychiatric inpatients, in accord with our "building block" or incremental research strategy, began with examination of the modeling component alone. Before examining these studies in detail, some reflections on their conceptualization and execution as a group seem warranted. In our first investigation, Liberman (1970) sought to enhance two classes of behavior in psychiatric inpatients by means of modeling procedures. His effort was largely successful with regard to one criterion behavior, patient self-disclosure, but unsuccessful in altering a somewhat more complex behavior, namely patient attraction to treatment staff. We interpreted this pair of findings as yet another example of a phenomenon apparently characteristic of several of the research programs examined in this book; that is, complex criterion behaviors call for complex, or at least more powerful, interventions for their successful alteration. We sought to reflect the spirit of this notion in our second and third inpatient investigations, in which Friedenberg (1971) and Walsh (1971) utilized somewhat more elaborate modeling displays for attraction, and obtained moderately more favorable effects.

In none of these studies, however, were the effects of modeling especially enduring, thus suggesting the likely value of augmenting the use of modeling with yet other procedures or combinations of procedures. This development of increasing power in our independent variable interventions found expression in the remaining investigations reported in the present chapter. Our procedures in these subsequent studies were those we have already described as Structured Learning Therapy—modeling, role playing, and social reinforcement—plus, in our most recent research, direct attempts to maximize transfer of training. While this brief preview has sought to describe, in overview, the fact that added interventions have, in a number of our investigations, resulted in added training effectiveness, we in no sense wish to communicate a sense of completeness. Our training "package" is, and hopefully will continue to be, "in progress." Note also, that as this research program has developed, we have explicitly shifted away from our initial type of dependent variable, i.e., skills primarily useful to patients for successful participation in traditional psychotherapy (self-disclosure, attraction, accurate role expectations, etc.), to skill targets more directly useful to patients in their daily functioning (social interaction, focusing, role taking, etc.).

### Self-Disclosure

Let us turn now to the specific inpatient studies we have conducted thus far. As noted above, Liberman's (1970) experimental goal was to examine the effectiveness of modeling procedures for enhancing both self-disclosure and attraction to treatment staff—two dependent variables we will examine more fully elsewhere in this book. It is sufficient to note at this point in our presentation that self-disclosure and related variables (self-exploration, self-reference, openness) have frequently been demonstrated to relate in important ways to a favorable therapeutic outcome (Drag, 1968; Jourard, 1969), and much the same conclusion is appropriate for attraction and related relationship variables (Gardner, 1964; Goldstein, 1971).

### *Procedure*

Subjects were 84 male alcoholic inpatients in a state hospital for alcoholics. The median age was 43, median length of hospitalization, 23 days. None had concomitant diagnoses of organicity, and all were sober at the time of their experimental participation. All study patients were participating in intensive (15 hours per week) short-term group psychotherapy.

Six experimental conditions were constituted: four modeling conditions and two control conditions. The modeling conditions were operationalized in terms of four tapes of initial psychotherapy interviews constructed for this investigation (see Appendix, pp. 213–230). These tapes depicted an alcoholic patient who expressed either *(1)* high attraction–high disclosure, *(2)* high attraction–low disclosure, *(3)* low attraction–high disclosure, or *(4)* low attraction–low disclosure vis-à-vis the psychotherapist on the tape. Therapist statements were identical on all four tapes. Our pilot procedures revealed these tapes to be credible as psychotherapy sessions and satisfactory depictions of the various attraction-disclosure combinations. Our two control conditions may be described as the *neutral tape* and *no tape conditions*. The *neutral tape condition* consisted of a discussion between two (unidentified) people about the nature of psychotherapy, what kinds of people typically receive it, the professionals offering it, etc. This (no treatment) tape sought to control for the attraction–disclosure conditions' attentional component. This tape and the four modeling tapes were identical in length. The *no tape condition* sought to control for the act of tape listening per se.

The study's predictions were that patients exposed to a high attraction model would later display greater attraction to their own interviewer than would patients exposed to either a low attraction model, a neutral tape, or no tape. Similarly, exposure to a high-disclosing model was predicted to lead to greater disclosure in an actual interview than was exposure to a low-disclosing model, a neutral tape, or no tape.

The 84 patients were randomly assigned to the study's six conditions. For patients assigned to the four modeling conditions, experimental procedures began by each patient being given (by an $E$ unaware of the study's hypotheses) the following instructions:

In recent years, more and more people experiencing emotional and psychological problems related to alcoholism have been obtaining help from psychotherapists. We are interested in learning more about psychotherapy and the reactions of alcoholics to this form of treatment.

In order to obtain information concerning alcoholics' reactions to therapy, we are going to play a tape of part of an actual psychotherapy session that took place in another state. This recording is from an initial therapy session with an alcoholic patient that took place in a hospital. By the way, it's important to mention that this patient has given us his permission to use his tape for these purposes. Here is some of his background:

This patient was in his mid-to-late thirties, and before coming to the hospital he was just about at the end of his rope. His family had threatened to leave him, he was losing his job, and he was about one step removed from total social and economic ruin. However, since this recording of his initial therapy session was made, he has shown great improvement. He has since been discharged from the hospital; he has obtained a well-paying job, and one which he says he enjoys; he has been able to stay dry, according to him, without too much trouble; and he's reported lately that he's beginning to get back with his family.

This history of the patient you are about to hear on the tape is true, but we know that "success stories" like this don't happen every day. Nevertheless, we would like to find ways of treating alcoholism so that these successes will happen more often.

One way to begin to find out why this patient was so successful in therapy is to start by looking at his first therapy session.

As you listen to the tape, we would like you to put yourself in the place of a patient and imagine how you, as a patient, would react to a similar situation.

These pretape instructions sought to optimize the patient's perceptions of the model as being similar to him in background and personality, as being rewarded for his behavior, and as being successful in his efforts—in response to the frequent finding in the modeling research literature that reward consequences to the model influence the amount of observer modeling which occurs. Each S then listened to the taped therapy session appropriate for his experimental condition. The same procedure held for the *neutral tape condition* patients, except that their pretape instructions were:

In recent years, more and more people experiencing emotional and psychological problems related to alcoholism have been obtaining help from psychotherapists. We are interested in learning more about psychotherapy and the reactions of alcoholics to this form of treatment.

In order to obtain information concerning alcoholics' reactions to therapy, we are going to play a tape in which two people talk about psychotherapy. Please listen carefully.

*No tape condition* patients participated in none of the above procedures, and began their study participation with the second (interview) phase of the investigation. For these patients and, after tape listening, for patients in the five tape conditions, E introduced the interviewer (another E) who stated:

I would like to ask you some questions about yourself and I would like you to answer them as honestly and as truthfully as you can. As you can see, what we say in here will be tape-recorded. However, the recordings will be held in strictest confidence. No one else here in the hospital will hear what you say unless you request it. OK?

Each study patient then participated in an individual intake-like interview during which he was asked exactly the same questions which had been addressed to the patient on the four modeling tapes. These questions were:

1. I wonder if you could tell me what you see as the causes of your drinking problem?

2. Now, try to describe to me what you see as your strong points and your weak points.
3. Now I'd like you to tell me the kinds of things that get you angry. . . . What are some of the things you do about your anger; how do you handle it?
4. What about the kinds of things that get you anxious, or fearful?
5. Now, I'd like you to tell me what your parents were like . . . If you had a choice, in what way would your parents be different?
6. There's one more question I'd like to ask. Most people have some sort of sexual problem. I wonder if you could tell me what sort of difficulties you've had in this area?

Following this interview, the first E administered a Client's Personal Reaction Questionnaire (CPRQ) to each patient. Over the course of an extended series of investigations (e.g., Ashby, Ford, Guerney, & Guerney, 1957; Goldstein, 1971) considerable predictive and construct validity has come to be associated with this measure of the patient's attraction to or liking for his psychotherapist. This testing session completed the study's experimental procedures.

### Results and Discussion

The tape-recorded interviews were content-analyzed for disclosure following content-analysis procedures of Ashby et al. (1957).* These data and the CPRQ attraction data constituted the study's dependent variable information. Preliminary to data analysis relevent to the study's hypothesis, a correlational analysis was performed between the study's dependent variable data and an array of demographic information obtained on each patient. The purpose of this analysis was to identify any variables usable for adjustment purposes in a covariance analysis. One such variable, IQ, was identified as a significant premanipulation correlate of subsequent attraction scores (Pearson $r = .23$; $df = 82$; $p < .05$). The subsequent analysis of covariance on attraction scores, however, failed to reveal any significant main or interaction effects. Thus, this study failed to find an attraction enhancement effect by modeling with the study patients. Analysis of variance on the study's disclosure data, in contrast, did yield a significant overall effect ($F = 2.36$; $df = 5.78$; $p < .05$). Tukey a tests performed on all possible cell comparisons revealed that patients exposed to the high-disclosure model were significantly more disclosing in their own interview than were patients exposed to the low-disclosure model,

---

* Interjudge reliability—Pearson $r = .93$.

but only when both models displayed low attraction toward the taped therapist. In addition, high-disclosure modeling led to significantly greater patient disclosure than did no tape listening. Thus this initial study provided partial evidence that one criterion, self-disclosure, could be enhanced by means of modeling procedures.

### Attraction

Our second inpatient investigation was conducted by Friedenberg (1971). In conceptualizing this study, we sought to be responsive to the growing body of research literature that increasingly highlights the importance of nonverbal behavior in the communication of interpersonal messages. Mehrabian (1969a), Mehrabian and Friar (1969), and Wiener and Mehrabian (1968) have reported evidence concerning the "message-value" of postures, positions, movements, and facial expressions in the communication process between two persons. Dittman, Parloff, and Boomer (1965), Ekman and Friesen (1968) and Scheflin (1964) are among the increasing number of researchers seeking to incorporate and expand this domain in psychotherapy-relevant contexts. It was based on such findings that we sought in this investigation to examine the value of nonverbal modeling cues for enhancement of patient attraction.

### *Procedure*

Our study sample consisted of 60 male psychiatric inpatients. Forty-two were diagnosed schizophrenic, the remainder psychoneurotic (14), manic-depressive (2), and unspecified psychosis (2). Average age was 44 years; average length of hospitalization, 8 years, 1 month. The patients were randomly assigned to four experimental conditions in a 2 × 2 factorial design involving two levels of modeled attraction to interviewer displayed nonverbally (high, low), and two levels of modeled attraction to interviewer displayed verbally (high, low). To implement these conditions, we developed and piloted four modeling videotapes. Interviewer questions, framed to be consistent with those frequently asked in the initial psychiatric interview, were identical on all tapes:

1. I wonder if you could tell me about the kinds of things that make you feel good . . . what you like . . . what makes you happy?
2. Can you tell me what kinds of things worry you . . . things you don't enjoy . . . things that get you upset?
3. You know that people get along well with some people and not so

well with others; could you tell me something about people you don't get along well with?

4. Everyone gets angry at some things some of the time; what kinds of things get you angry?

5. If you wanted to change something about yourself, like the way you act with people, what would it be?

Taped patient responses to these questions were also constant across tapes, with the exception that the tape utilized in the two high verbal attraction conditions included several additional comments by the taped patient (model) expressing high attraction to the taped interviewer. Low attraction statements were substituted for these on the low verbal attraction tapes (see Appendix, pp. 232–235). Both of these sets of attraction statements have been demonstrated in our earlier modeling studies to reliably result in corresponding levels of attraction when employed with a college student patient population (Goldstein, 1971).

Nonverbal cues of attraction consisted of postural portrayals reflecting polar positions on the nonverbal attitude continuum demonstrated by Mehrabian (1969b). Thus, the high attraction cue complex consisted of the videotaped patient-model sitting 27 inches from the interviewer, leaning forward 20°, showing eye contact over 90% of the time, and directly facing the interviewer (shoulder orientation of 0°). Low nonverbal attraction cues employed included having the model sit 81 inches from the interviewer, leaning backward at a 30° angle, showing eye contact less than 10% of the time, and facing partially away from the interviewer (shoulder orientation of 30°). The four resultant videotapes, reflecting the study's four experimental conditions, were the four possible combinations of high and low verbal and nonverbal modeled attraction (High-High; High-Low, Low-High, Low-Low). The videotaped interviewer displayed identical neutral behavior on all four tapes—no forward or backward lean, 50% eye contact, and direct shoulder orientation.

Subjects participated individually, and began their participation by receiving the following instructions:

Hello, I'm Mr. Friedenberg. If at any time while I'm talking, you get confused, just stop me, O.K.?

We're doing some research on better ways to help patients, and I'd like your help. We asked the people on the ward who would be able to help us, and you were one of the people they said could help us a lot. All you have to do is answer some questions. Since this research is not a part of your treatment, none of the answers that you give will be passed on to anyone here at the hospital, O.K.?

Today, we have a videotape recording of an interview between a patient and his interviewer in another hospital in New York State. After you watch this interview, we would like you to tell us your feelings about the interview you saw and heard. Then, we would like you to talk for a little while with the interviewer that you will see and hear on the tape. He is here today.

The patient on the tape has told us that we could use this tape for our research. This interview happened a short time after he came to the hospital. He was 35 years old, and was in pretty bad shape. His wife was going to leave him and he had lost his job. Since this interview, he has come a long way. He has been discharged from the hospital. He has a good job, which he says he likes a lot. And he's back together again with his wife. Now, can you tell me what you remember about what I just said? (If patient recalls adequately, continue.)

Now, we'll play the tape. Please watch and listen carefully to the tape, because we'll ask you questions about it when it's done. If the tape is too long, we can stop it so you can rest a while, but I don't think you'll have to rest because it's pretty short, about ten minutes.

The appropriate modeling videotape was then displayed, immediately after which each patient responded to a modified version of the CPRQ, which was read to him by an experimental assistant. Patient scores on this measure were viewed as our initial index of modeled attraction. As an opportunity to obtain a second, more behavioral, such measure, each patient was then requested to participate in a brief interview with the same interviewer he had seen on the modeling tape:

To help us learn more about interviewing, we would now like you to talk for a little while with the interviewer you saw and heard on the tape. Your interview will be tape-recorded, but what you say will be kept confidential. No one else here at the hospital will hear what you say unless you want them to, O.K.? Also, two of my associates will watch the interview to see if we can find out things about improving them. Now, I'd like to you to meet your interviewer.

Each interview was tape recorded and observed by two raters who recorded various aspects of each patient's nonverbal behavior (forward lean, eye contact, and degree of shoulder rotation). After the interview each patient completed a second CPRQ.

### Results and Discussion

Two significant findings emerged from the several analyses conducted across this study's data. Planned comparisons conducted between the High-High and Low-Low groups revealed significantly greater postvideotape attraction $(F = 16.38; df 1, 56; p < .01)$ and significantly less within-interview silence $(F = 72.50; df 1, 15; p < .001)$ for the group exposed to a high attraction (verbal and nonverbal) model. No similarly significant results emerged on these criteria in comparisons involving mixed models, or for any comparisons on the study's other criteria: nonverbal behavior during the interview, verbal openness or guardedness during the interview, and postinterview attraction to interviewer.

Thus, as noted at the outset of this chapter, a modeling effect for attraction did emerge in this investigation. It failed to prove robust, however, and was no longer evident on most interview criteria, which served as our immediately following test for minimal transfer. Extrapolating from the comparative findings and strength of experimental intervention in this and the Liberman study, we examined in our next investigation a purportedly more powerful set of procedures designed to maximize further the likelihood of attraction modeling.

### Attraction and Conformity Pressure

Walsh (1971) sought to influence patient attraction by a combination of modeling and conformity pressure procedures. Our interest in the latter type of intervention grew initially from the many demonstrations in the social psychological research literature indicating the power of conformity pressure in altering a wide array of perceptual and social judgments (Asch, 1951; Blake & Brehm, 1954; Blake & Mouton, 1961; Crutchfield, 1955; Sherif, 1936). More recently, our own research has made successful use of conformity pressure procedures to alter attraction-to-therapist in middle-class, college student Ss (Goldstein, 1971; Himmelsbach, 1970; Walsh, 1970). Walsh (1971) brought this line of investigation and our concern with modeling procedures together in a study involving 60 female psychiatric inpatients. As in the Friedenberg (1971) study, most were diagnosed schizophrenic, and were screened into the study sample based on a screening and pretesting procedure oriented toward establishing that each study patient possessed sufficient comprehension and attention span for adequate participation in study procedures. The 60 patients were randomly assigned to five experimental conditions in a 2 × 2 plus control factorial design involving the presence and absence of high attraction modeling and the presence and absence of high attraction conformity pressure.

In overview, Ss began participation by exposure to an audiotape of a therapy interview on which the patient (model) expressed either high attraction on several occasions to the taped therapist or verbalized no such attraction statements. Following this, Ss were exposed (or not exposed) to conformity pressure oriented toward the perception of a high level of attractiveness of the taped therapist. Subjects rated the attractiveness of the therapist at this point in time. All Ss then participated in a live interview with the same therapist they had heard on the tape recording, after which they again rated their attraction to him. The modeling and conformity pressure procedures were omitted for control Ss, whose study participation began with, and was limited to, the live interview and post-interview ratings.

### Procedure

The two tapes used during the modeling phase of this investigation (*High Attraction* modeling and *No Attraction* modeling), each the product of satisfactory pilot examination, were approximately 10 min long, and differed only in that 10 statements expressing patient attraction to the therapist were incorporated into the High Attraction tape (see Appendix, pp. 232–235). Both tapes sought to be maximally responsive to research on modeling enhancement by having the model (taped patient) and the observer (S) of the same sex, approximate age, and background; by displaying the behaviors to be modeled with high frequency; by structuring the model as successful; and by indicating in yet other ways that the model was rewarded for the behaviors displayed.

All Ss were seen individually. Instructions were either presented by tape recording or read directly to subjects, so that no reading was required of them. Their participation began by being provided the following instructions:

Hi. I'm Mr. Walsh from Syracuse University. We're doing some research on interviews. We're trying to find ways to make them better, and we wondered if you'd help us. All we'd like you to do is answer some questions. Since this is research and not treatment, no one here at the hospital will hear any of the answers you give, unless you want them to. OK?

If S agreed to participate, the following instructions were read to him if he was in one of the four groups required to listen to the tape recorded interview:

What we'd like you to do today is listen to a tape-recorded interview between a patient at another State Hospital and her interviewer. Then we'd like you to answer some questions about that interview so we can find out what you thought about it. Finally, we'd like you to talk for a few minutes with the interviewer that you'll hear on the tape. He's here today. OK?

Let me tell you a little about the patient that you'll hear on the tape. First of all, she gave us her permission to use this interview for our research, so she knows other people will be listening, and that's OK with her. When this interview took place, she was about 35 years old and had been in the hospital a couple of weeks. Things weren't going very well for her then—she'd lost her job and her husband had threatened to leave her. Since then, things have gotten a lot better for her. She's out of the hospital now. She has a new job which she says she likes. And she's back together again with her husband. So things have gotten better for her.

You'll be able to hear the tape through these earphones. You will be Number 4. There will be three other people in rooms down the hall listening to the same tape you listen to. So after the tape, when they ask Number 4 to say something into the microphone, say your answer into this. You'll hear some questions about the interview after you listen to it, and I'd like you to answer these by saying out loud one of the answers on the sheet in front of you—"strongly agree, slightly agree, not sure, slightly disagree, or strongly disagree." I'll read a couple of practice statements so you'll know what I mean.

Which of those five answers would you give about yourself if you heard this: "I like to watch television." How about this: "I like to go to the dentist."

The tape lasts about ten minutes. If that seems too long to you, just tell me and we'll stop. Also, if you can't hear the tape, tell me that too. You can put on your earphones now.

Subjects then listened to the appropriate modeling tape (see Appendix, pp. 232–235). Immediately after tape listening, the following instructions, for purposes of implementing the conformity pressure phase of this investigation, were presented:

We would now like to find out what you, and three other people who are listening, thought about the interview you just heard. Before we begin, we would like those of you who are listening to introduce yourselves by speaking into the microphone. The first member of our group is a head nurse at another State Hospital. Would you give us your name, please, Number 1: "Susan Preston." The second member of our group is a social worker. Would you give us your name, please, Number 2: "My name is Melissa Blake." The third member of our group is a recreational therapist. Would you give your name, please, Number 3: "I'm Sheila Coleman." The fourth member of our group is a patient here at the hospital. Would you give us your name, please, Number 4: "_____."

I will read to all of you some statements about the interview, and I want you to answer these by saying out loud one of the answers on the sheet in front of you. You may say either "strongly agree, slightly agree, not sure, slightly disagree, or strongly disagree." Mr. Walsh will write down your answers.

Subjects in the two groups not exposed to conformity pressure then heard 13 items from the tape rating form of the CPRQ (Goldstein, 1971). A 5-sec pause occurred after each item so the S could answer.

Before answering the 13 CPRQ items, Ss in the two groups exposed to conformity pressure heard the following:

We would like each of you to know how the other people in this group answer each statement. After I read a statement, I would like each of you to give your answer into the microphone when I call your number. Do not answer until I call your number. Each of you will be able to hear what the other people in the group say.

Conformity pressure was exerted in a manner similar to that used in our earlier studies (Goldstein, 1971; Himmelsbach, 1970; Walsh, 1970). Subjects in the two High Attraction Conformity Pressure groups heard the tape-recorded responses of the three female confederates before answering each of the first nine CPRQ items. On seven of the nine items, the three confederates answered unanimously in the direction of high attraction (strong agreement on positive items, strong disagreement on negative items). They displayed disagreement on two items as a means of including added credibility to the deception. As a minimal test of the effects of conformity pressure in the absence of such pressure, no confederate responses were heard during the last four CPRQ items.

Following these procedures, each S was provided the following additional instructions, and then participated in a 10-min interview structured around the same interview questions used in Friedenberg's (1971) investigation:

To help us learn more about interviewing, we would now like each of you to talk with the interviewer you heard on the tape. Your interview will be tape recorded, but what you say will be kept confidential. No one else here at the hospital will hear what you say unless you want them to. We would like Number 4 to speak to the interviewer first. OK? You may now remove your earphones.

Following the interview, which was tape recorded for later content analysis, each S again completed CPRQ ratings of his attraction to the interviewer. This completed the study's data gathering procedures.

### Results and Discussion

Our major experimental predictions were that modeling and conformity pressure would lead to significantly greater posttape and postinterview attraction than would the absence of both, and that the two procedures combined would yield a greater effect than either singly. Analyses of variance were conducted across the study's attraction data as tests of these predictions. These analyses are presented in Table 6.1.

TABLE 6.1
ANALYSES OF VARIANCE ($F$ VALUES) FOR POSTTAPE AND POSTINTERVIEW
ATTRACTION

| Measure | Modeling | Conformity | Modeling $\times$ Conformity |
|---------|----------|------------|------------------------------|
| Posttape attraction | 11.74** | 13.02** | 11.12** |
| Postinterview attraction | .13 | 1.6 | 1.9 |

** $p < .01$.

Post hoc cell comparisons by means of Tukey b tests on the posttape attraction data reveal all three treatments to differ significantly from the no modeling–no conformity pressure condition, but no significant differences among the three treatments. As Table 6.1 also indicates, no significant effects for postinterview attraction were obtained. A number of other comparisons, most of an exploratory nature, were made on data obtained during this investigation. Most such comparisons yielded negative results. Thus, no between condition differences emerged on the posttape CPRQ items administered in the absence of conformity pressure, or on patient openness, guardedness, self-referring statements, or silence during the live interview. As we had done in Friedenberg's (1971) study, we arranged the interview room so that the interviewee's chair was physically light, on wheels, and placed facing a corner of the room eight feet from where the interviewer would be sitting. Upon entering the room, the interviewer suggested that the interviewee "pull up the chair." Subjects exposed to the high attraction modeling tape pulled up the chair, i.e., sat themselves significantly closer to the interviewer than did those not exposed to this tape.

This study's major findings may be evaluated briefly. Once again, modeling procedures resulted in significant levels of patient change. But, also once again, these changes failed to persist into an immediately following interview test for minimal transfer. Conformity pressure yielded like effects and like failure of transfer. Combining the two procedures failed to yield a more powerful or a more transferable effect.

These three investigations summated in our thinking to the position that what may be necessary for more substantial, enduring, and transferable patient change is a more powerful implementation of modeling procedures, perhaps oriented toward more behavioral and less attitudinal skill targets and, as the early chapters of this book suggest, augmented by opportunities for the patient observers to behaviorally rehearse what they have seen, and receive social approval as their rehearsal enactments increasingly approximate the behavior of the model. That is, we were led to more fully conceptualizing Structured Learning Therapy—a conceptualization we put to direct test in our next investigation.

### Social Interaction I

Withdrawal, apathy, and minimal social interaction have long been recognized as major descriptive features of schizophrenia and other functional psychotic disorders. Diverse attempts to explain the bases for such behavior in institutionalized patients have been formulated, including (1) deficiencies in social motivation and social skill (Cameron, 1944); (2) deficiency in role-taking ability (Bloom & Arkoff, 1961; Helfand, 1956); (3) an effort to reestablish the capacity for stabilized thinking and perception by avoiding stimuli that evoke complex response hierarchies (Broen, 1968; Freeman, 1960); (4) as deriving from long-term familial and environmental patterns of social isolation (Faris & Dunham, 1960; Jaco, 1954); and (5) as behavior maintained and "enhanced" by the reinforcement contingencies made available in many staff-oriented, large mental hospitals (Dunham & Weinberg, 1960; Paul, 1969; Ullmann & Krasner, 1969). Concurrent with these several efforts to determine causality, numerous and varied attempts have been made to alter such minimal social interaction behavior in schizophrenic patients. Early interventions oriented toward these ends tended to be primarily informal and unsystematic, relied largely upon subjective criteria to evaluate their efficacy, and were typically reported as successful in terms of such criteria. The specific techniques utilized were, for the most part, changes in ward or hospital organization, use of attendants in more therapeutic-like and less singularly custodial capacities, use of patient-run groups, and directive attempts to raise the level of patient social motivation (Galioni, Adams, & Tallman, 1953; Hyde, 1953; Kraus, 1954; Merry, 1956; Miller, 1954; Miller & Clancy, 1952; Rees & Glatt, 1955). During the past decade, two major approaches to schizophrenic withdrawal behavior, social interaction, and resocialization have emerged. The first, growing from clinical programs such as those noted above, has been most frequently described as the milieu therapy approach (Artiss, 1962; Cumming & Cumming, 1962; Kraft, 1966). Here patients are given considerable responsibility, an array of group activities are implemented, group pressures toward social interaction and related goals are exerted, staff-patient status lines are blurred or diminished and, in more general terms, attitudes and behaviors necessary for satisfactory posthospital adjustment are reflected in the structure and operation of within-hospital activities. The few experimentally well-controlled examinations of milieu therapy programs have yielded evidence indicating at least moderate, and sometimes considerable success in enhancing patient social predispositions (Appleby, Scher, & Cumming, 1960; Kasius, 1966; Pace, 1957; Sanders, Smith, & Weinman, 1967). Yet, as Paul (1969) correctly observes with regard to these investigations, "The greatest weakness to date appears to lie in a failure to include systematically specific focus on instrumental role training . . . [Paul, 1969, p. 87]." This explicit instrumental role training focus combines with a special emphasis upon overt social *behavior* and a rationale derived from laboratory investigations of learning and reinforcement to form the second major approach to enhancing social interaction and resocialization in schizophrenia—the social learning approach.

Most of these social learning investigations have explicitly reflected operant conditioning principles. King, Armitage, and Tilton (1960) developed what they termed an operant-interpersonal methodology, one relying primarily upon shaping procedures. Compared to patients participating in either verbal therapy or recreational therapy, operant-interpersonal patients displayed significantly higher levels of verbalization, motivation to leave the ward and interest in occupational therapy. Ullmann, Krasner, and Edinger (1964) also provided an early demonstration of the use of operant procedures to successfully alter verbal-interpersonal behavior in a schizophrenic sample. Investigations such as these subsequently led to what thus far is the major application of operant principles to schizophrenic social behavior, the token economy. These programs too have begun to yield moderate and at times considerable evidence for their efficacy in reducing withdrawal and apathy and enhancing social interaction behavior in schizophrenic samples (Atthowe & Krasner, 1968; Ayllon & Azrin, 1965; Schaefer & Martin, 1966; Steffy, Torney, Hart, Craw, & Martlett, 1966).

Thus, both the milieu therapy and social learning (particularly operant) approaches to social interaction enhancement among schizophrenics rest on positive, if beginning, evidence and stand as promising approaches for further development and examination. The investigation we now wish to present (Gutride, Goldstein, & Hunter, 1972a) sought to examine the efficacy of Structured Learning Therapy when oriented toward similar ends. In its current form it is patently less expensive in several respects than either milieu or token economy approaches. Whether it is also an effective approach was the central empirical question of this study.

### Procedure

The initial S pool for this investigation was 133 asocial psychiatric inpatients in a state mental hospital. Inclusion in this pool was a function of a screening procedure jointly conducted by $E$ and the psychiatrist and chief nurse on each of nine hospital wards. Screening criteria were such that a patient was included if in the joint judgment of the screening panel, the patient consistently displayed social interaction difficulties or deficiencies. Since we desired asocial patients with a functional diagnosis, those diagnosed alcoholic, organic, mentally retarded, or as hospitalized for drug abuse were excluded from study participation. Thirty-five of the patients thus selected were discharged from the hospital during the 12-week period of Structured Learning Therapy, and 11 additional patients were unable or unwilling to complete the study's posttesting, thus reducing the study sample to a final $N$ of 87. Since, as will be noted, we were also interested in this investigation in the possible differential effectiveness of our training procedures as a function of patient acute–chronic status, patients of both types were included in our sample. Acute status was defined as being in the hospital less than one year and having had no more than two prior hospitalizations. Patients in the hospital for longer than one year and having had more than two prior hospitalizations were defined as chronic for purposes of this investigation. The final $N$ consisted of 30 acute and 57 chronic patients. Within each of these two categories, patients were randomly assigned to experimental (training) and control (no training) conditions such that 15 acute and 30 chronic patients constituted the experimental group, and 15 acute and 27 chronic patients made up the control group sample. Diagnostically, 75% of both the experimental and control samples were schizophrenic. The remainder in each group consisted primarily of patients diagnosed psychotic depression, schizoid personality, or inadequate personality.

In overview of the study procedures, all patients, and each ward psychiatrist and chief nurse began their participation by completion of test materials selected or developed to obtain both covariate data and baserate information on pretraining level of patient social interaction. Experimental group patients then participated in a 4-week Structured Learning Therapy program designed to enhance their level of overt social interaction. During this period, control group patients participated in no special study procedures. Posttraining observational and psychometric measurement of social interaction behavior was then obtained across all study patients.

The training program's goals were explained to all study patients and their active participation invited. Control patients were told in addition that due to equipment failure, their program participation would be delayed a few weeks. The pretesting that was conducted consisted of four measures, all directly or indirectly relevant to social interaction. First, for possible covariance usage, each ward psychiatrist completed the Psychotic Inpatient Profile (Lorr & Vestre, 1968) on each study patient residing on his ward. It was the Seclusiveness and Disorientation subscales of this instrument that we viewed as potential covariates, since each appeared on an a priori basis to be likely influences upon patient social interaction. Also at this point in time, the Ward Atmosphere Scale (Moos, 1969) was completed by each patient, its Affiliation and Autonomy subscales being those of potential interest to us for later covariance analysis. Base-rate dependent variable testing at this juncture included the FIRO (Schutz, 1967), in whose Inclusion subscale we were interested, and the POMS (McNair & Lorr, 1964), used to determine the influence upon mood of alterations in social interaction behavior.

Four modeling videotapes were developed by us for use as this study's stimulus materials. Each depicted several variants on a single social interaction theme. Concretely, the first tape contained enactments indicating how one individual (the model) can interact with another individual who approaches him. The second, how an individual (the model) can initiate interaction with a second person. The third, how an individual (the model) can initiate interaction with a group of people. Finally, continuing this progression reflecting increasing complexity of social interaction, the fourth tape depicted how an individual (the model) can resume relationships with relatives, friends and co-workers from outside the hospital. In several respects, in both the development and experimental usage of these modeling displays, we again sought to be responsive to laboratory research findings that have identified characteristics of the observer, the model, and the modeling display that function to enhance the level of vicarious learning which occurs. This included our portrayal of several heterogeneous models; the introduction and summarization of each tape by a high status narrator (hospital superintendent and clinical director), who sought by his introduction to maximize observer attention and by his summary to reemphasize the nature of the specific, concrete social interaction behaviors; portrayal of the model's characteristics as similar to that of most participating study patients (age, sex, patient status); and frequent and readily observable reward provided the model contingent upon his social interaction behavior.

Experimental group patients were constituted into eight subgroups of five to eight each and met with two group leaders three times per week for a 4-week period. The group leaders were 20 undergraduate volunteers who underwent a 12-hour training program in the application of modeling, role playing, and social reinforcement immediately prior to the beginning of the investigation. Each of the four modeling tapes served as stimulus materials for three consecutive group meetings. Each session began with the modeling tape display, during which the group leaders actively drew attention to those model behaviors representative of effective social interaction. At frequent intervals the sound was turned off and the importance of nonverbal aspects of social interaction was highlighted, e.g., forward leaning, eye contact, smiling, etc. Each tape was immediately followed by an "idiosyncratizing" group discussion in which the behaviors and circumstances depicted were related to each patient's personal experiences and environmental demands. The remainder of each session was devoted to role playing both the depicted and personalized social interaction sequences. Initially, the group leaders were active guides and participants in the role-play enactments, though as the sessions continued, the patients themselves took increasing responsibility for role allocation and enactment. The role-playing enactments were themselves videotaped and played back to the group for comment and corrective feedback. Both the group leaders and, frequently, other group members provided the role-play enactor with frequent social reinforcement as his depiction more and more approximated that of the videotaped models.

Posttesting across experimental and control patients was conducted during the week following completion of the Structured Learning program. All patients individually completed both the FIRO and the POMS. Since our main dependent variable concern was with neither attitudinal (FIRO) or mood (POMS) criteria, but with overt social interaction *behavior*, certain behavioral observation criteria were developed and measured. The first may be termed *Standardized Observation* of patient social interaction behavior. Each patient was brought to a waiting room and requested to wait a brief period prior to taking the FIRO and POMS. A second "patient" (an experimental accomplice) was already seated in this room, apparently also waiting to complete his posttesting. Their subsequent interaction, during which the accomplice sought to behave in a prearranged, standardized manner, was observed through a one-way mirror by a rater trained to rate, at 30-sec intervals, the presence or absence of the following interactional patient behaviors:

1. patient eye contact
2. forward leaning
3. physical contact
4. smiling
5. initiates conversation
6. responds to conversation
7. talks 10 or more consecutive seconds.

During this 5-min period of standardized observation, the accomplice sought to behave in a friendly and interested manner and, on a schedule set at 30 sec, 60 sec, 90 sec, 2 min, 3 min, and 4 min, would ask one of the following questions if the patient were not talking at that given point in time:

le.*      Were you in the program?
1c.      Are you in the program?
2e.      How many people were in your group?
2c.      How many people are coming from your ward?
3e.      What did you think of the program?
3c.      What do you think of the program?
4e.      Would you go through this again?
4c.      Do you really want to go through this?
5e & c.  What time is it?
6e &c.   What do you do when this is over?

Our second observational criteria may be termed *Naturalistic Observation* of patient social interaction behavior. Eight raters were trained in the use of a social interaction checklist developed by us for this investigation, by means of which they could rate the following interactional patient behaviors:

1. eye contact
2. forward leaning
3. physical contact
4. smiling
5. initiates conversation
6. responds to conversation
7. talks 10 or more consecutive seconds
8. seated alone
9. seated with others.

Interrater reliability for these ratings, determined during three training sessions, yielded an overall percentage agreement (taking raters two at a time in all possible pairings) of 85%. Patients were observed by these raters during mealtimes for the 2-week period immediately following the posttesting described above. Each rater was randomly assigned to rate 10 or 11 patients; each patient was observed for one 10-min period. In addition, each rater completed Semantic Differential ratings on each patient whose behavior they had observed. These ratings were on the dimensions: *(1)* general social skill, *(2)* interaction with others, and *(3)* social impact upon others.

---

* e: Question asked to experimental patients.
  c: Question asked to control patients.

In addition to this investigation's major comparisons involving the presence and absence of Structured Learning Therapy, our design was such to permit two sets of exploratory questions to be addressed to our data. In response to Magaro's (1969) cogent arguments predicting differential treatment responsiveness to interventions such as ours as a function of acute versus chronic status, acute–chronic was utilized as our second experimental variable. Finally, to complete our 2 × 2 × 2 design, we chose to inquire into the possible additivity of treatment interventions by utilizing as our third variable, presence versus absence of psychotherapy– psychotherapy being defined for this investigation as participating in two or more sessions per week of individual or group psychotherapy.

## Results and Discussion

*Covariance Check.* As noted earlier, based upon scale descriptions and items, as well as relevant research, we selected the Seclusiveness and Disorientation subscales of the Psychotic Inpatient Profile and the Affiliation and Autonomy subscales of the Ward Atmosphere Scale as potential covariates for our social interaction dependent measures. A correlational analysis comparing patient scores on these four subscales against each of the 16 scores reflecting overt social interaction behavior (Naturalistic and Standard Observation scores) revealed the appropriateness of this a priori covariate selection. Each subscale score correlated at .25 or greater with five or more social interaction scores. Based upon this outcome, a series of 2 × 2 × 2 analyses of covariance was conducted across the study's data. The results of these analyses are reported in Table 6.2.

*Main Effects.* A moderate number of main effects emerged for our three treatment variables on several of our dependent variable measures. Such effects were, for the most part, on the overt or rater judgment measures of social interaction behavior, with relatively less apparent influence being exerted by our interventions on either attitude or mood criteria. Structured Learning Therapy yielded significant differences on four of the seven specific social interaction behaviors rated under Standard Observation conditions. Mealtime (Naturalistic) overt behavior ratings, however, demonstrated no effects for Structured Learning Therapy, though the judges who had completed these behavior ratings rated such patients as significantly more socially interactive on two separate Semantic Differential dimensions, and as marginally so on a third. Psychotherapy, in contrast, appears to have had essentially no effect upon social interaction behavior or more global ratings thereof—at least as far as this simple effects analysis is concerned. In fact, on two of the four criteria for which were found significant main effects for psychotherapy (Natur-

## TABLE 6.2
ANALYSES OF COVARIANCE ($F$ VALUES) FOR SOCIAL INTERACTION

| Measure | Source[a] |
|---|---|
| *Standard Observation* | |
| 1. forward leaning | SLT (97.91***) |
| 2. smiling | SLT (7.56***); PTX (4.47**) |
| 3. responds to conversation | SLT (31.35***); SLT × AC (3.12*) |
| 4. talks 10 or more consecutive seconds | SLT (5.51**) |
| *Naturalistic Observation* | |
| 1. eye contact | AC (7.47***); SLT × PTX (4.90**); SLT × AC (2.85*) |
| 2. forward leaning | PTX (4.11**) |
| 3. initiates conversation | AC (3.74*) |
| 4. responds to conversation | AC (4.21**); SLT × PTX (5.48**) |
| 5. talks 10 or more consecutive seconds | AC (9.61***) |
| 6. seated alone | SLT × PTX (8.56***); SLT × AC 3.54*) |
| 7. seated with others | SLT × PTX (11.83***) |
| *Social Behavior Ratings* | |
| 1. general social skills | SLT (3.32*); AC (5.23**); SLT × PTX (4.83**); SLT × AC (5.38**) |
| 2. interaction with others | SLT (5.11**); SLT × PTX (4.69**); SLT × AC (2.93*) |
| 3. social impact upon others | SLT (36.99***); PTX (8.22***); AC (20.79***); SLT × PTX (27.19***); SLT × AC (7.55***) |
| POMS | |
| 1. tension–anxiety | SLT × AC (3.48*) |
| 2. depression–dejection | PTX (4.33**); SLT × PTX (4.00**) |
| 3. anger–hostility | SLT (4.13**); PTX (2.79*); AC (3.15*); SLT × PTX (3.57*); PTX × AC (14.09***) |
| 4. fatigue | AC (3.65*); SLT × PTX (3.94*) |
| 5. confusion–bewilderment | PTX × AC (3.92*) |
| 6. total mood disturbance | SLT × PTX (4.46**); PTX × AC (7.22***) |

[a] Source key: SLT—Structured Learning Therapy; PTX—Psychotherapy; AC—Acute-Chronic.

* $p > .05 < .10.$    ** $p < .05.$    *** $p < .01.$

alistic Observation: forward leaning, and Semantic Differential: social impact upon others), the direction of the difference showed significantly higher score for patients *not* participating in psychotherapy. Finally, on the Naturalistic Observation and Semantic Differential scores for which significant main effects emerged on the acute–chronic variable, all such differences favored the acute as compared to the chronic patients.

None of our three treatment variables significantly influenced patients' self-reported (FIRO) predisposition to either seek social interaction with others or want others to seek social interaction with them. Patient self-reported mood was affected almost as little by our interventions when examined singly, although all three interventions had moderate to considerable impact upon reducing anger–hostility.

*Interaction Effects.* Analysis of the joint influence of our treatment each of which post hoc comparisons were conducted by means of Scheffe variables yielded a number of significant interaction effects in response to tests.* No significant interactions were obtained on any of the Standard Observation social interaction criteria for any of our treatment variables. Structured Learning Therapy and psychotherapy, however, interacted to yield several significant effects on the Naturalistic Observation criteria, on the judges' Semantic Differential ratings of patient social interaction, and on certain patient mood dimensions. Post hoc analyses on these data may be summarized as indicating:

1. For acute and chronic patients combined, psychotherapy plus Structured Learning Therapy yields significantly more positive scores than does psychotherapy alone on:
   a. Naturalistic Observation: seated with others
   b. Naturalistic Observation: responds to conversation initiated by others
   c. POMS: total mood disturbance

In contrast to the suggestion provided by this small number of consistent post hoc analyses that perhaps Structured Learning Therapy augments the effects of psychotherapy on our criteria, it should be noted that we obtained no significant results to indicate the converse, i.e., a more positive effect upon patient social interaction of psychotherapy plus Structured Learning Therapy, as compared to Structured Learning Therapy alone.

---

* These post hoc analyses were calculated for those $F$s significant at $p < .05$ or better. No such analyses were calculated for those $F$s reported in Table 6.2 as significant at $p > .05 < .10$. These are included in Table 6.2 simply to report possible trends in our results.

2. For acute and chronic patients combined, and in the absence of psychotherapy, Structured Learning Therapy yields significantly more positive scores than does the absence of Structured Learning Therapy on:
   a. Naturalistic Observation: seated with others
   b. Naturalistic Observation: responds to conversation initiated by others
   c. Naturalistic Observation: eye contact
   d. Semantic Differential: general social skill
   e. Semantic Differential: interaction with others
   f. Semantic Differential: social impact upon others
   g. POMS: depression–dejection
   h. POMS: total mood disturbance

3. For acute and chronic patients combined, and in the absence of Structured Learning Therapy, psychotherapy yields significantly more positive scores than does the absence of psychotherapy on:
   a. Naturalistic Observation: seated alone (infrequency of)
   b. Naturalistic Observation: seated with others
   c. Naturalistic Observation: responds to conversation initiated by others
   d. Naturalistic Observation: eye contact
   e. Semantic Differential: interaction with others
   f. Semantic Differential: social impact upon others
   g. POMS: depression–dejection
   h. POMS: total mood disturbance

4. For acute and chronic patients separately, and in the absence of psychotherapy, Structured Learning Therapy yields significantly more positive scores than does the absence of Structured Learning Therapy on:
   a. Semantic Differential: general social skill
   b. Semantic Differential: social impact upon others

Though both types of patients are rated significantly higher on these dimensions if they participate in Structured Learning Therapy, as compared to patients of each type who do not, the ratings obtained by acute patients are significantly greater than those assigned to the chronic patients.

5. For Structured Learning Therapy and no Structured Learning Therapy patients combined, and for acute patients only, psychotherapy yields significantly more positive scores than does the absence of psychotherapy on:

a. POMS:   anger–hostility
b. POMS:   total mood disturbance

On these same two mood dimensions, for patients in psychotherapy only, acute patients obtained significantly more positive scores than did chronic patients.

Finally, it should be noted that no significant three-way interactions emerged from these analyses; with one possible exception, no significant effects were obtained for any of our treatments on either the Expected Inclusion or Wanted Inclusion scores of the FIRO; and on none of our several dependent variable measures were there significant differences between male ($N = 50$) and female ($N = 37$) patients.

The major focus of this investigation concerned the effects of Structured Learning Therapy on patient social interaction skills as reflected in both overt social interaction behavior as well as global ratings of such behavior, patient predisposition to social interaction, and patient mood. With the exception of our predispositional measure, a moderate number of significant effects of each of the above types emerged. We view these findings as providing satisfactory, though certainly only tentative and initial, evidence for the efficacy of these procedures for social interaction skill training.

Psychotherapy, too, yielded a significant influence upon a number of our dependent measures, but with a very few exceptions this was the case only in the absence of Structured Learning Therapy. That is, while there was evidence on a small number of criteria suggesting that Structured Learning Therapy augmented the effects of psychotherapy, there was considerably more evidence on other, but closely related, criteria which may be interpreted as suggesting an opposite effect; i.e., that Structured Learning Therapy and psychotherapy are mutually inhibiting to some degree. More concretely, this possibility is a tentative interpretation which may be drawn from comparing the almost total absence of significant main effects for psychotherapy (computed across both acute and chronic patients receiving and not receiving Structured Learning Therapy) and the several significant interaction effects involving psychotherapy (which, while also computed across acute and chronic patients, involved only those *not* receiving Structured Learning Therapy). This possibility of mutual inhibition is a speculative inference and should be viewed as such. To the extent that it is valid, it suggests the value of further inquiry into questions concerning the additivity, "subtractivity," or mutual exclusiveness of such treatment interventions.

For the most part, our data analysis revealed that on those criteria on which Structured Learning Therapy or psychotherapy were effective, they were effective for both acute and chronic patients, although in some instances, they were significantly more effective for the acute patients. Almost by definition, as the work of Magaro (1969) and others suggests, the acute patient, especially if he is also of good premorbid personality, will frequently be an individual whose interpersonal skill repertoire is essentially intact, but is not finding appropriate overt expression due to the interference of his psychopathology. The chronic patient, especially if he is also of poor premorbid personality, is much more likely to have an inadequate or deficient repertoire of interpersonal skills as a result of long term lack of practice—both during his hospitalization(s) and, frequently, before. The acute patient's more adequate interpersonal skill repertoire, therefore, likely accounts for not only those few instances in which acute patients obtained significantly higher scores than did chronic patients, but also probably explains the several significant Naturalistic Observation criteria main effects, all of which favored the acute patients. More important, however, because we view the acute patient as an individual with a relatively intact (but nonoperating) interpersonal skill repertoire and the chronic patient as one deficient or lacking in such skills, it is the chronic patient whom we view as the preferred target for Structured Learning Therapy—at least for social interaction skills. In this regard we would propose that one of the more important findings of this investigation is that in most of those instances in which Structured Learning Therapy did yield a significant effect, it did so not only for acute patients, but also for the chronic patient sample.

We noted earlier that our modeling displays were presented in a sequence we conceptualized as hierarchical, from the apparently more simple, less threatening, and less demanding type of social interaction to that seemingly representing greater complexity, potential threat, and demanding more social skill. For example, we sought to teach patients appropriate behavioral means for responding to conversation initiated by others, before seeking to teach behaviors by which one might appropriately initiate conversation with others. Inspection of our findings contains at least a suggestion that, across treatments and type of patient, the simpler and perhaps less threatening skills were learned better than the more complex types of social interaction behaviors. For example, there were four significant or near significant effects for "responds to conversation," but only one for "initiates conversation"; three significant or near significant effects for "eye contact," but none for "physical contact." To the extent that our inferences here regarding the simplicity and complexity of given behaviors are correct, it may be appropriate to consider the desirability in future implementations and evaluations of Structured Learning Therapy of (1) a more extended series of sessions, (2) proportionately greater time and materials devoted to the more complex behaviors representative of the given skill, and/or (3) the augmentation of Structured Learning Therapy with yet other intervention procedures. Both Structured Learning Therapy and psychotherapy, as defined in this investigation, proved superior to the absence of either in the level of resultant patient social interaction on several criteria. In discussing these findings, we have attributed them to the specific effects of each treatment. It is possible, however, that the (an) active ingredient in these interventions is one they share in common, namely, the attention provided each patient by an institutionally sanctioned change agent, and the opportunity and practice thus provided each patient to engage in social interaction with the change agent. As a control for such a potential nonspecific therapeutic ingredient, some form of attention control group that also provided social interaction opportunities for the patient would have been a clearly desirable addition to this study's design. Our second attempt to enhance social interaction skills largely reflected these several added training and experimental control dimensions.

## Social Interaction II

### Procedure

The Ss for this investigation (Gutride, Goldstein, & Hunter, 1972b) were 106 psychiatric inpatients at a state mental hospital. Though all carried diagnoses of a functional disorder, and most were diagnosed schizophrenic, it was not formal diagnoses to which we were responsive for selection purposes. As in our earlier study seeking to enhance social interaction skills, it was overt deficit behavior in this skill domain which led to a given patient's acceptance into the study sample. Also as before, screening for acceptance was conducted by a panel consisting of one of the Es, the ward psychiatrist, and the nurse most familiar with the patient's daily behavior. A total of 12 wards were drawn upon for this purpose. Once a given patient was selected as a possible participant, he was individually provided the following invitation and orientation by E:

You probably know that we have a closed circuit television studio on the first floor of Building Four. We can take pictures of people doing things and then show them back what they look like. This seems to be one of the best ways of learning about yourself. We've developed a program in which we want to improve the social atmosphere in the dining halls at mealtime. As you know, people usually go to meals, eat, and leave, and there's practically no conversation or relaxation. So we are going to use the television equipment to show you how we can interact with others, we'll practice interacting with others, and see ourselves doing it. You were selected for this program by your doctor and nurse because they thought you would enjoy it and get a lot out of it. The program beings in two weeks, and next week we'd like to give you some questionnaires to fill out which you'll also fill out at the end of the program so we can evaluate the effectiveness of the program. They won't be seen by your doctor or nurse.

Of the 146 patients invited, 28 declined. Twelve of the remaining 118 were either discharged or failed to appear during the course of the study, leaving the final study sample of 106 patients. All participating patients, for pretesting purposes, were administered the POMS (McNair & Lorr, 1964) and the FIRO (Schutz, 1967).

Five experimental conditions formed the investigation's experimental design, in a 1 × 5 format. Within certain hospital administrative restrictions, patients were randomly assigned to one of the following:

1. Structured Learning Therapy (5 weeks), plus transfer training (2 weeks); $N = 46$
2. Structured Learning Therapy (5 weeks), plus Structured Learning Therapy (2 weeks); $N = 14$
3. Structured Learning Therapy (5 weeks); $N = 13$
4. Companionship control (7 weeks); $N = 18$
5. No treatment control; $N = 15$

The Structured Learning Therapy for experimental conditions 1, 2, and 3 consisted (during the first 5 weeks) of meeting with two group leaders, in groups of six to ten patients each, three times per week for sessions lasting one hour each. Thus, Structured Learning Therapy during the first 5 weeks of the program consisted of a total of 15 meetings per group. Five modeling videotapes were developed for this investigation, all oriented toward displaying optimal social behavior in an eating and mealtime context (see Appendix, pp. 235–245). As in our other investigations, we sought to enhance the level of observer modeling by using several heterogeneous models; by including on each tape an introduction and summarization by a high status narrator who sought to increase attention and provide reinforcement to the model; by displaying several instances of each behavior we were seeking to teach; by utilizing models similar in age and dress to most observers; by scheduling the tapes in order from least to most complex; and by providing frequent and obvious social reinforcement to the model throughout all five tapes. In outline form, the content of these modeling displays was:

1. The most rudimentary social eating behavior, e.g., how to hold a knife and fork, use of napkin, posture at the table, etc.
2. Very simple social behaviors, e.g., what and how one might say something when joining an already occupied table, excusing oneself when passing by someone in a tight space between tables, helping someone with their tray, etc.
3. Somewhat more lengthy, if still brief, interactive behaviors, e.g., offering to get seconds for someone, greeting other patients or dietary personnel, asking for the salt, excusing oneself from the table, etc.
4. A series of longer, more complex conversations, all of which were positive in tone
5. A series of negative social interactions, e.g., someone yelling at you to get out of his way, someone spilling something on or near you, etc.

Following tape presentation, in the three Structured Learning Therapy conditions, a brief "idiosyncratizing" discussion was held in which patients had the opportunity to relate the behaviors depicted to their own typical behavior and real-life environments. Role playing then ensued, during which the behaviors displayed were rehearsed. Group leaders, as part of the role playing, placed special emphasis on pointing out (on the modeling display), portraying (during live modeling), and eliciting (during role playing) various aspects of body language relevant to successful social interaction, e.g., smiling, eye contact, posture, gestures, and so forth. To maximize the opportunity to provide patients with social reinforcement contingent upon correct enactments, or to provide other performance feedback, all patient role playing was itself videotaped and immediately displayed. The foregoing describes the first 5 weeks of participation for patients in Conditions 1, 2, and 3. At the completion of this series, study procedures were varied for each of these three groups.

1. Structured Learning Therapy plus Transfer Training. We have briefly mentioned earlier in this chapter our feelings about the importance for enduring patient change of active efforts aimed at enhancing transfer of training. We will elaborate our rationale and procedures for doing so at some length in Chapter 9. It will suffice at this point to indicate that we feel a major determinant of such successful transfer is performance feedback, primarily in the form of reinforcement received by the patient in his posttraining, real-life environment for enactments of his newly acquired behaviors. To implement such feedback, one of the group

leaders and an *E* joined patients for every lunch and dinner meal for a period of 2 weeks following initial (5 weeks) training. Patients observed during this period to be enacting the target behaviors were immediately provided social reinforcement. Patients not doing so, were provided further modeling or prompts.

2. *Structured Learning Therapy plus Structured Learning Therapy.* In planning this experiment, we realized that patients receiving the initial training plus transfer training might later perform more adequately than those receiving the initial training only, *not* because the former received *transfer* training, but simply because the first group received *more* training. That is, the extra 2 weeks of training might have proven to be the responsible variation, not the fact that it occurred in situ, etc. To control for this possibility, patients in this second condition received 2 additional weeks of Structured Learning Therapy *in the training studio* after their initial 5 weeks of training. One tape was re-presented and role played each day, with the last (sixth) day of additional training devoted to a general discussion and summary.

3. *Structured Learning Therapy.* Patients assigned to this condition participated in the initial five-week, 15-session program only.

4. *Companionship Control.* We have commented above on the importance in behavior change research of controlling for effects which may be attributable to interpersonal attention from a change-agent. In the present study, patients in the three Structured Learning conditions may change more than those receiving no treatment (Condition 5) not because of what we perceive as the active ingredients in Structured Learning, but because of the attention given patients by group leaders offering interest, concern, involvement, etc. Thus the need for an appropriate experimental control. We operationalized this attention control condition by providing each patient with an undergraduate student companion for the number of hours (15) equal to that involved in Structured Learning participation. The companion–patient pairs engaged in a wide variety of activities (walks, cards, etc.) and a broad range of conversations. The companions sought to be warm, nonjudgmental, empathic friends. Such companionship has been tentatively demonstrated to yield a variety of positive effects, several of which are clearly describable as enhanced social behavior (Beck, Kanto, & Gelineau, 1963; Gruver, 1971; Holzberg, Knapp, & Turner, 1967; Umbarger, Dalsimer, Morrison, & Breggin, 1962).

5. *No-Treatment Control.* Patients assigned to this condition participated in no Structured Learning Therapy or transfer training, nor were

they assigned a student companion. Their only study involvement was participation in pretesting and posttesting activities.

Posttesting was conducted following completion of these several interventions. In addition to readministration of the FIRO and POMS, two sets of systematic observations were made of patient social behavior. The first, Standard Observation, involved bringing each patient individually into the TV studio which, for postmeasurement purposes, had been furnished with tables, chairs, silverware etc.—to simulate the hospital's dining hall. The patient was told he and a helper would "go through a make-believe meal" and that the patient "should do whatever he thought best in each situation which would occur." A series of simulated situations or tasks were then initiated by E and the helper (accomplice), such as waiting on the food line, getting one's food, sitting at an already occupied table, the spilling of food, and so forth. The patient's responses to each situation were observed through a one-way mirror and rated for the presence and absence of both situation-specific appropriate responses (e.g., excusing oneself if appropriately passing someone on line; sitting at an occupied table; acknowledging others at table, etc.) and more generally appropriate social responses (e.g., eye contact, smiling, initiating and responding to conversation, etc.)

Each patient's mealtime social behavior was also observed in the hospital dining hall. Naturalistic Observations involved the observation of the first 15 min of one randomly chosen meal for each participating patient. Raters recorded, at 30-sec intervals, the presence or absence of the following behaviors:

1. talking on line
2. sits at occupied table
3. acknowledges others as he sits down
4. puts napkin in lap
5. initiates conversation at table
6. responds to conversation
7. talks 10 consecutive seconds
8. smiles
9. gestures
10. eye contact
11. uses napkin correctly before leaving
12. acknowledges others when leaving

The final study measure was a global rating form, cast in Semantic Differential format, completed by all naturalistic observers on the dimensions: *(1)* general social skills, *(2)* interaction with others, and *(3)* social impact on others.

### Results and Discussion

The major findings of this investigation are presented in Table 6.3. As Table 6.3 indicates, several significant findings emerged between treatment conditions. As a group, they largely confirm the major results of our earlier attempt to enhance social interaction behaviors, though no significant POMS or FIRO results were obtained. Social behaviors specific to a mealtime context and more generally applicable social behaviors were both enhanced by Structured Learning participation. While the usefulness of Structured Learning Therapy for these purposes thus appears further supported, no consistent evidence is apparent in these results to suggest the relative superiority of any of the three implementations of Structured Learning Therapy. That is, transfer training as operationalized seems to have added only relatively little to the impact of the five week Structured Learning Program. In Chapter 9 we will consider at some length a potentially more powerful and comprehensive operationalization of transfer training. It is also generally true of our findings that 7 weeks of Structured Learning participation (5 + 2) yielded no greater skill enhancement than did participation for 5 weeks. All three Structured Learning conditions, however, yielded consistent, and at times considerable, increments in social interaction behaviors which were significantly greater than that following from companion control and no treatment control conditions. The effects of Structured Learning Therapy, therefore, appear to be attributable to factors beyond the interpersonal attention inherent in its procedures. Such interpersonal attention, in the form of the companion control condition, yielded essentially no effects on our criteria beyond no treatment participation.*

To this point in the present chapter, we have focused primarily upon our Structured Learning attempts to alter an array of overt patient social behaviors. These several social-interpersonal skill dimensions were originally chosen as targets for modification due to their clear and critical relevance to matters of patient discharge, posthospital adjustment, inter-

---

* We are currently conducting a third investigation of the effects of Structured Learning Therapy on the social interaction skills of schizophrenic inpatients (Sutton-Simon ,1973). This study, as is explained in connection with the study presented later in this chapter dealing with patient role taking, uses what is hopefully a more powerful type of modeling display, one combining "behavioral" and "cognitive" modeling portrayals (see Appendix, pp. 245–284 ).

## TABLE 6.3

### Analyses of Variance (F Values) and t Tests for Social Interaction

| Measure | Source[a] |
|---|---|
| *Standard Observation* | |
| 1. excuses self on line $(F = 4.51**)$ | SLT+TT > COMP |
| | SLT+C > COMP |
| | SLT+N > COMP |
| 2. sits at occupied table $(F = 2.39*)$ | SLT+TT > COMP |
| | SLT+N > COMP |
| 3. acknowledges others when sitting down $(F = 3.48*)$ | SLT+TT > COMP |
| 4. smiles $(F = 2.78*)$ | SLT+TT > SLT+N |
| | SLT+C > SLT+N |
| 5. proper use of napkin $(F = 2.96*)$ | SLT+TT > COMP |
| 6. acknowledges others when leaving $(F = 2.78*)$ | SLT+TT > COMP |
| | SLT+C > COMP |
| *Naturalistic Observation* | |
| 1. talking to others on line $(F = 2.70*)$ | SLT+TT > SLT+N |
| | SLT+C > NTR |
| | SLT+N > COMP |
| | SLT+N > NTR |
| 2. sits at occupied table $(F = 3.40*)$ | SLT+TT > COMP |
| 3. initiates conversation $(F = 3.85**)$ | SLT+TT > SLT+C |
| | SLT+TT > SLT+N |
| | SLT+C > COMP |
| | SLT+C > NTR |
| | SLT+N > COMP |
| | SLT+N > NTR |
| 4. responds to conversation $(F = 5.00**)$ | SLT+TT > NTR |
| | SLT+C > NTR |
| | SLT+N > NTR |
| | SLT+N > COMP |
| | COMPT > NTR |
| 5. smiles $(F = 2.42, p > .05 < .10)$ | SLT+C > NTR |
| | SLT+N > COMP |
| | SLT+N > NTR |
| 6. gestures $(F = 2.35*)$ | SLT+N > COMP |
| | SLT+N > NTR |
| 7. acknowledges others when leaving $(F = 2.89*)$ | SLT+C > COMP |
| | SLT+C > NTR |
| *Social Behavior Ratings* | |
| 1. general social skills | — |
| 2. interaction with others $(F = 2.07*)$ | SLT+TT > NTR |
| | SLT+C > NTR |
| | SLT+N > NTR |
| | COMP > NTR |
| 3. social impact upon others $(F = 2.51*)$ | SLT+TT > NTR |
| | SLT+C > NTR |
| | SLT+N > NTR |
| | COMP > NTR |

[a] Source key: SLT-TT—Structured Learning Therapy (5 weeks) + transfer training (2 weeks); SLT-C—Structured Learning Therapy (5 weeks) + Structured Learning Therapy (2 weeks); SLT-N—Structured Learning Therapy (5 weeks); COMP—Companion control (5 weeks); NTR—No treatment control.

$* p < .05.$  $** p < .01.$

131

personal need satisfaction, etc. But there remain a host of other skills relevant to an individual's ultimate adjustment and satisfaction. Several of these additional skills are of an affective nature. Two in particular appear relevant to satisfactory personal and interpersonal functioning and, as such, became the training targets for our next two Structured Learning Therapy investigations. Their appropriateness as training targets is augmented, in the context of the present book, by evidence examined earlier suggesting the possibility of special deficiencies in these skill domains among lower-class individuals. As our initial studies in these domains, each of these investigations may be appropriately viewed as pilot efforts, i.e., attempts to define conditions and measures, examine procedures and, hopefully, discern hypothesized trends in the data.

### Focusing–Experiencing

The target skill for our first attempt (Orenstein, 1972) to examine the impact of Structured Learning Therapy upon affective behavior was focusing-experiencing. Central to the definition of these phenomenological constructs is one's ability to be aware of, tuned in to, or accurately perceive one's current feelings. While attention to one's affective state has been an important component of a number of therapy systems (Chessick, 1969; Ford & Urban, 1963; Perls, Hefferline, & Goodman, 1951) its most recent major emphasis is represented by the Rogerian-existential viewpoint. Rogers (1957) viewed psychotherapy largely as a means of helping the client increase his awareness and use of his ongoing affective experience, toward the goal of reorganizing his feelings, values, and perceptions. In work growing from and greatly elaborating upon this original Rogerian viewpoint, Gendlin and his co-workers have developed and investigated the companion concepts of focusing and experiencing. Gendlin describes experiencing as a concrete, ongoing, internal process made up of feelings that provide the basic data a person uses in relating to his world. Furthermore, it is viewed as a "felt" process, i.e., phenomenological, inwardly sensed, and preconceptual (Gendlin, 1961b, 1964). In companion with Gendlin's conceptual and philosophical elaboration of the experiencing construct, he and others have conducted a series of investigations examining its significance in the context of psychotherapy. Starting with correlational research on the Rogerian Process Scale (Walker, Rablen, & Rogers, 1960), of which experiencing was one "strand" or subscale; in later, similar work with an elaboration of this subscale, the Experiencing Scale (Gendlin & Tomlinson, 1961; Klein et al., 1969); and in more recent studies designed so that directionality could be more fully determined (Kiesler, 1971; Rogers, Gendlin, Kiesler, & Truax, 1967), evidence has begun to accumulate that the ability to experience, as defined above, is likely an important contributor to successful psychotherapy. It both correlates in a significant, positive manner with certain change scores and differentiates between more and less successful clients. While these findings do not yet yield a definitive conclusion regarding the value of experiencing in psychotherapy, they are powerful enough to lead one to wonder if an individual's experiencing level can be enhanced. Gendlin (1969) has also raised this question and recently begun to examine a procedure designed to turn an individual's attention inward, to train a person to experience more fully and accurately, to help an individual become more aware of his ongoing feelings. He calls this procedure *focusing*, and seeks to teach it by means of a set of standardized instructions called the *Focussing Manual*. It was one of the main purposes of our present investigation to examine the relative efficacy of the *Focussing Manual* and Structured Learning Therapy for purposes of enhancing patient experiencing.

It is important to note that our interest in experiencing and training of focusing skill to enhance experiencing is *not* for purposes of aiding the process of individual psychotherapy. While such a benevolent outcome may occur, and is desirable, we view experiencing as a valuable human skill independent of one's involvement or lack of involvement with psychotherapy. It is to Gendlin's credit that although the experiencing construct developed historically in a psychotherapeutic context, he has come to view it as a worthwhile skill for people in general, and has already sought to teach it by means of his *Focussing Manual* to normal high school (Gendlin, Beeke, Cassens, Klein, & Oberlander, 1968) and college (Gendlin, 1969) students.

## Procedure

Seventy-five female inpatients in a moderately sized state mental hospital constituted the patient sample for this investigation. Their selection from the hospital's population of female inpatients was conducted by a panel consisting of *E*, the ward psychiatrist on each of the six participating wards, and each ward's head nurse. Selection criteria were operationalized primarily in terms of the panel's judgment that the given patient was deficient in his awareness of his important feelings (deficient in experiencing), but had potential growth in this respect. That is, as in our earlier studies, selection for inclusion in the study's sample was a function of apparent deficit in the target skill, and not formal diagnosis.

In overview of this study's procedures and design, participating patients were first interviewed to obtain base-rate experiencing data; pretested to obtain both potential covariate (intelligence, adjustment, and attraction to interviewer) and dependent variable base-rate (mood) information; assigned to experimental condition utilizing a 1 × 5 design; administered the appropriate treatment intervention; and then both reinterviewed and readministered the mood measure.

The initial (and postmanipulation) interviews were conducted by six female interviewers, each of whom was blind as to the study's hypotheses. The interviewers were satisfactorily trained for, and used, a nondirective approach in conducting their interviews. They were instructed ". . . to show a receptive interest in each individual, his thoughts, feelings, and self-attitudes, and a willingness to understand any communication which the patient might be willing to make." Beyond such instructions, when necessary, they were instructed to use the following prompts: "What's that like for you?"; "What else about you?"; and "How's that?" Each interview lasted 30 min.

Each patient was then administered a premanipulation test battery. The findings of Gendlin et al. (1968) and Roger's (1957) theoretical statement suggest, respectively, that intelligence and adjustment may be significant correlates of experiencing. To capitalize on these possibilities for possible covariance control purposes, the Vocabulary subtest of the Wechsler Adult Intelligence Scale and the MACC Behavioral Adjustment Scale (Ellsworth, 1971) were administered to each patient. Rogers et al. (1967) have also reported a substantial positive relationship between experiencing and clients' perceptions of their therapist. Thus, also for possible covariance analysis purposes, each patient was administered a Client's Personal Reaction Questionnaire, which we and others have used extensively elsewhere as a reliable measure of patient attraction to his interviewer (Ashby et al., 1957; Goldstein, 1971). For exploratory purposes, in response to our own speculation that our treatment procedures might influence not only patient experiencing but also his mood state, the Multiple Affect Adjective Checklist (Zuckerman & Lubin, 1965) was also administered at this point in time. This checklist yields anxiety, hostility and depression subscores.

Following pretesting, patients were randomly assigned to the study's five treatment conditions.

1. *Structured Learning Therapy.* Each patient assigned to this condition met individually with an E different from the one who had tested her for two 40-min Structured Learning sessions. Two 15-min modeling displays of focusing behavior were developed for this investigation and used, one each, in these two sessions. The modeling displays (see Appendix,

pp. 284–290) essentially potray female models *(1)* instructing themselves to focus, *(2)* focusing, and *(3)* rewarding themselves for focusing.
The 25 min remaining, after the viewing of each tape, were used in discussion, role playing, provision of feedback and social reinforcement by
*E*, and, at times, redisplay of segments of the modeling videotape.

2. *Focussing Manual.* Each of the 15 patients assigned to this experimental condition met individually with the same *E* for two 40-min sessions during which the procedures of the *Focussing Manual* were
conducted three times per session. *Focussing Manual* procedures, in overview, involve instructions from *E* to the patient to relax, pay special attention to certain feelings, problems, and changes in these feelings during
the course of the session. The *E*, in a paced instructional sequence seeks
to help the patient attend to, perceive, and focus upon his feelings, their
labels, and their changing nature.

3. *Brief Instructions.* Since it is the obligation of the therapy researcher to be seeking not only therapeutic effectiveness in his procedures, but also inexpensiveness in their application, we wondered about
the consequences of simply and briefly telling patients to focus. (A more
extended rationale for the use of brief instructions is presented in the following chapter.) Immediately prior to their post manipulation interview,
each patient assigned to this condition was told by *E* that:

> The interview you will now have with Mrs. _____ will be most helpful to
> you if you see what your feelings are and talk about them during the interview.
> You will get the most out of it if you pay attention to what you feel and talk to
> your interviewer about it.

4. *Attention Control.* Since patients' level of experiencing in their
second (postmanipulation) interview may be greater than that character-
izing their first interview because of the interpersonal attention and concern inherent in the Structured Learning and *Focussing Manual* procedures, controlling for attention appeared necessary. Patients assigned to
this condition met individually with the same *E* for two 40-min sessions.
The first session was oriented around the notion, presented to the patient,
that one can often understand oneself better by thinking about, examining, and discussing one's family. During this session *E* asked a series of
questions about the patient's family, its status, and its history. The second
session was structured on the analogous idea that review of one's past can
also aid self-understanding. Thus, the focus of this meeting was on the
patient's childhood, adolescence, school days, job and dating history, etc.

5. *No-Treatment Control.* Patients assigned to this condition re-

ceived no study intervention between their first and second interviews. This condition, therefore, yielded base-rate information regarding changes in experiencing due to having spoken to the interviewer previously.

Following these procedures, each patient was again individually interviewed by the interviewer who had seen her previously. The same interview format, duration, and setting were used for each patient. Immediately after the interview, each patient was readministered the Multiple Affect Adjective Checklist. This completed the study's procedures for each patient.

The two classes of dependent variable criteria were mood changes as reflected by the Multiple Affect Adjective Checklist and, more centrally, changes in mode and peak experiencing level in patients' second (postmanipulation) interview as compared to their premanipulation interview level. To obtain Experiencing level scores, content analysis of the interview tapes was conducted using Gendlin and Tomlinson's (1961) Experiencing Scale (interjudge reliability = .85). This is a 7-point scale exemplified by a score of 1 for interview content which is unequivocally external; 3 for personal reactions to external events or limited self descriptions; 5 for problems or propositions about feelings or personal experiences; and 7 for content that is a full, easy, and integrated presentation of experiencing of feelings.

### Results

Covariance analyses conducted across the experiencing data yielded no significant between-condition differences. On both the mode and peak experiencing level change scores, Structured Learning Therapy, *Focussing Manual*, Brief Instructions, Attention Control, and No-Treatment Control failed to differ significantly. The anxiety subscale of the patient mood measure, in contrast, did yield a seies of significant change score differences between conditions ($F = 2.82$; $df = 4.72$; $p < .05$). Post hoc (Scheffe tests) analyses in response to this finding revealed that patients undergoing Structured Learning Therapy become significantly *more* anxious from first to second testing than do patients in each of the other four study conditions. In direct contrast to this apparent anxiety-enhancement effect, patients provided *Focussing Manual* procedures become significantly *less* anxious than patients in each of the four other study conditions.

Our view of the meaning and implications of this experimental outcome will be presented later in this chapter, after we first present our final inpatient study. It sought to alter a patient skill which is directly complementary to focusing–experiencing, and thus can perhaps best be reflected upon jointly with the present study.

## Role Taking

Our second study* dealing with an affective skill grew from both our earlier investigations of social interaction behavior and a parallel research program (see Chapter 8) making successful use of Structured Learning procedures to heighten the level of empathy offered by hospital personnel. The training target for this present study was patient role-taking skill. We have detailed in Chapter 2 the purported deficiency of many lower-class individuals with regard to this skill. This apparently not infrequent, generalized inadequacy in apprehending the feelings of others combined with our desire to choose a skill domain which was specifically useful for posthospital adjustment to lead us to a program of Structured Learning Therapy for role-taking skill in a marital context. The ability to adequately take the role of one's spouse has been the focus of considerable study in the marriage and family research literature. Taylor (1967) demonstrated that the smaller the discrepancy in self–other perceptions within a married couple (i.e., the greater their role-taking accuracy), the greater their reported marital satisfaction. Stuckert (1963) and Tharp (1963) have independently reported concurring results, though each used both different measures and much more heterogeneous samples of couples than did Taylor. Using yet other dependent variable indices of marital satisfaction, adjustment or happiness, Kotlar (1965), Levinger and Breedlove (1966), and Navran (1967) each found marital role-taking skill to be a significant determinant of outcome. These several findings, especially when viewed in the context of other research underscoring the crucial role of marital stability and satisfaction for adequate posthospital adjustment, gave added support to our choice of training target.

### Procedure

As our first research effort using Structured Learning Therapy for enhancement of role-taking skill, this investigation was quasi-exploratory in nature. Subjects were 30 female schizophrenic inpatients who volunteered to participate. Each was married, each had a recent history of sig-

---

* The collaboration of Drs. Norman Stein, Stephen Driscol, and John Sheets in the conceptualization and execution of this investigation is very much appreciated.

nificant marital problems, and each would be interacting with her husband during and/or immediately after the period of Structured Learning Therapy via the occurrence of home visits, discharge, etc. The 30 patients were randomly assigned to three experimental conditions: *(1)* Structured Learning Therapy; *(2)* attention control; or *(3)* no-treatment control.

The 10 patients assigned to the first experimental condition met, in groups of 5, with two group leaders for three 2-hour Structured Learning Therapy sessions. Attention control patients also met in groups of 5 with the same group leaders, but for three 2-hour *discussion* sessions. No-treatment patients participated only in the study's pre-testing and post-testing. Three modeling tapes were developed for use in this investigation (see Appendix, pp. 290–315). Each sought to display in a highly concrete and repetitive manner the two behavioral "learning points" that together formed our operational definition of role taking: *(1)* What is he feeling; and *(2)* How can I best tell him I understand his feeling. In an effort to examine the impact of a potentially more powerful modeling display than was used in our earlier studies, the format of each tape consisted of six scenes. Each display lasted 15–20 min. The scenes depicted follow.

*1. Narrator's Introduction.* The (high status) narrator sought to briefly introduce the learning points, maximize observer attention, and heighten observer expectation of reward (i.e., her own marital satisfaction) as a function of applying the learning points constituting the skill of role taking.

*2. Identification Scene.* An actor portraying a husband and an actress portraying a wife enacted a common conflict event (low role taking) characteristic of many marriages in general, and marriages among lower-class individuals in particular. The major purpose of this scene was to maximize observer identification with the taped model.

*3. Instruction Scene.* The wife-actress is heard meeting with her doctor and describing the content of the Identification scene conflict in some detail. The doctor empathizes with and supports the wife, but gradually —using the concrete incidents of the conflict—provides her with detailed instructions regarding the nature, use, and value of the two role-taking learning points. The wife practices these satisfactorily and receives social reinforcement from the doctor for doing so.

*4. Rehearsal Scene.* The wife is portrayed at home alone, privately rehearsing her use of the learning points in anticipation of her husband's return from work. This scene was included in response to Meichenbaum's research on self-instruction, a process not unrelated to Bandura's (1969) emphasis upon the importance of covert rehearsal for the retention of key behavioral modeling behaviors. Self-instruction, quite literally, involves teaching subjects to talk to themselves. Thus, schizophrenic patients were taught by Meichenbaum (1971a) to tell themselves to "pay attention," "avoid distraction," "be coherent and relevant," and "make themselves understood." Impulsive school children were trained to tell themselves to "slow down," "be careful," and "avoid being hasty" (Meichenbaum & Goodman, 1971). Similarly, both snake-phobic (Meichenbaum, 1971b) and test-anxious (Meichenbaum, Gilmore, & Fedoravicius, 1971) Ss were provided analogous self-instruction training. While these studies were largely exploratory in nature, and thus must be interpreted with considerable tentativeness, their combined results indeed suggest the likely importance of this class of cognitive mediation for the alteration of an array of maladaptive behaviors.

5. *Modeling Scene.* The husband and wife are home alone. The wife makes full and frequent use of her role-taking skill, as the husband portrays increasing responsiveness to her efforts in the form of praise, openness, and reciprocal role-taking behavior.

6. *Narrator's Summary.* The narrator reappears and summarizes the foregoing successful use of role taking, reiterates its value and nature, explains the rehearsal purposes of the role-playing session which is to follow tape playing, and urges the observers to make use of role-taking behaviors in their own marriages.

In order to determine the most appropriate content for each modeling display, within the format outlined above, in-depth survey efforts were conducted involving both the relevant professional literature and several persons engaged in daily clinical practice with lower-class patients. These efforts suggested the likelihood that the three most frequent dimensions of affect involved in lower-class marital crises are hostility, apathy, and lack of affection. The content of our modeling displays was, therefore, developed around these three affective themes. Both scripting and enactment were conducted by lower-class individuals and by professionals having extensive contact with such persons.

The attention control–discussion group condition was incorporated into the study's design in response to the possibility that the act of focusing for a total of 6 hours upon marriage and marital conflict—by the patient, other group members, and the group leaders—might itself cause patients to become more aware of, and empathic with their husband's affective behaviors. While these discussions were relatively free-wheeling at times, they were structured largely around the following topical areas:

1. What has your marriage been like?
2. How have you and your husband handled problems between you?

3. How would you like your husband to be different?
4. How would you like to be a different kind of wife?
5. What might you do to improve your relationship with your husband?

Three measures were individually administered to all study patients immediately before and after the one and one-half week period during which Structured Learning and attention-discussion were implemented.

1. *Direct Test of Modeling* (see Appendix, pp. 315–316). Four husband statements were selected from each of the three modeling displays and tape recorded by the same actor portraying the same affective qualities (hostility, apathy, lack of affection) he had portrayed when offering each statement on the modeling tape. The Direct Test of Modeling tape was played to each patient individually. The patient was asked to pretend that the taped speaker was *her* husband, and to respond to each statement with what she would actually say to him; 45 sec were provided for each response. The test form, with all taped statements, was given to the patient to follow along as the tape was played. All responses were recorded by the tester, not the patient, on another copy of this form.

2. *Generalization Test for Role Taking* (see Appendix, p. 317). Since the Direct Test items also were redisplayed and responded to extensively during the role-playing segments of the Structured Learning Therapy sessions (and thus could elicit well-practiced, role-taking responses with little external validity), it was important to test for role-taking skill on similar items for which there had been no training or practice. Nine such items, three for each affective dimension, were derived for this purpose from the role-taking subscale of the Yale Marital Interaction Battery (Buerkle & Badgley, 1959). These (Generalization Test) items were recorded by an actor different from the one employed for the Modeling Tape and Direct Test enactments. Patients were again asked to respond as if the statements were directed at them by their own husbands.

3. *Inferred Meanings Test* (R. Hall, 1969). This measure was included in our test battery as an index of general role-taking ability, independent of a marital context. Twenty brief sentences were presented two times each by means of a tape recording. For our version of this tape, we re-recorded all test items (sentences) using an actor whose own background was socioeconomically lower class. After the patient heard each sentence the second time, the tester presented four alternative meanings, and it was the testee's task to choose that alternative most veridical with his estimate of the actor's feelings as judged from his tone of voice, verbal emphasis, and other verbal qualities. For example, items and response alternatives utilized included:

1. I don't have a bad heart.
   a. But I have other problems.
   b. I'm not sure about it.
   c. I don't like the question.
   d. Simple fact.
2. We hope you will help us.
   a. We really have no hope.
   b. Even though others have failed.
   c. We need help very badly.
   d. Simple fact.
3. I have lots of friends.
   a. But no really close ones.
   b. I really don't.
   c. I don't like the question.
   d. But she does not.

### Results and Discussion

One-way analyses of variance were computed across the study's three conditions for the three types of dependent variable data described above. The results of these analyses are presented in Table 6.4.

A post hoc (*t*-test) analysis between study conditions on Direct Test of Modeling scores revealed no significant differences. Thus, the significant result that did emerge on this criterion must be considered marginal. Its limitation to trend-like, or suggestive, implications is further pointed to by the absence of a significant generalization effect on the other two study measures.

It would seem instructive, in seeking to understand both these and our focusing–experiencing findings, to briefly reexamine our major findings for the Structured Learning studies presented thus far in this chapter. Elaborating procedurally upon our earlier modeling studies, we undertook two investigations that sought to enhance an array of concrete social interaction behaviors. A minimum of 15 hours of Structured Learning

TABLE 6.4

ANALYSES OF VARIANCE (*F* VALUES) FOR ROLE TAKING

| Measure | $F$ |
|---|---|
| Direct test of modeling | 5.21* |
| Generalization test of modeling | .76 |
| Inferred meanings test | 1.20 |

* $p < .05$.

participation was required of study patients. In both experiments, considerable gain in social interaction skill emerged. We then turned to two skill targets whose behavioral referents were less easy to define, display, and observe. The focus in these last two studies was on altering patient skills possessing intrapersonal more than interpersonal referents. While we feel both studies were well designed and well executed in other respects, it now seems desirable that training for such skills be considerably more extensive than was done. If anything, focusing and role taking now appear to us to be *more* difficult skills to learn than does social interaction behavior, and thus future studies with these or similar target skills should involve at minimum the same type of 15-hour, 5-week program used successfully with social interaction, and perhaps longer programs.

A relatively complex skill, such as role taking, may be taught in a more successful and enduring manner not only by lengthening the duration of training. Training also may be enhanced by dividing the training target into its component subskills. Recall that in teaching role taking to schizophrenic women we sought to teach them to *both* identify what the model was feeling and respond to the model by describing to him her perception of his feelings. It seems likely that this double requirement, perception plus verbal communication, was a fairly difficult task—especially for Ss who are purported to experience major difficulties in attending to, processing, and responding to affective interpersonal stimuli. When we later simply asked study and other patients to *label* the model's feelings, a remarkably high level of accuracy emerged. Thus, our current plans regarding optimal procedures for teaching role taking involve two separate Structured Learning sequences. The first we call "accurate affective perception," its focus is upon teaching the patient to correctly perceive and identify a wide array of affective displays. *After* completion of such training, patients would then participate in an analogous sequence focusing upon "acurate affective communication." Focusing–experiencing, we would propose, may be analogously dividable into component subskills for training with such patient populations.

Beyond issues of length of training and skill complexity reduction, there exists yet a third domain of concern. It will be recalled that in our attempt to increase focusing–experiencing, Structured Learning recipients became significantly more anxious over the period of training than did all other study patients. This single finding, while quite substantial within the context of that one experiment, has not yet been tested elsewhere in our research program. Thus, we cannot yet speak to its generality, to whether Structured Learning attempts to teach related skills (such as role taking) similarly appear to suffer from increased competing stimuli in the form of heightened anxiety. And, if it should be a reliable finding, does it indeed function to inhibit skill learning as we have just implied? *(Focussing Manual* patients showed significantly less anxiety, but also failed to improve significantly in focusing–experiencing.) If Structured Learning should prove anxiety enhancing for certain (e.g., intrapersonal) skills, does it do so for certain types of patients only, e.g., schizophrenics—who, Arieti (1955) and others have suggested, become schizophrenic in the first place largely in response to the onslaught of overwhelming anxiety. Beyond such questions of type of training × type of skill × type of patient interaction effects, what mechanisms or constructs may be proposed as linking anxiety enhancement to Structured Learning? Are patients who are being taught such skills by Structured Learning made more anxious by the "threat" of being asked to look inward, or by what they in effect see when they do look inward? Or, more parsimoniously, is the possible link between Structured Learning and increased anxiety more a matter of the possible threat associated with task novelty, task difficulty or other, yet unspecified, experimental demand characteristics? Or, finally, is such a link artifactual, spurious, or simply nonexistent?

These several speculations and suggested investigative directions complete our presentation of our Structured Learning Therapy studies with lower- and working-class inpatient samples. We now wish to turn to our related efforts with lower- and working-class outpatients.

# Chapter 7

## STRUCTURED LEARNING AND THE LOWER-CLASS OUTPATIENT

For a variety of reasons, our outpatient research series has not as yet developed as fully as have our efforts with either psychiatric inpatients or potential paraprofessional therapists. The fact that we have conducted fewer studies with outpatient samples, however, is not by any means to suggest that we view such research as less valuable. The extensive documentation presented in Chapter 1 regarding the overwhelming failure of most contemporary treatment approaches with the lower-class and working-class outpatient is, it seems to us, much more than sufficient testimony to the necessity of further outpatient studies of Structured Learning Therapy and other prescriptive treatment attempts. With the proviso that we view them as but a beginning, therefore, let us turn to our outpatient investigations.

As in our inpatient and paraprofessional research, our initial focus has been upon the modeling component. Our first training target was the alteration of unassertive or overly dependent behavior. This skill was chosen largely in response to material presented in Chapter 2 suggesting that overdependence upon external authority is purportedly a particularly salient characteristic of lower-class individuals. Furthermore, it is a characteristic noted by Kohn (1969) and Roman and Trice (1967) to augment vulnerability to environmental or intrapsychic stress, especially under ambiguous circumstances or situations demanding highly independent behavior. Our first three investigations, therefore, sought to increase appropriate independent or assertive behavior in samples of lower- and working-class patients.

144

## Independence I

Early attempts to enhance independent behavior by means of interview techniques were not notably successful (e.g., Browne, 1964; Heller & Goldstein, 1961). Wolpe and Lazarus (1966) have recently drawn attention to assertiveness, or enhanced independence, as a meaningful target for behavior modification efforts with several types of diagnostically diverse patients, and A. A. Lazarus (1966) has provided quasi-experimental evidence for the value of a broad spectrum behavior modification approach towards this end. More recently, focusing upon behavior rehearsal as their primary intervention, McFall and Marston (1970) were similarly able to effect significant if moderate alterations in independent behavior. Taken as a group, these reports imply that behavioral techniques may well serve as effective means for enhancing independent behavior. The effectiveness of the particular behavioral interventions noted above, however, is still more suggestive than conclusive, and leads to the prediction that yet other behavior modification procedures may more adequately lead to independence enhancement. With this as additional motivation, we undertook the present series of investigations to bring modeling techniques to bear upon such goals.

### Procedure

Subjects for our first study were 90 psychiatric outpatients who had voluntarily sought psychotherapy at a large, public, psychiatric clinic. Within sampling limitations specified below, they were randomly selected from a much larger pool of ongoing clinic patients. Half were male, half female. Our goal was a psychoneurotic sample, therefore psychotic and organic patients (based upon the clinic's official diagnoses formulated at intake) were excluded. Thus, all participating patients were formally diagnosed psychoneurotic, mostly neurasthenic or some classification of character disorder. Within each sex category, patients were randomly assigned to three experimental conditions, (1) independence modeling, (2) dependence modeling, and (3) no-modeling control. The independence modeling group reflects the major clinical thrust of this investigation, to examine the efficacy of modeling procedures for independence enhancement. The dependence modeling condition appears to contain little potential clinical utility, but was included to provide a second experimental test of the effectiveness of modeling interventions with a patient sample. The control group—controlling primarily for attention—was incorporated for obvious comparison purposes.

Our stimulus materials consisted of 50 tape-recorded interpersonal situations involving two persons. In each situation, one person (stimulus person) instigates frustration or a threat to independent behavior for the second person (target person), and the latter must respond in a (forced choice) independent or dependent manner. These situations were (1) the 30 developed by Borgatta (1951) as a role-play form of the Rosenzweig picture-trustration study (1947), plus (2) 20 similar situations developed by us for this investigation. Using his situations, Borgatta (1951) was able to provide at least partial evidence that Ss react to the role-play format in a manner quite similar to the way they react to real, overt threats to independent behavior. Heller and Goldstein (1961) subsequently provided additional evidence for the construct validity of this procedure as an overt measure of independent–dependent social responsiveness. Since 20 of the situations were newly developed by us, and all 50 were "new" in role-play format in a Dutch patient context, pretesting was necessary to obtain information regarding stimulus pull. That is, since these situations were to be used for both premeasurement and postmeasurement purposes, and as our modeling display stimuli, it was necessary to establish that no situation disproportionately elicited independent or dependent responses independent of our modeling intervention. Toward this end, the situations were submitted to two successive panels of judges, consisting of three and eight psychologists respectively, who responded to each situation in terms of their estimate of its pull of independent or dependent responses. The pooled judgments of panel members were utilized to rewrite both the situation descriptions and the alternative responses such that no single situation pulled either an independent or dependent response more than two-thirds of the time. Pretesting on a pilot sample of nine patients demonstrated that this a priori equalization for stimulus pull was successful.

Examples of the situations utilized, and the response alternatives presented with the situations include:

1. $E_1$: You and your husband are standing before the closed front door of your house. You are looking for your keys in your purse. Your husband says to you:*

   $E_2$: Why did you have to lose the keys now!

   *Independent response alternative:* Well, where are *your* keys?

   *Dependent response alternative:* Do you remember where I put them?

---

* $E_1$, as is explained further below, presented the situation on a tape recording. $E_2$'s presentation, to aid in the interpersonal reality of the depiction, was presented live to the patient.

2. $E_1$: A friend asks you to go downtown to buy a special present for her mother. However, you buy a different present because the one she wanted is sold out. She says to you:

$E_2$: I think it's rubbish!

*Independent response alternative:* Then you should have gone yourself.

*Dependent response alternative:* I'll change it for you.

3. $E_1$: You are in a shoe shop and you have tried on a number of shoes. The saleslady says to you:

$E_2$: It's time that you chose a pair.

*Independent response alternative:* I'll keep trying till I find a pair that completely suits me.

*Dependent response alternative:* Okay, I'll take these.

The 50 situations were tape recorded by $E$ and two models, six tapes being necessary to reflect the three experimental conditions plus the use of male and female models.

The experimental procedures involved first providing the patient with the following, orienting instructions:

We have asked you to come in today for a routine investigation in which every patient will participate. It will be important for you, but we will benefit from it as well, because it will give us information about the effectiveness of our methods. In a moment we will describe several everyday situations. We would like you to respond to each description by telling us what you would say if you were in such a situation. We ask you to tell us what you would say.

An example of such a situation would be: It is Friday afternoon, 5:00, and you are about to go home from work. Your boss appears and says: "We've just received some work we didn't expect. It must be completed. Everybody will have to work overtime." The tape will then say: "What is your answer?" When you hear that, we ask you to say in two or three sentences what you would say in reality. You could for instance reply to this situation by saying: "Couldn't you have said this a little sooner. I already have an appointment for tonight." or "O.K., what do you want me to do?" or whatever you would want to say. You should only give the answer you yourself would give.

Fifty interpersonal, independence-relevant situations were then presented, in what may be conveniently conceptualized as three experimental phases.

*1. Base Rate (situations 1–10).* All participating patients heard the first 10 situation descriptions. No response alternatives were provided during this base-rate series. Instead, the patient was requested to respond in terms of whatever he felt he would actually say in such a situation in real life; 30 sec were provided for each response.

2. *Modeling (situations 11–40).* The implementation of this phase varied with experimental condition. Control group patients listened to the 30 situations; after each of which they were presented with a card on which was typed two response alternatives, one independent and one dependent, in counterbalanced order; and were asked to choose and read the one which most closely represented what they felt they would actually say; 15 sec were allotted for each such response. Patients in the independent modeling condition heard the same 30 situations, but on a randomly distributed 20 of these situations they also heard a rewarded model (successful patient of the same sex as the patient) state an independent response. On the remaining 10 situations in this phase, the patients were presented with the two response alternatives and asked to choose that alternative which most closely represented what they would actually say. When their choice was the independent alternative, $E$ responded with appropriate social reinforcement. Choice of the dependent response elicited no $E$ reinforcement. Directly parallel procedures were implemented in the dependent modeling condition, with dependent responses being modeled and reinforced.

3. *Posttest (situations 41–50).* This phase was identical in procedure to the pretest phase. No model or response alternatives were presented. All patients provided free responses to each situation.

Our criteria of patient change in independence–dependence were *(1)* posttest minus base rate independence and dependence change scores, and *(2)* a trials analysis across the 10 response situations during Phase 2, to identify any growth in independence or dependence over the course of modeling exposure.

### Results

A 5-point rating scale for independence–dependence was developed for use in judging patient base-rate and posttest free responses, the rating categories ranging from clearly independent to clearly dependent. Patient free responses were coded, randomized (to keep judges blind as to patient experimental condition and phase of testing), and submitted to four graduate student judges pretrained to an interjudge reliability coefficient of .85 in the use of this scale.

These ratings were analyzed by means of a 2 × 3 (sex by experimental condition) analysis of variance, as presented in Table 7.1. Our experimental predictions were that: *(1)* exposure to an independent model would lead to significantly greater increases in independence than would no-modeling (control) procedures; *(2)* exposure to a dependent model

TABLE 7.1

ANALYSIS OF VARIANCE OF INDEPENDENCE–DEPENDENCE CHANGE SCORES BY
PATIENT SEX AND MODELING CONDITION

| Source | df | MS | F |
|---|---|---|---|
| Sex (A) | 1 | 21622.50 | 6.76* |
| Experimental condition (B) | 2 | 22580.27 | 7.06* |
| A × B | 2 | 1645.83 | .51 |
| Error | 84 | 3198.61 | — |

\* $p < .05$.

would lead to significantly greater increases in dependence than would
no-modeling (control) procedures; and (3) exposure to an independent
model would lead to significantly greater increases in independence than
would exposure to a dependent model. No sex differences predictions
were made. Post hoc (*t*-test) analyses conducted in response to the significant main effects for sex and condition constituted tests of these predictions on our change score criterion. These results are presented in Table
7.2.

These findings indicate a significant effect for independence modeling,
as compared to no modeling, for both male and female patients. Dependence modeling also led to significant increases in dependent responses for
female patients, but failed to exert a similar influence upon male patients.
Directly analogous results emerged from a trend analysis of changes in
independence–dependence choices on the 10 forced-choice response

TABLE 7.2

POST HOC COMPARISONS OF INDEPENDENCE–DEPENDENCE CHANGE SCORES BY
PATIENT SEX AND MODELING CONDITION

| Sex | Conditions compared | t |
|---|---|---|
| Male | Independent–Control | 2.06* |
| Female | Independent–Control | 3.01** |
| Male and female | Independent–Control | 3.59** |
| Male | Dependent–Control | .22 |
| Female | Dependent–Control | 3.26** |
| Male and female | Dependent–Control | .64 |
| Male | Independent–Dependent | 2.10* |
| Female | Independent–Dependent | 2.45* |
| Male and female | Independent–Dependent | 2.56* |

\* $p < .05$.
\*\* $p < .01$.

trials interspersed among the phase two modeling trials. Both male and female patients demonstrated significant increases in independent response choices when exposed to an independent model, whereas only female patients increased in dependent response choices as a function of exposure to a dependent model. Before seeking to reflect upon the implications of these findings, we wish to present two additional investigations, both of which sought to replicate and extend the major results noted above.

### Independence II

We observed earlier that considerable attention has been paid in the laboratory to modeling enhancers, i.e., characteristics of the observer, model, or modeling display that function to augment the subsequent level of vicarious learning and performance. One such modeling enhancer is the observer's attraction to the model (Bandura & Huston, 1961; Grusec & Mischel, 1966). In another context, we have reported a series of investigations in which we were successful in raising the level of patient attraction to his psychotherapist (Goldstein, 1971). Perhaps our most reliable procedure for doing so involved use of trait structuring, i.e., describing the as-yet-unmet psychotherapist to the patient as "warm," "experienced," or in related positive trait terms. This procedure, which has also proven repeatedly successful in enhancing subject attraction in a variety of laboratory contexts (Asch, 1946; Beilin, 1960; Divesta & Bossart, 1958; Kelley, 1950), has yielded significant increments in patient attraction to therapist in our studies using separate samples of (1) nonpatient college students, (2) adult, psychotic inpatients, and (3) normal and disturbed adolescents. Considering together these several laboratory and clinical demonstrations of attraction enhancement, along with the evidence noted above in which observer attraction to the model augmented the level of subsequent modeling, we sought in our second investigation to determine if trait structuring of the model would increase observer modeling when the observers were psychiatric patients and the experimental setting a clinical one.

### *Procedure*

The clinical setting; screening inclusion, and exclusion criteria; diagnostic distribution; and recruitment procedures characteristic of our first experiment were essentially identical for the present investigation. Our sample consisted of 30 male and 30 female outpatients randomly selected from the residual pool (after the first experiment) of patients attending the Clinic.

Our experimental design was 2 × 3 factorial (plus control) in which were represented patient sex (male versus female) and trait structuring (warm structuring and independent model; cold structuring and independent model; no structuring and independent model), plus a no-structuring–no-modeling control group. Twenty patients (10 male, 10 female) were randomly assigned to each of the three trait structuring and modeling experimental conditions. The no-structuring–no-modeling control group was *not* constituted for this investigation. Since the same patient population was drawn upon in our first experiment, at approximately the same point in time, and run through study procedures identical to those used in the present investigation, the same control group data was used for comparison purposes in this second experiment. As noted, study procedures involved the same 3-phase, 10-situation (base rate, 30-situation modeling display, plus forced choice response format, 10-situation posttest) sequence as the first experiment, with two exceptions. First, only independence modeling was provided, since we felt this to be by far the more clinically relevant target. Second, after the 10 base-rate situations, but before exposure to the model, patients were provided the following trait structuring regarding the model.

### Warm Structuring

Now we'll do it in a slightly different way. In what follows you will again hear some situations, but you will not always have to answer. Sometimes the tape will give the answer for you. The answers you will hear are given by a patient who has been successfully treated. People who know him well all consider him a very sympathetic and outgoing person, someone with a warm personality. You'll probably also notice this when you hear his voice on the tape. Be sure to listen carefully to the answers this patient gives.

However, answers will not always be given on the tape. In some situations we would again like to have the answer that you would give. But this time you do not have to respond in your own words. We will give you a card on which there are two answers. You will have 15 seconds to choose that answer which looks most like the answer that you would give in such a situation.

*Cold Structuring.* Instructions for this condition were the same as the foregoing, except that in lieu of the "sympathetic, outgoing, warm" description of the model, patients were told: "People who know him well all find him aloof in social interactions, a rather unsympathetic person, someone with a rather cold personality. You'll probably also notice this when you hear his voice on the tape." No-structuring patients were provided the same information about the tape and response procedures, but were not provided structuring of the model.

Based upon the research findings noted earlier, our experimental predictions were: (1) greater independence modeling in all three modeling conditions as compared to the no-modeling control condition, i.e., a replication of the result of the first experiment; (2) greater independence modeling as a function of warm structuring of the model, in comparison to both no structuring and cold structuring; and (3) greater independence modeling in the no-structuring condition in comparison to cold structuring of the model.

### Results

To examine our first prediction of a modeling effect for independence, $t$-test comparisons on posttest minus base-rate independence change scores were made for each experimental condition against the no-modeling control group. Both the warm structuring–independence modeling ($t = 2.86$; $p < .05$) and the no structuring–independence modeling ($t = 3.56$; $p < .05$) conditions increased significantly more in independence than did control group patients. This finding held for males and females separately and in combination. No significant difference emerged between the cold structuring–independence modeling and control conditions.

As was the case in the earlier experiment, a trend analysis by condition across the 10 Phase 2 response situations revealed a highly significant increment across trials for each condition separately, as well as all conditions combined. On both criteria, therefore, exposure as we have operationalized it to an independent model results in significant increments in observer independence.

A 2 × 3 analysis of variance was performed to examine the effects of trait structuring as either an enhancer (Hypothesis 2) or an inhibitor

**TABLE 7.3**

ANALYSIS OF VARIANCE OF INDEPENDENCE CHANGE SCORES BY PATIENT SEX AND STRUCTURING CONDITION

| Source | df | MS | F |
|---|---|---|---|
| Sex (A) | 1 | 453 | .09 |
| Experimental condition (B) | 2 | 20647 | 4.44* |
| A × B | 2 | 5465 | 1.18 |
| Error | 54 | 4653 | — |

* $p < .05$.

(Hypothesis 3) of independence modeling. This analysis is presented in Table 7.3.

The significant main effect for experimental condition led to post hoc cell comparisons (t test) collapsing across sex categories. This analysis revealed no significant warm–no structuring difference, a significant warm–cold difference $(t = 2.25; p < .05)$, and a significant no-structuring vs. cold structuring difference $(t = 2.82; p < .01)$.

Thus, this investigation yielded an overall modeling effect; evidence that cold structuring of the model yields significantly less modeling than either warm structuring or no structuring; and no confirmation of our prediction that warm structuring of the model would lead to modeling enhancement.

## Independence III

Instructions to the observer regarding the desirability and explicit nature of the behaviors to be modeled is a second modeling enhancer with laboratory roots and potential clinical relevance. Bandura (1969) has commented in this connection:

> Much social learning is fostered through exposure to *behavioral modeling cues* in actual or pictorial forms. However, after adequate language development is achieved, people rely extensively upon *verbal modeling cues* for guiding their behavior. Thus, for example, one can usually assemble relatively complicated mechanical equipment, acquire rudimentary social and vocational skills, and learn appropriate ways of behaving in almost any situation simply by matching the responses described in instructional manuals. If the relevant responses are specified clearly and in sufficient detail, verbally symbolized models may have effects similar to those induced by analogous behavioral displays [pp. 145–147; italics in original].

The effectiveness of such verbal modeling cues, as both an enhancer of behavioral modeling cues and as an intervention used alone, has been demonstrated in laboratory contexts by Bandura and Mischel (1965) and Masters and Branch (1969). An investigation reported by Whalen (1969) demonstrated the value of instructions as a modeling enhancer in increasing self-disclosure behavior in a college student sample. Our own research group has conducted two further relevant investigations. Perry (1970) provided some evidence for the value of instructions as a modeling enhancer in teaching empathy to a sample of ministers, and Lack (1971) reported a similar outcome in her study involving teaching self-disclosure behavior to a sample of psychiatric attendants. The present study was undertaken to test the predictions that: *(1)* our independence-modeling procedures would lead to heightened independence in a psychotic inpatient sample; *(2)* this modeling effect would be enhanced by providing such patients with prior instructions regarding the nature and value of independence modeling; and *(3)* to explore the effect upon patient independence of such instructions operating alone, with no subsequent behavioral modeling of independence.

## Procedure

Our initial patient pool for this investigation consisted of patients residing on what in terms of years in hospital and patient symptomatic chronicity was the most chronic male patient ward in a large, provincial, mental hospital.* Approximately 250 patients resided on this ward and, our pretesting of the study procedures revealed, most were unable to sufficiently comprehend, or respond to, our instructions and materials. Thus, our final sample was not a randomly selected one from this ward. Instead, the chief psychiatrist and two ward psychiatrists constituted a panel that selected for us 54 patients who, in their collective judgment, would be able to participate in the experiment's procedures. These patients each had a primary diagnosis of schizophrenia. All had been hospitalized at least 8 years.

Patients were randomly assigned to four experimental conditions in a 2 × 2 factorial design involving the conditions: *(1)* modeling and instructions; *(2)* modeling; *(3)* instructions; and *(4)* no modeling–no instructions control. With two exceptions, our experimental materials and procedures were identical to that used for independence modeling in our first experiment. After the 10 base-rate situations, the following instructions were provided patients assigned to conditions 1 and 3; those in condition 1 also received our usual modeling procedures; condition 3 patients received these instructions only:

In a research project conducted by Smith and Jones in America in 1969, it was found that people who find it difficult to have contact with others gave weak and dependent answers, but when they could act more independent it was easier for them to be with people and have real contact with them. A research project of the Rockefeller Foundation for Psychological Research showed that people who were shy felt much happier after learning in therapy to give more independent answers in difficult or embarrassing situations.

---

* We have included this study involving inpatients in the present section for purposes of clarity and exposition, since both its procedures and target skill are so similar to those involved in the preceding outpatient investigations.

This means that if someone gets in an unpleasant situation, such as being accused of something he did not do, he should not pipe down, but should stand up for his rights and not let himself get pushed into a corner. For example, if your boss tells you at 5:00 that you have to work overtime, and you answer: "You should have told me that earlier, now I have an appointment for tonight." That is an independent answer. Or, as another example, if you have worked hard all week and you want to go to bed early, but a friend comes to visit you and stays on and on, and you tell him: "I'm sorry but I'm tired and want to go to sleep. Come back another time." That would be another typical independent answer. If you had said nothing, and waited till he had gone by himself, that would be a typical dependent act.

This research shows us that it is good for people with problems like you may have to give independent answers in the following situations.

### Results

A 2 × 2 analysis of variance was performed on posttest minus baserate independence change scores to examine the effects of modeling and instructions on independence. These results are presented in Table 7.4.

A post hoc analysis ($t$ tests) revealed that patients in each of the three experimental conditions increased in independence significantly more than no instructions–no modeling control patients. That is, modeling plus instructions ($t = 3.12; p < .01$), modeling ($t = 2.85; p < .02$), and instructions ($t = 3.42; p. < .01$) patients each gained in independence significantly more than controls. There were no significant differences between these three conditions. Again, therefore, the overall modeling effect was replicated. Furthermore, while instructions alone also yield a significant increase in independence, the combined results are such that we do not have evidence for a modeling-enhancement effect. Modeling and instructions appear to be substitutive, not additive, in this investigation.

The major finding emerging from these three investigations is the twice-replicated significant modeling effect for independence. One psy-

**TABLE 7.4**

ANALYSIS OF VARIANCE OF INDEPENDENCE CHANGE SCORES BY PATIENT SEX
AND INSTRUCTIONS CONDITION

| Source | df | MS | F |
|---|---|---|---|
| Modeling (A) | 1 | 228.02 | 4.75* |
| Instructions (B) | 1 | 252.88 | 5.26* |
| A × B | 1 | 212.16 | 4.42* |
| Error | 52 | 48.03 | — |

*$p < .05$.

chotic and two neurotic samples were taught via exposure to a model to verbalize more independent responses. These investigations, it must be noted, provide no evidence regarding the durability or transfer of such enhanced (verbal) independence beyond the immediate training settings. Both of our inquiries into the operation of modeling enhancers with clinical populations yielded findings somewhat different from the normal subject-laboratory context results from which we were extrapolating. Structuring a neurotic sample that the model is warm yielded results no different from that following no structuring. Yet, describing the model as cold yielded a modeling decrement in comparison to warm-structured and no-structuring conditions. We have no ready explanation for the failure of warm structuring to function as a modeling enhancer, save to suggest that its roots may lie in the disordered interpersonal relationships or inaccurate interpersonal perception which are probably much more characteristic of a neurotic, than a normal, sample.

Since we have long believed that if two treatments are equally effective, the least "expensive" (in time, money, effort, etc.) is to be preferred, our findings on instructions and modeling raises an important question. Working with a chronic psychotic sample, we found in essence that telling patients to respond independently and providing two verbal modeling examples was as effective as a considerably more elaborate behavioral modeling display. This finding rather clearly raises questions about optimally versus maximally strong interventions. Further experimental examination of these procedures, singly and in combination, seems obviously warranted. In doing so, however, one would do well to compare such interventions not only on such intermediate criteria (e.g., changes in verbal behavior) as were used in our investigations, but also on more ultimate criteria, such as changes in patient independent behavior in his real-life environment.

## Role Induction and Patient Mood

We have essentially taken the position throughout this book that traditional insight-oriented psychotherapy is generally inappropriate for the typical lower-class or working-class patient. Considerable evidence in support of this position was presented in Chapter 1. Yet, we also noted a major exception to this generalization—traditional psychotherapy preceded by Role Induction Interview procedures. Both our own and others' earlier research on the outcome-relevant implications of patient prognostic and role expectancies (Goldstein, 1962; Heine & Trosman, 1960;

Overall & Aronson, 1963), and studies on ambiguity reduction (Bordin, 1955a; Heller, 1967; Robbie, 1963) and the provision of structure (Clemes & D'Andrea, 1965; Goldstein et al., 1966; Holland, 1965) strongly support the basic role-induction finding. When provided with sufficient clarification of expectancies and specific patient role training, lower- and working-class patients can indeed profit from traditional psychotherapy (e.g., Hoehn-Saric et al., 1964; Nash, Hoehn-Saric, Battle, Stone, Imber, & Frank, 1965; Sloane et al., 1970; Strupp & Bloxom, 1971). The major focus of the present investigation (Ben, 1972) was patient mood change. We sought to examine the separate and combined effectiveness of role induction and modeling as means of altering selected mood states. In addition, we attempted to obtain information about the effects of our experimental interventions on the patient's evaluation of his subsequent interview relationship.

## Procedure

Subjects for this investigation were 70 lower-class men who had sought psychotherapeutic assistance at a community clinic for alcoholics. All had major drinking problems reflected in their personal, marital and/or employment functioning. None had been to this particular clinic before.

In overview of the study's procedures, after agreeing to participate, each patient was pretested to determine the nature of his mood state on several mood dimensions at that point in time. Assignment to experimental condition, and the study's experimental manipulations followed. Our design format was 2 × 2 plus control and involved the presentation of audiotaped intake interviews displaying the presence vs. absence of role induction, crossed with the presence vs. absence of taped patient (model) mood improvement; or a no-tape control condition. All patients then completed the mood measure a second time, as well as a measure reflecting their attraction toward the taped interviewer. Each patient was then individually interviewed and retested on these mood and attraction measures to examine the relevance to an actual intake interview of our role induction and modeling manipulations. The foregoing is a summary description of this investigation's procedures. Having provided this overview, we now wish to present the study's methods and measures in greater detail.

The initial base-rate testing of participating patients consisted of the Psychiatric Mood Scales, or POMS, (McNair & Lorr, 1964). The POMS has been demonstrated to be a reliable measure of affective state on the dimensions of Tension–Anxiety, Anger–Hostility, Depression–Dejection,

Vigor, Fatigue, and Confusion. It was the Tension–Anxiety, Anger–Hostility, and Depression–Dejection subscales of this measure in which we were particularly interested, as decreases in their level formed our operational definition of mood improvement. As such, the patient-model on two of our modeling tapes overtly displayed decreases in such affective expressions over the course of the taped interview.

Patients were then randomly assigned to one of four modeling conditions or to a no-modeling control condition. The four modeling conditions, in each of which a modeling tape was played to the patient, were operationalized in such a manner that role induction was crossed with modeled mood improvement by the taped patient-model (see Appendix, pp. 317–337). Instructional material (Part 1) and credibility-enhancing interview segments (Part 2) both appeared on all four modeling tapes. Following this material, a series of interviewer statements (Part 3) is heard on the two role induction tapes only, which explicitly clarify the nature of treatment, the respective roles and responsibilities of therapist and patient, and which provide related information. No such statements are presented on the two no-role induction tapes. Our second independent variable, modeled mood improvement, was operationalized by having the taped patient-model, on the two mood improvement modeled tapes, display progressively decreasing feelings of tension, hostility, and depression.

To determine the effects of these interventions on patient mood, the POMS was readministered. All study patients followed their posttesting by participating in an individual interview with a second E. The interview schedule utilized was such that the questions put to each study patient were identical to those asked of the taped model as Part 2 of the modeling tapes. These questions, which were adapted from our earlier studies (Goldstein, 1971) were:

1. Could you tell me what *you* see as the causes of your drinking problem?
2. You said you have had a drinking problem for about __ years. What brings you to the clinic about it at this time?
3. How has your family reacted to your drinking?
4. How has it affected your work?
5. How has your drinking problem affected other parts of your life?
6. Now, could you try to tell me how you feel about yourself?
7. Most people get angry. Could you tell me the kinds of things that get you angry? What do you do when you get angry?
8. What about the kinds of things that get you anxious or fearful? What do you do about the things that get you anxious or fearful?

9. Now, could you tell me about your parents? What were they like? If you had your choice, in what way would your parents be different?

Our overall prediction regarding the data derived from this interview was that patients exposed to the role-induction interview, and especially those both hearing this interview and hearing the interviewee (model) display mood improvement, would themselves experience greater mood improvement and greater attraction to their interviewer than those not exposed to these interventions.

## Results and Discussion

Analyses of variance and Dunnett's tests for comparison with a control conducted across patient mood change data revealed two consistent sets of significant effects. On each of the three mood states portrayed as diminishing on our modeling displays, Tension–Anxiety, Anger–Hostility, and Depression–Dejection, there emerged a significant role induction × modeling interaction effect and a significant modeling tape vs. no-modeling tape effect. That is, patients exposed to *both* role-induction material and a model displaying progressive reduction in Tension–Anxiety, Anger–Hostility, and Depression–Dejection themselves improve significantly more on all three of these mood dimensions than do patients exposed to either role induction, or a model displaying mood improvement, or to neither of these interventions. Here, then, is clearly an instance in which modeling procedures combined with the structuring or ambiguity reduction of the role-induction material yield a series of effects which modeling alone (and role induction alone) were unable to accomplish. From this perspective, it may be appropriate to tentatively view the provision of structure or the reduction of ambiguity as an additional and clinically relevant modeling enhancer.

Dunnett's test comparisons of the four modeling tape groups (combined and separately) against the no-tape control reveal, again on each of the three modeled mood improvement dimensions, a significant series of effects. Thus, if a patient hears one of our modeling tapes, even if role induction material is omitted and/or mood improvement is not portrayed, there still follows a greater decrease in Tension–Anxiety, Anger–Hostility, and Depression–Dejection than is the case for patients hearing no modeling tape. This rather straightforwardly seems to be an attention effect, and simple supports the apparently generally accepted notion that treatment-relevant attention from clinic personnel can and does have an ameliorative effect on patient mood state. Beyond these two sets of significant effects, for combined role induction and mood improvement modeling as compared to the other tape conditions, and for all tape conditions as compared to no-tape display, no other significant mood effects emerged. Vigor, Fatigue, and Confusion, alteration of none of which was modeled, remained essentially unaltered by the study interventions.

It will be recalled that study patients were examined for their attraction to both the taped and live interviewers. Analyses of these data across study conditions reveal findings largely consistent with the mood improvement results presented above. Both posttape and postinterview CPRQ attraction to the respective interviewers was significantly greater for patients hearing both role-induction material and a patient-model displaying mood improvement, as compared to the model only or no role induction—no modeled mood improvement tapes. The combined tape did not yield effects significantly different from the role induction—no modeled mood improvement tape. Thus, as was true for each modeled mood improvement dimension, a combination of both the role induction and modeled mood improvement interventions yielded the most enhancing effect upon patient attraction. Dunnett's test comparisons with the control again indicated all four tape groups to significantly differ from the no-tape control, this time in their attraction to the live interviewer. (No-tape controls were, by definition, not exposed to the taped interviewer, and thus this comparison could be made only for attraction to the live interviewer.) Again we view this latter finding as essentially an attentional effect.

The primary thrust of the findings just presented, beyond their suggestion of an additional modeling enhancer and a possible relationship enhancer, seems to center on the issue of mood improvement. Mood alteration is a ubiquitous goal in diverse efforts to assist the psychiatric outpatient. The present investigation, while certainly but a mere beginning, clearly suggests the possible usefulness of modeling procedures toward these ends. Perhaps even more powerful effects upon patient mood will follow, as was the case for other targets in our inpatient studies, when modeling procedures were combined with activities designed to help the patient behaviorally rehearse alternative responses, and receive reinforcement for correct efforts at doing so. Such Structured Learning Therapy attempts to effect enduring mood change loom as a promising path for future empirical research efforts.

*Part 3*

# PARAPROFESSIONAL TRAINING

# Chapter 8

## STRUCTURED LEARNING AND
## THE WORKING-CLASS PARAPROFESSIONAL

### Introduction

In earlier chapters we presented considerable evidence that the components of Structured Learning, singly and especially in combination, exert a significant influence upon several types of behavior change. Such effectiveness has been shown by us and by others in both laboratory and clinical contexts, across age levels, class lines, and target behaviors. The apparently wide applicability of these learning approaches led us to speculate about, and investigate, their utility with yet another type of population relevant to the mental health needs of the lower-class and working-class patient: the paraprofessional psychotherapist and other high patient-contact personnel.

The recent but very rapidly growing utilization of paraprofessionals—nurses, attendants, aides, correctional personnel, student companions, ministers, housewives—to serve in therapeutic and quasi-therapeutic roles has resulted in growing concern with the adequacy of their training. A variety of approaches—didactic and experiential, traditional and innovative—are currently being employed (Ellsworth, 1968; Garfield, S. L., 1969; Grosser et al., 1969; Guerney, 1969). The evidential base for most of these approaches, however, is primarily descriptive testimonials. Their roots are rarely in basic research on learning and behavior change or similarly substantive domains, and systematic evaluation of their efficacy is largely absent.* In this context, and with the demonstrated value of the

---

* Two significant exceptions to these generalizations are the training procedures that have been developed by Truax and Carkhuff (1967) and by Ivey (1971) and his

**163**

components of Structured Learning serving as impetus, we undertook a series of investigations examining the value of Structured Learning for purposes of paraprofessional training. As was the case for our patient studies, we began our investigative efforts by focusing upon the modeling component alone.

A major concern of our initial paraprofessional investigation was responsive to the fact that a large number of agencies offering psychotherapeutic and related services have championed the use of workers variously termed "indigenous," "neighborhood," or "community." The use of such personnel, it is held, will greatly diminish or eliminate a number of the discrepancies which have been shown to exist between the middle-class (professional) psychotherapist and the lower-class patient. Their shared experiential and subcultural histories should purportedly minimize discrepant expectancies, values, relationship difficulties, etc. In addition, and most relevent to the present study, therapist bias under these conditions, it is proposed, should be minimal. As a step in this direction of supposedly more optimal therapist–patient pairing, we utilized working-class, potential paraprofessionals as Ss and presented our study materials in such a manner that the operation of therapist bias could be discerned. While such Ss are clearly not "indigenous," or "neighborhood," their socioeconomic backgrounds and life styles represent a major step in the direction away from the more credentialed M.D.- or Ph.D.- level psychotherapist.

Having defined our experimental intent in this investigation as both the examination of modeling procedures for paraprofessional training purposes, and focus upon the possible interactive role played by social class-determined therapist bias in the successful implementation of these procedures, we wish to turn now to a brief presentation of our dependent

---

co-workers. Both the training in facilitative conditions by the former, and Ivey's work on microcounseling represent systematic efforts to construct and evaluate change-agent skill training programs. Each approach consists of a large number of components, among which are modeling and role playing. Accumulating evidence has begun rather clearly to support the value of these programs, and thus their further use and development is most certainly to be encouraged. One major problem inherent in each approach, however, concerns their prepackaged nature. "It" may work, but as was true for the criticisms of global outcome research in psychotherapy, what "it" is, or, stated more heuristically, which components of the program are active and thus should be maximized, and which are ineffective and should be dropped is not discernible when one evaluates only complete programs. We much prefer a "building-block" research strategy in which separate components and combinations thereof are systematically evaluated for their incremental validity. Such series of parametric studies are often not conducted, and yet are vital if maximally effective combinations of procedures are to be identified.

variables—variables we view as an esssential component of the successful change-agent's (professional or paraprofessional) skill repertoire. Despite divergence on numerous theoretical and procedural grounds, almost all approaches to psychotherapy come together in the prime importance for successful outcome which they accord the therapist–patient relationship. Research findings in support of this position are abundant (Gardner, 1964; Goldstein, 1971; Truax & Carkhuff, 1967). While almost all of this converging theoretical and research material derives from work with and by "credentialed" psychotherapists, it seems a reasonable a priori assumption to posit that relationship forces are of equal potency when the treatment giver has little therapeutic experiences and fewer diplomas on his wall. In fact, as implied above, a major stimulant to the paraprofessional movement has been the very notion that a major, positive consequence of paraprofessional–patient life style commonality should be an enhanced therapeutic relationship.

Since no actual patients participated in this (analogue) study, it was only the paraprofessional's contribution to the therapeutic relationship we sought to investigate. Operationally, we defined this contribution in terms of a measure of therapist *attraction* to a portrayed patient. Relationship thus defined has proven in a number of our earlier studies (Goldstein, 1971) to be a consistently fruitful operational approach. Not only, however, does therapeutic outcome depend in large measure on the therapist's attraction toward, or liking of, the patient. The behavioral, in-therapy consequents of such an interpersonal disposition must be appropriately communicated to the patient. Our earlier research has demonstrated that two such consequents of high levels of therapist attraction are communication of accurate empathy and nonpossessive warmth. The research programs conducted by Carkuff (1969), Rogers *et al.* (1967), and Truax and Carkhuff (1967) provide considerable evidence regarding the impact of these two classes of therapist behavior. Thus, in the present investigation, attraction, empathy, and warmth were selected as the primary dependent variables.

## Procedure

One hundred thirty-five nurses and attendants employed in a state mental hospital were utilized as this study's sample. Ninety-four were registered nurses, 10 were licensed practical nurses, and 31 were attendants. The two nurse subsamples represent the total available nursing population at the hospital; the 31 attendants were randomly selected from a total pool of approximately 500 attendants. Since no significant differences emerged in a series of between-subsample comparisons on our dependent measures, all Ss were treated as a single sample in the various data analyses. Mean age was 38, with an age range 21–68; mean number of years of nursing or attendant experience was 14, with a range 1–40 years; 114 Ss were female, 21 male.

Nine experimental conditions were constituted in a 3 × 3 factorial design, and Ss were randomly assigned to these conditions. The two independent variable dimensions thus represented (modeling and social class structuring) were each implemented at three levels (modeling: high attraction, low attraction, neutral; social class structuring: middle, lower, no social class structuring). Concretely, each group of 15 Ss began study participation by reading two pages of orienting instructions, as E read these same instructions aloud to them. With the exception of one paragraph, that presenting the social class status of the patient they were about to hear, the initial instructions were identical for all nine groups of Ss. Their instructions were:

In recent years, more and more psychiatric nurses working in mental hospitals have begun to serve as psychotherapists for their patients. While the number of nurse-psychotherapists is not yet large, it is growing as the number of training programs and courses increase. The goal of the research in which you are participating today is to learn more about the kind of job a nurse can do as a psychotherapist. In a few moments you will hear a tape recording of part of an actual psychotherapy session, a session which took place in a state hospital located outside New York State. It is the patient's first session. The psychotherapist is a psychiatric nurse who has been conducting psychotherapy sessions as a regular part of her work for the last four years. Most of her psychotherapy patients, as is true of the one you will hear on the tape, have been diagnosed as alcoholic. The particular patient you will hear is a 39-year-old male who, at the time of the interview, was in the third week of his second hospitalization for alcoholism.

Since the main goal of this research is to better understand the job of nurse-psychotherapist, when the tape is over we will ask you to fill out a questionnaire which will give us some of your opinions about the patient on the tape. However, we can learn about what nurses can do as psychotherapists not only by getting your opinions about the people on the tape, but also by asking you what you would say to the patient if you were his psychotherapist. Therefore, when the tape starts, listen carefully to what both the patient and the nurse-therapist have to say. At various times during the taped session, the session will stop and you will hear a voice say, "What would you say?" and then the voice will say a number. On the work sheet after this page you will see blank spaces numbered 1, 2, 3, etc. These correspond to the numbers you will hear. Write what *you* would say to the patient in these spaces. For example, let us suppose that the patient on the tape said: "I've really been feeling terrible lately," then you heard a voice on the tape say: "What would you say?—One," and you decide that if you were the therapist you'd comment: "Can you tell me more about that?" You would write this comment in the blank space numbered one. As another example, if you would say: "It sounds like things have been pretty bad," you would write that in the blank space. It is *your* comment we wish you to write in, whatever you would say to the patient. Please write as clearly as you can. There will be 45 seconds each time for you to write your comment. To assure anonymity, we ask you *not* to sign your name on the work sheet or any other place on the booklet. Are there any questions?

In the three experimental conditions in which we wished to lead the subjects to believe that the portrayed patient was socioeconomically middle class, the following statement was added to the first paragraph of instructions:

With regard to the patient's background, he, like his father, obtained a college degree in Business Administration, has worked pretty steadily as an insurance salesman, and began drinking heavily, a number of years ago both at cocktail parties and when dining out with customers.

For the three conditions in which we sought to structure the patient as lower class, the following statement was included:

With regard to the patient's background, he, like his father, completed only a grade school education, worked (when he had work) mostly as a laborer, and began drinking heavily a number of years ago at both neighborhood bars and alone.

For the third level of social class structuring, i.e., no class structuring, no social class-relevant information was added to the basic instructions stated above.

The experimenter then played one of three modeling tapes to each 15-S group. These tapes, constructed by us, depicted a 20-min segment of an initial psychotherapy session (see Appendix, pp. 338–346). Patient statements on all three tapes were identical. The therapist statements varied in terms of the level of attraction displayed by the taped therapist toward the taped patient. In the 3 high-attraction conditions, 12 statements by the taped therapist expressing positive affect, respect, liking, and so forth, were added to the basic therapist script. Examples of such high-attraction verbalizations are: "I'm not clear why your wife would act that way, I find you a rather easy person to talk with." "You seem to be really trying to make your marriage work. I respect people who really try like that." "Well, you won't get that from me. I'm really glad you were assigned to me." Statements expressing a low level of therapist attraction toward the patient were substituted for the high-attraction statements in the tape used for the three low-attraction conditions. For example: "I think I understand a little why your wife would act that way, I find it somewhat hard to talk with you myself." "You don't seem to be trying to see her side of it. I find it hard to respect people who don't at least try to do that." "Well, maybe you deserve to be nagged at times." The therapist statements on the tape played for the three conditions involving no display of therapist attraction (high or low) toward the patient consisted only of the basic therapist script. This script or portrayal was composed of 38 patient statements and 38 therapist statements, half of the latter were directive in nature (e.g., questions, declarative statements), and half were essentially nondirective (e.g., reflections of feeling, restatements of content).

As we noted in Chapter 5, research on modeling techniques suggests a number of display, observer, and model characteristics that serve to maximize the level of modeling that occurs. In constructing the modeling tapes, we once again sought to be as responsive as possible to these research findings by building into the tapes an array of such modeling maximization characteristics. More specifically, as one form of likely reward to the (taped therapist) model on all three study tapes, the taped patient repeatedly expressed high attraction to the taped therapist. Bandura (1969) and Lefkowitz et al. (1955) have shown that the greater the status of the model, the more likely is the observer to imitate, and thus our pretape instructions incorporated a statement indicating that the nurse-psychotherapist on the tape was highly experienced. A female actress was chosen for the therapist depiction in response to Bandura et al.'s (1963a & b) and Rosenblith's (1959, 1961) finding that same sex individuals are more frequently modeled. Investigations reported by Bandura (1969) and Campbell (1961) concur in finding more frequent modeling, the more frequently is the behavior to be modeled displayed. Thus, in both the high- and low-attraction tapes we incorporated 12 statements by the therapist expressing high or low attraction to the patient, this being the maximal number we felt it was possible to include in the therapy tapes were they to remain credible depictions of a psychotherapy session.

Pilot trials involving these modeling tapes, as well as all other study procedures, were run on a sample of 9 psychology graduate students and on a group of 21 psychiatric nurses from a state hospital other than the one at which the study was conducted. The resultant pilot data rather clearly supported both the credibility of the modeling tapes as bona fide psychotherapy sessions, and the discriminability present within the three levels of social class structuring and the three levels of therapist attraction.

As suggested by the orienting instructions presented earlier, seven 45-sec pauses occurred at irregular intervals in each modeling tape. Each pause was immediately preceded by a voice on the tape (another *E*) asking: "What would you say?" Subjects then individually wrote down what they would say to the patient at that particular point were they seeing him in psychotherapy.* A subsequent content analysis of these statements using a modification of the Truax and Carkhuff (1967) scales for empathy and warmth provided this study's "in-therapy" data on what we view as the behavioral consequents of therapist attraction.† Subject attraction to the taped patient, our other major criterion of modeling, was measured by use of the Therapist's Personal Reaction Questionnaire (TPRQ), which was administered immediately following the completion of the modeling tape. This questionnaire has been utilized in a large number of investigations of the psychotherapeutic relationship, investigations whose results combine to quite clearly point to its rather substantial reliability and validity as a measure of therapist attraction to the patient (Goldstein, 1971). Also at this point in time, as an exploratory attempt to discern additional consequents of modeled attraction, ratings were obtained from each S tapping her estimation of the taped patient's insight, socialization skills, degree of disturbance, and prognosis (Strupp, 1960).

This investigation's hypotheses were as follows.

*1. Modeling Hypothesis.* A high level of displayed therapist attraction will result in higher levels of subject attraction, empathy, and warmth toward a taped patient than will be evidenced when no therapist attraction is displayed. Display of no therapist attraction will result in higher levels of subject attraction, empathy, and warmth than will display of a low level of therapist attraction.

*2. Social Class Hypothesis.* Structuring Ss' perceptions of the taped patient as socioeconomically middle class will result in higher levels of attraction, empathy, and warmth toward a taped patient than will no social class structuring. No social class structuring will, in turn, result in higher levels of attraction, empathy, and warmth than will lower-class structuring.

---

* This procedure is modeled after that developed by Strupp and Jenkins (1963) for their several psychotherapy investigations utilizing filmed therapist-patient interactions.

† Interjudge reliabilities for this content analysis were $r = .84$ for empathy, and $r = .71$ for warmth.

3. *Interaction Effect Hypothesis.* The combination of a high level of displayed therapist attraction and structuring of the taped patient as middle class will result in higher levels of subject attraction, empathy, and warmth than will a no attraction display–no social class structuring combination. The latter, in turn, will yield higher dependent variable scores than will the combination involving a low level of displayed attraction and lower-class structuring.

### Results and Discussion

Preliminary to an analysis of the study's hypotheses, results were examined on two items that had been included in the posttape test booklet as a check on the success of structuring of the taped patient's social class. One item asked S to choose, from among a range of dollar amount alternatives presented, her estimate of the taped patient's total earnings during the year prior to his hospitalization. A $\chi^2$ computed on middle-class versus lower-class structuring by rated earnings of $11,000 or $8,000 versus $5,000 or $2,000 yielded a highly significant result ($\chi^2 = 60.83$; $p < .001$). The second item included as a check on our structuring, straightforwardly asked S to indicate whether she judged the patient's social class background to be upper, middle, or lower class. As above, the comparison of class structuring (middle versus lower) against rated class (upper or middle versus lower) yielded highly significant support for the success of our social class structuring ($\chi^2 = 40.03$; $p < .001$).

A series of analyses of variance were conducted across the study's dependent variable data. On our analyses for modeling main effects, no significant result emerged for either TPRQ attraction or in-therapy empathy. A highly significant main effect for modeling, however, did emerge for warmth ($F = 6.88$; $df = 2,126$; $p < .01$). Further analysis seeking the sources of this effect (post hoc cell comparisons via Tukey $b$ tests) revealed that Ss exposed to a high-attraction displaying model, or to a model displaying neither high nor low attraction, offered significantly greater warmth in their in-therapy comments than did Ss exposed to a model displaying low attraction to the taped patient. Fully consistent with this finding is the result indicating a main effect for modeling ($F = 4.65$; $df = 2,126$; $p < .01$) on Ss' ratings of degree of patient disturbance. Post hoc comparisons in response to this finding revealed Ss exposed to a model displaying low attraction to the patient rated him as significantly more disturbed ($p < .05$) than did Ss exposed to a model displaying either high or no attraction toward the identical patient.

With regard to the study's second hypothesis, analyses of variance examining our social class structuring predictions revealed no significant main effects for either measure of in-therapy behaviors, empathy, or warmth. Social class structuring did, however, have a significant influence upon TPRQ attraction $(F = 3.58; df = 2,126; p < .05)$. Post hoc cell comparisons on these data revealed that Ss led to perceive the patient as middle class were significantly more attracted to him $(p < .05)$ than were Ss for whom no social class structuring was provided. No similarly significant comparisons involving lower-class structuring emerged.

The analyses of variance results bearing upon the joint influence of modeling and social class structuring (Hypothesis 3) provide a substantial series of findings, with significant interaction effects emerging for attraction $(F = 2.87; df = 4,126; p < .05)$; empathy $(F = 2.62; df = 4,126; p < .05)$; and warmth $(F = 3.93; df = 4,126; p < .01)$. Between-cell comparisons following the analyses of variance revealed a number of significant differences. Structuring the patient as lower class in combination with displaying neither high nor low therapist attraction led to significantly higher levels of posttape attraction than was the case for S groups exposed to a combination of either lower-class structuring and low-attraction modeling or no social class structuring and low modeled attraction. Contrary to prediction, the lower-class structuring–no modeled attraction group also yielded higher posttape attraction than that from he Ss provided no social class structuring and a high-attraction model.

The cell comparisons conducted on the study's in-therapy empathy data yielded no significant results. Thus, the statistically significant interaction effect for structuring and modeling on empathy must be considered as marginal in nature. Analogous post hoc comparisons conducted on the in-therapy warmth data, in contrast to the foregoing, yielded a large number of significant cell differences. Subjects structured that the patient was middle class and hearing a high level of displayed attraction responded at a higher level of warmth to the patient than did (1) Ss structured lower class and hearing a low-attraction model; (2) Ss structured middle class and hearing a low-attraction model; or (3) Ss provided no social class structuring and hearing a high-attraction model. Furthermore, when neither social class structuring nor modeled attraction were provided, Ss responded significantly more warmly than when lower-class structuring and low modeled attraction were offered.

The focus of this analogue investigation involved examination of the effects of modeling and social class structuring on certain major dispositional (attraction) and in-therapy (empathy and warmth) performance consequents for a group of potential paraprofessional pscychotherapists. Both modeling and social class structuring, considered separately, yielded moderately significant effects on a portion of the study's dependent measures. The level of modeled attraction influenced both the warmth expressed by the Ss "to" the taped patient and their ratings of his degree of disturbance. Thus, Ss hearing a taped therapist express a low level of attraction to a patient, respond to such a modeling display by expressing significantly less warmth than Ss hearing a model displaying either high or neither high nor low attraction. They also perceive him as significantly more disturbed.

The effects of social class structuring taken alone were not particularly powerful in this investigation. Such structuring was reflected in neither measure of in-therapy behavior, and only somewhat weakly in the nurses' stated attraction to the patient. From such an absence of findings, one might posit that this study's Ss, almost all of whose daily patient contacts involve lower-class and working-class patients, fail to share the purported professional therapist bias against such nonmiddle-class patients. If one were to embrace this conclusion, it would appear that some research substantiation is thus provided for the greater "commonality of background" rationale partially underlying the growing usage of paraprofessional and indigenous change-agents. However, examination of this investigation's interaction-effect findings, in which the combined influence of structuring and modeling was examined, leads to a rather different conclusion. Although not totally consistent across all comparisons, the several significant interaction effects and post hoc cell comparisons on attraction, empathy, and warmth, combine to demonstrate very substantially that Ss' perception of a patient's social class, when combined with observation of a model's behavior toward such a patient, exerts a powerful influence upon both their evaluation of, and behavior toward, that patient. It will be recalled that among the major types of behavior modification demonstrated to follow from exposure to a model is what Bandura (1969) has termed "disinhibitory effects." This term reflects the circumstance of an individual performing an act that was part of his behavioral repertoire *prior* to his observation of a model performing the same act or behavior, but that was rarely enacted for reasons such as negative social sanctions. Observation of the model under these conditions, it is held, serves as a disinhibitor, releaser, sanction, or more generally, implicit permission to act. Thus, for example, Bandura *et al.* (1963a&b) and Epstein (1966) have demonstrated significantly greater aggressive behavior in boys observing an aggressive model when no punishment is accorded the model consequent to his aggressive behavior. We would speculate, therefore, that social class structuring alone had no effect upon empathy and warmth and only a weak effect upon attraction, not because of insufficient commonality of background between change-agent and patient but, instead, because overt expression of social class bias is widely and strongly disapproved. Such a perceptual and behavioral predisposition, however, when combined with the disinhibiting, repeated permission to act provided by observing an experienced and rewarded model, does indeed lead to overt expressiveness of social class bias.

In summary of this investigation, we may note that its findings indeed provide some initial evidence in support of modeling as an effective paraprofessional training procedure, as well as a partial basis to begin questioning the widely held commonality of background assumption underlying much paraprofessional recruitment, selection, and training.

### Self-Disclosure

Our second investigation of the effectiveness of modeling procedures in a paraprofessional training context had therapist self-disclosure as its dependent variable focus (Lack, 1968). Mowrer (1963) has observed:

> Professional therapists have long presented a pedagogical anomaly: namely, failure to demonstrate the very accomplishments which they urge upon their patients. . . . It is hardly surprising if "closed" therapists have singularly failed to produce "open" patients [p. 332].

Mowrer hypothesizes a salutory, almost reciprocal, effect of therapist self-disclosure upon patient self-disclosure, a relationship he views as proceeding via a modeling process. Jourard (1969) and his co-workers have examined this notion extensively. Employing a variety of paradigms, types of subjects, and experimental contexts, a markedly consistent finding has emerged: self-disclosure by one member of a dyad indeed facilitates self-disclosure by the other (Drag, 1968; Heifitz, 1967; Jaffe, 1968; Jourard & Landsman, 1960; Jourard & Richman, 1963; Korman, 1967; Resnick, 1968). These findings formed the basis for our own attempt to increase paraprofessional therapist self-disclosure via modeling procedures.

The investigation's second independent variable was instructions to self-disclose. As we have noted above with regard to psychotherapy in general, one must seek to determine the training procedure or set of procedures that is not only most effective but, given effectiveness, that is least expensive—of time, effort, cost, etc. If telling subjects what to do (instructions) proves as effective as the more costly development and use of modeling enactments, then the former procedure is to be preferred.

The present investigation, therefore, was implemented by a 2 × 2 factorial design involving the presence and absence of both modeling and instructions for self-disclosure.

## Procedure

Subjects for this investigation were 60 female psychiatric attendants employed at a large state mental hospital. Ss were randomly assigned to four experimental conditions: *(1)* instructions plus modeling; *(2)* instructions; *(3)* modeling; and *(4)* control. Each S was run individually, and began her study participation by hearing the following instructions (material in brackets were omitted for Ss in experimental conditions 3 and 4).

In recent years, more and more psychiatric attendants working in mental hospitals have begun to serve as psychotherapists for their patients. While the number of attendant-psychotherapists is not yet large, it is growing as the number of training programs and courses increase. The goal of the research in which you are participating today is to learn more about the therapeutic job attendants can do as psychotherapists. In a few moments you will hear a tape recording of part of an actual psychotherapy session, a session which took place in a city outside of New York State. It is the patient's first session. The psychotherapist is a psychiatric attendant who has been conducting psychotherapy sessions as a regular part of her work for the last four years, and who has also been involved in teaching other attendants how to serve as effective psychotherapists. The psychiatrists and nurses she works with view her as quite competent and generally successful with her patients. Most of her psychotherapy patients, as is true of the one you will hear on the tape, have been diagnosed as alcoholic. The particular patient you will hear is a 39-year-old male who, at the time of the interview, was in the third week of his second hospitalization for alcoholism.

[As you listen to the taped session, be particularly aware of the therapist's openness about herself. According to leading therapists of several different schools of thought about therapy, openness and frankness by the therapist about herself or himself are highly important qualities. This involves sharing by the therapist, when she meets with her patients, of her own past experiences, and also a sharing of her feelings about the patients, and about the therapeutic relationship. Research has very clearly shown that therapist openness about her own experiences is desirable in order to help the patient be more open about his problems, especially if the patient is having difficulty discussing these problems. Much research demonstrates this to be true—when the therapist discloses things about her own experiences, feelings, and even her problems, it encourages patients to disclose their experiences, feelings and problems. This is very important for a patient to do in order to be helped by psychotherapy. *At high levels of therapist openness,* the therapist may discuss personal ideas and freely volunteer information about her personal concerns, attitudes, and past experiences. She gives the impression of a person, who, through her own experiences, has come a long way toward understanding herself and the world, and who is willing to extend her experiences along these lines in order to be helpful to the patient. At low levels of therapist openness, the therapist either avoids talking about herself, or does so in a fashion which has no relation to the patient, and it begins to sound as if she is more concerned with her own problems than those of the patient. The therapist you will hear is exhibiting high levels of openness about herself.]

Since the main goal of this research is to better understand the job of the psychiatric attendant, when the tape is over we will ask you to fill our a questionnaire which will give us some of your opinions about the patient on the tape. However, we can learn about what attendants do as therapists not only by getting your opinion about the people on the tape, but also by asking you what you would say to the patient if you were his therapist. Therefore, when the tape starts, listen carefully to what both the therapist and the patient have to say, being particularly aware of how the therapist communicates honesty and openness. At various times during the taped session, the session will stop and you will hear a voice say, "What would you say?" and then the voice will say a number. On the work sheet after this page you will see blank spaces numbered 1, 2, 3, etc. These correspond to the numbers you will hear. Write what *you* would say to the patient in these spaces, [*trying to be as open and frank as you can be* about yourself. For example, let us suppose that the patient on the tape said: "I've really been feeling terrible lately, I lost my job and everything seems hopeless," then you hear a voice on the tape say: "What would you say —One." You may decide that if you were the therapist you would comment: "It sounds like things have been pretty bad, I know what you mean, I once lost my job and had a terrible time getting up the energy to look for another one." You would write this comment in the blank space numbered one. This is just one example.] It is your comment we wish you to write in, whatever you would say to the patient. Please write as clearly as you can. There will be one minute each time for you to write your comment. To assure anonymity, we ask you *not* to sign your name on the work sheet or any other place on the booklet.

After you have heard the tape, we will ask you to conduct an interview. Are there any questions?

Following these instructions, each S listened to a 35-min tape recording of a purported therapy interview between an attendant-psychotherapist and an alcoholic patient. One of two tapes were utilized, depending upon experimental condition. Both these tapes were modifications of that used in the investigation described above. Each contained 38 therapist statements. On the tape used in the *instructions plus modeling* and the *modeling* conditions (see Appendix, pp. 346–353) 19 of these statements were self-disclosing comments by the taped therapist-model. These statements were rated at levels 3 or 4 of the Carkhuff (1969) self-disclosure scale. For example, in response to the taped patient's initial statements regarding his drinking behavior the therapist replied:

Sounds like drinking began socially for you, sort of the way smoking did for me, but for a long time I didn't consider myself a smoker. Do you think you're an alcoholic now?

And later in the tape:

It sounds like its pretty hard for you at home. Your description of your wife reminds me of a supervisor I once had in my first hospital job. When she got an idea it had to be carried out on the spot. I hated that situation, but there were good things about the job also, so I couldn't bring myself to leave. I bet you would find it hard to leave also.

The second tape, used in the *instructions* and *control* conditions (see Appendix, pp. 354–360), contained no therapist self-discosing statements, but in all other respects was identical to that just described. On both tapes the patient role was portrayed by a male actor, the therapist by a female. At 11 points on each tape, always following a patient statement, a voice on the tape would ask, "What would you say?" A 1-min pause ensued, during which time $S$ was to enter on a form provided what she felt she would say to the patient at that juncture were she therapist. These written statements, as will be noted below, were later content-analyzed for subject self-disclosure. We were also interested in learning whether at least minimal transfer would occur following these interventions, and thus required each $S$ to conduct a brief psychotherapeutic interview. Following the tape listening procedure, each $S$ was told:

As I mentioned before, you will now be asked to conduct an interview. The person we will ask you to interview will act the role of a patient. He is an actor, playing the role of a patient, and we would like you to interview him as though this were his first psychotherapy session. We have prepared a series of cards on which you will find a number of topics which are generally discussed during a first therapy interview. We will give you a moment to examine these cards, and then we will introduce you to the actor-patient. You will be asked to end the interview after 15 minutes.

The interview topics listed for each $S$-interviewer were parents, anxiety or nervousness, sexual difficulties, drinking problems, anger, strong points, and weak points. To maximize the reality of the interview, the interviewee was in fact a nondrinking, ex-alcoholic who was currently a member of Alcoholics Anonymous. An extended series of role-play interviews were conducted with this interviewee-actor, thus training him to enact the role of an acute, hospitalized alcoholic patient in a relatively standardized manner across interviews. He was not informed as to the nature of the investigation and its experimental conditions. All interviews were tape recorded for later content analysis of interviewer self-disclosure.

Subject statements written as if they were by the taped patient's therapist from the tape display phase of this study, and verbal statements from the interview phase, were both content analyzed in two ways. The first was the Carkhuff (1969) Scale for the Measurement of Facilitative Self-Disclosure in Interpersonal Processes. At the lowest level of self-disclosure on this scale, the therapist seeks to remain detached from the patient and discloses nothing about his own feelings or experiences. At level two, the therapist may not appear to be avoiding such disclosure, but nevertheless does not volunteer personal information. Behavior at level three is exemplified by the therapist communicating an openness to volunteering personal information, but this information is primarily abstract and reveals little about the therapist as a unique individual. At level four, the therapist freely volunteers information about personal concerns in both depth and detail. At level five, the therapist reveals intimate and detailed material that might be embarrassing under different circumstances or if revealed to an outsider. To reflect the possibility that S self-disclosure could occur in two somewhat different forms, the Carkhuff Scale content-analysis data was analyzed in two different formats: (1) mean level—to reflect frequent but more moderate levels of self-disclosure; and (2) percentage above level three—to reflect the occurrence of infrequent but high levels of self-disclosure.

As an apparent step in the direction of self-disclosure, but not necessarily involving actual disclosure, individuals may make self-referring statements. To evaluate the occurrence of such behavior, our second content-analysis procedure involved use of Davidoff's (1969) Scale for Rating Self-Referring Statements. Use of this scale reflects essentially a frequency count of such self-referring statements as *I, me, we,* and *us;* and the words *my, mine, our,* and *ours* when they refer to S's own physical or mental experiences. Interjudge reliability, in the content analyses of the written and interview data respectively, were .96 and .91 for the Carkhuff scale; and .97 and .98 for the Davidoff scale.

### Results and Discussion

Analyses of variance were conducted across the study's data. These results are presented in Table 8.1.

These findings indicate, with regard to subject written responses to the taped patient, a series of significant main and interaction effects for both modeling and instructions. Thus, Ss exposed to either a high self-disclosing model and/or instructions to self-disclose, display reliably higher levels of self-disclosure and self-reference in written responses to an audiotaped patient than Ss not so exposed or instructed. Post hoc cell comparisons across these Phase I data (Tukey *a* test) revealed a single series of significant differences—Ss exposed to *both* instructions and a high self-disclosing model displayed significantly higher levels of self-disclosure and self-reference than did Ss exposed to either modeling alone, instructions alone, or no intervention. Thus, in direct contrast to our earlier study of instructions and modeling to increase independent behavior in schizophrenic patients, in the present investigation the two interventions do indeed appear to function in an additive manner.

The second series of analyses of variance presented in Table 8.1 present our Phase 2 findings, i.e., S self-disclosure and self-reference vis-à-vis an actor-patient being interviewed by S. In partial contrast to the Phase 1 findings, here effects for modeling alone emerged—but they emerged strongly, i.e., on all three dependent measures. No similarly significant effects for instructions, nor interaction effects, were obtained. Thus, Ss exposed to a high self-disclosing model, in contrast to those not so exposed, display significantly higher levels of self-disclosure and self-reference in their verbal communications to a live (actor) patient.

For exploratory purposes, this study's dependent variable data and a number of items of demographic information on Ss were intercorrelated.

TABLE 8.1
ANALYSES OF VARIANCE (*F* VALUES) FOR SELF-DISCLOSURE AND SELF-REFERENCE

| Measure | Instructions | Modeling | Modeling × instructions |
|---|---|---|---|
| *Phase 1 (written data)* | | | |
| Self-disclosure (mean level) | 11.19** | 7.87** | 3.61 |
| Self-disclosure (%) | 15.13** | 7.07* | 4.28* |
| Self-references | 14.47** | 10.05** | 5.21* |
| *Phase 2 (interview data)* | | | |
| Self-disclosure (mean level) | .71 | 11.92** | .01 |
| Self-disclosure (%) | .48 | 12.69** | .39 |
| Self-references | 1.18 | 7.85** | .01 |

\* $p < .05$.     \*\* $p < .01$.

Inspection of the resultant correlational matrix revealed significant relationships between the three self-disclosure and self-reference scores and both subject age (negative) and education (positive). That is, across experimental conditions, younger, more educated Ss offered higher levels of self-disclosure and self-reference than did older, less educated subjects.

This investigation's findings provide, first of all, further evidence for the value of modeling procedures in the training of therapy-relevant skills. In contrast to our earlier finding with a patient sample, instructions to Ss were demonstrated on one set of criteria to serve an incremental function such that, when combined with modeling, they yielded an effect more powerful than either procedure alone.

We included in this investigation the requirement that each S interview an actor-patient as a means of providing a minimal test of transfer. Results indicated that the effects of modeling, but not instructions, did indeed endure in an immediately following interview context. While such a finding is valuable, we would caution, based on our entire research program, that the likelihood of even such minimal transfer appears to be very much a function of target skill complexity. For example, it will be noted in the investigations described below that the somewhat more complex skill, empathy, failed to transfer until much more substantial training interventions were utilized.

### Empathy I

Our third paraprofessional therapist study (Perry, 1970) utilized a somewhat more complex experimental design, focused upon empathy as the target skill, and again sought to examine the independent and interactive effects of modeling and instructions as skill training procedures. Although the value of therapist empathy as an active therapeutic ingredient appears to have been somewhat oversold during the past decade (Shapiro, 1969), the cumulative evidence regarding its therapeutic impact nevertheless remains impressive (Carkhuff, 1969; Hart & Tomlinson, 1970; Truax & Carkhuff, 1967).

We employed a 2 × 3 factorial design reflecting two levels of instructions for empathy (presence and absence) and three levels of displayed empathy (high, low, no model). As in our investigation of self-disclosure, the present study involved two phases: (1) Ss heard instructions and listened to a modeling tape of a purported therapeutic interview, during which they wrote on 12 occasions what they would say were they therapist; and (2) each S conducted a brief interview with a pseudo-patient. To complete this brief overview of the investigation, it may be noted that in addition to empathy, content analyses on both the written and interview material from Ss were also performed for *respect* (regard or concern for the helpee's feelings, experiences, and potentials) and *genuineness* (personal involvement used in a nondestructive and facilitative way)—two other dimensions of therapist behavior frequently demonstrated to be facilitative of patient change.

## *Procedure*

Subjects for the investigation were 66 clergymen, representing a number of religious denominations, who volunteered to participate. All had had some minimal counseling training and were currently associated to varying degrees with a local pastoral counseling institute. They were randomly assigned to the study's six experimental conditions, and began participation by individually being presented with the following premodeling tape instructions (material in brackets was omitted for Ss assigned to the three *no instructions for empathy* conditions):

In recent years more and more upset and disturbed people have been seeking help from professionals of all sorts, from psychiatrists, psychologists, social workers, clergymen, teachers, physicians. Clergymen have been very effective as counselors for years and many are spending increasing time in this way. The goal of the research in which you are participating today is to learn more about the therapeutic job a clergyman can do in counseling. We hope to learn more about effective therapeutic ingredients.

In a few moments you will hear a tape recording of selected excerpts from an actual counseling session which took place in a city outside of Washington state. It is the client's first session. The counselor is a minister who has been doing a great deal of therapeutic counseling in his ministry for the past four years and is highly thought of by his colleagues for the quality of his counseling. Many of his clients, as is true of the one you will hear on the tape, are alcoholics. The particular patient you will hear is a 39-year-old male who, at the time of the interview, had been hospitalized once for alcoholism.

[As you listen to the taped session, be particularly aware of the empathy extended to the patient by the counselor. According to therapists of many different schools of thought about therapy, empathy is a major therapeutic ingredient. By empathy is meant the communication to the client that you understand him, understand where he is *at that moment,* and that you communicate understanding of not only his obvious words, but also the less obvious feelings and content. There is a sensitive awareness and appreciation of the client's feelings. Researchers have defined empathy thus—

At a *high* level of accurate empathy the message "I am *with* you" is unmistakably clear—the therapist's remarks fit perfectly with the client's mood and content. His responses not only indicate his sensitive understanding of the obvious feelings, but also serve to clarify and expand the client's awareness of his own feelings or experiences.

At a *low* level of accurate empathy the therapist may go off on a tangent of his own or may misinterpret what the patient is feeling. At a very low level he may be so preoccupied and interested in his own intellectual interpretations that he is scarcely aware of the client's "being."

The counselor you will hear is exhibiting a *high* level of accurate empathy.

A large number of research studies give weight to the importance of the therapeutic relationship and specifically to empathy. For example, Truax (1961) compared therapy sessions of 8 hospitalized patients, 4 of whom showed clear improvement and 4 who showed clear deterioration on a variety of personality tests after 6 months of intensive therapy. He found that psychotherapists whose patients improved were consistently and significantly rated higher on accurate empathy than psychotherapists whose patients deteriorated on the tests. Other studies as well have found high correlations between evaluations of constructive personality change and level of accurate empathy extended by the therapist (Barrett-Lennard, 1962; Bergin & Soloman, 1963; Truax, 1963; Truax, Carkhuff, & Kodman, 1965). Thus, empathy as a therapeutic ingredient appears to contribute a great deal to therapeutic improvement.]

Since the main goal of this research is to better understand the job of the pastoral counselor, when the tape is over we will ask you to fill out a questionnaire which will give us some of your opinions about the client on the tape. However, we can learn about what clergymen do as counselors not only by getting your opinion about the people on the tape, but also by asking you what you would say to the client if you were counseling him. Therefore, when the tape starts, listen carefully to what both the client and the counselor have to say, being particularly aware of how the counselor communicates his sensitive understanding of the client. At various times during the taped session, the session will stop and you will hear a voice say, "What would you say?" and then the voice will say a number. On the work sheet after this page you will see blank spaces numbered 1, 2, 3, etc. These correspond to the number you will hear. Write what *you* would say to the client in these spaces, [*trying to be as empathic as you* can be. For example, let us suppose that the client on the tape said: "I've really been feeling terrible lately," then you hear a voice on the tape say: "What would you say—one." You may decide that if you were the counselor you would comment: "It sounds like things have been pretty bad," so you would write this comment in the blank space numbered one. This is just one example.] It is your comment we wish you to write in, whatever you would say to the client. Please write as clearly as you can. There will be 45 seconds each time for you to write your comment. To assure anonymity, we ask you *not* to sign your name on the worksheet or any other place on the booklet. If you have any questions, please press the STOP button on the tape recorder and get the experimenter. If you have no questions, turn to the worksheet on the next page.

One of three modeling audiotapes (see Appendix, pp. 361–377) were then played to each S, depending upon his experimental condition. Each portrayed a therapeutic interview and contained 12 pauses preceded by instructions to Ss to write what they would say if they were treating the client. The client's statements were identical on all three tapes. Taped therapist statements varied by experimental condition. Therapist statements on the high-empathy modeling tape were judged by two independent raters to reflect an average empathy level of 3.8 on the Carkhuff scale.* Analogous therapist statements on the low-empathy modeling tape were independently rated at an average of 1.5. On both these tapes we sought to incorporate a maximal number of modeling enhancers. Thus, we presented the largest number of modeling displays possible within the limits of interview credibility; explicitly underscored the model's competence and status; minimized competing stimuli; and, most important, maximized apparent reward to the model in a response-contingent manner. The study's third tape was developed for the no-model conditions and, as such, contained no therapist statements, but only those of the client.

Following exposure to instructions and tape, each S conducted a 15-min interview with an actor trained to play the same alcoholic patient role as utilized in our study concerned with self-disclosure (Lack, 1968). Interview procedures and topics were also the same as in the earlier investigation. The actor-patient was kept unaware of the nature of the investigation and its hypotheses. All interviews were tape recorded for later content analyses for interviewer *empathy, respect,* and *genuineness.*

### Results and Discussion

Interjudge reliabilities were determined separately for the written (in response to the taped patient) and verbal (in response to the live actor-patient) S responses for the three criterion variables. The reliabilities for empathy, respect, and genuineness, respectively, were .82, .69, and .66 for the written data; and .88, .83, and .79 for the verbal data.

A series of analyses of variance for instructions, modeling, and their interaction were conducted across the study's data. These results are shown in Table 8.2. In this table, baseline results reflect the level of the given characteristic displayed by the interviewer after hearing the pretape instructions, but before exposure to the taped model. Phase 1 results re-

---

* The first four interchanges on both this tape and the low-empathy tape involved minimal or no counselor statements. In this manner, S responses during this segment could be considered baseline responding, free from any possible modeling effects.

flect scores obtained during and after exposure to the model; and Phase 2 scores are derived from the interviews conducted by Ss.

As Table 8.2 indicates, there emerged no instructions × modeling interaction effects, only a single main effect for instructions, and several main effects for modeling. Post hoc analyses of these data reveal, for each of the significant, Phase 1 modeling findings, a significant cell difference favoring Ss exposed to the high-empathy model, as compared to low-empathy modeling exposure. Subjects exposed to no model obtained criterion scores intermediate to high- and low-empathy modeling Ss. None of the cell comparisons involving no-modeling Ss yielded significant differences.

Thus, this study's findings contrast in two important respects with our earlier attempt to train self-disclosure. While modeling procedures proved clearly effective as an initial training approach in each study, the present investigation—unlike our result with self-disclosure—provided no evidence of an even minimally enduring effect. That is, on a transfer task represented by an interview occurring immediately after the experimental manipulation, modeling effects clearly discernible during the manipulation had disappeared. Note also that while instructions had indeed led to significant effects when self-disclosure was the target skill, no such result emerged for instructions to be empathic. Perhaps both of these failures —of instructions and of even minimal transfer—are in part attributable

TABLE 8.2

ANALYSES OF VARIANCE (F VALUES) FOR EMPATHY, RESPECT, AND GENUINENESS

| Measure | Instructions | Modeling | Instructions × modeling |
|---|---|---|---|
| *Empathy* | | | |
| Baseline | .36 | — | — |
| Phase 1 | .40 | 6.47*** | .48 |
| Phase 2 | 1.18 | 2.71* | .75 |
| *Respect* | | | |
| Baseline | .00 | — | — |
| Phase 1 | .77 | 6.19*** | .64 |
| Phase 2 | 2.52 | .90 | .52 |
| *Genuineness* | | | |
| Baseline | 7.92*** | — | — |
| Phase 1 | .35 | 3.05** | .36 |
| Phase 2 | 1.35 | 1.32 | .07 |

$* p > .05 < .10.$     $** p < .05.$     $*** p < .01.$

to the relative complexity of empathic skill, i.e., to the fact that perhaps unlike self-disclosure, empathy simply cannot be taught by very simple means, or in any enduring sense with so brief and relatively nonpowerful a manipulation as was utilized in the present investigation. As will be noted shortly, such a nonenduring effect occurred once again, in a similar investigation of empathy training that we conducted for somewhat different goals. That investigation combined with the one described above to lead to research on much more extended and powerful training interventions—research examined below.

### Empathy II

It will be recalled that in the initial study involving a paraprofessional sample, we obtained some evidence for a disinhibiting effect, such that exposure to an experienced and rewarded model expressing social class-related biases appeared to increase the expression of such bias by observers. The investigation we now wish to present (Sutton, 1970) is a second such attempt to discern further possible antecedants and consequents of social class bias among paraprofessionals. Its second purpose, as noted above, was to examine efforts to enhance subject empathy via brief modeling procedures.

### *Procedure*

Subjects were 60 psychiatric attendants employed at a large state mental hospital. They were randomly assigned to four experimental conditions in a 2 × 2 factorial design involving structuring of a taped patient as middle-class or lower-class, and high or low taped therapist (model) empathy. Pretape listening structuring to Ss of the taped patient's social class was identical to that used in our earlier investigation of social class structuring (Goldstein, Cohen, Blake, & Walsh, 1971). The high- and low-empathy modeling tapes were identical to that used in the Perry (1970) study, except that in the present instance a female therapist–model was utilized.

### *Results and Discussion*

Two items were included in our posttape testing of Ss to serve as a check on the pretape social class structuring. Subjects structured that the tape patient was middle class rated his likely annual income ($\chi^2 = 37.69$; $p < .001$) and his social class standing ($\chi^2 = 139.18$; $p <$

.001) as significantly higher than did Ss structured that the taped patient was lower class. Thus, both items provide confirmation of the success of the structuring provided.

Subject written responses during 12 pauses in the modeling tapes, and subject verbal responses during a 15-min, posttape interview with an actor-patient, were each content analyzed for empathy (interjudge reliabilities = .94 and .89 respectively). Analyses of variance on these data are presented in Table 8.3.

These analyses once again reveal a significant modeling effect for empathy during Phase 1, and a rapid disappearance of this effect in an immediately following test for minimal transfer. In contrast to our earlier investigation of social class structuring, no such effect emerged in the present investigation. It seems appropriate to speculate that this difference in outcome may at least in part be attributable to sample differences in the two investigations. In the former study, 104 of the 135 participating Ss were nurses, and 94 of these were registered nurses. In the present investigation, all subjects were psychiatric attendants. It is possible that reflected here is a between-sample social class difference such that the attendant sample are themselves socioeconomically much more like the taped patient, share greater commonality of background and experience with him, and hence in fact hold less social class bias then existed in our sample of nurses. The growing degree of reliance upon indigenous workers in the paraprofessional therapist movement is such that speculations such as the foregoing appear to be worthwhile directions for continued empirical examination.

Reflecting upon these four paraprofessional therapist investigations as a group, it seems quite clear that the same types of conclusions are warranted as we were led to in our inpatient and outpatient studies. Modeling certainly appears to be a valuable approach to skill enhancement, but

TABLE 8.3

ANALYSES OF VARIANCE (F VALUES) FOR EMPATHY: A

| Measure | Structuring | Modeling | Structure × modeling |
|---|---|---|---|
| *Phase 1 (written data)* empathy | .27 | 11.72* | .43 |
| *Phase 2 (verbal data)* empathy | 1.15 | 3.03 | 3.71 |

* $p < .01$.

weak interventions lead to weak outcomes. Effects of a more enduring nature, and particularly effects which transfer to real-life environments, appear to demand considerably more powerful interventions. This perspective led to our next investigation, an examination of Structured Learning for paraprofessional skill enhancement. In response to its demonstrated value as an active therapeutic ingredient, and in light of the findings of our initial paraprofessional studies, we chose empathy once again as the target skill.

## Empathy III

### *Procedure*

Subjects were 74 student nurses employed at a moderately sized, public psychiatric hospital. Subject participation was voluntary, and in response to a hospital-wide invitation to a 10-hour course in "conversation training." Each nurse, as the initial step in study participation, completed a copy of the Hospital Training Questionnaire, Form A (see Appendix, pp. 377–380). The questionnaire, developed for this investigation, consists of 30 common problematic situations involving nurse–patient interactions. It was developed by soliciting a pool of such situations from senior hospital staff and then, in consultation with such personnel, selecting those situations of apparent greatest frequency and/or most difficulty in handling. The format of each item is such that a problematic patient statement is made or behavior reported and the nurse must offer a response. Our purpose in administering this questionnaire at the outset was to obtain base-rate, pretraining information regarding the level of nurse empathy. Toward this end, each nurse response was rated by two independent judges (interjudge reliability = .83) on the Carkhuff (1969) empathy scale. Following completion of this premeasure, the participating nurses were randomly assigned to experimental and control conditions. Experimental group Ss were constituted into groups of six to eight each, and participated in a 10-hour empathy training program. The groups were led by two Es and included in their membership, for reasons elaborated below, four head nurses on the hospital staff. The specific procedures constituting our Structured Learning program for this experiment were as follows:

1. Introduce the training program's purpose as *conversation training.* Describe it briefly as helping participants learn to converse in ways more helpful to their patients. *Do NOT use the word "empathy."*

2. Administer the study's base-rate measure, the Hospital Training Questionnaire, *Form A*. Read instructions aloud and be sure all participants understand.

3. Present and discuss the nature and meaning of empathy:

   a. Define in terms of the two learning points to be modeled later (What is the patient feeling? How can I best communicate to him that I understand his feelings?). Write these two learning points on the blackboard and leave it there throughout training.

   b. Define by distributing and discussing the Carkhuff empathy scale. Read the entire scale aloud as participants follow along. Leader give examples at each of the five levels. Constantly refer to the two learning points.

   c. Discuss ancillary topics:

       (1) Importance of empathy for patient change (mood, self-exploration, etc.)

       (2) Importance of empathy for participant (helper) self-esteem and skill development

       (3) Importance of empathy for hospital climate (and countervailing forces).

       (4) Means for identifying patient feelings (Learning Point One)

       (5) Means for communicating to patients that their feelings are understood (Learning Point Two)

       (6) Empathy versus sympathy

       (7) Empathy versus diagnosis or evaluation

       (8) Empathy versus directiveness or questioning (including when empathy is *not* appropriate)

       (9) Value of empathic attempts which are inaccurate

4. Distribute blank copies of the Hospital Training Questionnaire, *Form A*.

5. Two group leaders present the 30 Form A items, with one of the leaders serving as model, responding in each instance with a Level 3, 4, or 5 answer. Refer in doing so to both the two learning points and the Carkhuff scale. On the last 15 items, pause between protagonist (e.g., "patient") statement and model (e.g., "nurse") response and encourage participants to silently or covertly rehearse their own empathic response. Encourage brief discussion by participants of any items representing events which have occurred to them. In these instances, elicit how they handled the event.

6. One group leader presents the 30 Form A items again. Leader serves as protagonist (e.g., patient) and seeks helper (e.g., nurse)

responses to the first 10 items on a volunteer basis from the trainee Ss. Leader seeks responses to remaining 20 items from each participant in turn, on a nonvolunteer basis. Be sure *each* member has an opportunity to respond to three or more items (repeat items if necessary). The correct leader response to the member response is:

  a. If member response is *not* empathic (Level 1 or 2) provide conditional acceptance with no reinforcement (e.g., "That might be useful on occasion, but perhaps a better response would be . . ."). Leader then provides (models) an empathic response.

  b. If member response is empathic (Level 3, 4, or 5), provide social reinforcement (e.g., "very good," "that's excellent," "that really responds to the two learning points," etc.).

7. Leader presents 30 Form A situations again. First with other leader, and then with each participant, more extended helper-helpee empathic conversations are to be modeled and then role played. Continue referring to the two learning points. Provide social reinforcement whenever appropriate.

8. Urge members to apply learning points with patients on their ward before the second Structured Learning meeting.

9. At beginning of second meeting:
  a. Write learning points on blackboard.
  b. Be sure each member has a blank copy of Form A and the Carkhuff scale.
  c. Go over the Carkhuff scale as in first meeting.
  d. Discuss member thoughts on empathy and any attempts to apply it with patients since first meeting.

10. Leaders model and role play the 30 situations.

11. Leader and each group member in turn role play the 30 situations. Leader provides social reinforcement where appropriate.

12. Leader and members role play more extended conversations. Leader provides social reinforcement where appropriate.

13. Leaders model and role play the thirty situations if time permits.

14. Administer Hospital Training Questionnaire, Form B.

15. Mention follow-up testing will be conducted.

These several procedures consumed a 10-hour period, spread across two consecutive days. Immediately following the final modeling–role-playing sequence, the Hospital Training Questionnaire was readministered. This form of the questionnaire, Form B, contained the original 30 situations that had constituted Form A and that had been the focus of most of the training, plus 15 additional items to which subjects had not been previously exposed. The control group members, who had taken

Form A at the same point in time as had experimental group members, also completed Form B at this second point in time without, of course, any intervening empathy training.

As noted earlier, four head nurses participated in the empathy training program. Each served first as a participant in one of the five experimental groups, and then as an observer in a second such group. Our intention was to discern whether such persons could subsequently serve as, in a sense, paraprofessional trainers of paraprofessional therapists. Schematically, our overall procedural sequence was:

| Study phase | Procedure | Experimental group | Control group |
|---|---|---|---|
| 1. Experimental group training | Pretesting Training | Form A Empathy training, professional trainers | Form A No training |
| 2. Control group training | Posttesting, Training | Form B No training | Form B Empathy training; paraprofessional trainers |
| 3. Follow-up | Posttesting₂ Follow-up testing | Form B No testing | Form B — |

As the second major phase of our procedures, therefore, student nurses previously assigned to the control group condition then met with two, now-trained, head nurses for a 10-hour Structured Learning empathy training program. The format of these sessions paralleled directly that conducted by the Es with the experimental group Ss. The experimenters sat in on all sessions run by the paraprofessional trainers and served the role of nonparticipating observers. Following this training of the original control group members, Form B was readministered to them. One month later, with no further training interventions, Form B was administered for follow-up purposes to all Ss.

### Results and Discussions

Tests of four predictions were addressed to the study's data. A significant increase in the level of displayed empathy during the study's first phase was predicted for the experimental group nurses, in contrast to that evidenced by the control group members during what was, for them, essentially a no-training wait period. A comparison of experimental versus control change scores on the 30 situation items appearing on both Forms A and B indeed yielded the predicted effect $(t = 19.6; p < .001)$. Since these situations were the major stimulus materials for the training received by experimental group Ss, a separate comparison appeared warranted between the two groups on the 15 Form B situations on which no training had been conducted, e.g., a test for a generalization effect. Once again, experimental group Ss displayed significantly higher levels of empathy than did members of the control group $(t = 20.94; p < .001)$. Our third prediction sought to examine the effectiveness of the training implemented during the study's second phase, training conducted by the four head nurses. Our experimental comparison in this regard concerned the change in empathy scores displayed by members of the original control group as a function of their training, in comparison to that evidenced by them during the wait period (Phase 1). That is, the control group members served first as equivalent group controls for the nurse sample trained by the Es, and then as controls for themselves. This comparison, too, yielded a clearly significant increase in the level of empathy displayed $(t = 15.21; p < .001)$. Finally, in response to the failure of our earlier studies to yield sustained skill enhancement, we readministered Form B to all participating nurses one month after the completion of all training sessions. The 30-item scores derived from this testing were compared to subject Form A scores, i.e., their base-rate empathy levels. This comparison demonstrated that the enhanced level of nurse empathy had indeed sustained $(t = 10.01; p < .001)$.

This investigation's findings combine to provide further support for the usefulness of Structured Learning in the training of potential paraprofessional therapists and other personnel situated in high patient-contact positions. The effectiveness of the four head nurses, after but minimal training, in enhancing the level of empathy displayed by the original control group is a provocative finding indeed. While no doubt a great deal of training of paraprofessionals *by* paraprofessionals occurs informally, to date this function has been largely "owned and operated" in most formal senses by professional personnel. While this finding is but a mere hint of important, but untapped, training resources, it is perhaps sufficient to lead one to suggest that our further, serious attention to such possibilities may well be productive.

Finally, we began this presentation by indicating the major importance of the durability and transferability of the types of training gains we have demonstrated. While our one-month follow-up results are clearly a step in the right direction, at least as far as durability evidence is concerned, the issue of transferability is a rather different matter. Our pre, post, and follow-up measures were questionnaires and, as such, provide no transferability information regarding the actual level of nurse empathy displayed in daily work with patients on the hospital ward. Such is the ultimate criterion in investigations such as the present one, and while we were unable to obtain such data in this study, evidence of this type must be obtained before final conclusions can be drawn regarding the *clinical* efficacy of Structured Learning procedures used for paraprofessional training purposes. In our next paraprofessional investigation, we not only sought such necessary criterion data, but also to incorporate into our training procedures a technique that has been demonstrated in laboratory contexts to maximize the probability of transfer of training.

## Empathy IV

In general terms, the investigation we now wish to present is a replication and extension (to the issue of transfer of training) of the study examined above. Psychiatric hospital personnel were again the sample; empathy enhancement was again the target skill. Whereas the previous study was conducted in Holland with a sample consisting primarily of young student nurses, Ss for the current investigation were 20 staff nurses, 40 attendants, and 30 other high patient-contact personnel (OTs, RTs, etc.) in a large American mental hospital. Our experimental procedures and materials included, but elaborated upon, those employed in the earlier study. Specifically, three experimental groups, 30 Ss each, were randomly constituted:

1. Structured Learning plus transfer training
2. Structured Learning
3. No training control

### *Procedure*

Procedures and materials for Groups 2 and 3 were exact replications of those utilized for the experimental and control groups in the Dutch student nurse study. That is, Group 2 underwent a 10-hour Structured Learning program for empathy enhancement. Group 3 participated in no such training, but responded to the study measures at pre, post, and follow-up points in time. Group 1 Ss, in addition to participation in the 10-hour program, engaged in procedures intended to augment the likelihood that training program gains in empathy would subsequently find reliable expression in Ss' real-life environment, i.e., the ward. In Chapter 9 we will present in detail five procedures used with repeated success to augment transfer of training in laboratory contexts. One of these procedures, performance feedback, was implemented in the present investigation. Concretely, two of the individuals who had provided the initial Structured Learning training of empathy were assigned on a full-time basis for a 2-week period to the two wards on which the 30 Group 1 Ss worked. Their task, in general terms, was to provide Structured Learning in an everyday context. That is, each trainer spent 2 hours per day observing the actual, on-the-ward interactions of staff (Ss) and patients. Each S, furthermore, met with one of the two trainers for an individual, 15-min session each day. The S was asked to bring with him to these meetings verbatim notes of interactions he had had with patients that day. These notes and the trainer's observations formed the session's training stimuli. Interactions reported by the trainee or observed by the trainer in which the trainee offered the patient an empathic response (Levels 3, 4, or 5) were responded to by the trainer with social reinforcement. When the trainee had provided a Level 1 or 2 response, the trainer offered further modeling (e.g., "What you might have said was . . .") and role playing (e.g., "Now, why don't you tell me what you might say if the patient again says to you . . ."). While our extended rationale for this procedure will be presented in Chapter 9, we might briefly indicate here that such performance feedback was designed to be responsive to evidence indicating the value for transfer of reinforcement in vivo of "correct" responses provided *after* initial learning criteria have been met.

Our measurement procedures required all Ss to complete the Hospital Training Questionnaire, Form A, for base-rate measurement purposes prior to participation in Structured Learning; Form B of the questionnaire at the completion of such training; and to respond 2 weeks later to 15 tape-recorded "patient" statements—constructed in such a manner as to represent our measure of transfer. Items for this latter measure were derived from actual staff-patient interactions occurring on the three wards on which the study Ss worked. That is, we sought to approximate a measure of subject response to the actual patients with whom they interacted daily.

## Results and Discussion

Results of this investigation are presented in Table 8.4.
Post hoc analyses (*t* test) of these data reveal:
1. A replication of the significant effect of Structured Learning on empathy enhancement

2. A replication of the significant effect of Structured Learning on the generalization of empathy enhancement to new stimuli; not present at either premeasurement or during training
3. A significant transfer training effect for in vivo performance feedback

These results clearly lend force to our earlier conclusions. Structured Learning for paraprofessional empathy enhancement appears to be quite viable. Paraprofessionals again served successfully as trainers, this time "on-the-job," under what may indeed have been considerably more difficult circumstances than was the case in our first study's training center setting. Finally, beginning evidence has been provided for the successful use in a paraprofessional training context of a critical, laboratory-derived principle of transfer training.

### TABLE 8.4
ANALYSES OF VARIANCE ($F$ VALUES) FOR EMPATHY: B

| Source | $df$ | $MS$ | $F$ |
|---|---|---|---|
| Structured Learning | 2,86 | 19.81 | 143.50* |
| Generalization of Structured Learning | 2,86 | 22.69 | 126.05* |
| Transfer training | 2,83 | 20.13 | 93.00* |
| Structured Learning plus transfer training | 2,83 | 18.52 | 125.10* |

\* $p < .01$.

## Rules, Disapproval, and Reinforcement

Our final paraprofessional investigation (Schneiman, 1972) sought to test further the limits of applicability of Structured Learning by examining both a different type of skill and subject sample than were used in our earlier studies.* Teachers-aides are one of the most rapidly growing subgroups of paraprofessional workers in the United States today. During the 1969–70 academic year, 200,000 such persons were utilized in American elementary and secondary schools (Bennett & Falk, 1970), and projections foreseeing employment of over 1 million teachers-aides during the late 1970s have appeared (Harris, 1971). Regardless of even-

---

* Dr. Byron Egeland served as major adviser for this investigation.

tual absolute numbers, it seems certain that persons employed to provide on-the-job classroom assistance to teachers will be present in very substantial numbers in the years ahead. The nature and quality of their training, therefore, is a matter of considerable importance.

As has also been true for other subgroups of paraprofessionals, teachers-aide training has taken many different forms (Bowman & Klopf, 1968; Grambs, 1970; Matheny & Oslin, 1970) with most frequent emphasis upon didactic lecture procedures (Berliner, 1971; Goth, 1968; Hendrix, 1968; Hill, 1960; Olmstead, 1970). It was the overall goal of the present investigation to compare the effectiveness of this common didactic orientation to training with Structured Learning.

We selected as the training target for this study certain principles of contingency management relevant to a classroom setting. The application of behavioral assessment and behavioral treatment strategies and procedures has emerged in recent years as a major force in the management of classroom behavior (e.g., Buckley & Walker, 1970; Clark, Evans, & Hamerlynck, 1972; O'Leary & O'Leary, 1972). Becker, Madsen, Arnold, and Thomas (1967) sought to alter the disruptive classroom behavior of 10 children by training their teachers to systematically implement the principles of Rule-making, Ignoring, and Praising. Rule-making meant regularly making explicit to the child what behaviors were expected of him during each class period. Ignoring was defined as having the teacher avoid paying attention to any behaviors by the child that interfered with the teaching–learning process, except behaviors that might result in injury. Praise required the teacher to overtly attend to, and comment favorably on, those behaviors by the child that facilitated learning. Apparently as a function of these procedures, classroom observation revealed a substantial and consistent decrease in deviant behavior for almost all the participating children.

Madsen, Becker, and Thomas (1968) both replicated and extended these findings. Rule-making, Ignoring, and Praising again proved to be effective in reducing disruptive classroom behavior, with some evidence that the major contribution stemmed from the teacher's use of praise and related expressions of social reinforcement. Lorr (1970) substituted Mild Disapproval (a corrective statement that specifies the inappropriate behavior and presents an acceptable alternative) for Ignoring and found even more satisfactory behavioral outcomes. Thus, it was the ability to adequately implement the principles of Rule-making, Mild Disapproval, and Praise that formed the training goal for the present investigation. We have held throughout this book that Structured Learning appears to be appropriately prescriptive for lower-class and working-class populations.

In the present study we sought to examine the restrictiveness or breadth of this "prescription" by training and comparing both lower-class and middle-class teachers-aide samples.

## Procedure

Subjects for this investigation were 30 lower-class teachers-aides randomly selected from the population of such persons in a moderately large city school district, and 30 middle-class teachers-aides randomly drawn from a suburban school district. Two measures constituted the pretesting required of all participating teachers-aides. The first was a questionnaire, the Teacher-Aide Attitude Questionnaire. The development and format of this measure closely paralleled the Hospital Training Questionnaire used in the empathy training studies. That is, first a large pool of descriptions of aide–pupil interaction situations were obtained. The most frequently occurring of these situations, which also could be difficult or problematic for the aide to handle, were used in the final questionnaire. The aide was required to indicate what she believed she would say or do if the pupil made the statement presented, or if the event described occurred.

Our second premeasure was the Classroom Observation Instrument (Krumboltz & Goodwin, 1966). This instrument is essentially a procedure for recording certain classes of aide behavior (Rules, Disapproval, and Praise) and the pupil behaviors preceding them (Attending, Scanning, Social contacts, Disruptive). That is, one can record with this instrument the occurrence of the aide behaviors to be trained, and the antecedent pupil behaviors, since it is obviously enhancement of the *appropriate* use of Rules, Disapproval, and Praise in which we are interested, not sheer increases in their frequency. Each teacher-aide was individually observed for a 30-min period by a trained observer. Four observers were used for this purpose; average interobserver reliability was .89.

Following pretesting, and utilizing a 2 × 3 factorial design, aides were randomly assigned (within social class groupings) to three experimental conditions:

*1. Structured Learning.* Aides met in groups of 10 each for one 3-hour Structured Learning session. The modeling tape employed (see Appendix, pp. 380–386) was developed by us for this investigation, and used the same six-scene format that characterized our modeling displays for the study of patient role-taking: *(1)* narrator's introduction, *(2)* problem demonstration, *(3)* skill instruction, *(4)* skill rehearsal, *(5)* skill implementation, and *(6)* social reinforcement. Discussion, role playing, feedback, and provision of social reinforcement then followed, in a manner similar to that described several times earlier in this chapter.

2. *Didactic Learning.* Aides assigned to this experimental condition participated in a 3-hour lecture and group discussion session, led by the same *E* who had served as Structured Learning leader. Rule-making, Mild Disapproval, and Praise were defined and (verbally) exemplified at considerable length. Their role in the broader context of classroom management was elaborated. Group discussion focused on both the foregoing, as well as concrete examination of how the three principles might most effectively be utilized with specific children in the participant's classes.

3. *No-Treatment Control.* The 10 middle-class and 10 lower-class teachers-aides assigned to this experimental condition participated in the study's pretesting and posttesting only. They were exposed to no Structured or Didactic Learning procedures.

Following the foregoing interventions, posttesting was conducted. The Teacher-Aide Attitude Questionnaire was readministered; 30 additional min of aide–pupil interaction was observed and recorded on the Classroom Observation Instrument. While this latter measure, as the study's major measure of performance, is most consequential from an applied perspective, we also felt it necessary to incorporate a measure of performance at posttesting. We did so in the form of a Direct Test of Modeling. All participating aides were exposed (live) to a sample of the pupil interaction stimuli they had seen on the modeling tape and rehearsed during role playing. A child actor was employed for this purpose. He initiated three disruptive behaviors during the 5-min test period (refusal to sit with the aide, failure to pay attention to the aide when seated next to her, and disruptive noise-making when the aide was reading aloud), during which the aide's responses were observed and recorded using the Classroom Observation Instrument format.

### Results and Discussion

The major findings of this investigation are presented in Table 8.5.

The results presented in Table 8.5 indicate a rather clear and consistent pattern. The analyses of the Teacher-Aide Attitude Questionnaire data reveal that across social class levels both Structured and Didactic Learning are superior to no instruction in enhancing *S* acquisition of the target skills—at least as far as *S* ability to verbalize such skills is concerned. Of greater applied consequence is the aides' ability to actually *enact* the skill behaviors. Can they, first of all, perform the behaviors immediately after training and while still in the training setting? Results for the Direct Test of Modeling reveal an affirmative answer, again across social

TABLE 8.5

ANALYSES OF VARIANCE ($F$ VALUES) AND $t$ TESTS FOR RULE-MAKING, MILD
DISAPPROVAL, AND PRAISE

| Measure | Source[a] |
|---|---|
| *Teacher-Aide Attitude Questionnaire* | |
| 1. Rule-making | |
| a. between treatments  ($F = 32.86**$) | SL > NT |
|  | DL > NT |
| 2. Mild disapproval | |
| a. between treatments  $(F = 86.28**)$ | SL > NT |
|  | DL > NT |
| 3. Praise | |
| a. between treatments  $(F = 10.18**)$ | SL > NT |
|  | DL > NT |
| 4. Total | |
| a. between treatments  $(F = 67.97**)$ | SL > NT |
|  | DL > NT |
| *Direct Test of Modeling* | |
| 1. Rule-making | |
| a. between treatments  $(F = 24.23**)$ | SL > DL |
|  | SL > NT |
| b. between social classes  $(F = 17.06**)$ | MC > LC |
| 2. Mild disapproval | |
| a. between treatments  $(F = 33.79**)$ | SL > DL |
|  | SL > NT |
| 3. Praise | |
| a. between treatments  $(F = 17.67**)$ | SL > DL |
|  | SL > NT |
| b. between social classes  $(F = 10.05**)$ | MC > LC |
| 4. Total | |
| a. between treatments  $(F = 59.84**)$ | SL > DL |
|  | SL > NT |
| b. between social classes  $(F = 15.56**)$ | MC > LC |
| *Classroom Observation Instrument* | |
| 1. Rule-making | |
| a. between social classes  $(F = 10.78**)$ | MC > LC |
| 2. Mild disapproval | |
| a. between treatments  $(F = 4.53*)$ | SL > DL |
|  | SL > NT |
| 3. Praise | |
| a. between social classes  $(F = 10.11**)$ | MC > LC |
| 4. Total | |
| a. between treatments  $(F = 4.56*)$ | SL > DL |
|  | SL > NT |

[a] Source key: SL—Structured Learning; DL—Didactic Learning; NT—No
treatment; MC—Middle class; LS—Lower class.
* $p < .05$.      ** $p < .01$.

class levels, only for those aides trained by Structured Learning. That is, both middle- and lower-class aides receiving Structured Learning performed significantly more adequately on all three target skills (separately and combined) than did either Didactic Learning or no-treatment Ss. Across treatments it appears that middle-class aides demonstrated significantly more adequate performance than did their lower-class counterparts on two of the three skill dimensions.

Of greatest importance among these results is not what the aides *say* they would do, nor their immediate posttraining performance. Most consequential is their overt skill performance *in the classroom*. The Classroom Observation Instrument results do indicate substantial positive transfer from the training to application setting. In both their appropriate use of Mild Disapproval, and in their use of the three skills combined, aides receiving Structured Learning evidence performance superior to those receiving Didactic Learning or no treatment. While these findings also held separately for both social class groupings, there is again related evidence that middle-class aides perform more adequately than do lower-class aides.

We thus see from this investigation that a set of skills rather different in nature from those we have sought to teach earlier can also be taught reasonably successfully and rapidly by means of Structured Learning procedures. And furthermore, such procedures consistently proved more effective than a traditional lecture-discussion approach. Our current research, building on these findings, seeks to increase even more the carry over of adequate skill enactment from the training setting to the application setting. We are, in addition, going beyond the target skills of the Schneiman (1972) study, and are currently seeking to teach a full range of contingency management principles to large paraprofessional samples (Stein, Goldstein, Driscoll, & Sheets, 1973). The relative success of the efforts reported in the present chapter, it seems to us, both warrants and encourages such larger scale research examinations of Structured Learning for paraprofessional training.

*Part 4*

**CONCLUSION**

# Chapter 9

# FUTURE DIRECTIONS

We held at the outset of this book that successful treatment approaches for lower-class and working-class patients are singularly lacking, a position for which we presented considerable evidence in Chapter 1. In subsequent chapters, drawing upon research on class-linked child-rearing practices and personality development, language acquisition and usage, psychopathology, and a series of related areas, we sought to develop a rationale for a potentially more effective set of treatment procedures—a set we noted in Chapter 5 rests on a particularly sound base of laboratory research and clinical application with middle-class Ss and clients. We termed this approach, consisting of modeling, role playing, and social reinforcement, Structured Learning Therapy. We held this combination of procedures to be potentially "tailored to," or "prescriptive for," lower-class and working-class populations, particularly when used concretely to teach discrete interpersonal or personal skills. In Chapters 6–8 our initial research efforts testing Structured Learning Therapy were presented. Its utility for skill enhancement with both patient and paraprofessional samples was examined. Our evidence, we would hold, is most encouraging. It is beginning and tentative evidence, yet combines to suggest both the likely soundness of our rationale and the likely value of continued study and elaboration of Structured Learning Therapy. By "elaboration" we wish to underscore the need to avoid considering one's approach as "fixed" or "final." In fact, as will be seen shortly, we will present a particularly viable case for examining the addition of a fourth component to Structured Learning Therapy. It is all too common an occurrence in the fields of psychology and psychiatry that new therapies or therapeutic innovations somehow all too quickly become "traditional" or otherwise rigidified.

There is little about Structured Learning Therapy that is new: We only claim to have more systematically elaborated, applied, and evaluated a set of previously developed procedures than has been true in the past. There are but two broad conclusions we wish to draw from our series of investigations. First, we view the combined outcomes of these studies as further evidence for the value of laboratory investigation of basic change processes as a particularly sound base from which to derive psychothera-peutic interventions. To us, this conclusion has a host of implications, ranging from where one might most profitably point the therapy research-er for sources of truly useful hypotheses, to issues concerned with clinical psychology training—and in particular the continued value of the scien-tist-practitioner model. Our second overall conclusion is more directly clinical in nature, and holds that not only does further use and evaluation of Structured Learning Therapy appear most worthwhile, but, more gen-erally, we take our findings as support for the broader value of efforts to develop prescriptive, tailor-made, or idiosyncratic therapies, i.e., thera-pies more fully responsive to *significant* patient characteristics and less self-indulgently responsive to our preferred theoretical biases and upper middle-class life styles.

As suggested above, to us the best psychotherapy is "perpetually tran-sitional," never quite fixed or complete, always turning to the stimuli of new research and the feedback of clinical experience to improve its effec-tiveness. In the remainder of this chapter we wish to suggest some of the major directions in which Structured Learning Therapy might profitably move, and from which its effectiveness might increase. Some of these directions reflect explicit plans we ourselves have or are already imple-menting. Others, we hopefully leave with our encouragement to other in-vestigators.

### Transfer of Training

In spite of the rather consistent positive outcome of our research to date on Structured Learning, with but two exceptions these studies share a particularly significant weakness—a weakness present in the vast ma-jority of research on psychotherapy and behavior modification. We refer here to the absence of *active* concern about transfer of training. By "ac-tive" we mean the failure of the researcher, behavior modifier, or psy-chotherapist to implement interventions specifically designed to maximize the likelihood of significant positive transfer. Passive concern, e.g., follow-up measurement to discern if such transfer has occurred, is less rare, but active intervention is almost nonexistent. Whether it be two-thirds, one-half, or 90%; whether on global, specific, targeted, or other outcome criteria, it is clear that psychotherapy probably "works" rather frequently. But what does "works" mean? It is obviously one thing to obtain a significant $p$ value representing verbal or behavioral patient change measured immediately after one's therapeutic or experimental intervention, but quite another matter to effect *enduring* change in either a patient's real-life behavior or a therapist's subsequent clinical work. It is such enduring change which forms the goal of transfer training. We are now conducting investigations in which a full array of transfer training procedures are incorporated into our original modeling–role playing–social reinforcement approach. These procedures directly reflect the five separable characteristics of the training and/or criterion tasks that have been identified in laboratory contexts to function as transfer enhancers.

*1. General Principles.* Transfer of training has been demonstrated to be facilitated by providing S with general mediating principles governing performance on both the training and criterion tasks (Duncan, 1959; Goldbeck, Bernstein, Hillix, & Marx, 1957; Hendrickson & Schroeder, 1941; Judd, 1902; Miller, G. A., Heise, & Lichten, 1951; Ulmer, 1939; Woodrow, 1927). This same finding has been repeatedly substantiated in research on learning sets (Harlow, 1949), deutero-learning (Ruesch, 1957), advance organizers (Ausubel, 1963), and, perhaps most germane to our present research, also in studies of the effects of prior instructions on vicarious learning (Masters & Branch, 1969; Whalen, 1969).

*2. Response Availability.* Transfer of training has been demonstrated to be facilitated by procedures which maximize criterion response availability. It has been well established by now that, other things being equal, the response that has been emitted most frequently in the past will be emitted on subsequent occasions. This finding derives from studies of the frequency of evocation hypothesis (Underwood & Schulz, 1960); the spew hypothesis (Underwood & Schulz, 1960); and research on preliminary response pretraining (Atwater, 1953; Cantor, 1955; Gagne & Foster, 1949; Mandler, 1954; Mandler & Heinemann, 1956). This general result, which Mandler (1954) summarizes as ". . . learning to make an old response to a new stimulus showed increasing positive transfer as degree of original training was increased," is also consistent with research on overlearning. Overlearning is a procedure whereby learning extends over more trials than are necessary merely to produce *initial* changes in the S's behavior, a procedure that has been operationalized in the literature by running Ss through as many as 100 or more "extra" trials after criterion has been initially reached.

*3. Identical Elements.* In perhaps the earliest experimental concern with transfer enhancement, Thorndike (Deese, 1958) concluded that when there was a facilitative effect of one habit on another, it was to the extent that and because they shared identical elements. Ellis (1965) and Osgood (1953) have more recently emphasized the importance for transfer of similarity between stimulus and response members of the two tasks involved. Osgood (1953) concludes, ". . . the greater the similarity between practice and test stimuli, the greater the amount of positive transfer." This conclusion rests on a particularly solid base of experimental support, involving both motor (Crafts, 1935; Duncan, 1953; Gagne, Baker, & Foster, 1950) and verbal (Osgood, 1949, 1953; Underwood, 1951; Young & Underwood, 1954) behaviors. Implicit awareness of this principle of transfer enhancement has already been acted upon in the context of psychotherapy by investigators who have literally moved the therapy out of an office setting and into the patient's real-life, problem-relevant environment (Hsu, 1965; Jones, Kahn, & Wolcott, 1964; Lazarus, 1966; Stevenson, 1962), or who have enhanced the "real-lifeness" of certain stimuli in the office itself (Jones, 1960; Marlatt, 1968b).

*4. Stimulus Variety.* Callantine and Warren (1955), Duncan (1958), and Shore and Sechrest (1961) have each demonstrated that positive transfer is greater when a variety of training stimuli are employed. We have commented on this approach to transfer enhancement elsewhere, as it might be implemented in psychotherapy, by suggesting that one way would be to have each patient interact with more than one psychotherapist. Specifically, we proposed:

> The employment of several different therapists may . . . greatly increase the breadth of stimuli or the complexity of the total stimulus pattern to which the patient is exposed. The different personalities, styles, and even appearances of the separate therapists should become stimuli or cues for the desired responses. Since, presumably, all the therapists would be reinforcing responses in the same general class, the response class would become conditioned to a variety of interpersonal stimuli, and, since the exact form of the response is assumed to vary more when emitted in the presence of varying stimuli, greater response generalization should occur . . . [Goldstein *et al.,* 1966, p. 232].

*5. Performance Feedback.* Given successful implementation of both Structured Learning procedures and the four transfer principles discussed thus far, positive transfer may still fail to occur. As Tharp and Wetzel (1969) and many others have so fully demonstrated, stable and enduring performance of newly learned skills is very much at the mercy of real-life reinforcement contingencies. Absence of reinforcement is likely to lead to deterioration in skill enactment. We have described above two possible implementations of the performance feedback principle, in our use of two on-the-ward transfer trainers to help transfer and stabilize appropriate mealtime social behavior among patients and empathetic behavior by nurses. By this or other means, we view attention to systematic performance feedback as likely of great consequence, and certainly a high priority investigative concern.

## Procedural Refinement

A second potentially fruitful investigative path we would urge concerns efforts to refine the therapeutic use of modeling, role playing, and social reinforcement. Above all, such efforts require that the investigator remain fully in touch with, and innovatively responsive to, the continuing research literature in these three domains. More effective use of these Structured Learning components is likely to involve continued search for new characteristics of the model, the modeling display, and the observer which may function as modeling enhancers. It may involve new or altered procedures to increase observer attention, retention, and reproduction of the modeled behaviors. Procedures identified as increasing the likelihood that role-played behaviors will become an enduring part of the enactor's behavioral repertoire—improvisation, commitment, choice, and reward—are further areas of potentially worthwhile refinement. A great deal is known about procedures that facilitate or inhibit the effectiveness of reinforcement—nature, delay, magnitude, contingency basis, scheduling, and so forth. Each of these is a potential source for increasing the effectiveness of Structured Learning. Furthermore, for almost all of these modeling, role playing, and social reinforcement variables, there are matters of setting, frequency, duration, source, and relevance that might profitably be explored.

## Procedural Elaboration

Our understanding of the personality development, linguistic, and psychopathology research examined above led us to a treatment approach composed of modeling, role playing, and social reinforcement. We have stressed, however, that it would be most inappropriate to view this "psychotherapeutic prescription" as fixed or final. Research on behavior modification is thriving, and as it does new techniques are proposed and older techniques are better understood. Cognitive variables, wisely we feel, are increasingly being integrated with noncognitive concerns to form more powerful behavior change techniques. Such increased effectiveness is likely to be augmented even further by a rapidly growing technology in audiovisual and other fields. Which of these several behavior modification, cognitive, and technological developments will indeed add to the value of Structured Learning is a broad research question for the future.

One promising lead is already apparent. There has been a recent burgeoning of interest among persons concerned with psychotherapeutic effectiveness with utilization of audiovisual techniques. These developments are potentially relevant to all three components of Structured Learning. Perhaps obviously, the nature of one's modeling display is in large measure a function of audiovisual concerns. But this is also in part true for the nature and success of both role playing and social reinforcement delivery. In certain of our investigations, particularly the two Gutride et al. studies (1972a&b), patient role-play enactments were videotaped and played back to patients for critique, evaluation, and feedback purposes during the role-play periods. Considerable work has recently emerged on such self-confrontation (Bailey & Sowder, 1970; Berger, 1970; Bernal, 1969; Cornelison & Arsenian, 1960; Garner, 1970; Geertsma & Reivich, 1965; Moore, Chernell, & West, 1965), and the nature of this research clearly suggests that audiovisual feedback is a highly worthwhile area for future research, both generally and as a possible effectiveness-increasing addition to Structured Learning. Similarly useful application of audiovisual feedback may emerge when it is combined with Structured Learning procedures and used for therapist training purposes. This suggestion follows from both our own paraprofessional therapist studies and several reports of successful use of related audiovisual techniques for such training purposes (Benschoter, 1965; Gladfelter, 1970; Goldberg, 1967; Gruenberg, Liston, & Wayne, 1970; Kagan, 1970; Ruhe, Gundle, Haybourne, Forman, & Jacobs, 1960; Stoller, 1965; Yonge, 1965).

### New Clinical Applications

In our research to date we have worked almost exclusively with lower-class and working-class patient and paraprofessional samples. We have made much throughout this book of our goal of tailor-making treatments to samples, and feel that Structured Learning Therapy is an effective first approximation to a prescriptive therapy for the samples examined. Nevertheless, it must be recalled (Chapter 5) that most of the laboratory and clinical research that has been reported on modeling, role playing, and social reinforcement was conducted using middle-class samples. We would suggest, therefore, that a particularly worthwhile research undertaking would involve examination of the effectiveness of Structured Learning with middle-class patient and therapist samples. This suggestion is given added credence by the series of positive findings for middle-class teachers-aides exposed to Structured Learning in Schneiman's (1972) investigation reported earlier. Structured Learning procedures might also be profitably utilized with child and adolescent patients. While we have no direct evidence to support this suggestion, it should be noted that a considerable proportion of the laboratory research conducted by others on the components of Structured Learning, particularly modeling, employed child and adolescent Ss.

Related to these goals is the general desirability of seeking to develop and examine ever finer, increasingly specific therapeutic prescriptions. Our prescriptive basis, social class, is a broad basis indeed. We have found it to be a useful one at this stage in the development of Structured Learning Therapy, but would note that just as a social class designation highlights between-class differences and within-class commonalities, it also obscures within-class differences. Not only are any given group of lower-class individuals heterogeneous in many respects, but many of the dimensions on which they are heterogeneous may indeed be relevant for the planning and implementation of more individualized prescriptive treatments. Thus, social class as a basis for therapy construction must be considered but a beginning among many which are possible. Magaro's (1969) speculations (noted in Chapter 1) regarding the potential value of developing treatment approaches for hospitalized patients as a joint function of their social class and premorbid level of functioning is a likely positive step beyond our own prescriptive starting point. What other personality, demographic, behavioral, or related information will prove useful for the development of progressively more effective psychotherapeutic prescriptions remains, it seems to us, an exciting and challenging issue for further empirical study.

Not only may new clinical applications be sought by the use of new types of samples and increasingly individualized prescriptions, but also by examining skills we have not yet sought to teach. The following listing is certainly incomplete, but represents our effort to select skills for future investigation, by ourselves and others, that have been identified in the literature as: (1) those in which lower-class and working-class patients are often deficient, (2) those in which patients, independent of social class, are often deficient, and (3) those associated with successful performance as a psychotherapist. Consistent with our major emphasis upon prescriptive treatments, upon the notion of developing *both* change techniques and target skills to accord most fully with patients' life styles, recurring needs or characteristic environmental demands, the potential training targets listed below jointly reflect not only these bodies of relevant literature, but also major imputs we have actively and consistently sought from our lower-class and working-class patients.

1. *For lower-class and working-class patients:*
   a. *Internal control* (Gurin *et al.*, 1969; Masters, 1970; Reimanis, 1971; Rotter, 1966).
   b. *Interpersonal stress rehearsal* (Janis, 1958; Lazarus, R. S., 1966; Parad, 1965; Taplin, 1971).
   c. *Intentions seeking* (Kohn, 1959a & b, 1969).
   d. *Frustration tolerance* (Kohn, 1969, Levine & Scotch, 1970, Roman & Trice, 1967).
   e. *Tolerance for ambiguity* (Budner, 1962; Dibner, 1958; Dublin, 1968; Frenkel-Brunswik, 1949).
   f. *Need achievement* (Kleiner & Parker, 1963; McClelland, *et al.*; Atkinson, Clark, & Lowell, 1953; Sewell & Haller, 1959).
   g. *Reduction of information overload* (Miller, 1960; Schroeder & Suedfeld, 1970; Schroeder, Driver, & Streufert, 1965).
   h. *Accurate affective perception* (Beldoch, 1964; Cadman, Misbach, & Brown, 1954; Davitz, 1964; Ekman, Friesen, & Ellsworth, 1972).
   i. *Accurate affective responsiveness* (Davitz, 1964; Davitz & Mattis, 1964; Knapp, 1963).
   j. *Interpersonal trust* (Deutsch, 1960; Geller, 1966; Rotter, 1967).
   k. *Self-control of attention* (Broen, 1968; Ferster, 1965; McGhie, 1969; Meldman, 1970; Paul, 1969).
   l. *Impression management: healthy competent* (Braginsky, Grosse, & Ring, 1966; Fontana & Klein, 1968; Fontana, Klein, Lewis, & Levine, 1968.
2. *For lower-class and working-class paraprofessional therapists:*
   a. *Concreteness–specificity* (Carkhuff, 1969; Hart & Tomlinson, 1970; Truax & Carkhuff, 1967).
   b. *Immediacy* (Carkhuff, 1969; Hart & Tomlinson, 1970; Truax & Carkhuff, 1967).
   c. *Tolerance for ambiguity* (Crandall, 1969; Feldman & Rice, 1965; Riessman, 1969).
   d. *Attraction* (Byrne, 1971; Goldstein, 1971).

    *e. Supportiveness–reassurance* (Bugental, 1965; Parad, 1965).

    *f. Principles of contingency management* (Ayllon & Azrin, 1965, 1968).

This listing of personal and interpersonal skills that might profitably be examined in the context of Structured Learning completes our presentation. We wish to end on the simple note that the search for therapies that fit the patient seems an even more worthwhile endeavor to us. We urge others committed to both patient welfare and a fuller understanding of psychological change to actively join this search.

# MODELING SCRIPTS

**211**

Paraprofessional Skill-Enhancement Investigations

# PATIENT SKILL-ENHANCEMENT INVESTIGATIONS

### High Attraction–High Self-Disclosure

*T:**  I guess you don't like that very much . . . it makes you feel uncomfortable.

*P:†*  Yeah . . . but y'know, I . . . I don't feel uncomfortable talking to *you*. I sorta feel that you're . . . uh . . . that you're, I don't know . . . friendly or interested.

*T:*  OK . . . well . . . what I'd like to do now is ask you some questions about yourself. And I'd like you to answer them as best you can. First of all . . . I wonder if you could tell me what you see as the causes of your drinking problem.

*P:*  Hmmmm . . . that's a good question. I'm not really sure exactly what the causes are . . . but I know for sure that at this point I am an alcoholic and I obviously have a drinking problem. . . . I think it has something to do with my feeling depressed or nervous 'cause those are the times I drink the most. . . . Also, by the way, when I'm feeling sorta lonely . . . Before I came here, though, it got to the point where I couldn't stop and was drinking all the time. . . . Let's see . . . I think I started drinking sorta heavy in my middle 20s—humph, I used to think it was just social drinking then, but looking back, I gotta admit it was really more than just that. . . . But I really can't remember any one thing, you know, that really . . . that really "caused" it—except like I said before, when I'm feeling lonely or down in the dumps. . . . I sure would like to change, though . . . and get myself out of this mess.

---

* *T* represents Therapist throughout Appendix.
† *P* represents Patient throughout Appendix except where noted otherwise.

**213**

*T:*   OK . . . Now, try to describe to me what you see as your strong points and your weak points.

*P:*   Uh huh . . . well . . . one of my weak points is my alcoholism. At this point it's really my weakest. . . . Along with this I also get involved with telling lies . . . I don't like the way that sounds but that's really what it amounts to . . . you know, like I'll tell my wife or friends—and sometimes even myself—that I'll quit drinking or that I'll cut down to one a day. . . . Sometimes when I say this I even believe it myself, but then . . . I'll go ahead and keep drinking anyway . . . or . . . even worse, I'll sneak in a couple and then go around pretending and denying that I had any . . . and then I get to feeling guilty. (pause) . . . There are other things, too . . . for example . . . well, for example . . . lotsa times I feel I'm not as good as other people. . . . Sorta generally, I think . . . like when I'm working . . . I feel that the other guys on the job are better than me—not just because of my alcoholism . . . I try to tell myself that it's bullshit, but somehow I still feel inferior. . . . One thing, for example, I feel that I can't talk to people . . . that I can't carry on a conversation. (pause) . . . Jesus, y'know I've never really been able to be this frank to anyone about these things before. . . . Somehow, though, I feel pretty comfortable talking to you.

*T:*   Ok . . . well, what about the other kind?

*P:*   Oh, you mean my strong points. . . . Humph, I can't seem to think of as many strong points as I can weak points. Well . . . I'm here . . . and I feel that I really want to do something about my drinking. . . . I would consider that a strong point . . . . Also, I feel I'm a pretty friendly person —even when I'm not drinking! . . . And when I put my mind to something, I *used* to be able to get it done—except, of course, when it came to drinking.

*T:*   OK . . . now I'd like you to tell me the kinds of things that get you angry.

*P:*   Hmmmmm . . . that's a good question, too. . . . The kinds of things that get me angry. . . . Well, to tell the truth, I get angry at *myself* a lot, you know . . . like I said before . . . when I sneak around and pretend I'm not drinking when I really am . . . and when I can't keep my promises to stop. . . . Sometimes I even get angry with myself for being angry! . . . Like when someone criticizes me for doing something wrong. . . . I'll get angry at that person even though he was right. . . . And then I'll get angry at myself for being angry . . . 'cause the other guy was really right. . . . Also, when my wife gets after me for drinking or for yelling at the kids. . . . I'll get angry at her even though I know she's right. . . . It's hard for me to . . . to accept the fact that she's right . . . and I certainly can't admit it to her. . . . Let's see. . . . Another time I get angry is when I'm hurt—I don't mean physically hurt, but, you know, emotionally . . . like when my wife says something like 'you can go to hell for all I care' . . . or if she just *does* something that makes me feel like she doesn't care. . . . When she does these kinds of things, I feel bad, and either I blow up at her . . . or just boil inside and then go off drinking. . . . (pause) . . . . I get angry a lot about petty things, too . . . like when I've just missed a bus . . . or left the house forgetting something that I had to take with me . . . or if I stub my toe . . . or waiting in a restaurant a half hour before the damn waitress gets around to serving me—you know . . . things like that.

T:    Well . . . what are some of the things you do about your anger—how do you handle it?

P:    What do I do about it? . . . Well . . . I usually cuss or yell—either to myself or aloud. . . . Actually, I yell a lot at other people, too. . . . At the family—my parents, my wife—if I'm angry at her—or at the kids. . . . There are times, too, when I take my anger out against the family when the cause of my anger is something else. . . . Like if something on the job gets me pissed off . . . instead of yelling at the boss . . . or even talking to him about it . . . I'll wait 'til I get home and yell at the wife and kids. . . . Then she gets angry at me and we get into a real fight. (pause) . . . . Lotsa times it's hard for me to . . . to face . . . or . . . or come to grips with what's making me angry. . . . Sometimes I don't do anything about my anger—just keep it bottled up inside and hope it'll go away. . . . But it seems as if it never does. . . . Or else I'll either get depressed and start drinking . . . or take it out on something or somebody else. . . .

T:    OK . . . what about the kinds of things that get you anxious, or fearful?

P:    . . . Well . . . some of the same things that get me angry . . . also get me anxious and upset. . . . Like for instance, when I get very, very angry . . . lotsa times I can even feel myself shaking. . . . One thing I've been afraid of lately is that my wife . . . my wife . . . may leave me and take the kids. . . . I feel that I really need her and I don't know what I'm going to do if she leaves. . . . Another thing that I think ties in with this is a fear I have of being alone—I don't mean alone for like an hour or a day, or anything like that—I mean real loneliness . . . with no one around who really cares. (pause) . . . . Sometimes I worry about what people think of me. . . . Especially when I'm meeting new people. . . . I get very tense and nervous and try to make a good impression—and usually end up making a fool out of myself. (pause) . . . . Another thing . . . it's not easy to say, but I'm . . . I'm very afraid of failure— failure, in general, like with that inferiority stuff I told you about. . . . Like doing a lousy job in my work; . . . as a husband; . . . as a father; . . . . Actually . . . failure as . . . uh . . . as a person, or as . . . as a man. . . . Also, I have a fear in the back of my mind that one of these days I'm really going to get hurt—or even killed—from drinking so much.

T:    Well . . . how do you handle these things?

P:    Yeah . . . that's a good point . . . . Well . . . as far as doing things about it . . . I really haven't been very successful . . . I mean, it's sorta the same as anger . . . I may blow off some steam and try to unwind—like I'll go bowling or play golf . . . but it doesn't always work. . . . Other times, I'll go to sleep. . . . I know this is just an escape, but I sure don't feel nervous when I'm sleeping—although sometimes I do get bad dreams. . . . Lotsa times, though, I'll drink. . . . I know that's an escape, too, but it does give me relief for awhile. . . .

T:    All right. . . . Now, I'd like you to tell me what your parents were like.

P:    My parents . . . well . . . my parents and I have never really gotten along very well. . . . I care about them . . . you know—I care what happens to them— . . . but as far as any real deep feelings go . . . I have very little for them. . . . Excuse me . . . do you mind if I smoke? . . . Anyway, as I was saying . . . I don't really have any deep feelings for them. . . . There have been times, in fact, that I've hated them . . . (pause) . . . . Let's see . . . my father was a fairly good provider, but I remember that it was my mother who really wore the pants in the family. . . . One thing, though . . . I always got the feeling they weren't loving enough—I don't know if those are the right words for it—but, you know what I mean . . . that they didn't show enough caring . . . or . . . or affection. I don't think they were this way on purpose. . . . I just think that they couldn't show this caring—at least not to each other or to me. . . . They've always been sorta cold. . . . I'd like to be able to say that my father was an alcoholic and that he started me off on it . . . but that wasn't the way it went at all. . . . In fact, they hardly touched the stuff . . . so I can't blame them. . . . I feel that there's something about the way *I've* handled things that's gotten me into this mess.

T:    OK . . . tell me . . . if you had your choice, in what way would your parents be different?

P:    How would I like them to be different? . . . Well . . . I think mostly in the fact that they could've cared more—that in, that they could've showed it—you know, been warmer and not so cold. . . . That's mainly it, but of course, I wouldn't have minded it if they had been millionaires, as well! (pause) . . . . You know . . . I guess I said this before . . . but even though all you've been doin' the past 5 or 10 minutes is asking me questions . . . I still . . . for some reason or another . . . feel comfortable talking to you and being honest about myself. . . . For example, I feel that *you're* warm and that *you* care.

T:    Well . . . we all have various feelings about certain people. . . . I'm glad that you can *express* yours. There's one more question I'd like to ask. . . . Most people have some sort of sexual problem. . . . I wonder if you could tell me what sort of difficulties you've had in this area.

P:    Boy . . . you're not pulling any punches, are you! . . . (pause) . . . Well . . . (hesitates) . . . to be honest, I . . . I do have some problems with sex. . . . It's not easy to talk about . . . but . . . but I feel I can trust you. . . . Anyway . . . what it amounts to is that I have trouble in bed. . . .

*T:* How do you mean. . .

*P:* Well . . . I can't. . . . I can't get an erection—not always, but *most* of the time. . . . Don't misunderstand me . . . I really feel I love my wife . . . and she certainly is good looking enough . . . but for a long time now . . . I just haven't . . . haven't been able to make it in bed. . . . I don't know what it is . . . whether it's that I get nervous or what. . . . Hell . . . it got to the point where every time I tried, I was afraid that I wasn't going to be able to . . . and then, sure enough . . . I couldn't. It's gotten to the point, now, that I've even stopped trying. . . . I really feel rotten about the whole damn thing . . . not only for myself . . . but for my wife, too . . . Generally, she's been pretty good about the whole thing—but, Christ! . . . what can you expect! . . . (pause) . . . There is *one* way that I have been able to get an erection—and that's by . . . that's by masturbating—but, shit, that only makes me feel guilty and it sure ain't . . . it sure ain't the same as with my wife. . . . Even . . . even when I get an erection this way and then, before . . . before I come . . . if I right away try it . . . with my wife . . . as soon as I start to enter her . . . it disappears and just becomes . . . becomes limp again. . . . Let me tell you, Doc, . . . *it is frustrating as hell!* (pause) . . . You know . . . I was just thinking . . . I wouldn't be surprised if this sex bit also has something to do with my drinking problem. . . .

*T:* Well, it's good that you're giving some thought to these problems. (pause) . . . Well . . . thank you very much . . . that's all for now. . . . I know it's not been easy for you to talk about all these things, but I'm sure the information you've given me will be helpful. . . . We'll be getting in touch with you soon. . . .

*P:* . . . Hey, Doc . . . I'd like to be able to see *you* again. . . . Will I be able to?

## High Attraction–Low Self-Disclosure

*T:* I guess you don't like that very much . . . it makes you feel uncomfortable. . . .

*P:* Yeah . . . but y'know . . . I . . . I don't feel uncomfortable talking to *you* . . . . I sorta feel that you're . . . uh . . . that you're . . . I don't know . . . friendly . . . or interested.

*T:* OK . . . well, what I'd like to do now is ask you some questions about yourself . . . and I'd like you to answer them as best you can. First of all . . . I wonder if you could tell me what you see as the causes of your drinking problem. . .

*P:* Hmmm . . . that's a good question . . . I guess maybe I do have some-

what of a drinking problem . . . but . . . I'm not so sure I'm a real alcoholic—you know what I mean—. . . Yeah, I drink at times . . . but not
really that much . . . . Let's see . . . I guess I drink most when I'm feeling low or nervous . . . but then, that's not so unusual, is it? . . . I mean
after all . . . everybody probably drinks most when they're feeling that
way . . . (pause) . . . Let's see . . . when did I first start drinking?
. . . Well . . . although I had—you know—a couple of drinks here and
there in my teens . . . I guess I really didn't start drinking regularly until
my mid-20s . . . but even then . . . I guess it was really more of a
social drinking type thing . . . not really alcoholic drinking. . . .
(pause) . . . Y'know . . . maybe it's just that I *think* I have problems . . . .
Maybe that's really all there is to it . . . . I think that if I really tried
to stop—and, after all, I've been able to do it before— . . . I think
that if I really tried . . . I'd be OK. . . .

T:    OK . . . now, try to describe to me what you see as your strong points
and your weak points.

P:    Uh huh . . . my strong points . . . let's see . . . well . . . I would consider myself a pretty friendly guy—even when I'm not drinking—. . .
And when I put my mind to something . . . I usually get it done. . . . I
guess I'm fairly intelligent and fairly good looking. . . . I don't get angry very often . . . and I don't get tense or depressed very often, either
—although I'm sure a lot of other guys do . . . . Humph . . . this probably sounds to you as if I think I'm "Mr. Great," . . . but I guess we all
have a tendency to think highly of ourselves. . . . Let's see . . . what
else. . . I'm a good husband and father . . . but I bet my wife wouldn't
tell you that . . . but then, all she does is nag, anyway. . . . In fact
. . . she's probably a big reason why I keep drinking . . . I think anybody would drink with a wife like that. . . . Another thing on the strong
side—I guess I said this before—. . . but I do get along pretty well with
people. . . . In fact, that probably has something to do with my drinking, too . . . 'cause a bunch of us usually get together and go to a
bar. . . . I'm pretty good at my job—in fact, I do quite well— . . . the
boss doesn't always agree with me . . . but *I* think I am . . . I did miss
some days once in awhile . . . but not all that many. . . . Besides,
other guys missed days, too . . . (pause) . . . Jesus, y'know . . .
I've never really been able to talk like this to anyone before. . . . Somehow, though . . . I feel pretty comfortable talking to you.

T:    OK . . . well, what about the other kind?

P:    Oh yeah . . . my weak points . . . ha, ha, . . . almost forgot about
those. . . . Maybe that's because I really don't think I have that
many. . . . Let's see . . . I guess maybe you could call my drinking a
weak point . . . but after all . . . I really don't drink that much . . . and
I have been able to stop from time to time . . . and for fairly long
periods. . . . Hell, I know a lot of guys with problems a lot worse than
mine . . . and I don't mean just drinking! . . . At least I'm not a junkie!

*T:*   OK . . . now I'd like you to tell me the kinds of things that get you angry.

*P:*   Hmmm . . . that's a good question, too. . . . The kinds of things that get me angry. . . . Well, to tell the truth, I really don't think I get angry that much—I guess maybe I get *annoyed* at times—. . . but not really *angry*. . . . And when I do get annoyed, it's mostly just at little things. . .—you know—. . . normal annoyances like missing a bus; . . . stubbing my toe; . . . forgetting something I needed and then having to go back and get it;. . . you know . . . the same things that everybody gets annoyed at. . . (pause) . . . Oh yeah . . . I get annoyed at my wife once in awhile, too . . . but, hell . . . it's her own fault . . . Like whenever I'd say I'd stop drinking . . . She'll keep asking me if I had any . . . or say that my breath smells funny . . . and even when she's not asking me all these questions—I'm sure she's thinking that I sneaked in a couple, or that she doesn't believe me. . . . Well . . . anyway . . . I keep tellin' her that when she keeps getting on my back like that, *she drives* me to drink. . . . Also my kids . . . Christ! . . . not a moment's peace . . . I get home from work and just want to relax for awhile . . . and they're yelling . . . And comes the weekend—which is the only chance I get to sleep late—and they're running around, screaming . . . or fighting with each other. . . . Hell, anybody would get annoyed at that! . . . And then there's the job . . . . I swear I don't know why I stay there. . . . With all the time I've put in for them . . . you'd think they'd show some appreciation . . . but, no . . . what do I get . . . criticism! . . . I wouldn't even mind it so much if they were right—but most of the time, they're not. . . . With all these things to put up with . . . a guy wouldn't be *normal* if he *didn't* drink.

*T:*   Well . . . what are some of the things you do about your anger . . . how do you handle it?

*P:*   Hmmm . . . yeah . . . what *do* I do about it? . . . Well, since I don't get angry that much . . . there's really not that much to handle. . . . I know you're probably thinking that's contradictory to what I said before . . . but not really . . . I mean, sure I get annoyed at times . . . but really not that often—and when I do, it usually doesn't last. . . . Most of the time it just goes away by itself. . . .

*T:*   OK . . . what about the kinds of things that get you anxious, or fearful?

*P:*   Well . . . I really don't *get* these feelings very often. . . . Sure, *normal* type fears . . . like if I'm driving along and see some maniac coming straight at me . . . but anybody would get upset in a situation like that . . . (pause) . . . I guess I've been this way as far back as I can remember. . . . Even in school, when everybody else used to get scared before a test . . . it never really used to upset me that much. . . . Sure, I guess I got sorta nervous once in awhile . . . but nothing compared to the other guys. . . . I'm sorry if I disappoint you by not having any of these fears . . . . Oh . . .—wait a minute—. . . I just remembered . . .

when I was a kid, I used to be a little bit afraid of dogs. . . . But actually, there was a very simple explanation for it . . . I don't think it was anything unusual . . . it was just that once, when I was coming home from school . . . a dog bit me . . . And I was afraid of dogs for about a year after that. . . . Really, though, I guess my fear was just a normal reaction—especially since I was just a kid at the time. . . . Now, dogs don't bother me at all. . . .

T:     Well . . . how do you handle these things? . .

P:     Yeah . . . that's a good point . . . except that I don't get nervous that often . . . so there's really nothing much to handle. . . . I really don't know what else to say. . . .

T:     All right . . . now, I'd like you to tell me what your parents were like.

P:     My parents . . . there's a real story. . . . You asked before what I thought was the cause of my drinking . . . well, I guess I've been giving them to you—my wife; . . . my job; . . . and now my parents. . . . In fact, my parents probably had the most to do with it . . . . I mean . . . aren't they responsible for how a person grows up and what he turns out to be? . . . Excuse me . . . do you mind if I smoke? . . . For example, "love" . . . I don't think they knew what the word meant—or maybe they did for my older brother . . . but not for me! . . . I'm sure you've heard this story before . . . but they were always comparing me to him . . . "why can't you be like your brother, blah, blah, blah" . . . as if I had anything to do with it—they're the ones that made me what I was. . . . That's what gets me the most—there was nothing I could do about it . . . then—or now. . . . You probably think I'm blaming everything on them—saying that they're the cause of my troubles— . . . well, I don't think I'm that far wrong. . . . Although they, themselves, didn't drink that much—in fact, they hardly touched the stuff— . . . they sure knew how to drive a person to it!

T:     OK . . . tell me . . . if you had your choice . . . in what way would your parents be different?

P:     How would I like them to be different? . . . Well, for starters . . . how about different parents, altogether. . . . I'm sure I would've been much better off that way. . . . In fact, I'm sure I wouldn't have started drinking so much, either . . . (pause) . . . You know . . . I guess I said this before . . . but even though all you've been doin' the past 5 or 10 minutes is asking me questions . . . I still . . . for some reason or another . . . feel comfortable talking to you and telling you these things. . . . For example, I feel that *you're* warm . . . and that *you* care.

T:     Well . . . we all have various feelings about certain people; . . . I'm glad that you can *express* yours. There's one more question I'd like to ask. . . . Most people have some sort of sexual problem . . . I wonder if you could tell me what sort of difficulties you've had in this area.

P:     Boy . . . you're not pulling any punches, are you! . . . Well . . . to tell the truth . . . I don't think I have any difficulties in this area . . . it's my *wife* you should be talking to. . . .

T: How do you mean?

P: Well . . . *I've* been fine . . . but over the past couple of years . . . she's been sorta turned off—actually *she's* the one that needs the help. . . . I guess maybe she figures that she's had her children and now there's no reason to go to bed anymore. . . . Well . . . whatever it is . . . her attitude sure drives me up a wall! . . . See what I mean when I say that she's one of the reasons I drink—with that kind of attitude to put up with . . . who wouldn't! . . . Humph . . . to listen to her, you'd think I was at fault. . . . Whenever I go out at night she's always asking where I'm going . . . and what I'm doing—as if she thinks I'm going out with other women. . . . But I don't. . . . I don't know why I don't . . . I certainly have good reason to . . . I'm sure other guys in the same situation, would. . . . It wouldn't be so bad if she'd just leave me alone *all the time* . . . but she's always either complaining or nagging or asking me questions . . . and then when *I* want to get some satisfaction . . . it's no go . . . (pause) . . . You know . . . I've been thinking . . . what with my parents, my wife, and my job . . . I've been getting pretty much of a raw deal. . . . I'm beginning to see that these are the causes of my drinking . . . and if I can change some of *these* things . . . I oughta be OK. . . .

T: Well . . . it's good that you're giving some thought to these problems . . . (pause) . . . Well . . . thank you very much . . . that's all for now. . . . I know it's not been easy for you to talk about all these things, but I'm sure the information you've given me will be helpful. . . . We'll be getting in touch with you soon.

P: . . . Hey, Doc . . . I'd like to be able to see *you* again . . . will I be able to?


## Low Attraction—High Self-Disclosure

T: I guess you don't like that very much . . . it makes you feel uncomfortable. . . .

P: No . . . not really . . . but I do feel uncomfortable talking to you like this. . . .

T: OK . . . well, what I'd like to do now is ask you some questions about yourself. And I'd like you to answer them as best you can. First of all, I wonder if you could tell me what you see as the causes of your drinking problem?

P: Isn't that what I'm here to find out? . . . I mean . . . I figured that's what *you* people were supposed to tell *me* . . . well . . . OK . . . I'm not really sure exactly what the causes are . . . but I know for sure that at this point I *am* an alcoholic and I obviously have a drinking problem. . . . I think it has something to do with my feeling depressed or nervous, 'cause those are the times I drink the most. . . . Also, by the way, when I'm feeling sorta lonely. . . . Before I came here, though, it got to the point where I couldn't stop and was drinking all the time. . . . Let's see . . . I think I started drinking sorta heavy in my middle 20s— humph . . . I used to think it was just social drinking then, but looking back, I gotta admit it was really more than just that. . . . You doctors are always talking about things in the mind . . . but I really can't remember any one thing, you know, that really . . . that really . . . "caused" it—except like I said before, when I'm feeling lonely or down in the dumps. . . . I sure would like to change, though . . . and get myself out of this mess. . . .

T:   OK . . . now try to describe to me what you see as your strong points and your weak points.

P:   Humph . . . are these questions really supposed to help me! . . . OK . . . well . . . one of my weak points is my alcoholism . . . at this point it's really my weakest. . . . Along with this I also get involved with telling lies—I don't like the way that sounds but that's really what it amounts to— . . . you know, like I'll tell my wife or friends—and sometimes even myself—that I'll quit drinking or that I'll cut down to one a day. . . . Sometimes when I say this I even believe it myself, but then . . . I'll go ahead and keep drinking anyway . . . or, even worse . . . I'll sneak in a couple and then go around pretending and denying that I had any . . . and then I get to feeling guilty . . . (pause) . . . There are other things, too . . . for example . . . well, for example . . . lotsa times I feel I'm not as good as other people . . . Sorta generally, I think . . . like when I'm working . . . I feel that the other guys on the job are better than me—not just because of my alcoholism. . . . I try to tell myself that it's bullshit . . . but somehow I still feel inferior. . . . One thing, for example . . . I feel that I can't talk to people . . . that I can't carry on a conversation . . . (pause) . . . Oh, yeah . . . there's another thing, too. . . . I don't like to admit it . . . but I . . . I get to feeling lonely a lot.

T:   OK . . . well . . . what about the other kind?

P:   Oh . . . you mean my strong points. . . . Humph . . . I can't seem to think of as many strong points as I can weak points . . . well . . . I'm here . . . and I feel that I really want to do something about my drinking. . . . I would consider that a strong point. . . . Also . . . I feel I'm a pretty friendly person—even when I'm not drinking! . . . And when I put my mind to something, I *used* to be able to get it done—except, of course, when it came to drinking. . . .

T:   OK . . . now I'd like you to tell me the kinds of things that get you angry.

P:   . . . I don't know . . . these questions seem like a waste of time to me. . . . You want to know when I get angry, huh? . . . Why is it you doctors always try to get us to say that we're "hostile" about something? . . . well . . . never mind. . . . To tell the truth, I get angry at *myself* a lot . . . you know . . . like I said before . . . when I sneak around and pretend I'm not drinking when I really am . . . and when I can't keep my promises to stop. . . . Sometimes I even get angry with myself for being angry! . . . Like when someone criticizes me for doing something wrong. . . . I'll get angry at that person even though he was right. . . . And then I'll get angry at myself for being angry . . . 'cause the other guy was really right. . . . Also, when my wife gets after me for drinking or for yelling at the kids . . . I'll get angry at her even though I know she's right. . . . It's hard for me to . . . to accept the fact that she's right . . . and I certainly can't admit it to her. . . . Let's see . . . Another time I get angry is when I'm hurt . . . I don't mean physically hurt, but, you know, emotionally . . . like when my wife says something like "you can go to hell for all I care" . . . or if she just *does* something that makes me feel like she doesn't care. . . . When she does these kinds of things, I feel bad . . . and either I blow up at her . . . or just boil inside and then go off drinking . . . (pause) . . . I get angry a lot about petty things, too. . . . Like when I've just missed a bus . . . or left the house forgetting something that I had to take with me . . . or if I stub my toe . . . or waiting in a restaurant a half hour before the damn waitress gets around to serving me . . . you know . . . things like that. . . .

T:   Well . . . what are some of the things you do about your anger—how do you handle it?

P:   How do I handle it? . . . well . . . I usually cuss or yell—either to myself or out loud. . . . Actually, I yell a lot at other people, too . . . at the family—my parents; . . . my wife—if I'm angry at her—, or at the kids. . . . There are times, too, when I take my anger out against the family when the cause of my anger is something else. . . . Like if something on the job gets me pissed off . . . instead of yelling at the boss . . . or even talking to him about it . . . I'll wait 'til I get home and yell at the wife and kids. . . . Then she gets angry at me and we get into a real fight . . . (pause) . . . Lotsa times it's hard for me to . . . to face . . . or . . . or come to grips with what's making me angry. . . . Sometimes I don't do anything about my anger—just keep it bottled up inside and hope it'll go away. . . . But it seems as if it never does. . . . Or else I'll either get depressed and start drinking . . . or take it out on something or somebody else. . . .

T:   OK . . . what about the kinds of things that get you anxious, or fearful?

P:   What kind of questions *are* these? . . . It sounds to me that this is the same as before . . . 'cause some of the same things that get me angry, also get me anxious and upset. . . . Like, for instance, when I get very, very angry . . . lotsa times I can even feel myself shaking. . . . One thing I've been afraid of lately is that my wife . . . my wife . . . may leave me and take the kids. . . . I feel that I really need her and I don't know what I'm going to do if she leaves. . . . Another thing, that I think ties in with this, is a fear I have of being alone—I don't mean alone for like an hour . . . or a day, or anything like that— . . . I mean real loneliness . . . with no one around who really cares . . . (pause) . . . Sometimes I worry about what people think of me . . . especially when I'm meeting new people . . . I get very tense and nervous and try to make a good impression . . . and usually end up making a fool of myself . . . (pause) . . . Another thing . . . it's not easy to say . . . but I'm . . . I'm very afraid of failure—failure, in general . . . like with that inferiority stuff I told you about . . . like doing a lousy job in my work; . . . as a husband; . . . as a father; . . . actually, failure as . . . uh . . . as a person, or as . . . as a man. . . ./Also, I have a fear in the back of my mind that one of these days I'm really going to get hurt—or even killed —from drinking so much.

T:    Well . . . how do you handle these things?
P:    What do you mean, "how do I handle these things?" . . . . If I were able to handle them I wouldn't be here. . . . I obviously haven't been very successful. . . . I mean . . . it's sorta the same as anger . . . I may blow off some steam and try to unwind—like I'll go bowling or play golf . . . but it doesn't always work. . . . Other times . . . I'll go to sleep . . . I know this is just an escape, but I sure don't feel nervous when I'm sleeping . . . although sometimes I do get bad dreams. . . . Lotsa times, though, I'll drink. . . . I know that's an escape, too, but it does give me relief for awhile.

T:    All right . . . now, I'd like you to tell me what your parents were like.
P:    . . . I really don't see the point of these questions . . . but if you really want to know . . . OK . . . my parents . . . well . . . my parents and I have never really gotten along very well. . . . I care about them . . . you know—I care what happens to them— . . . but as far as any real deep feelings go . . . I have very little for them. . . . Hey, is it OK if I I smoke? . . . d'ya got a light? . . . Anyway . . . as I was saying . . . I don't really have any deep feelings for them. . . . There have been times, in fact, that I've hated them . . . (pause) . . . Let's see . . . my father was a fairly good provider . . . but I remember that it was my mother who really wore the pants in the family. . . . One thing . . . though . . . I always got the feeling they weren't loving enough—I don't know if those are the right words for it—but, you know what I mean . . . that they didn't show enough caring . . . or . . . or affection. . . . I don't think they were this way on purpose . . . I just think that they couldn't show this "caring" . . . at least not to each other or to me. . . . They've just always been sorta cold. . . . I'd like to be able to say that Father was an alcoholic and that he started me off on it . . . but that wasn't the way it went at all . . . . in fact they hardly touched the stuff . . . . so, I can't blame them. . . . I feel that there's something about the way I've handled things that's gotten me into this mess.

*T:* OK . . . tell me . . . if you had your choice, in what way would your parents be different?

*P:* How would I like them to be different? . . . Well . . . I think mostly in the fact that they could've cared more—that is, that they could've showed it—. . . you know . . . been warmer and not so cold. . . . That's mainly it . . . but, of course, I wouldn't have minded it if they had been millionaires, as well! . . . (pause) . . . You know . . . it just occurred to me . . . . All you've been doin' the past 5 or 10 minutes is asking me questions. . . . I get the feeling you're not really interested in what I'm saying . . . that you just want to . . . sorta . . . put me on the spot. . . .

*T:* Well . . . we all have various feelings about certain people. . . . . I'm glad that you can *express* yours. . . . There's one more question I'd like to ask. . . . Most people have some sort of sexual problem. . . . I wonder if you could tell me what sort of difficulties you've had in this area.

*P:* Humph . . . I was wondering when you'd get around to asking something like that! Why is it you guys always think that there's gotta be something "sexual"? . . . (pause) . . . well . . . (hesitate) . . . to be honest . . . I . . . I do have some problems with sex . . . and I find it hard to talk about it to you. . . . Anyway . . . what it amounts to is that I have trouble in bed. . . .

*T:* How do you mean?

*P:* Well . . . I can't . . . I can't get an erection—not always, but *most* of the time. . . . Don't misunderstand me . . . I really feel I love my wife . . . and she certainly is good looking enough . . . but for a long time now . . . I just haven't . . . haven't been able to make it in bed. . . . I don't know what it is . . . whether it's that I get nervous, or what. . . . Hell . . . it got to the point where every time I tried, I was afraid that I wasn't going to be able to . . . and then, sure enough . . . I couldn't. . . . It's gotten to the point, now, that I've even stopped trying. . . . I really feel rotten about the whole damn thing . . . not only for myself . . . but for my wife, too. . . . Generally, she's been pretty good about the whole thing . . . but, Christ! . . . what can you expect! . . . (pause) . . . There is *one* way that I have been able to get an erection—and that's by . . . that's by masturbating—but, shit, that only makes me feel guilty and . . . it sure ain't . . . it sure ain't the same as with my wife. . . . Even . . . even when I get an erection this way and then, before . . . before I come . . . if I right away try it . . . with my wife . . . as soon as I start to enter her . . . it disappears and just becomes . . . becomes limp again. . . . Let me tell you, Doc . . . *it is frustrating as hell!* (pause) . . . You know . . . I was just thinking . . . I wouldn't be surprised if this sex bit also has something to do with my drinking problem. . . .

*T:* Well . . . it's good that you're giving some thought to these problems . . . (pause) . . . well . . . thank you very much . . . that's all for now

. . . I know it's not been easy for you to talk about all these things . . . but I'm sure the information you've given me will be helpful. . . . We'll be getting in touch with you soon.

*P:*    Doc . . . I . . . I don't mean anything personal . . . but do you think it would be possible for me to see *somebody else* next time?

## Low Attraction—Low Self-Disclosure

*T:*    I guess you don't like that very much . . . it makes you feel uncomfortable. . . .

*P:*    No . . . not really . . . but I do feel uncomfortable talking to you like this. . . .

*T:*    OK . . . well . . . what I'd like to do now is ask you some questions about yourself. And I'd like you to answer them as best you can. First of all, I wonder if you could tell me what you see as the causes of your drinking problem?

*P:*    Isn't that what I'm here to find out! . . . I mean . . . I figured that's what *you* people were supposed to tell *me*. . . . well . . . OK . . . I guess maybe I do have somewhat of a drinking problem . . . but I'm not so sure I'm a real alcoholic—you know what I mean. . . . Yeah, I drink at times . . . but really not that much. . . . Let's see . . . I guess I drink most when I'm feeling low or nervous . . . but then, that's not so unusual, is it? . . . I mean, after all . . . everybody probably drinks most when they're feeling that way . . . (pause) . . . Let's see . . . when did I first start drinking . . . well . . . although I had, you know, a couple of drinks here and there in my teens, I guess I really didn't start drinking regularly until my mid-20s. . . . But, even then . . . I guess it was really more of a social drinking type thing . . . not really alcoholic drinking . . . (pause) . . . Y'know . . . maybe it's just that I *think* I have problems. . . . Maybe that's really all there is to it. . . . Nothing personal . . . but you doctors are always talking about things in the mind. . . . I think that if I really tried to stop—and, after all, I've been able to do it before—. . . I think that if I really tried . . . I'd be OK.

*T:*    OK . . . now, try to describe to me what you see as your strong points and your weak points.

*P:*    Humph . . . are these questions really supposed to help me! . . . OK . . . my strong points . . . let's see . . . well, I would consider myself a pretty friendly guy—even when I'm not drinking. . . . And when I put my mind to something . . . I usually get it done. . . . I guess I'm fairly intelligent and fairly good looking . . . I don't get angry very often . . . And I don't get tense or depressed very often, either—although I'm sure a lot of other guys do. . . . Humph . . . this probably sounds to you as if I think I'm "Mr. Great" . . . but I guess we all have a tendency to think highly of ourselves. . . . Let's see . . . what else . . . I'm a good husband and father . . . but I bet my wife wouldn't tell you that . . . But then, all she does is nag, anyway. . . . In fact . . . she's probably a big reason why I keep drinking. I think anybody would drink with a wife like that. . . . Another thing on the strong side—I guess I said this before—but I do get along pretty well with people. . . . In fact, that probably has something to do with my drinking, too, 'cause a bunch of us usually get together and go to a bar. . . . I'm pretty good at my job—in fact, I do quite well—. . . the boss doesn't always agree with me . . . but *I* think I am. . . . I did miss some days once in awhile . . . but not all that many. . . . Besides, other guys missed days, too. . . .

T:    OK . . . well . . . what about the other kind?

P:    Oh, yeah . . . my weak points . . . ha, ha . . . almost forgot about those. . . . Maybe that's because I really don't think I have that many. . . . Let's see . . . I guess maybe you could call my drinking a weak point . . . but after all . . . I really don't drink that much, and I have been able to stop from time to time . . . and for fairly long periods. . . . Hell, I know a lotta guys with problems a lot worse than mine . . . and I don't mean just drinking! . . . At least I'm not a junkie!

T:    OK . . . now I'd like you to tell me the kinds of things that get you angry.

P:    . . . I don't know . . . these questions seem like a waste of time to me. . . . You want to know when I get angry, huh? . . . well . . . like I said before . . . I really don't think I get angry that much—I guess maybe I get *annoyed* at times, but not really angry. . . . Why is it that you doctors always try to get us to say that we're "hostile" about something? Anyway . . . when I do get annoyed . . . it's mostly just at little things . . . You know, normal annoyances like missing a bus; stubbing my toe; forgetting something I needed and then having to go back and get it . . . you know . . . the same things that everybody gets annoyed at. . . . Oh, yeah . . . I get annoyed at my wife once in awhile, too . . . but, hell . . . it's her own fault. . . . Like whenever I'd say I'd stop drinking . . . she'll keep asking me if I had any, or say that my breath smells funny . . . and even when she's not asking me all these questions—I'm sure she's thinking that I sneaked in a couple, or that she doesn't believe me. . . . Well, anyway, I keep tellin' her that when she keeps getting on my back like that, *she drives* me to drink. . . . Also my kids . . . Christ! . . . not a moment's peace. . . . I get home from work and just want to relax for awhile . . . and they're yelling . . . And comes the weekend— which is the only chance I get to sleep late—and they're running around, screaming . . . or fighting with each other. . . . Hell, anybody would get annoyed at that! . . . And then there's the job . . . I swear I don't know why I stay there. . . . With all the time I've put in for them, you'd think they'd show some appreciation . . . but, no . . . what do I get—criticism! . . . I wouldn't even mind it so much if they were right—but most of the time, they're not. . . . With all these things to put up with, a guy wouldn't be *normal* if he *didn't* drink.

*T:*   Well . . . what are some of the things you do about your anger . . . how do you handle it?

*P:*   How do I handle it? . . . Well, first of all, I told you that I don't get angry that much . . . so there's not really that much to handle. . . . I know you're probably thinking that's contradictory to what I said before . . . but not really . . . I mean, sure I get annoyed at times . . . but really not that often—and when I do, it usually doesn't last. . . . Most of the time it just goes away by itself.

*T:*   OK . . . what about the kinds of things that get you anxious, or fearful?

*P:*   I told you before . . . I really don't *get* these feelings very often. . . . Sure, *normal*-type fears . . . like if I'm driving along and see some maniac coming straight at me . . . but anybody would get upset in a situation like that . . . (pause) . . . I guess I've been this way as far back as I can remember. . . . Even in school, when everybody else used to get scared before a test . . . it never really used to upset me that much. . . . Sure, I guess I got sorta nervous once in awhile . . . but nothing compared to the other guys. . . . I'm sorry if I disappoint you by not being some kind of "nervous Nellie" . . . I know you doctors always like to find some sort of . . . what do you call it . . . some sort of . . . "Neurosis" . . . in a person. . . . Oh—wait a minute—I just remembered . . . when I was a kid, I used to be a little bit afraid of dogs. But actually, there was a very simple explanation for it. . . . I don't think it was anything unusual . . . it was just that once when I was coming home from school, a dog bit me. . . . And I was afraid of dogs for about a year after that. . . . Really, though, I guess my fear was just a normal reaction—especially since I was just a kid at the time. . . . Now, dogs don't bother me at all.

*T:*   Well . . . how do you handle these things?

*P:*   How do I handle what? . . . What do you mean, "How do I handle these things?" . . . I told you I don't get nervous that often, so there's really nothing much to handle. . . . I really don't know what else I can say.

*T:*   All right . . . Now, I'd like you to tell me what your parents were like.

*P:*   I really don't see the point of these questions . . . but if you really want to know . . . OK. . . . Hey, is it OK if I smoke? . . . D'ya got a light? (pause) . . . My parents . . . there's a real story. . . . You asked before what I thought was the cause of my drinking . . . well, I guess I've been giving them to you—my wife; my job; and now my parents. . . . In fact, my parents probably had the most to do with it. . . . I mean, aren't they responsible for how a person grows up and what he turns out to be? . . . For example, "love"—I don't think they knew what the word meant—or maybe they did for my older brother . . . but not for me! . . . I'm sure you've heard this story before . . . but they were always comparing me to him . . . "why can't you be like your brother, blah,

blah, blah" . . . as if I had anything to do with it—they're the ones that made me what I was. . . . That's what gets me the most—there was nothing I could do about it, then—or now. . . . You probably think I'm blaming everything on them—saying that they're the cause of my troubles—. . . well, I don't think I'm that far wrong. . . . Although they, themselves, didn't drink that much—in fact, they hardly touched the stuff—they sure knew how drive a person to it!

T:   OK . . . tell me . . . if you had your choice, in what way would your parents be different?

P:   How would I like them to be different? . . . Well, for starters, how about different parents, altogether. . . . I'm sure I would've been much better off that way. . . . In fact, I'm sure I wouldn't have started drinking so much, either . . . (pause) . . . You know . . . it just occurred to me. . . . All you've been doin' the past 5 or 10 minutes is asking me questions. . . . I get the feeling you're not really interested in what I'm saying . . . that you just want to . . . sorta . . . put me on the spot.

T:   Well . . . we all have various feelings about certain people; I'm glad that you can *express* yours. There's one more question I'd like to ask. . . . Most people have some sort of sexual problem . . . I wonder if you could tell me what sort of difficulties you've had in this area.

P:   Humph. . . . I was wondering when you'd get around to asking something like that! . . . Why is it you guys always think that there's gotta be something "sexual?" . . . Hell . . . it's my wife you should be talking to. . . .

T:   How do you mean?

P:   . . . Well . . . *I've* been fine . . . but over the past couple of years, she's been sorta turned off—actually . . . *she's* the one that needs the help! . . . I guess maybe she figures that she's had her children and now there's no reason to go to bed anymore. . . . Well . . . whatever it is . . . her attitude sure drives me up a wall! . . . See what I mean when I say that she's one of the reasons I drink—with that kind of attitude to put up with . . . who wouldn't!! . . . humph . . . to listen to her, you'd think I was at fault. . . . Whenever I go out at night she's always asking where I'm going . . . and what I'm doing—as if she thinks I'm going out with other women. . . . But I don't . . . I don't know why I don't. . . . I certainly have good reason to. . . . I'm sure other guys . . . in the same situation . . . would. . . . It wouldn't be so bad if she'd just leave me alone *all the time*. . . . But she's always either complaining or nagging or asking questions . . . and then when *I* want to get some satisfaction . . . it's no go. (pause) . . . You know . . . I've been thinking . . . what with my parents, my wife, and my job . . . I've been getting pretty much of a raw deal! . . . I'm beginning to see that these are the causes of my drinking . . . and if I can change some of *these things* . . . I oughta be OK.

T:   Well . . . it's good that you're giving some thought to these problems

. . . (pause) . . . well . . . thank you very much. . . . That's all for now. . . I know it's not been easy for you to talk about all these things, but I'm sure the information you've given me will be helpful. . . . We'll be getting in touch with you soon. . . .

P:     Doc . . . I . . . I don't mean anything personal . . . but do you think it would be possible for me to see *somebody else,* next time?

## Control Tape*

A:     What does psychotherapy involve?

B:     Well, psychotherapy includes various kinds of counseling and guidance, individual, group, child and family therapy, and psychoanalysis. In a series of regularly scheduled meetings, a trained professional works *with* a person (or sometimes a group of persons) to help him change his feelings, attitudes, and behavior so as to relieve his emotional tensions and enable him to live more effectively.

A:     Are there many people in this country who have used psychotherapy?

B:     Roughly one in four adult Americans thinks he has had emotional problems serious enough to call for professional help. One in seven has sought such help. So says the report of a nation-wide poll conducted for the Joint Commission on Mental Illness and Health, a group set up in 1955 by Congress to assess the nation's mental health status and resources.

A:     Who did all these people see, and what kinds of problems did they have?

B:     Of those adults who sought help for their troubles, 42% went to their clergyman, 29% to their family physician, 18% to a psychiatrist or psychologist, and 10% to a social agency or marriage clinic. Their commonest problems had to do with marriage, personal adjustment, and children. Whatever their distress, they were more or less "normal" people able to carry on in the community. Aside from these, about three-quarters of a million Americans are hospitalized for serious mental illness. They occupy about half of all our hospital beds. Perhaps 300,000 others urgently require some form of hospitalization, but do not get it. There is plenty of other evidence of the toll taken by emotional ills. Military records show that during World War II, 865,000 draftees were rejected on psychiatric grounds, and 43% of all disability discharges (980,000) were for similar reasons. We have an estimated 4.5 million alcoholics, and every year some 20,000 suicides. Emotional disturbance plays a key part in these tragedies, and in narcotics addiction, prostitution, crime, and juvenile delinquency as well. It leads to many serious accidents. It cuts down efficiency and productivity, too.

---

* Adapted from Ogg, E., *Psychotherapy—A helping process,* Public Affairs Pamphlet No. 329, New York: Public Affairs Committee, 1962.

A:   I hear a lot about psychotherapy nowadays. How come people are afraid of going into therapy?

B:   Despite wide popular interest in psychology, people in persistent emotional trouble rarely turn to a professional helper until their difficulties become acute. Therapists for emotional problems (as distinct from grave mental illness) are relatively new. Many people think therapists treat only "crazy folk." To seek psychological help then would be to admit being "wrong in the head." "It's my nerves—I'm not nuts—there's nothing the matter with me," such people argue, even when they are suffering. Most of us have been brought up to believe that we should be able to manage our life problems on our own. When we fail, we're reluctant to admit it. It seems better to keep our skeletons in the closet and put up as brave a front as we can before the world.

A:   Are there any other reasons?

B:   There is also the common fear of entering into the unknown. While on one level we may want to change ourselves and our lives because they are so unsatisfactory, on another we're afraid of change. What will the "head-shrinker" do to us? This slang term for the psychotherapist expresses the dread of being changed, perhaps in a way we won't like, by a being with powers beyond our understanding.

A:   Is there really that much difference between average people and the so-called "mentally ill"?

B:   Although the origins of mental illness are still unclear, attitudes toward it today are more hopeful. The mood-improving drugs have made even the most severely disturbed patients more manageable and often more open to treatment. Some can live for the most part in their own or foster homes, getting drugs and psychotherapy in a clinic, and even going to work. So the gulf between mental sufferers and people in general is beginning to narrow. We can see now that there is in fact no sharp dividing line between them. Mental illness can range from mild emotional difficulties that hamper but do not cripple to bizarre and extreme behavior that calls for hospitalization, much as physical ills can range from colds to serious heart attacks.

A:   When's the best time to go into therapy?

B:   It makes sense to seek help before difficulties pile up. An interview with a professional at the beginning of a problem with a child or adolescent, for example, may uncover hidden pressures on the youngster which can be corrected, thus heading off more serious trouble. The fact that he can't solve the difficulty by himself doesn't mean he's weak-willed or headed for a mental crack-up. Few people, even the most intelligent, can see their own emotional problems clearly—they're too tangled up in them. That's why many citizens, including psychotherapists, enlist professional aid to clarify their difficulties. Instead of being an admission of failure, the decision to seek help is often the first step in coming to grips with a problem.

*A:* How does psychotherapy work? What . . . what do most people expect?

*B:* Psychotherapy is so close to common sense that most patients quickly understand what it is about. The effects of a cruel father or a rejecting mother on a person's development are not hard to understand, although expert help is needed to overcome them. Of those who do seek psychological help, most start out with certain misconceptions. Some look for a quick, even "magical," cure. Their wish to lean on someone stronger than they are prompts them to see the therapist as a superhuman character who is never anxious or depressed or sick, but always able to handle his own and other people's problems with unerring skill. Many believe he will uncover a single cause for all their difficulties, and then prescribe how to get rid of it. They expect the professional to do all the work and guarantee success. It may be a long time before a patient can give up such wishful thinking. But sooner or later he must learn that there are no "wonder" cures in psychotherapy.

*A:* What's the goal of psychotherapy and how fast does it work?

*B:* Emotional difficulties of long standing have tangled roots rather than a single cause. To uncover those roots takes time and work—work on the part of the patient as well as the therapist. When they are exposed, the therapist offers no prescriptions. The patient may already be suffering from too many prescriptions; all his life family and friends have been telling him what to do! A central aim of therapy is to help him grow to the point where he will be able to make his own decisions and act on them. This cannot be accomplished overnight. It may take months or even years.

*A:* How does the therapy relationship work?

*B:* To benefit from the relationship, you must be able to *experience* it. Many people can't at first. They are too distrustful, too much in the habit of talking mechanically without conveying any real meaning or wanting to, too distracted, or too bored and out of touch with their own feelings. So your therapist may have to work first on whatever blocks your capacity to experience the relationship. If both of you are engaged as whole people, you're sharing a real experience. Live interest is the test. By learning to experience in this way you become your whole self.

## High Attraction–No Attraction*

*T:* Hi, I'm Mr. Bevin. How are you today?

*P:* Fine. I feel pretty good today.

*T:* Well, I have five questions that I'd like to ask you, and I'd like you to an-

---

* Ten attraction statements made by the patient were included on the High-Attraction Modeling Tape, but not on the No-Attraction Modeling Tape. These statements are in parentheses in the script.

swer each question for a couple of minutes. At the end of two minutes you'll hear a bell and then I'll ask you to go on to the next question. I wonder if you could tell me what kinds of things make you feel good—what you like—what makes you happy.

P:  Well, I—I think what makes me really happy are my children. My husband and me, we used to take 'em to the zoo and—and on picnics and—and really have a lot of fun. Things haven't been like that lately though. My husband and me ain't been together much. I guess there are other people that make me happy too though. You know—well—people like Mary. She's a nurse here and—and she talks to me. Well and—and sometimes she takes us for walks around the hospital. You know I—I can tell her about my problems and she always listens to me and tries to help me. (You listen to me just like she does. I really like that.)

T:  I'm glad to hear that. How does Mary help you?

P:  Ah, I don't know. She's just nice to me. I wish everyone was like Mary. (You're a lot like her—I don't know—because you listen to me. I—I get the feeling that you really understand what I'm saying.) S—Sometimes (bell) I just really feel like talking.

T:  That means it's time for the next question. Can you tell me what kinds of things worry you—um—things you don't enjoy, things that get you upset.

P:  Well, I guess my husband gets me most upset. He doesn't seem to care about me. And, well, he ignores me a lot and—and I—I feel bad because —well—I—I just—I don't think he really loves me. Ah, there are other things that upset me too like—well—well, like—like last week somebody here in the hospital took my bracelet. I think I know who took it, but I —I can't do anything about it. I really get hurt when people just don't care about what happens to me. (B—But somehow I—I get the feeling that you care.)

T:  I think I understand how you feel. Ah, are there any other things that upset you?

P:  (sigh) Yah. Like—like last week, Sandy, that—that girl down the hall threw her shoes through a window. That really got me upset. And—well I—I get upset when people just don't have time to talk to me too. Like Linda. She's another nurse here. And ah I just don't know, if—if you want to talk to her, she'll just tell you that she's too busy. (I'm glad you're not like that.) It's always bothered me when I wanted to talk to somebody and they—they (bell) just didn't have time to listen to me.

T:  Let's go on to the next question. You know that people get along well with some people and—well—not so well with others. Could you tell me something about people—ah—you don't get along with?

P:  Well, let's see—one person I don't get along with is my mother. I guess I never have. She used to drink all the time and she'd come home drunk. She'd—and she'd beat us kids or she'd yell at my dad. I think a lot of the time she wishes I'd never been born. (It's funny but you're the first person I ever told that to. I don't know why I was able to tell you that. It must be something about the way you asked me—or the way you listen to me. Other doctors have asked me about my parents, but I never—I never told them about my trouble with my mother. I really feel good that I could tell you that.)

*T:* I can—I can really understand what you're saying. Anyone here at the hospital that you don't get along with?

*P:* Well there's—there's one attendant, Jane. Well, she's always telling me what to do and—and when to get up and when to go to breakfast. You know, stuff like that. I don't like people telling me what to do like that. (I'm glad you're not bossy like that. I really feel good talking to you.) It seems like people are always (bell) trying to tell me what to do.

*T:* It's time for the next question. Everyone gets angry at some things some of the time. Um, what kinds of things get you angry?

*P:* Well, the way my husband acts. Well, like—like he comes home from work and—and right away he has to have a beer and he—he just sits there the rest of the night drinking his beer and watching TV. He just— he just doesn't ask me how I'm doin'—he doesn't really care. You know I—I work hard all day and I come home and I—I clean the house and fix the supper and he just doesn't care. Sometimes I get so mad I'd like to throw his beer at him. (You know I—I usually don't tell people things like this, but I feel good telling you.)

*T:* I'm glad you can tell me things like that. What happens when you get angry?

*P:* Well, I—I—I guess I get very quiet. You know but—but inside I'm—I'm really burning up I'm so angry. I guess I—I really just wanna run away. I get really angry too when—when people tell me—well, when they tell me I'm stupid. (I bet you'd never do that.) Sure, I—I make mistakes sometimes just like everybody else. But it seems like (bell) I'm always being blamed for doin' things wrong.

*T:* This will be the last question. If you wanted to—if you wanted to change something about yourself,—ah—like the way you act with people, what would it be?

*P:* Well I—I'd like to be more friendly with people. But I—I guess I just don't know how to talk to 'em. I just sit and listen and—and think how stupid I am and—and wonder why I can't think of anything else to say. (But I don't feel that way with you. It's really easy for me to talk to you.)

*T:* Ah, anything else that—that you'd like to change about yourself?

*P:* Well, I—I wish I wouldn't be so confused all the time. Well, like—like sometimes I just don't know what to believe. I think I'm doin' somethin' good and—and somebody'll come along and say I ain't doin' it right. I really try hard but (bell)—but people just don't seem to care about what I'm doin'.

T:   Our time's up but—um—I do want you to know that—ah—I understand your feelings and I—I really hope things work out for you.

P:   Thank you. (You know, I—I really enjoyed talking to you. I got a lot off of my shoulders. I hope we can talk some more real soon.)

### Social Interaction: Tape 1

#### *Narrator's Introduction*

Hello, I'm Dr. K., Superintendent of the hospital. I want to welcome you to our new television studio, and I am very pleased you are participating in the television role-playing program. I am positive that if you involve yourself in it, we will see some very important progress being made with your problems. This program can help us all to improve the social atmosphere in which we live. Even though you will be concentrating on socializing in the dining halls, I think the effect will be far greater.

This week, we are starting with the absolute basics of social interaction—simple eating behavior. You know that people can look sociable or not sociable just in how they eat. So we will be concentrating on using napkins, and forks and knives, not because we don't know how, but to really make us aware of how just eating behavior can contribute to socializing. I think we will also have some fun figuring out what to do in some situations that are amusing to look at, but which can be pretty troublesome when they happen. Watch this tape carefully as it demonstrates eating behaviors that can really affect your sociability.

#### *Scene 1*

*Narrator:* Put your napkin in your lap.

Patient A sits down at dining hall table, takes his napkin off the table, unfolds it, puts it in his lap.

*Narrator:* Good.

Patient A smiles.

Patient B sits down at dining hall table, takes his napkin off the table, unfolds it, puts it in his lap.

*Narrator:* Good.

Patient B smiles.

Patient C sits down at dining hall table, takes his napkin off the table, unfolds it, puts it in his lap.

*Narrator:* Good.

Patient C smiles. Patients A, B, and C eating.

*Narrator:* Also use your napkin during the meal when you need it.

Patient A eating, takes napkin off his lap, wipes his mouth, puts napkin back in his lap.

*Narrator:* Very good.

Patient A smiles.

Patient B eating, takes napkin off his lap, wipes his mouth, puts napkin back in his lap.

*Narrator:* Very good.

Patient B smiles.

Patient C eating, takes napkin off his lap, wipes his mouth, puts napkin back in his lap.

*Narrator:* Very good.

Patient C smiles.

*Narrator:* That was good, that's how to use your napkin.

## Scene 2

*Narrator:* Proper eating posture. Don't lean over your food. Sit up straight,

Patient D sitting with good posture between patients E and F who are hunched over the table.

*Narrator:* (to patient D) Good, that's the way to sit.

Patient D smiles. Patients E and F look at patient D, then at each other, then both straighten up. Patient D congratulates them and they all smile and then resume eating.

Patient G sitting with good posture between patients H and I who are hunched over the table.

*Narrator:* (to patient G) Good, that's the way to sit.

Patient G smiles. Patients H and I look at patient G, then at each other, then both straighten up. Patient G congratulates them and they all smile, and then resume eating.

*Narrator:* Good, you've all got it now.

## Scene 3

*Narrator:* Using your knife and fork properly.

Patient A holding a fork correctly.

*Narrator:* This is the way to hold a fork.

Patient A smiles.

Patients B and C each holding a fork incorrectly. Patient B changes to correct grasp.

*Narrator:* (to patient B) That's it, now.

Patient B smiles.

Patient C changes to correct grasp.

*Narrator:* That's the way. You've all got it now.

Patient C smiles. Patients A, B, and C resume eating, each holding fork correctly.

*Narrator:* Let's watch how we eat with a fork. We always hold the fork in an upright position.

Patients A, B, and C each hold their fork in correct position.

*Narrator:* Also remember forks don't have sides, so bring them to your mouth slowly.

Patients A, B, and C each bring their fork to their mouth slowly.

*Narrator:* Good, you've all got it now.

Patients A, B, and C smile.

## Scene 4

*Narrator:* Using your knife and fork together.

Patients A, B, and C are all sitting and eating. Each is using his knife and fork properly.

*Narrator:* You don't saw hard or fast with a knife, you just take your time and press gently. Notice how you hold the food with your fork. Very good, everyone!

Patients A, B, and C smile, and then resume eating.

*Narrator:* Here is everyone eating together. Aren't they doing beautifully?

Patients A, B, C, D, E, and F unfold their napkins, put it in their laps, put food on their correctly held forks, raise the fork to their mouths slowly, cut their food carefully and wipe their mouths with their napkins.

*Narrator:* Ladies and gentlemen, that's tremendous.

### Narrator's Summary

Now that you've seen the actors demonstrate the importance of good eating posture and using your napkin, fork, and knife properly, you will have a chance to do it yourselves, and by seeing yourselves on television, learn just how sociable you can look through good eating habits. Sit up straight, use your napkin, hold your knife and fork properly, and I guarantee that you will not only look good, but feel good as well. "Try it, you'll like it."

## Social Interaction: Tape 2

### Narrator's Introduction

Hello, I'm Dr. P., Assistant Superintendent of the hospital. This is the second week of the program, and you are off to a good start after concentrating on eating habits. Now we begin looking at socializing itself. Today we will be concentrating just on things you can do, with very little talking, that can make all the difference in the world in social interaction. We will look at how we can pass someone in line, move out of someone's way, and make room for someone at our table. It sounds simple, and it is, but when you see it and do it, you will recognize how much it adds to the social atmosphere. So watch the tape carefully and note how these simple behaviors create a pleasant social interaction. Watch the way the actors look at one another, smile, and speak to one another, rather than just act as if no one was there.

## Scene 1

Patients A, B, C, D, E, and F standing on line at food counter of the hospital dining hall waiting to be served. Patient A is served and walks with tray past rest of line, saying, "Excuse me, please" to each patient he passes close by. Same behaviors enacted by patient B, and then by patient C.

Patients G, H, and I are seated at Table 1 and are eating. Patient A approaches them. They wave and smile at him, and then move their trays to make room for him. Patient A smiles and thanks them.

Patient B approaches Table 1 (now full) and then moves toward adjacent table (Table 2). Patient G pulls his seat in to let patient B get to Table 2 more readily. Patient B smiles and thanks patient G. Same behaviors are repeated by patient G with patient C, who joins patient B at Table 2.

### Narrator's Summary

You saw that when someone wanted to move down the line, he excused himself and he looked at the people he talked to. When a group of people saw someone coming, they looked at him, smiled, and let him go by. When someone came to a table, the others said hello, smiled, looked at him, and made room for him. These are friendly and sociable ways to do things and now you will be doing them and seeing yourselves so you can learn first-hand how these things can make you even more sociable than you already are.

## Social Interaction: Tape 3

### Narrator's Introduction

Hello, I'm Dr. S., Clinical Director of Building #4. This program is moving right along, and we are going to be spending this week on even more varied dining hall behaviors that can contribute to a good social atmosphere. How many of us ever take the time to talk to the people behind the counter, or even to just thank them when they serve us our food? When people are having trouble with trays, do we help them? Do we sit with each other or sit alone? If we want something, do we ask for it? When we leave the table, do we let the others know? Well, the actors are going to demonstrate these things, and I want you to watch the tape carefully to see how much friendlier doing these things makes the dining hall atmosphere. Note that it's not just the talking, but the eye contact, the smiling, and the gesturing that really make the actors look sociable.

## Scene 1

Narrator: Talk to the people who serve you your food.

Patients A, B, and C, each in turn, approach the food server at the dining hall food counter, say, "How are you?" receive their food, and thank the food server.

## Scene 2

*Narrator:* Help each other if someone has trouble.

Patients A and B are walking off the food line. Patient B has difficulty carrying his tray. Patient A removes some items from B's tray and together they rearrange B's tray. Patient B thanks patient A and they both smile.

Patient C passes Table 1 and shows considerable difficulty balancing his tray. Patient D gets up from the table and helps C rearrange and support his tray. Patient C thanks patient D and they both smile.

## Scene 3

*Narrator:* If you see someone sitting alone, join him.

Patient E approaches patient F sitting alone at Table 1. Patient E sits down next to F, saying as he does, "I'd like to join you."

Patients A and B approach Table 2, at which patient G is sitting alone. Patient A tells G he looks lonely and that they would like to join him. Patient G smiles approval and A and B sit down.

## Scene 4

*Narrator:* If you want something at the table, ask for it.

Patients D, E, and F are seated at table and are eating. Patient E looks around, asks patient F to please pass the salt. F does so. E thanks F. Same behaviors enacted by patient B with A and C, and by patient H with G and I.

## Scene 5

*Narrator:* If you want more food, go get seconds. And ask others if they want more.

Patients D, E, F, and G are eating at Table 1. Patient F finishes the food in his plate, wipes his mouth with his napkin, puts his napkin down, and then says, "I think I'll get some seconds, anyone want anything?" Patients D, E, and G thank him but decline. Patient F gets up, walks to food line, greets food server and asks for and receives seconds.

Patients A, B, and C are eating at Table 2. Patients B and C finish eating, wipe their mouths with their napkins and then put their napkins down. Patient B says, "I'm still hungry." Patient A states, "Why not get seconds?" Patient B says he will and patient C says he will go with him. Patients B and C get up, walk to food line, greet food server, ask for, and receive, seconds.

## Scene 6

*Narrator:* When you finish your meal, don't just get up and run. Sit a while, and then tell people you're leaving.

Patients C, D, E, and F are seated at Table 1, eating. D finishes his food, wipes his mouth with his napkin, puts the napkin down, sits 2 min and says, "I

think I'll go wash up." He then gets up, saying, "I'll see you all later." Patients
C, E, and F reply affirmatively.

Patients G and H are seated at Table 2, eating. They finish, use and replace
their napkins correctly, and remain seated 2 min, engaged in small talk. Patient
G invites H to play ping pong. H accepts and they both get up and leave.

## Narrator's Summary

You saw that when you greet the people behind the counter who serve your
food, you seem much friendlier than when you say nothing. If you help someone with their tray, or say hello when you sit at a table, others like your sociability. When you want salt, or seconds, you saw how asking for it, rather than
just taking it or doing nothing, is the best way. You even watched the actors
offer to bring seconds back for each other, and that is really nice. Finally,
when you are done with your meal, you saw how much better it is to tell people you are leaving the table rather than just getting up and walking out. For
all of these things, you saw how looking at the people you are speaking to, and
gesturing put you in your most social light. I recommend that you practice and
do these things from now on, because I know that they can make important
differences in how you feel about yourself and how others feel about you.

## Social Interaction: Tape 4

### Narrator's Introduction

Hello, I'm Dr. H., Clinical Director of the Extended Care Units. This week
is the fourth week of the program, and we are ready to start looking at complete social interaction in the dining hall. In other words, we will be practicing holding conversations with one another during mealtimes. The dining table
is often the best place to just relax, enjoy each other's company, and talk. Yet,
so many people just eat and run. We will watch the actors demonstrate how to
hold conversations at the dining table. They will look at one another, smile,
lean toward one another, gesture, and show interest in each other as they speak
and listen. It doesn't matter what they talk about, but the way they talk makes
them feel friendly, and others see them as friendly. So watch this tape carefully
and see how mealtime conversations can really be pleasant.

### Scene 1

Patients A, B, and C seated at table. Patient C comes over, and the following
conversation ensues:

A:    It's not too bad. Do you like it?
B:    Well, yes, it's better than it was yesterday.
C:    Good morning, is that seat taken?
A:    No, no; go ahead, sit down.

C:   I don't know how people can sleep on such a beautiful morning.

A:   Right.

C:   It's a beautiful, beautiful day.

B:   It snowed during the night.

C:   Did it?

B:   Yes.

A:   Just a few flurries; nothing much. That would make you want to sleep later in the morning, I guess—a little snowy out.

C:   Not me.

A:   You're one of these peppy kinds, huh?

C:   Oh, if it's a good day, I like to get up early, get an early start, have breakfast early, so I can be hungry by lunch time.

A:   I don't have any trouble about eating; how about you?

B:   No, not really. Uh, would you care to take a walk outside after we eat? I love to walk in the snow.

C:   Make the first tracks . . . That's fun!

B:   I've finished my coffee. I think I'll get another cup. Anyone else want some more coffee?

A:   No, thanks.

C:   Yeah. . . . oh, why don't you wait, I'll finish my meal then I'll get more.

B:   Ah, I'm looking forward to an invigorating walk this morning.

C:   Where're you going to walk?

B:   Oh, anywhere; where ever nobody else has been; I'm just going to make brand new tracks in the snow.

C:   Want company?

B:   Yes, you want to join me?

C:   Maybe . . . no, I don't think I will. Thank you anyway.

B:   How come?

C:   I don't have boots.

### Scene 2

Patients *D, E, F, G,* and *H* seated at table.

D:   This is very good coffee, don't you think?

E:   Yeah, I'll tell you, I'm trying something different though. I get tired of saccharine . . . the after-taste and all . . . I'm trying the sugar and the coffee really has improved. Before that . . . uh, I don't know, I get tired of coffee, it was just bad.

D:   I don't like any of those artificial sweeteners.

F:   I don't like anything artificial.

D:   They say that the worst thing for you is the bleach from refined flour. Natural grains, natural flour, the health foods and that sort. . . . I really believe there's a lot to that.

F:   Did anybody know that new sugar substitute . . . the protein. . .

E:   Yes. Where did they discover that?

*F:*    I'm not sure; down in South America, I think.

*D:*    In Africa?

*F:*    Tribes have been using it for years.

*D:*    I think what it does, it makes your taste buds so sensitive to sweets that . . . if it's the same thing I saw on another show, that you keep tasting sweet, even if you're tasting something bitter, for an hour or so, that it lingers with you.

*F:*    They might perfect it though.

*D:*    Are you superstitious?

*F:*    Yeah. I try to think that I'm not superstitious, but I'm superstitious.

*D:*    Do you know where the three on a match superstition came from?

*F:*    No.

*D:*    From World War I. They'd line up in the trenches and the third one would get shot. The third one was unlucky.

*F:*    How did superstitions come from talking about saccharine?

*E:*    That's funny; you talk about sugar and artificial sweeteners hurting you and cigarette smoking doesn't help you any. That's for sure.

*F:*    Do you smoke?

*E:*    No.

*F:*    That figures. It's easy for you to say.

*G:*    Anybody see the Copy Cats last night?

*D:*    Yeah. That was a good show. It really was. Boy, those people are so talented. Just wonder how some people get so lucky . . . they have everything.

*E:*    I've heard a lot about that show, but I've never . . . never seen it.

*G:*    Do you watch the movies on television?

*F:*    I love movies . . . old movies.

*G:*    They have more this year . . . two a night now. They took the Merv Griffin show off and they have movies instead of that. Which is a help.

*F:*    If I lived in New York city, I'd never go to bed. I'd watch movies all night long.

*G:*    Do you stay up to watch them?

*F:*    Well, sometimes.

*E:*    Well, I think it's going to get to a point shortly where if they show nothing but movies, all the other programs will be taken off the air. I, for one, don't enjoy old movies. I prefer a good talk show. How about you?

*H:*    I like talk shows I guess; you know, it . . . it keeps you . . . other peoples opinions are good . . . they're important. I'd just as soon watch a talk show as an old movie.

*E:*    I realize they have a problem with the women as far as sports are concerned but there's certainly a lot of good sports on television.

### Narrator's Summary

You saw the actors talk to one another in a relaxed, pleasant way. You saw that everyone participated and that when they did, they looked at one another, smiled, gestured, and leaned toward one another. What they were talking about was really unimportant. The way they talked, however, made all the difference. While you practice having conversations at mealtime in the remainder of your group session, try and remember these ways of talking.

### Social Interaction: Tape 5

#### *Narrator's Introduction*

Hello, I'm Miss T., the Supervising Nurse. This is the fifth week of the program here in the studio, and I think we have come a long way in learning how we each can contribute to a good social atmosphere here in the dining hall. The only thing we haven't really discussed yet is what to do in situations that could be unpleasant. We all know that people sometimes spill things or drop their trays, and this can be very embarrassing. Yet, there are ways that we can act even then which can really show how social we are. The actors will show you what these ways are. Basically, it involves remaining calm and pleasant, offering a helping hand, and not making a big fuss over it. You will see that even here, things like eye contact, pleasant smiles, and gestures can do a lot to turn an unpleasant situation into a friendly one. So watch this tape carefully.

### *Scene 1*

Patients *A, B, C, E,* and *F* are on food line in hospital dining room. Patient *A* is at head of line. The following conversation ensues:

*A:*    I'm sorry; I'm Johnson, from Room 803. My doctor has me on a salt-free diet; I think there's a special platter here for me.
*D:*°  I don't remember seeing that.
*A:*    Yes, he just put me on that yesterday.
*D:*    I probably have it back here; I'm sorry Mr. Johnson.
*A:*    Alright.
*B:*    You know, you're holding up the whole line. Will you hurry it up, please!
*A:*    I'm sorry, but I'm on a special diet and she mistakingly gave me the wrong platter. I'll be through in a minute, but I'll tell you, why don't you come right on by here. It's perfectly all right.
*B:*    O.K. Sure.
*D:*    I believe this is it.
*A:*    Yes, it is, thank you very much.

### *Scene 2*

Patient *E* is standing in the aisle between tables. He bends over, places his tray on the table and begins taking the dishes off, blocking the aisle with his

---

° D represents Dietician in this dialogue.

body as he does. Patient C walks over, seeking to pass through the aisle. The
following conversation ensues:

C:    Listen, my food's getting cold; could I get by here?
E:    Oh, I'm sorry, I didn't even see you. Here, why don't you go on through
      here. I'm so sorry.
C:    Thanks.

## Scene 3

Patients E and F are standing in the dining hall with coffee cups in their
hands and are having a conversation. Patient G comes over and, showing sur-
prise at seeing patient F, shouts patient F's name loudly.

G:    Roberta!
E:    Look out! (As she spills coffee on patient D) Oh, I'm sorry.
F:    Oh, I hope that doesn't stain.
E:    Oh, here, let me help you.
F:    Think nothing of it. It's perfectly O.K.
E:    She called back, and. . . .
F:    You were saying something to me. . . .
      Yeah, well, anyway. . . .

## Scene 4

Patients G, H, and I are seated at a table, eating.

H:    Ah, that was very good tonight. Does somebody have a cigarette?
I:    Yeah, here.
H:    Oh, thank you . . . ooh, I'm sorry (sleeve dips in I's plate of food)
I:    That's all right. . . . Bob Brown . . . that was rather awkward . . . can
      I help you there?
H:    No, that's O.K.
I:    Here's your cigarette.
H:    Oh, thank you. I could use one now.
G:    Would you like one?
I:    Yes, thank you.

## Scene 5

Patients F, G, and H are seated at a table, eating. Patient F reaches for the
salt shaker and knocks over a glass of liquid. He apologizes briefly, cleans up
the spillage, and resumes eating.

### Narrator's Summary

You saw that when these accidents occurred, people remained calm, offered
a helping hand, and were pleasant. They did not make a big fuss, they just
cleaned up and went on with their meal. Eye contact, smiling, gestures, and

leaning toward one another made them seem friendly, even in these difficult situations. You will now have a chance to practice these things and see first-hand how you can handle them in the best way possible.

## Social Interaction—Behavioral Modeling: Tape 1

### Narrator's Introduction

Hello, I'm Dr. Turner from Denver State Hospital. You are now going to see some very important movies which will show you how some patients at another hospital were able to get to know and talk to another person who came over to them. I want you to pay close attention to these movies and notice what these patients did in order to get to know the person who came over to them.

It is important to watch these movies to see what the patients did because psychological research has shown that when people do get to know and talk with others, they feel better and are happier. We know that if you watch closely and learn what these patients did and if you do these things yourself, you too will feel better and be happier. I want you to notice how the patients did four very important things:

First, the patients answered questions and made conversation with the person who came over to them.

Second, the patients asked questions and started up conversations themselves with the person who came over to them.

Third, the patients tried to understand what the other people said to them and they tried to make the other people understand what they were saying. The patients tried to make sense and talk about the same thing the other people were talking about.

Fourth, the patients tried to talk alot. They did not answer with just a yes or a no, but they explained what they wanted to say. They tried to talk for a longer time.

When the patients in the movies did these four things, that is: *(1)* when they answered questions and made conversation; *(2)* when they asked questions and started conversations; *(3)* when they tried to make sense and make sure the other people understood them; and *(4)* when they talked for a long time the patients felt better and happier. We and others have actually done this, with many patients just like you, and we found that they always feel better and are happier. Since we want you too to feel better and since we also want you to be happier, we want you to do all these things, just like the patients in the movies. So pay close attention and learn what to do. Thank you.

### Scene 1

$M^\circ$ is seated by himself, doing nothing.

---

$^\circ$ *M* represents Model throughout the Appendix.

*P:* Hello, my name is Tom. What's your name? (Extends hand.)

*M:* I'm Steve. (Shakes hands and looks at *P.)*

*P:* How are you today?

*M:* Fine thanks, and you?

*P:* Just fine thanks. You must be new here. I don't think we've ever met before.

*M:* Yes, I am new. I just got here yesterday and I haven't met anyone yet.

*P:* Well, then I'm really happy to meet you. It's always nice to meet new people and to have new friends to talk to.

*M:* Yes it is. I'm glad that you came over to talk to me. Have you been at the hospital for a while?

*P:* Yes, for about 2 months.

## Scene 2

*M* is seated in front of TV alone.

*P:* Hi John. Can I watch TV with you?

*M:* Sure, I'd like to have some company. (Looks at *P.)*

*P:* That's nice of you to invite me to watch TV with you.

*M:* I'm watching a basketball game. Syracuse is playing Fordham and Syracuse is winning. It's a very exciting game. I hope you like to watch basketball. (Looks and smiles at *P.)*

*P:* Yes, I do very much. I'm glad that you invited me to watch the game with you.

## Scene 3

*M* is seated alone, reading newspaper.

*P:* Can I see a section of the newspaper?

*M:* Sure, which section would you like? (Looks at *P.)*

*P:* The sports page if you've finished it already. Do you read the sports page?

*M:* Yes I do. I like reading about football and hockey. I've finished that section so here it is (Looks at and leans toward *P.)*

*P:* Thanks alot. That's nice of you to share your newspaper. I also like to follow the football and hockey scores.

*M:* Good. . . . Maybe then we can talk about our favorite teams after you read the sports news. Who do you think will go to the superbowl this year?

*P:* I don't know but I think it'll be Dallas again. Say, y'know, I really like talking to you about sports.

## Scene 4

*M* is walking down hallway by himself.

*P:* Hi, I'm Jim. What's your name?

*M:*   My name is Joe.
*P:*   I'm going to the dining room. Are you too?
*M:*   Yes, I was on my way over there also.
*P:*   Well, I'm not sure I know the way to the dining room yet. Could you tell me how to get there?
*M:*   Why don't you walk with me. Then I could show you the way there. It's not a long walk but it's kind of complicated.
*P:*   That's very nice of you to offer to take me to the dining room. It's also nice to have someone to talk to when you're new at a place.
*M:*   Yes, I know just what you mean. Let's go over to the dining room now. (Puts arm on *P*'s shoulder.)

### Scene 5

   *M* is putting on his hat and coat, standing near a doorway.

*P:*   Where are you going?
*M:*   I'm going out for a walk. (Looks at *P*.)
*P:*   Hey, that sounds good. Can I go with you?
*M:*   Sure, if you'd like to. I thought I would go over to the community store.
*P:*   That's a good idea. I could also use some cigarettes from the store, so I think I'll walk with you.
*M:*   Good, then let's go together. Why don't you get your coat while I wait here for you.
*P:*   O.K. I'll be right back.

### Scene 6

   *M* is sitting at a table, eating alone.

*P:*   Anybody sitting there (nods in direction of empty chair)?
*M:*   No, no one is sitting there. Why don't you sit down.
*P:*   Thanks, it's nicer to sit with someone at dinner than to sit by yourself.
*M:*   Yes, it is. Food isn't bad tonight.
*P:*   No? What is it?
*M:*   It looks like hash, but it tastes much better.
*P:*   You know, the food isn't bad here at the hospital.
*M:*   No, it's not. Especially the desserts. Sometimes the cooks make apple pie that's just great. I always eat two portions of it.
*P:*   I know the apple pie is really good, but you know, all the food tastes better when you have company while you eat. That's why I wanted to sit with you and talk with you over dinner.

### Scene 7

   *M* is standing on line in cafeteria.

*P:*   Could you hand me a tray? I can't reach them.
*M:*   Sure. It's easier for me since I'm closer. Do you have a fork?

*P:*    Not yet. I don't have any silverware.

*M:*    Here let me help you. Here's a fork and a spoon and here's some napkins. Do you need anything else?

*P:*    Thanks, but that's all I need. You're a very helpful person. It's nice to meet people who help out others.

*M:*    Thanks, I like to help other guys.

*P:*    That's a good way to make friends . . . help people out when they need it.

### Scene 8

M is seated alone on park bench.

*P:*    It's a really nice day, isn't it?

*M:*    It really is. I like sitting out here in the sunshine. (Looks at *P.*)

*P:*    It's so warm today and the sun feels so good.

*M:*    Maybe this means that winter is finally over. No more freezing cold and no more snow. Maybe we'll even have an early spring.

*P:*    That would be great. Then we could sit out here all the time and enjoy the good weather. It would also give us the chance to spend more time together to talk.

*M:*    I like having company when I sit out here.

*P:*    Me too. It's always good to have someone to talk to.

### Scene 9

M is sitting alone.

*P:*    How do you feel today?

*M:*    Much better, thanks. I think I'm almost all over my cold.

*P:*    That's good.

*M:*    I think that the medicine you gave me yesterday really helped.

*P:*    I'm glad to hear that, but just to be sure, you'd better take your medicine now.

*M:*    O.K.

*P:*    Would you like me to sit here for a while to talk?

*M:*    I'd like that very much. I wanted to talk to you about that letter we started writing to my son. Do you think you'd have the time now to help me finish it?

### Scene 10

M is sitting alone.

*P:*    Hi. How would you like to come with me down to O.T. to make something?

*M:*    What could I do at O.T.?

P:     Well, you could paint, or make an ashtray or work with clay. There are lots of things to do at O.T.

M:     You know, some of the things you mentioned sound pretty interesting. I think I'd enjoy trying to make something.

P:     I think you'd enjoy it too. I remember that you once told me that you paint.

M:     (Smiles.) Yes, I used to do oil paintings. Still life, like fruits and flowers. I was pretty good too. Will there be other people at O.T.?

P:     Sure.

M:     Hmm, then I could also make new friends there.

P:     That's a good idea. I'm sure you could make new friends there. C'mon, let's go.

## Narrator's Summary

You just saw some very important movies which showed you how some patients were able to get to know and talk to another person who came over to them. You saw how the patients did four important things:

1. They answered questions and made conversations with the other people.
2. They asked questions and started conversations with the other people.
3. They tried to make sense and make sure the other people understood them.
4. They tried not to talk with just yes or no, they tried to talk alot.

Because these patients were able to get to know and talk with the person who came over to them they felt much better and they were happier. When we talk with people, we are healthier and we have more fun. We want you to feel better and be happier too, so now we want you to do all the things you saw the patients in the movies do, right here with the other people in your group. Thank you.

## Social Interaction—Behavioral Modeling: Tape 2

### Narrator's Introduction

Hello, I'm Dr. Turner from Denver State Hospital. You are now going to see some very important movies which will show you how some patients at another hospital were able to get to know and talk to another person they went over to. I want you to pay close attention to these movies and notice what these patients did in order to get to know the person they went over to.

It is important to watch these movies to see what the patients did because psychological research has shown that when people do get to know and talk with others, they feel better and are happier. We know that if you watch closely and learn what these patients did and if you do these things yourself, you too will feel better and be happier. I want you to notice how the patients did four very important things:

First, the patients answered questions and made conversation with the person they went over to.

Second, the patients asked questions and started up conversations themselves with the person they went over to.

Third, the patients tried to understand what the other people said to them and they tried to make the other people understand what they were saying. The patients tried to make sense and talk about the same thing the other people were talking about.

Fourth, the patients tried to talk alot. They did not answer with just a yes or a no, but they explained what they wanted to say. They tried to talk for a longer time.

When the patients in the movies did these four things, that is: *(1)* when they answered questions and made conversation; *(2)* when they asked questions and started conversations; *(3)* when they tried to make sense and make sure the other people understood them: and *(4)* when they talked for a long time the patients felt better and happier. We and others have actually done this, with many patients just like you, and we found that they always feel better and are happier. Since we want you too to feel better and since we also want you to be happier, we want you to do all these things, just like the patients in the movies. So pay close attention and learn what to do. Thank you.

### Scene 1

P seated alone in chair, doing nothing.

M:   Hi, my name is Jack. What's your name? (Extends hand to P.)
P:   I'm John.
M:   I guess you're new here because we haven't met before. I always like to welcome new people and help them to get to know their way around.
P:   Thanks, that's very kind of you. I was feeling kind of lonely, not knowing anyone, until you came over to me.
M:   Would you like to meet some of the other guys on the floor. I could introduce you to the nurses and the doctors up here if you'd like.
P:   I would like that. It would be nice to make some new friends, have some people to talk to.
M:   Well, come on then. I'll show you around. (Puts arm on P's shoulder.)
P:   That's great. I'm really glad you came over to me.

### Scene 2

P sitting by himself, sobbing quietly. M puts arm around him.

M:   You seem to be kind of sad. Is there something I can help with?

P: I'm just kind of upset.

M: Is there anything you'd like to talk about?

P: It's my son. I haven't gotten a letter from him in over a month.

M: I'm sorry to hear that, but there's probably nothing to worry about. Your son is probably just very busy with work and hasn't had the time to sit down and write to you.

P: I know, but I can't help but worry.

M: I know how you must feel. Would you like me to help you write a letter to him? That way, you could find out what's going on.

P: I'd really appreciate that. You know, whenever I have a problem, you always seem to be able to help me out.

## Scene 3

P and M sitting watching TV.

M: Do you like this program? (Looks at P.)

P: Yes, very much. This is one of my favorites.

M: Mine too. I always enjoy watching cowboy programs and "Gunsmoke" is one of my favorites too. I missed it last week. Did you see it?

P: Yes, it was good. It was about a big bank robbery.

M: Gee, that sounds like a good one. I'm sorry I missed it.

P: If you'd like, I could remind you every time it's on.

M: Thanks, that's a good idea.

P: Sure. I like having company when I watch TV.

## Scene 4

P sitting alone.

M: (Puts hand on P's shoulder.) How would you like to play a game of cards?

P: Sure, I'd like to play, but I don't know many card games.

M: Do you know how to play gin rummy?

P: No, I don't.

M: Well, I could teach you. It's not a real hard game.

P: That would be nice. I'd like to learn a new card game.

M: Good, then once you know how to play, we can play cards together all the time. I could even teach you other games besides gin rummy. How about poker too?

P: Sounds like a real good idea.

## Scene 5

P standing alone.

M: (Puts arm on P's shoulder.) Say, I'm going for a walk over to the store. Would you like to walk over there with me?

P:     You're going to the store? Are you going to buy anything?

M:     Yes, I need some toothpaste. Besides, I just feel like going for a walk, get a little exercise.

P:     You reminded me. I need some toothpaste too and I wouldn't mind the walk either.

M:     Well, then, why don't you put on your coat and walk over there with me?

P:     I think I will. You know Tom, it was very thoughtful of you to mention it to me.

### Scene 6

*P sitting, eating alone.*

M:     Is anyone sitting in this seat?

P:     No, I don't think so.

M:     Could I sit here then?

P:     Sure, be my guest. I always like to have people to eat with, to talk to over dinner.

M:     Yes, I know what you mean. Having people to eat with makes dinner more fun.

P:     How do you like the food tonight?

M:     It's not bad. The hamburgers are pretty good, but the mashed potatoes are lumpy. What do you think of it?

P:     Pretty good.

M:     Say, what did you think of last night's food. Remember, we had chicken. That was pretty good wasn't it?

P:     Yeah, it was.

### Scene 7

*P walking down hallway.*

M:     Excuse me. I'm on my way to the O.T. room, but I think I got lost. Do you know where the O.T. room is?

P:     Yes, I know where it is. You go down this hall and then turn left.

M:     Thanks alot. Say, do you ever go there?

P:     No, I've never been to O.T.

M:     You ought to go. It's alot of fun. You can make things there, like ashtrays and paintings.

P:     That sounds pretty good. I've thought of going but I never had anyone to go with before.

M:     Well, why don't you come with me now? (Puts arm on *P*'s shoulder.)

P:     Thanks alot for offering to take me with you. You say they have painting over there?

M:     Yes, and lots of other things. I make ashtrays and hotplates. I make them out of different colored tiles.

P:   I think I'd like to do that, too, now that I have someone to go with.

## Scene 8

M and P, sitting and reading newspapers.

M:   Say, Joe, did you read the sports page yet?
P:   Yes, I saw it already.
M:   Did you read the article on the Syracuse Blazers?
P:   Yes, I read it, aren't they fantastic this year.
M:   Yeah, it looks like they are heading for a championship playoff game this year. I bet the people from Syracuse are real proud.
P:   That would be great. They haven't been in a playoff since the 50s.
P:   You know Tom, it's nice having someone around you can talk to about sports. I really like talking to you about the hockey games.
M:   Me too.

## Scene 9

M approaches a person dressed like a staff member.

M:   Good morning, Nurse Hall. How are you this morning?
N:   I'm fine thanks. And how are you today, Mr. Roberts?
M:   I'm fine. I'd like to go out for a walk today, now that the weather is so nice. Would you like to go with me?
N:   That sounds like a fine idea. I'll go for a walk with you if I have the time.
M:   Well, I sure hope you have the time because it's too nice a day to stay indoors.
N:   You're right. I'm glad you asked me to go with you, Mr. Roberts.

## Scene 10

M approaches a person dressed like a doctor.

M:   Hi, Doctor Allison.
D:   How are you feeling this morning, Mr. Drew?
M:   I'm feeling fine thank you.
D:   That's good to hear.
M:   Yes, I'm not at all upset today, like I was yesterday.
D:   I'm glad to hear that. I bet our talk yesterday had a lot to do with your feeling better today.
M:   I think so, Doctor. I know I felt much better after we talked about my problem.
D:   Sometimes when we talk about our problems, we work them out and then we feel better afterwards.
M:   Well, I know this much . . . if I ever get upset and start worrying again like I did yesterday, I'll come to talk to you about it.
D:   That's a good idea. Maybe I could help you if we talked about it.

## *Narrator's Summary*

You just saw some very important movies which showed you how some patients were able to get to know and talk to another person they went over to. You saw how the patients did four important things:

1. They answered questions and made conversation with the other people.
2. They asked questions and started conversations with the other people.
3. They tried to make sense and make sure the other people understood them.
4. They tried not to talk with just yes or no, they tried to talk alot.

Because these patients were able to get to know and talk with the person they went over to they felt much better and they were happier. When we talk with people, we are healthier and we have more fun. We want you to feel better and be happier too, so now we want you to do all the things you saw the patients in the movies do, right here with the other people in your group. Thank you.

## Social Interaction—Behavioral Modeling: Tape 3

### *Narrator's Introduction*

Hello, I'm Dr. Turner from Denver State Hospital. You are now going to see some very important movies which will show you how some patients at another hospital were able to get to know and talk to groups of people. I want you to pay close attention to these movies and notice what these patients did in order to get to know the group of people.

It is important to watch these movies to see what the patients did because psychological research has shown that when people do get to know and talk with others, they feel better and are happier. We know that if you watch closely and learn what these patients did and if you do these things yourself, you too will feel better and be happier. I want you to notice how the patients did four very important things:

First, the patients answered questions and made conversation with the group of people.

Second, the patients asked questions and started up conversations themselves with the group of people.

Third, the patients tried to understand what the other people said to them and they tried to make the other people understand what they were saying. The patients tried to make sense and talk about the same thing the other people were talking about.

Fourth, the patients tried to talk a lot. They did not answer with just a yes or a no, but they explained what they wanted to say. They tried to talk for a longer time.

When the patients in the movies did these four things, that is: *(1)* when they answered questions and made conversation; *(2)* when they asked questions and started conversations; *(3)* when they tried to make sense and make sure the other people understood them; and *(4)* when they talked for a long time the patients felt better and happier. We and others have actually done this, with many patients just like you, and we found that they always feel better and are happier. Since we want you too to feel better and since we also want you to be happier, we want you to do all these things, just like the patients in the movies. So pay close attention and learn what to do. Thank you.

## Scene 1

Three people sitting, M approaches them.

*M:*    Hi, I'm new here. Can I sit with you?
*P1:*   Sure, just pull up a chair.
*M:*    My name is Tony.
*P2:*   I'm Bill, and this is Carl, and this is George.
*P3:*   We were just talking about the weather.
*M:*    Isn't it great that winter's almost over?
*P3:*   Yes, before we know it, it will be spring.
*M:*    Great, we'll get rid of all this snow and everything will be green again.
*P1:*   The hospital is real pretty then. You'll like walking around the hospital grounds in the spring.
*M:*    You guys go for walks in the spring then?
*P2:*   Yes, we do. We walk around and then just sit in the sun and talk.
*M:*    That must be very relaxing, just walking around with good friends and then sitting here to talk. I wonder if I could go with you then?
*P1:*   That would be nice. We'd be very happy to have you join us.

## Scene 2

Three people at a table, playing cards.

*P1:*   Well, what shall we play?
*P2:*   I'd like to play hearts.
*M:*    Did I hear you mention that you're going to play hearts? That's one of my favorite card games. Can I play too? I haven't played hearts in a long time and I'd really like to.
*P3:*   Sure. Sit down. The game is even better with four people.
*M:*    I didn't know anyone who played hearts up here until just now.
*P1:*   We always play cards and you're welcome to join us any afternoon.
*M:*    Thanks alot.
*P2:*   Good, a new card player. I'm glad that you asked to join us.
*P3:*   Why don't you deal?
*M:*    O.K., let's see if I remember how to shuffle the cards. I'm supposed to deal out all the cards until there's none left, right?
*P1:*   That's right. Gee, it sure is nice to have you play cards with us.

### Scene 3

Two people on cafeteria line, M approaches them.

M:   Hello, everyone. What's for lunch?
P1:  Looks like tuna fish.
M:   Good, I like tuna fish. Could you hand me a tray?
P2:  You like tuna fish? We get it so often here at the hospital that I've gotten tired of it.
M:   I know, but I don't mind. (Another person gets on line behind M) Here, let me get you a tray. Looks like we're having tuna fish for lunch again.
P3:  Not again! That's twice in one week. Why can't they give us anything else?
P1:  You know, when you have to wait on a line, kidding around with your friends makes the time go faster.
M:   Yes, it does. It's alot of fun to kid around with friends.

### Scene 4

Two people walking down hallway, M approaches them.

M:   I'm on my way to the O.T. room. Where are you guys going?
P1:  We're going there, too.
P2:  Why don't you come along with us?
M:   I think I will. Have you ever been to O.T. before?
P1:  Sure, we go there all the time.
M:   I've never gone there before. What do you do there?
P2:  Oh, lots of different things. We can paint or make ashtrays, they have alot of interesting things.
M:   I didn't know you could paint there. That's something I'd like to do.
P1:  Yes, it's alot of fun. Also, at O.T. we spend time with our friends.
M:   Hmm, that's sounds pretty good, I could paint and also make some new friends.
P2:  Well then, you're going to the right place. You'll have a good time there. I'm glad you've decided to go with us.
P1:  Why don't you walk over there with us now so that we can show you around. We could even introduce you to Mrs. Richards. She's in charge over there.
M:   Thanks alot.

### Scene 5

Three people at a table eating, M approaches with a tray.

M:   Anybody sitting there?
P1:  No, why don't you sit down there?
M:   Thanks, I always enjoy having dinner with friends, it's much nicer than eating alone. How's the food tonight?

P2:  Not bad. The meat is kind of well done for me though.

M:  Me too, but they can't cook the meat so that it'll suit everybody. I guess we have to get used to the different way the food is made here.

P3:  Yeah, I know what you mean. I don't mind that so much, but you know what I wish? I wish I could get a candy bar here in the hospital. I really miss candy bars.

M:  You can get a candy bar right here in the hospital. Didn't you know that?

P3:  No, I didn't. Where can I get one?

M:  Over at the community store. I go over there just about every afternoon to buy something.

P3:  You do? Could I go with you?

M:  Sure, I'd like to have some company.

P3:  I'm glad that you sat down with us. I never would have thought about going over to the store to buy some candy if you had't mentioned it. Thanks alot.

## Scene 6

Three people sitting and working on a puzzle. M approaches.

M:  I see you're working on a puzzle. It looks very interesting.

P1:  It is. We get together every afternoon and work on it for awhile.

M:  Would you like some more help?

P2:  Sure, just pull up a chair.

P3:  Working on this puzzle together also gives us some time together, you know, just to sit around and shoot the breeze.

M:  I can see that. That's a very relaxing way to spend the afternoon. That's something I'd like to do, too. You know, I haven't worked on a puzzle in years. What part of the puzzle are you working on?

P2:  I think I have the sky here. See those clouds?

M:  Those are the pieces I have, too. Why don't we put them together and see if we could get more done that way.

P2:  That's a good idea. Good thing that you came over here and asked to help us. We'll have this puzzle done in no time.

## Scene 7

Three people putting on outer clothing, M approaches them.

M:  Hi, where are you going?

P1:  We're going out for a walk.

M:  Going any place in particular?

P2:  We were just going to sit outside for a while and then go over to the community store to get a Coke.

M:  Can I go with you?

P3:  If you'd like to come, we'd like to have your company.

*M:*   Today seems like a good day for a walk. I think I will go with you.

*P1:*   Then you could also stop off and have a Coke with us at the community store. That should be fun.

*M:*   Yes it should. Also, at the store, I'll be able to get another pack of cigarettes. Let me just get my coat. Wait here for me. I'll be back in a minute.

## Scene 8

Two people sitting and talking, *M* approaches them.

*M:*   Hi, I just got here yesterday and I don't know anyone yet. My name is Dave.

*P1:*   My name is Tom, and this is Joe.

*P2:*   Well, now you know us, so why don't you sit down and talk to us for a while.

*M:*   Thanks. I was feeling kind of lonesome until now, not knowing anyone and not knowing my way around the hospital.

*P1:*   We know what you mean. We've been through that too. It's lonesome when you don't know anyone. That's why it's good that you came over to talk to us.

*P2:*   If you'd like, we could introduce you to the other men on the floor.

*M:*   I'd really appreciate that. You're both very helpful, really make a guy feel right at home. That way, I could get to know everyone on this floor.

*P1:*   Sure, you could make some new friends. Would you like a cigarette?

*M:*   Yes, thanks. I forgot to bring any with me.

*P2:*   You can buy cigarettes right here in the hospital if you want to. Over at the store.

*M:*   I can? I didn't know that. Say, would you show me how to get to the store?

*P1:*   We'll take you over there if you'd like. See, it really pays to try to get to know the people around here. You can learn alot about the hospital.

## Scene 9

*M* approaches two others, sitting.

*M:*   I'm going over to the patient's library to read a book. Would you like to come with me? I'll read aloud if you like.

*P1:*   You'd read aloud to us? Hey, that sounds like something I'd enjoy.

*P2:*   Me too. I can't read as much as I used too. My eyes aren't so good anymore. I think I would enjoy hearing you read.

*M:*   Good, because I like to read to other people. My favorite books are detective stories. Would you like to hear one of those?

*P1:*   I would. Those are my favorites also. I like to try to figure out how the mystery ends before I get to the end of the book.

M: Well, I'll let you pick out whichever one you like to hear.
P2: That's real nice of you. You always think of good things to do.
P1: Say, let's go over to the library now. This is a real treat for us.

## Scene 10

Two people sitting on a bench talking. M sits down with them.

M: Hi. What are you guys talking about?
P1: Oh, we were just talking about the hospital.
P2: Just things in general, the nurses, the doctors, the food.
M: Well, I think the nurses and doctors are pretty good around here. What do you think?
P1: I think so, too. Especially Miss Thompson, the nurse on our floor.
M: I know, she's a very kind person. Whenever I have a problem or there's something that's bothering me, I always go over to her to talk about it.
P1: Me too. The other day, I was worried about having to go for an X ray, so she and I sat down and talked about it for a while. She explained everything to me.
M: I know what you mean. Last week, I was supposed to go home on a weekend pass. She and I had a long talk about it because I was kind of nervous about seeing my family again. She really helped me calm down.
P2: I think it makes you feel better to talk to people when you have a problem.
M: Sure, we even do that with our friends. You know how we always talk things over together, anything that's on our mind.
P1: You know, that's right. We even help each other out by talking things over.

## Narrator's Summary

You just saw some very important movies which showed you how some patients were able to get to know and talk to groups of people.

You saw how the patients did four important things:

1. They answered questions and made conversation with the other people.
2. They asked questions and started conversations with the other people.
3. They tried to make sense and make sure the other people understood them.
4. They tried not to talk with just yes or no, they tried to talk alot.

Because these patients were able to get to know and talk with the groups of people they felt much better and they were happier. When we talk with people, we are healthier and we have more fun. We want you to feel better and be happier too, so now we want you to do all the things you saw the patients in the movies do, right here with the other people in your group. Thank you.

### Social Interaction–Behavioral Modeling: Tape 4*

#### *Narrator's Introduction*

Hello, I'm Dr. Turner from Denver State Hospital. You are now going to see some very important movies which will show you how some patients at another hospital were able to get to know and talk to some of their friends and relatives from outside the hospital. I want you to pay close attention to these movies and notice what these patients did in order to get to know their friends and relatives better.

It is important to watch these movies to see what the patients did because psychological research has shown that when people do get to know and talk with others, they feel better and are happier. We know that if you watch closely and learn what these patients did and if you do these things yourself, you too will feel better and be happier. I want you to notice how the patients did four very important things:

First, the patients answered questions and made conversation with their friends and relatives.

Second, the patients asked questions and started up conversations themselves with their friends and relatives.

Third, the patients tried to understand what the other people said to them and they tried to make the other people understand what they were saying. The patients tried to make sense and talk about the same things the other people were talking about.

Fourth, the patients tried to talk a lot. They did not answer with just a yes or a no, but they explained what they wanted to say. They tried to talk for a longer time.

When the patients in the movies did these four things, that is: *(1)* when they answered questions and made conversation; *(2)* when they asked questions and started conversations; *(3)* when they tried to make sense and make sure the other people understood them; and *(4)* when they talked for a long time the patients felt better and happier. We and others have actually done this, with many patients just like you, and we found that they always feel better and are happier. Since we want you too to feel better and since we also want you to be happier, we want you to do all these things, just like the patients in the movies. So pay close attention and learn what to do. Thank you.

#### *Scene 1*

*M* is getting ready to leave hospital with spouse.

P:     I'm happy that you'll be coming home.
M:    I'm happy too, but I'm a little worried that things won't be O.K.
P:     I can understand that you'd be worried.

---

* Throughout this tape *P* will represent Person in whatever role is called for by the nature of the dialogue.

M:  Yes, I'm afraid that I'll start getting nervous again, you know, let little things get on my nerves.

P:  Well, I'm glad you're telling me about this now. This way, we can talk about the things that might make you nervous, and talking about those things sometimes makes you feel better.

M:  I know. That's why I'd like to talk to you about our family budget. If we can work out a good budget now, I won't start worrying about the bills, like I did before I came to the hospital.

P:  Good idea. We can make plans for our budget right now. I can tell . . . you must really be feeling better.

M:  Yes I am, and talking with you about our problems helps alot.

## Scene 2

Parents visiting M.

P1:  How are you John? Are you feeling better?

M:  I'm feeling fine Dad, and the medicine they give me helps alot.

P2:  Are they treating you well here?

M:  Fine, all the doctors and nurses are very kind.

P1:  How's the food here John? You seem to be losing a little weight.

M:  The food isn't bad, but I like your cooking better, Mom. I especially miss the cookies you used to bake for me.

P2:  How would you like me to bake some and then bring them here?

M:  I'd like that very much. Would you make a real big batch so that I would have enough to share with my friends? How about those peanut butter cookies you used to make?

P2:  Sure, I could make those.

P1:  You know, son, it's really good to see you. You really seem to be alot better. I like talking with you, especially now when you seem to be so happy.

M:  Well, Dad, I like having you visit me.

## Scene 3

M, out on a pass, runs into some friends.

P1:  Harry, it sure is good to see you. How have you been?

M:  Fine, just fine. I haven't seen you guys in months. What have you been up to?

P2:  Nothing much. Still working down at the factory.

M:  How are things down at the factory, all my old buddies?

P1:  Not bad. Bill Johnson got promoted to foreman, and Pete and I switched to the night shift.

M:  No kidding. Bill's a foreman now. That's a great promotion for him. How come you guys went onto the night shift. That's a pretty tough schedule.

*P2:* More money. They gave us $10 a week raise for nights.

*M:* Well listen, it was really good seeing you again. Say hello to your wives for me.

*P1:* Same here. I've always enjoyed seeing you Harry. Why don't you stop over at the factory some time to visit some of the guys. I know they'd like to see you.

*M:* Maybe I will. I'd like to talk to some of my old friends again.

### Scene 4

M's spouse is visiting him in the hospital.

*M:* Are the kids behaving well, doing their homework, and helping you around the house?

*P:* Yes they are. They've been very cooperative.

*M:* Good. That makes me feel better. Sometimes I worry about them.

*P:* Well, no need to worry. We just want you to relax and feel better.

*M:* I am feeling much better. I think the hospital is helping me alot.

*P:* I'm glad to hear that. I forgot to tell you, the kids got their report cards last week.

*M:* How were their marks?

*P:* Pretty good. Susan got two A's and Tim got one.

*M:* Sounds like they are both doing well in school. I'm glad to hear that. I enjoy having you visit me, Martha, especially when you bring me such good news from home.

*P:* I enjoy visiting you too, Sam, telling you about the kids and what's doing at home. You really sound as if you're much better.

### Scene 5

M in store.

*P:* Can I help you?

*M:* Yes, I'd like to buy a pen.

*P:* Any particular kind?

*M:* Yes, a blue ball point pen, not an expensive one.

*P:* I have two different kinds. This one is 20¢, and this one is 30¢.

*M:* I like this one better. I'll take this one. How much is it with the tax?

*P:* That will be 33¢.

*M:* Here's 35¢.

*P:* And here's your change. I'll put the pen in a bag for you.

*M:* Thank you for the service.

### Scene 6

Friends visit M.

*M:* Hello, Al. How are you Tony?

*P1:* It's good to see you, Ken.
*P2:* Yeah, Ken. How are you doing?
*M:* Fine, really good. Say, I'm glad you guys came out to see me.
*P1:* Well, we were wondering how you were. We haven't seen you in a while.
*M:* Well, I can't complain. The nurses and doctors here are helping me. I think I've gotten better with their help.
*P2:* You seem to be much better, you seem to be happier and more relaxed.
*M:* That's the way I feel. Say, why don't you guys tell me what's going on in town. I like to catch up on the news.
*P1:* Everything is O.K. My boss asked me to put in alot of overtime last month. I was really working hard.
*M:* You must have been very busy. And how about you, Tony?
*P2:* Things aren't so great at the store. Business has been kind of slow.
*M:* I'm sorry to hear that. Business will probably pick up soon. Hey, how are your wives?
*P1:* Fine.
*P2:* Fine.
*M:* That's good to hear. Gee, I'm glad to see you.
*P1:* We're happy that we came out here to see you, and to tell you about what's going on at home.

## Scene 7

*M* in store.

*M:* I'd like to buy some writing paper and some envelopes.
*P:* Did you want some fancy paper or just some white letter paper?
*M:* The white paper will be fine. I just want to write some letters to my friends.
*P:* This is what I have. This box with envelopes for $2.00 and this pad of paper with a package of envelopes for $1.50.
*M:* Hmm. This is a hard choice. Which one has more paper?
*P:* This one.
*M:* Then I'll take this one. I want alot of paper.
*P:* That will be $1.60 with the tax.
*M:* Here's $2.00.
*P:* I'll give you your change and put this in a bag for you.
*M:* Thank you very much. Good-bye.
*P:* Good-bye.

## Scene 8

*M* is visited by parents.

*P1:* Hello, Jim. We've come to take you home for the weekend.
*M:* Hello, Mom, hello, Dad. Boy, that would be great. I'd like to go home for the weekend with you, spend some time with you, and even see my brother and his wife.

*P2:*   I'm glad to hear that. Your brother will be coming over for dinner tonight with his wife.

*M:*   Will they be bringing the kids?

*P1:*   No, he thinks that they are too young to stay out so late.

*M:*   That's too bad. I'd like to see the kids. Maybe I could take a walk over to their house on Sunday and visit with them. That way I could get to see the kids.

*P2:*   That's a good idea. I know they'd like to have you visit with them.

*M:*   It sounds like this weekend is going to be alot of fun.

*P1:*   We're very happy that you'll be coming for a visit son. We haven't had a real long talk in a while. I like having those talks with you.

*M:*   Me too, Dad.

## Scene 9

M's spouse is visiting.

*P:*   Hello, dear. I'm so glad to see you. How are you?

*M:*   Not bad, Thelma, things are going O.K.

*P:*   I'm glad to hear that. Is there anything you need?

*M:*   Hmm. Let me see. I would like you to bring some magazines. My friends and I read all the magazines and then we talk about the articles.

*P:*   I'll bring you some when I visit next week. I'm happy to hear that you have alot of friends here in the hospital.

*M:*   Yes, it's nice having people to talk to around here, but I still miss being at home with you and the kids. How are they?

*P:*   The children are both working hard in school. Tommy just made the basketball team.

*M:*   That's great.

*P:*   Yes, and he said that he'd really like to have you come to watch him play. He'd enjoy having his father at one of his games.

*M:*   I'd like that too. It would make me proud to see him play basketball. I've always enjoyed spending time with him.

*P:*   Good, then maybe you could go with him next week.

## Scene 10

M's children visit him.

*P1:*   Hi, Dad. We came to see you.

*M:*   Hello, Edna. Hello Tom. Some company, how nice.

*P2:*   Look, Dad, we brought you a sweater. Do you like it?

*M:*   Let's see it. Blue, my favorite color. This is something I could really use up here. It gets so chilly at night on the floor.

*P1:*   Yes we know, Dad, that's why we thought you could use it.

*P2:*   Well, Dad, what have you been up to?

M:    Oh, nothing much. I've been going to O.T. alot lately. I'm making some ashtrays for the house. I make them out of little tiles. They come out pretty nice.

P1:    Just like you, Dad, always puttering around.

M:    Yes, and I'm even thinking of taking up painting. They have all the stuff I'd need right down in O.T. I'd like to try my hand at it.

P2:    Sounds good, Dad. You'll be so busy around here that you won't have time to visit with us.

M:    Of course not. I always have time to see my children. I enjoy your visits. And we enjoy coming out here to see you too, Dad, we like hearing what you're up to.

## Narrator's Summary

You just saw some very important movies which showed you how some patients were able to get to know and talk to their friends and relatives. You saw how the patients did four important things:

1. They answered questions and made conversation with the other people.
2. They asked questions and started conversations with the other people.
3. They tried to make sense and make sure the other people understood them.
4. They tried not to talk with just yes or no, they tried to talk alot.

Because these patients were able to get to know and talk with their friends and relatives they felt much better and they were happier. When we talk with people, we are healthier and we have more fun. We want you to feel better and be happier too, so now we want you to do all the things you saw the patients in the movies do, right here with the other people in your group. Thank you.

## Social Interaction—Cognitive Modeling: Tape 1

### Narrator's Introduction

Hello, I'm Dr. Turner from Denver State Hospital. You are now going to see some very important movies which will show you how some patients at another hospital were able to get to know and talk to another person who came over to them. I want you to pay close attention to these movies and notice what these patients did in order to get to know the person who came over to them.

It is important to watch these movies to see what the patients did because psychological research has shown that when people do get to know and talk with others, they feel better and are happier. We know that if you watch closely and learn what these patients did and if you do these things yourself, you too will feel better and be happier. I want you to notice how the patients did four very important things:

First, the patients answered questions and made conversation with the person who came over to them.

Second, the patients asked questions and started up conversations themselves with the person who came over to them.

Third, the patients tried to understand what the other people said to them and they tried to make the other people understand what they were saying. The patients tried to make sense and talk about the same thing the other people were talking about.

Fourth, the patients tried to talk a lot. They did not answer with just a yes or a no, but they explained what they wanted to say. They tried to talk for a longer time.

When the patients in the movies did these four things, that is: (1) when they answered questions and made conversation; (2) when they asked questions and started conversations; (3) when they tried to make sense and make sure the other people understood them; and (4) when they talked for a long time the patients felt better and happier. We and others have actually done this, with many patients just like you and we found that they always feel better and are happier. Since we want you too to feel better and since we also want you to be happier, we want you to do all these things, just like the patients in the movies. So pay close attention and learn what to do. Thank you.

### Scene 1

P: Hello, my name is Tom How are you?

M: Hmm, let me see, what am I supposed to do. I'm new here and I don't know anyone yet, but I do want to get to know the other people on the floor. So what should I do? There are four things I'm supposed to do. (1) I'm supposed to answer questions when somebody asks me something, try to make conversation when someone comes over to me. (2) I'm supposed to also talk to them, ask them questions. O.K. so far. (3) I'm supposed to make sense, talk so that Tom here can understand me. (4) I'm supposed to talk a lot, not just say yes or no. O.K., I think I know what to do. I'll talk to Tom now. That way, I can get to know him. I'll answer the questions he asked me. First, I'll tell him my name, then I'll tell him that I feel fine. That will answer his questions. I could also ask him questions about himself . . . that'll start a conversation. But I have to remember to ask good questions, something that he'd be interested in. I'll ask him how long he's been here at the hospital and how he likes it. Those are good questions. He'll understand what I'm saying. Hey, that's pretty good, I figured it all out. Pretty smart of me.

### Scene 2

P: Hi, John, can I watch TV with you?

M:    Hmm, Jim just asked me a question. That means I should do something now. But what am I supposed to do? I'm supposed to do four important things. First, I'm supposed to answer questions and talk with someone when they come over to me. Second, I'm supposed to talk with, try to get a conversation going when someone comes over to me. Pretty good so far, but I also have to make sure that I make sense. That's the third thing I have to do. I have to talk about what Jim's talking about and make sure that he understands what I'm saying. Also, I shouldn't answer just yes or no, I have to talk alot. O.K., I'd like him to watch TV with me, so I'll tell him that. I could also tell him what program I'm watching. That makes sense. That's something he'd be interested in. Pretty good so far, see, now I know just what to do.

## Scene 3

P:    Can I see a section of the newspaper—the sports section if you've finished with it?

M:    Hmm, Tom asked me for the sports section of the newspaper. I've finished reading it so what should I do now? I know, I'm supposed to answer his question and try to talk with him. That's one of the things I learned to do. Whenever someone comes over to you and says something to you, you should answer them. But there are other things I learned to do. I know, I also am supposed to talk with them, try to start up a conversation. O.K., I think I'll try that. But I have to remember . . . make sense. Talk about the same thing that Tom is talking about, talk about things he'll be interested in. That's the other thing I learned to do. But I also have to talk alot. Not just yes or not answers. There, that was the last thing I learned to do. O.K., so now I'll tell Tom that he can have the sports section because I've finished reading it. That's good because that answers his question and it also makes sense. Now I can even make conversation. Maybe I could tell him about some of the sports news. I'll tell him about some of the hockey teams. That's good, he'll be interested in that. Hey, I'm pretty good at this, aren't I? I really learned what to do when someone comes over to talk to me.

## Scene 4

P:    Hi, I want to go to the dining room, but I can't find it. Are you going there?

M:    Hey now, what should I do? This guy stopped me and asked me about the dining room. Now what am I supposed to do when someone asks me a question. I know, (1) I should answer the question. (2) Maybe I should even talk some more with him. (3) Make sense, talk so that he understands me. (4) Talk alot. Don't just say yes or no. O.K., now I'll try to do all those things. He wants to know if I'm going over to the dining room. I know where the dining room is so I could tell him that. I could even tell him that I'd like him to walk over there with me. That's pretty good, I'll tell him that. That's a good way to start a conversation and I think it's something that he'd be interested in. That's very smart of me to say that. Now I know just what to do.

## Scene 5

P:  Where are you going?

M:  John just asked me a question. I paid attention to what he said and I understood him. Good, now what should I do? I should answer him, that's the first thing I should do. But I have to remember to make sense, talk about the same things he's talking about, that's the second thing I have to do. But also, I shouldn't just answer his question with a yes or a no, I have to talk alot. That's the third thing I have to do. There's one other thing I have to do, that's talk with him, maybe even ask him a question. O.K., I know all the things I'm supposed to do. So what should I say? I should tell him where I'm going. That will answer his question. I'll tell him that I'm going to the store. That makes sense. Pretty good so far. What if he asks if he can go with me? What should I do then? I know, I'll answer that question also. I'll tell him that I'd like him to come with me. That's a good answer because I won't just say yes or no, I'll explain myself. Hey, not bad, I figured out what to do all by myself.

## Scene 6

P:  Is anybody sitting there?

M:  Hmm, I'm sitting here eating by myself and Bill just asked me if anyone is sitting there. Now what should I do? First thing is that I should answer his question. Whenever somebody asks you something, you're supposed to answer them. What else? I know, I should try to talk to him, strike up a conversation. That's the second thing I should do. Now what's the third thing I should do? I know, I have to make sense, make sure that Bill can understand what I say. Then there's one other thing I have to do; oh, I remember, I have to talk alot, not just say yes or no. O.K., now I'll try it out. I'll answer his question, I'll tell him that no one is sitting there. That's good. But then I'll talk to him. I'll tell him that I'd like it if he sat there. That's a good thing to say, he'll be interested in that. Good, that makes alot of sense. That's pretty smart of me.

## Scene 7

P:  Could you hand me a tray? I can't reach them.

M:  Now, there are four things I'm supposed to do when someone says something to me. What are those four things. Oh yeah, (1) I'm supposed to answer their question. That's right, but I'm supposed to answer their question in the right way. That's (2) Talk so that I make sense, talk about the same thing they are talking about. What else. (3) Talk to them, say something to them that will start up a conversation. (4) Talk alot, don't talk with just a couple of words, say alot of things. O.K., I remembered everything I should do. So now I'll tell him that I can get him a tray. That answers his questions and it makes sense. So far, so good. Also, that's alot more than just saying yes or no, and that's good, too. Now what should I say to make conversation with him? I know, I'll ask him if he needs a fork. Pretty sharp of me. I know just how to talk to people when they say something to me.

## Scene 8

P:     It's a really nice day isn't it?

M:     Hey, Bob just struck up a conversation with me. Let's see if I remember what I should do. (1) Talk to him when he strikes up a conversation. (2) Try to start a conversation with him. (3) Those are two very important things to do, but what else is there? Oh yes, (3) Make sure that he understands what I say, talk about the same things he talks about. (4) Talk alot. Don't just say yes or no. O.K., I'll try it right now. Bob's talking about the weather, so I'll talk about the weather. I'll answer him and say, 'Yes it is a nice day.' Good, but I should also say something else, something to make conversation. I know, I'll ask him if he likes to sit out here on such nice days. That's good, he'll understand that. Very good, I figured out just how to talk to Bob.

## Scene 9

N:     How do you feel today?

M:     Hmm, the nurse just asked me something, how I felt today. O.K., let's see if I know what to do. (1) I'm supposed to talk with people when they come over to me. (2) I'm supposed to try to start conversation with them. (3) I'm supposed to talk alot. (4) I'm supposed to talk so that they'll understand me, talk about something they are interested in. Now, I'll do those things. I'll answer the nurse's question by telling her how I feel, I'll tell her about my cold. Then I'll make more conversation, I'll explain how the medicine helped me alot. That's good, I'll be talking alot and making sense. That's very important. You know, I really am good at figuring out how to talk to people.

## Scene 10

D:     Would you like to come to O.T. with me to make something?

M:     The O.T. director just asked me if I want to go to O.T. with him. Now I'm supposed to do four things.
(1) Answer when people ask me questions or make talk with me. (2) Ask them questions, tell them things. What else am I supposed to do?

Oh, yeah. *(3)* Make sense, and *(4)* talk alot. O.K., I remembered all the important things I have to do. Let's see if I can do them now. I'll talk about O.T. That makes sense because that's what the O.T. director is talking about. I'll tell him I would like to go to O.T. But then I'll try to talk some more. I'll ask him a question, like What can I do at O.T. That's perfect. That's really perfect. That's real sharp of me to figure that out.

## Narrator's Summary

You just saw some very important movies which showed you how some patients were able to get to know and talk to another person who came over to them. You saw how the patients did four important things:

1. They answered questions and made conversations with the other people.
2. They asked questions and started conversations with the other people.
3. They tried to make sense and make sure the other people understood them.
4. They tried not to talk with just yes or no, they tried to talk alot.

Because these patients were able to get to know and talk with the person who came over to them they felt much better and they were happier. When we talk with people, we are healthier and we have more fun. We want you to feel better and be happier too, so now, we want you to do all the things you saw the patients in the movies do, right here with the other people in your group. Thank you.

## Social Interaction–Cognitive Modeling: Tape 2

### Narrator's Introduction

Hello, I'm Dr. Turner from Denver State Hospital. You are now going to see some very important movies which will show you how some patients at another hospital were able to get to know and talk to another person they went over to. I want you to pay close attention to these movies and notice what these patients did in order to get to know the person they went over to.

It is important to watch these movies to see what the patients did because psychological research has shown that when people do get to know and talk with others, they feel better and are happier. We know that if you watch closely and learn what these patients did and if you do these things yourself, you too will feel better and be happier. I want you to notice how the patients did four very important things:

First, the patients answered questions and made conversation with the person they went over to.

Second, the patients asked questions and started up conversations themselves with the person they went over to.

Third, the patients tried to understand what the other people said to them and they tried to make the other people understand what they were saying. The patients tried to make sense and talk about the same thing the other people were talking about.

Fourth, the patients tried to talk a lot. They did not answer with just a yes or a no, but they explained what they wanted to say. They tried to talk for a longer time.

When the patients in the movies did these four things, that is: *(1)* when they answered questions and made conversation; *(2)* when they asked questions and started conversations; *(3)* when they tried to make sense and make sure the other people understood them; and *(4)* when they talked for a long time the patients felt better and happier. We and others have actually done this, with many patients just like you, and we found that they always feel better and are happier. Since we want you too to feel better and since we also want you to be happier, we want you to do all these things, just like the patients in the movies. So pay close attention and learn what to do. Thank you.

## Scene 1

*M:*  Hmm, that's a new man on the floor and I'd like to meet him, become his friend. Now what should I do, what should I do to become his friend? There are four important things I should do to become his friend. *(1)* I should go over and talk to him, maybe ask him a question, try to start up a conversation. *(2)* Also, I should answer him if he asks me a question or says something to me. Yeah, that's right. But there are some other things I also have to remember to do, now what were they? Oh, yeah, *(3)* I should make sense, talk about something that he's interested in. *(4)* Talk alot, don't just say a couple of words, say alot of things. O.K., I'll try it now, I'll go over to the new guy and first, I'll tell him my name. Then, I'll ask him what's his name. That'll get a conversation going. Then, I'll answer his questions if he asks any. And all the time, I'll try to make sense and talk alot. Here goes. You know, I really know how to make friends and get to know other people.

## Scene 2

*M:*  Uh oh, Bill seems kind of sad. I think I'll go over to him. But what will I do when I go over to him. I learned to do four things, now what are they again? *(1)* Start up a conversation. *(2)* Answer him if he talks to me or starts up a conversation. *(3)* Make sure that I talk about the same things that he talks about, make sense. *(4)* Talk alot. Very good, I remembered everything. Now let's see if I can do all these things. I can go over to him and ask him what he's sad about . . . that'll start the conversation. Then we can talk about his problem. That's good. We'll talk alot and I'll make sense. Now what should I do if he asks me a question about his problem?

I know, I'll answer him, I'll tell him what I think. That's good because it makes sense, it's talking about the same thing he's talking about. Pretty smart of me, I just figured out what to do.

## Scene 3

M: Carl and I are sitting here, watching TV together. I'd like to get a conversation going because I'm a pretty friendly guy. Now what are those four things I have to remember to do? *(1)* Say something to him, maybe ask him a question. *(2)* Speak to him if he says anything to me or if he asks me a question. *(3)* Make sure that he understands what I'm saying and talk about things I think he'll be interested in. *(4)* Talk for long times, not just a couple of words. O.K., I've got it all. So what should I say now, let's see . . . why don't I ask him how he likes this TV program. That's a smart thing to say. That'll get a conversation started and it makes sense. This TV program is something I know he's interested in. Hmm, pretty good so far. O.K., what else? We could talk some more about TV, like what's my favorite program, what's his favorite program. Hey, you know, I'm a pretty smart guy to figure out how to get a conversation going.

## Scene 4

M: I'd like to play cards with someone, but no one has asked me. What do I have to do to get someone to play cards with me? I learned what to do. I learned those four things. I have to go over to someone and talk to them about it, ask them if they'd like to play cards. That's right that's the first thing I have to do. Now, what's the second? I know, if they ask me any questions, I have to answer them. The third thing I have to do is make sure that the person understands me, talk so that I make sense. And then the fourth thing I have to do is talk alot, not just yes and no, but use alot of words. O.K., I'll try it now. I'll go over to Dave and ask him to play cards with me. Then I'll tell him that I'd like to play gin runny but if he doesn't know how to play, I can teach him. Hey, that sounds great. Also, I'll answer any questions he has. I'm sure he'll play cards with me after I say all that to him.

## Scene 5

M: I'm going for a walk over to the community store, but I think I'd like some company. Now what should I do in this kind of situation? I learned what to do before. I learned that if I want company and if I want someone to talk to, I have to go over to them and strike up a conversation. That's right. That's the first thing I have to do. Now what's the second thing? The second thing is that if anyone asks me a question or says anything to me, I have to answer them. All the time though, I have to make sense, talk about something I think they'll be interested in. That's the third thing I learned. The fourth thing I learned was that I have to talk alot. I can't just say yes or no. I remembered everything. That's pretty smart of me. Now I'll try it. I'll go over to Bob and ask if he'd like to take a walk with me. If he asks me where I'm going I'll tell him that I'm going to the community store. That's good because it answers his question, it makes sense and its alot of talk. Gee, I'm really good at this, I really know how to get along with people.

## Scene 6

M:  I don't want to eat alone. That's not a friendly thing to do, so what should I do? Hey, that's John over there. I'd like to sit with him, so I'd better do those four things I'm supposed to do in these kinds of situations. Go over to him and talk with him or ask him a question. That's (1) Answer his questions if he asks me any. That's (2) Make sure that what I say makes sense, talk so that he can understand me. That's (3) Talk a lot. That's (4) O.K., I think I'll do all that now. I'll say, "Can I sit at your table and eat dinner with you?" Yeah, that's the way to do it. That's the friendly thing to do. That way I'll have company for dinner for sure. I really am good at figuring out how to be friendly.

## Scene 7

M:  Uh oh, I think I got lost on my way to the O.T. room. What should I do? I know, I can ask somebody to show me the way to the O.T. room . . . go over to that guy over there and ask him a question. That's the first thing I learned to do. Now what's the next thing I learned to do? Oh yeah, I have to answer any questions that he asks me or talk to him if he says anything to me. Gee, I've really learned how to get along with people. But there are still other things I have to remember to do. The third thing is, I have to talk so that he can understand me, make sense. The fourth thing is, I have to talk alot. Don't just say yes or no, explain what I mean. O.K., here goes, I'll go over to him and ask him how do I get to the O.T. room from here. Hey, since I'm such a friendly guy, I think I'll even ask him if he'd like to go to O.T. with me. That makes alot of sense. I sure have learned alot. I know exactly what to do to talk to people.

## Scene 8

M:  Say, these sports articles are pretty good. I'd really like to talk to someone about them. I could talk to Joe about these articles. Now what am I supposed to do when I want to talk to someone? There are those four things I learned. (1) Say something to Joe, ask him a question, or strike up a conversation. (2) Answer his questions or talk to him when he says something to me. *(3)* Talk about something that he'd be interested in, talk about the same thing he's talking about, make sense. *(4)* Talk alot, explain myself, don't just say yes or no. Boy, I really know what I'm doing, don't I? So now I'll ask Joe if he read the article on the hockey team. Then I can ask him what he thinks of the hockey team . . . that'll start off a good conversation. Gee, I really know how to talk with other people.

## Scene 9

M:    There's the nurse. I wonder if she'd like to take a walk with me. I'd like that because I like spending time with other people. Maybe I'll ask her, yes, that's what I'll do. Now what are those four things I learned to do in this kind of situation? I should go over to that person and ask them something or say something to them. Next, I should answer them if they say anything to me. Third, I should talk about something I think they'd be interested in, something that makes sense. Fourth, I should talk alot, talk for a long time. O.K., I'll go over to her and ask her if she'd like to take a walk with me. That'll get the conversation started. Then, if she asks me where I want to go, I'll tell her . . . I'll say I want to go over to the community store. That's good because she'll be able to understand that and it's also alot of talk. I really learned how to handle these kinds of situations. I figured that out all by myself.

## Scene 10

M:    There's the doctor I talk to. Gee, I'd like to talk to him now. But how do I get to talk to him? There are those four things I'm supposed to do in order to get to talk to people. *(1)* Go over and say something to the other person. *(2)* Answer when the other person says something to you. *(3)* Talk about something you think the other person is interested in. *(4)* Don't talk with just yes or no, talk a lot. O.K., now I have to remember to do all those things. I'll go over to the doctor and say, "Thank you for talking with me yesterday and helping me with my problem." That's good. It will start a conversation. It also makes sense and it's alot of words. I really am a sharp guy. I can figure out how to talk to the doctor.

### Narrator's Summary

You just saw some very important movies which showed you how some patients were able to get to know and talk to another person they went over to. You saw how the patients did four important things:

1. They answered questions and made conversation with the other people.
2. They asked questions and started conversations with the other people.
3. They tried to make sense and make sure the other people understood them.

4. They tried not to talk with just yes or no, they tried to talk alot.

Because these patients were able to get to know and talk with the person they went over to they felt much better and they were happier. When we talk with people, we are healthier and we have more fun. We want you to feel better and be happier too, so now we want you to do all the things you saw the patients in the movies do, right here with the other people in your group. Thank you.

## Social Interaction—Cognitive Modeling: Tape 3

### Narrator's Introduction

Hello, I'm Dr. Turner from Denver State Hospital. You are now going to see some very important movies which will show you how some patients at another hospital were able to get to know and talk to groups of people. I want you to pay close attention to these movies and notice what these patients did in order to get to know the group of people.

It is important to watch these movies to see what the patients did because psychological research has shown that when people do get to know and talk with others, they feel better and are happier. We know that if you watch closely and learn what these patients did, and if you do these things yourself, you too will feel better and be happier. I want you to notice how the patients did four very important things:

> First, the patients answered questions and made conversation with the group of people.

> Second, the patients asked questions and started up conversations themselves with the group of people.

> Third, the patients tried to understand what the other people said to them, and they tried to make the other people understand what they were saying. The patients tried to make sense and talk about the same thing the other people were talking about.

> Fourth, the patients tried to talk alot. They did not answer with just a yes or a no, but they explained what they wanted to say. They tried to talk for a longer time.

When the patients in the movies did these four things, that is: (1) when they answered questions and made conversation; (2) when they asked questions and started conversations; (3) when they tried to make sense and make sure the other people understood them; and (4) when they talked for a long time the patients felt better and happier. We and others have actually done this, with many patients just like you, and we found that they always feel better and are happier. Since we want you too to feel better and since we also want you to be happier, we want you to do all these things, just like the patients in the movies. So pay close attention and learn what to do. Thank you.

### Scene 1

M:   Look at those guys over there talking. Gee, I'd like to talk with them too. I'm new here and I don't know anyone yet. Now what am I supposed to do in this kind of a situation? What are those four things I'm supposed to do? Oh, I remember, first I should go over to them and start up a conversation. Second, I should talk with them and answer any questions they ask me. Third, I have to make sense, talk about the same things they are talking about and talk about things I think they'd be interested in. There's one other thing I have to remember to do, now what is that? Oh, yes, fourth, I have to talk alot. Don't answer questions by just saying yes or no, explain what I mean. O.K., I've got it now. Now I'll do the first thing. I'll go over to them and tell them my name. I'll say I'm new here and I don't know anyone yet. There—that's right. I'm pretty smart when it comes to figuring out how to make new friends.

### Scene 2

M:   Say, those guys are going to play a card game. Gee, I'd really like to play. So what should I do? I should ask them if I could play. That's just like the four things I learned to do. *(1)* Go over to them and ask them a question, or start talking to them. *(2)* Answer questions that they ask me or answer them when they talk to me. *(3)* Make sure they understand what I'm saying. *(4)* Talk alot. O.K., I learned what to do, now I'll try it out. First, I'll go over to them and ask them if I can play cards with them. That's good. Then, I'll tell them that I haven't played cards in a long while, but it is something I really enjoy. That's making conversation. So far, so good. Then, if they ask me what games do I know, I'll say, I know how to play gin rummy and hearts . . . that should answer their question. That's all very good. I think they'll be interested in what I say. I'm really proud of myself, I really know how to get along with people, how to talk to them.

### Scene 3

M:   Hmm, I'm standing on line waiting, with nothing to do. What's a good thing to do now? I know, I could do those things I learned to do, those things that help you get along better with people. First thing I have to do is go over to those guys and start talking to them. Then, second, I'll talk to them when they say something to me. O.K., but I have to remember, to always do the third thing, and that's make sense, talk about something they'd be interested in, or talk about the same thing they're talking about. And then there's the fourth thing, I have to talk alot. When they ask me something, I can't just answer yes or no. I have to say alot. O.K., I'll try it now. I'll ask the guys what's for lunch . . . that'll start a conversation going. That also makes sense because I know that's something they'd be interested in. Good, I think I'll try it. I really learned how to get along with people, I must really be a smart guy.

## Scene 4

*M:*  Hmm, I'm on my way to the O.T. room, but I sure would like to have those guys for company. You know, walk with them and talk with them over there. Now what are those four important things I'm supposed to do in this kind of a situation. Let's see if I can remember what I have to do to be a friendly guy. First, I have to go over to the guys and say something to them or even ask them a question. Second, I have to talk to them if they say anything to me or ask me a question. Third, I have to make sure they understand what I'm saying, talk so that I make sense. Fourth, I have to talk alot, try to explain what I mean. I'll try to do all those things now so the guys will go to O.T. with me. First, I'll tell them that I'm going to O.T. and then I'll ask them if they'd like to go with me. That's right. That'll start a conversation. Then, if they ask me what is there to do at O.T., I'll tell them. I'll say that I paint pictures and make ashtrays. That'll answer their question. Good, and everything will make sense and it'll be alot of talk. Gee, you know, I'm pretty sharp when it comes to figuring out how to talk to people.

## Scene 5

*M:*  Gee, I'd really like to sit with those guys because it's such fun to have someone to eat dinner with but what should I do. I know, I should do those four things I learned to do to make friends and get along with people. (1) Start talking to the guys. (2) Answer when the guys talk to me. (3) Make sense, talk so they can understand me. (4) Talk alot, not just a couple of words. O.K., let's see if I can do all those things right now. I'll start talking to them by asking if anyone is sitting in that chair. Then, if they say no, I'll ask if I can sit there. That's a good way to start a conversation. Then, whatever they're talking about, I'll also talk about. If they ask me how I like the food, I'll tell them. All that sounds very good. It shows that I really know what to do, I really am proud of myself.

## Scene 6

*M:*  Those guys are working on a puzzle. That looks like fun. I'd like to work on the puzzle with them. How could I get them to let me join them. I could try those four things I learned to do in these kinds of situations. First, I have to go over to them and start up a conversation. Second, I have to answer them when they talk to me. Third, I have to talk about things I think they'll be interested in. Fourth, I have to say alot, not just a couple of words. O.K., I remember everything I have to do, now I'll try it. I'll go over to where they are sitting and say, "Hi, fellas, I see you're working on a puzzle. It looks interesting." Then I'll ask them if I can help them. So far, so good. That's the start of a conversation and everything makes sense. Also, that's alot of talk. You know, I must have really learned alot because I know exactly how to talk to other people.

### Scene 7

M: Hey, it looks like some of my friends are going out for a walk. That's something I'd like to do with them. Now there's something I learned to do in just this kind of a situation. I learned that (1) I should go over to them and start talking to them, strike up a conversation, (2) I learned that when they talk to me or ask me a question, I have to answer them. (3) I learned that I have to talk so that they'll understand me, talk about things they'd be interested in. (4) I learned that I have to talk alot, not just a couple of words. O.K., I've remembered everything I'm supposed to do, now I'll do it. I'll walk over to them say, "Hi, are you going out for a walk." If they say yes, I'll ask them if I can go along with them. They'll understand everything I say, that's very good. I still have to remember though, that if they ask me anything, I have to make sure to answer them. I'm getting very good at this. I really know how to be a friendly guy. That's something to be proud of.

### Scene 8

M: I'm new here and I don't know anyone yet. But I'm feeling kind of lonely and I'd like someone to talk to. Now there are those things I learned that can help you make friends and find people to talk to. What were they? Oh yes, I know. Talk to other people, make conversation. Answer other people when they make conversation with you. Talk so that other people can understand you and are interested in what you say. Talk alot, don't just use a couple of words. Those are four things I could do right now to get to know the other guys here. So the first thing I'll do is start a conversation. I'll go over to thoses guys and say, "Hi, I'm new here and I haven't met anyone yet." Then, I could tell them my name. Then I'll ask them what their names are. That should start off the conversation. Say, this is a great way to get to know people. I won't be lonesome any more, after I've talked to those guys. I'm really glad I thought of this.

### Scene 9

M: I think I'll go over to the patients' library to read a book. But I would like some company though, I'd like to read aloud to someone. So, what should I do? I guess now would be a good time to try out those important things I learned to get along with people. First, I'll have to go to some of my friends and talk to them, ask them if they'd like to go over to the library with me. Then, I'll have to listen to them and answer any questions they ask me. O.K., so far, I know what to do. But there are two other things I learned to do. I also have to talk so they'll understand me and I have to talk alot. Those are the four things. O.K., why don't I try them now. I'll go over to Jim and Bob and say, "I'm going to the patients' library to read a book." Then, I'll ask them if they'd like to go with me. I'll tell them I'll read aloud to them if they'd like. That should start up a conversation and that's alot of talk. It also makes sense and that's something important. Hey, you know, I'm pretty good at this. Then, if they ask me any questions, like what book am I going to read, I have to remember to answer them. Gee, I really am smart. I just figured out how to be friendly with Jim and Bob. They'll come to the library with me now for sure.

## Scene 10

M:    Say, those are my friends, Tom and John, sitting over there talking. You know, I'd really like to sit with them too, that would be fun. Now what should I do in this kind of a situation. Let's see. There are those four things I learned to do, those four things to get along with people. Now what are they? Oh yes, (1) Go over to them and start up a conversation or ask them a question. (2) Answer them when they talk to me or ask me a question. (3) Talk about the same thing they are talking about or talk about things I think they'd be interested in. (4) Talk alot. Don't answer just yes or no. O.K., I know the four things I'm supposed to do, so now I'll try them. I'll go over to Tom and John and I'll say, "Can I sit with you?" Then, if they say yes, I'll ask them what they are talking about and then I'll talk about the same thing. That's good, but I have to remember that everything I say has to make sense. Pretty sharp of me, huh? I just figured out how to get to know and talk with my pals.

## Narrator's Summary

You just saw some very important movies which showed you how some patients were able to get to know and talk to groups of people. You saw how the patients did four important things:

1. They answered questions and made conversation with the other people.
2. They asked questions and started conversations with the other people.
3. They tried to make sense and make sure the other people understood them.
4. They tried not to talk with just yes or no, they tried to talk a lot.

Because these patients were able to get to know and talk with the groups of people they felt much better and they were happier. When we talk with people, we are healthier and we have more fun. We want you to feel better and be happier too, so now we want you to do all the things you saw the patients in the movies do, right here with the other people in your group. Thank you.

### Social Interaction–Cognitive Modeling: Tape 4*

*Narrator's Introduction*

Hello, I'm Dr. Turner from Denver State Hospital. You are now going to
see some very important movies which will show you how some patients at another hospital were able to get to know and talk to some of their friends and
relatives from outside the hospital. I want you to pay close attention to these
movies and notice what these patients did in order to get to know their friends
and relatives better.

It is important to watch these movies to see what the patients did because
psychological research has shown that when people do get to know and talk
with others, they feel better and are happier. We know that if you watch closely and learn what these patients did, and if you do these things yourself, you
too will feel better and be happier. I want you to notice how the patients did
four very important things:

First, the patients answered questions and made conversation with
their friends and relatives.

Second, the patients asked questions and started up conversations
themselves with their friends and relatives.

Third, the patients tried to understand what the other people said to
them and they tried to make the other people understand what they
were saying. The patients tried to make sense and talk about the
same thing the other people were talking about.

Fourth, the patients tried to talk alot. They did not answer with just a
yes or a no, but they explained what they wanted to say. They tried
to talk for a longer time.

When the patients in the movies did these four things, that is: *(1)* when they
answered questions and made conversation; *(2)* when they asked questions and
started conversations; *(3)* when they tried to make sense and make sure the
other people understood them; and *(4)* when they talked for a long time
the patients felt better and happier. We and others have actually done this,
with many patients just like you, and we found that they always feel better and
are happier. Since we want you too to feel better and since we also want you to
be happier, we want you to do all these things, just like the patients in the movies. So pay close attention and learn what to do. Thank you.

*Scene 1*

P:    I'm very happy that you'll be coming home.
M:    Say, my wife just told me that she's very happy that I'll be coming home.
      Now I'm supposed to do certain things, things that you do to get to know

---

* Throughout this tape *P* will represent Person in whatever role is called for by
the nature of the dialogue.

your relatives better. First, I'm supposed to talk to them, maybe ask them something. Second, I should answer them when they talk to me. Third, I should talk alot, don't just say yes or no. O.K., then I'll answer my wife because she just said something to me. I'll tell her that I too am very happy that I'll be going home. There, that's a good thing to say, it makes sense and it's about the same thing she is talking about. Maybe I could even ask her something, like how are the kids. That should start up a conversation. Good, now I'll just have to be sure that I make sense so she'll understand me and I have to make sure that I talk alot. Say, I'm kind of proud of myself, I really learned how to talk to my wife.

## Scene 2

P:  How are you John, are you feeling any better?

M:  Hey, these are my parents here to visit me. Good, this will give me the chance to practice those four things I learned to do in order to get to know my family better. Now let's see if I can remember those four things. Oh yes, (1) I have to talk to them, try to start a conversation by either saying something to them or asking them a question. (2) I have to answer them when they talk to me or when they ask me a question. (3) I have to make sure that what I say makes sense, talk about something they'd be interested in or talk about the same thing they're talking about. (4) I have to also talk alot. O.K., I'll try to do all those things now. My Dad just asked me if I'm feeling better so I'll answer him. I'll say, "Yes, I'm feeling much better." Hmm, maybe I should even tell them something else . . . maybe that the medicine the nurse gives me really helps me alot. That's a good thing to say, that's like starting a conversation. I also think it's something they'd be interested in. You know, I really learned how to get along better with my parents. I'm pretty proud of myself.

## Scene 3

M:  Say, those are some of my old buddies from the factory. I'd really like to spend some time with them. Now what am I supposed to do in this kind of a situation, when I want to be with people. I know, I'm supposed to go over to them and talk with them, ask them questions, answer when they ask me questions, make conversation. That's right. Those are very important things to do. But there are other things I'm supposed to do, now what are they? Oh, I know, I'm also supposed to try to make sense, talk about something I think they'd be interested in. Also, I have to talk alot, explain what I mean, not just say yes or no. I've got that part, now let's see if I can do it. First, I'll go over to my buddies and say hello, tell them how good it is to see them again. Next, I'll ask them about news from the factory . . . that's a good thing to say because that'll get a conversation started. Also, I think that's something they'd be interested in talking about. So far, so good. Now what should I do if they ask me how I've been? I'll tell them that I'm doing O.K., That's what I'll say. Hey, all that sounds good. I really know how to handle this situation. I must be a sharp guy.

## Scene 4

M: Now this is my wife here. She came to visit me in the hospital. I'd like to talk to her, get along better with her. I guess I should do those four things I learned. First, I learned I should talk to others, ask them questions and make conversation. Second, I learned that I should answer others when they talk to me. Third I learned that I should talk about things that others would be interested in and also talk about the same things they are talking about. Fourth, I learned that I should talk alot. I shouldn't just say a couple of words. O.K., I remembered everything, now I'll do it. First, I'll ask my wife something, something about the kids, like how they are doing in school. Then I'll talk to her about how the kids are doing at home, if they are behaving. All that sounds good. It makes sense because I know it's something that she'd like to talk about and it's also alot of talk, more than just a couple of words. I'm really getting good at talking to my wife. I must be getting better.

## Scene 5

M: Now I'm going into this store to buy something but I have to talk so that the store clerk understands what I want. Maybe I had better do those four important things I learned. (1) Talk to others, ask them questions and make conversation. (2) Answer others when they talk to me. (3) Talk sense so that they know what I'm saying. (4) Talk for long times, not just a few words. So first, I have to talk to the clerk, tell him what I want. I'll say I want to buy a pen. That's good. Then if he asks me any questions, I'll have to answer him, but I have to make sure that my answer makes sense. O.K., I'm all set. Say, I can sure handle these situations. I'm getting pretty good at talking to people.

## Scene 6

M: Say, these are some of my friends from home. They came up to the hospital to visit me. That's great. This will give me the chance to practice those four things to get to know my friends better. Now let's see if I remember what those four things are. (1) Talk to them, ask questions, and make conversation. (2) Answer them when they talk to me. (3) Talk about things they'd be interested in and talk about the same things they talk about. (4) Talk alot, explain myself. So what can I say? I could ask Al and Tony what's new back home, like how their families are doing and how're their jobs. Those are good things to say. That should start a conversation. O.K., here goes. You know, I must be pretty smart to figure out how to talk to my friends.

## Scene 7

M:     Hmm, I want to go into the store to buy something, but first, I'd better make sure I know what to do. There are those four things I have to do. First, I have to talk to the clerk, tell him what I want. Second, I have to answer the clerk if he asks me anything or says anything to me. Third, I have to make sense. I have to talk so that he'll understand me. Fourth I have to talk alot. There, I've learned what to do, now let's see if I can do it. I'll go into the store and tell the clerk that I want to buy some writing paper and some envelopes. That's right, I'll start talking to him, but I have to remember, whenever I say anything, I have to make sure that it makes sense. Hey, you know, that's pretty good. I really know what to do in these situations. Pretty sharp of me, huh?

## Scene 8

P:     Hello, Jim, we've come to take you home for the weekend.

M:     Now, these are my parents here. They're talking about taking me home for the weekend. Gee, I should really talk to them. I should practice those four things that will help me to get along with them better. Let's see if I can remember what those four things are. The first thing is, I have to talk to my parents, say things to them, and ask them questions. The second thing is, I have to answer them when they talk to me or ask me questions. The third thing is, I have to talk so they'll understand me, talk about things they are interested in. Fourth thing is, I have to talk alot, talk for a long time. There, those are the four things I have to do. Now what should I say to my parents. They are talking about taking me home for the weekend, so I'll talk to them about that. I'll tell them that I'd really like to visit with them. Then I'll tell them that I'd also like to see my brother and his wife. Maybe I'll even ask them a question, a question about my brother. That sounds good. It's alot of talk and it also makes sense, it's something that I know they like to talk about. I think I must be getting better because I know just how to handle this kind of situation. I'm sort of proud of myself.

## Scene 9

P:     Hello, dear, I'm so glad to see you.

M:     My wife came to visit me. That's real nice of her. Now I'll be able to talk with her and practice those things I learned to do that help you get along better with your relatives. First, I'll make conversation with my wife, say something to her or ask her a question. Second, I'll answer her when she makes conversation with me, when she asks me a question. Third, I'll try to make sure that she can understand everything I say, I'll talk about the same thing that she's talking about and things that she'd be interested in. Fourth, I'll try to talk for a long time, not just yes and no answers. Here goes. I'll try to do all those things right now. First I'll tell my wife that

I'm happy that she came to see me. Then I'll ask her about the children, that's a good topic. That's something we both like talking about. Say, I figured out just how to talk to my wife. That shows that I am getting better and that I'm very smart.

## Scene 10

M:  Hey, my children are here to see me. That's nice of them. I sure do like having them visit with me. Now, what am I supposed to do when I have visitors, let me think, oh yeah, I have to do four things. (1) Start up a conversation with them, talk to them. (2) Answer them when they start up a conversation with me or ask me a question. (3) Talk about things that they are interested in and talk so that I make sense. (4) Talk for long times, say alot. Now I've got it, so what could I say to my children? Oh, I know, first I'll tell them that I'm happy to see them. Next, I'll ask them if they brought me that sweater I wanted. That's a good way to start a conversation. But I have to remember, when they talk to me, I have to talk sense. Say, I figured that out real easily. I really think I'm getting better. I'm kind of proud of myself.

## Narrator's Summary

You just saw some very important movies which showed you how some patients were able to get to know and talk to their friends and relatives. You saw how the patients did four important things:

1. They answered questions and made conversation with the other people.
2. They asked questions and started conversations with the other people.
3. They tried to make sense and make sure the other people understood them.
4. They tried not to talk with just yes or no, they tried to talk alot.

Because these patients were able to get to know and talk with their friends and relatives they felt much better and they were happier. When we talk with people, we are healthier and we have more fun. We want you to feel better and be happier too, so now we want you to do all the things you saw the patients in the movies do, right here with the other people in your group. Thank you.

### Focusing—Experiencing: Tape 1

### Narrator

This film is about a patient like yourself who came to a hospital like this one, but in another state, for help. Her name is Jane and you will see her in two scenes. In the first scene Jane meets with her doctor. He tells her how to (1) see what her main feeling is and (2) to pay attention to it. He has her do this by telling her to (a) relax, (b) to see what her main feeling is, (c) to concentrate on it, *(d)* to think of a problem that has to do with that feeling, *(e)* to concentrate on that, *(f)* to notice if the feeling changes, and *(g)* to describe how she feels again. These steps enable Jane to see what her main feeling is and to pay attention to it. This will help her understand herself better and she will feel good about that.

In the second scene, Jane goes back to the ward and tries to *(1)* see what her main feeling is and *(2)* pay attention to it by herself—that is, without the doctor's help this time. Watch Jane and listen carefully to the steps she uses. After the film is over, we would like you to try to see what *(1)* your main feeling is and *(2)* pay attention to it, in the same way that Jane did. This will help you understand yourself better, and could lead to your getting well faster. But we'll tell you more about how you can try this later. Now watch this. Here is *Scene 1* with Jane and her doctor.

## Scene 1

*Doctor:* Hi, Jane.

*Jane:* Hello, Doctor.

*Doctor:* I am going to help you see what your main feeling is and pay attention to it. I believe this will help you to get to know yourself better. Is that O.K. with you?

*Jane:* What do you mean?

*Doctor:* Well, by relaxing, seeing what your main feeling is, concentrating on it, noticing if it changes, and seeing what your new feeling is, you will be better able to understand yourself. It is very good to know what you are feeling. It helps you get better sooner. Are you willing to try it?

*Jane:* What's the basic idea again?

*Doctor:* To see what your main feeling is and to pay attention to it. Are you ready to try it?

*Jane:* Yes. I'm ready.

*Doctor:* First, relax. Stretch your arms and legs and then let them drop.

*Jane:* (Stretches) O.K. Doctor, how's that?

*Doctor:* That's fine. Now close your eyes and try to see what your main feeling is. Try to be aware of your main feeling.

*Jane:* (30 sec) I am feeling nervous. I don't know what it's about, I just feel nervous.

*Doctor:* I am sorry that you feel nervous, but it is very, very good that you have identified your main feeling. Now, pay attention to it. Pay attention to your feeling of nervousness.

*Jane:* (30 sec)

*Doctor:* Good. You have concentrated on your main feeling. Now pick a problem that has to do with that feeling—a personal problem.

*Jane:* (10 sec) Well, I feel nervous wondering about whether I'll get any visitors. I want some to come, but I'm scared that no one will come to see me, so I'm nervous.

| | |
|---|---|
| *Doctor:* | Good, you've picked a problem that has to do with your feeling. Now concentrate on the problem *and* the feeling. |
| *Jane:* | (30 sec) |
| *Doctor:* | Good. Now, notice if the feeling changes. |
| *Jane:* | (30 sec) Well, the more I pay attention to that feeling of nervousness, the more I begin to feel lonely—like I'll be all alone if no one comes. |
| *Doctor:* | Good. Describe your present feeling. |
| *Jane:* | I'm scared because I don't want to be alone. |
| *Doctor:* | Now you understand yourself better. That's very good Jane. You've relaxed, saw what your main feeling was, paid attention to it. Then you picked out a problem, noticed if the feeling changed and described your feeling again. I want you to go back to the ward and practice what you have just done; practice seeing what your main feeling is and pay attention to it. You have done very well. |
| *Jane:* | O.K. That was good. |

## Scene 2

| | |
|---|---|
| *Narrator:* | Jane has done a good job and knows herself a little better. She is now going to do what the doctor said: she will see what her main feeling is and pay attention to it. She is going to do this while she is sitting alone in a chair on the ward. Here's Jane. |
| *Jane:* | I'm going to try to do what the doctor said—to see what my main feeling is and to pay attention to it. First, I have to relax. (stretches) . . . now I'll close my eyes and see what I'm feeling. (30 sec) I'm feeling pretty excited today . . . I feel a happy kind of excitement. I'll concentrate on that. Let's see, the doctor said to pick out a problem that has to do with the feeling. . . . Well, one thing is that I never finish the things I start. I begin to do things and then I never finish them. I'll concentrate on that problem and the feeling. (30 sec) The doctor said to notice if my feelings change. (10 sec) Well, I don't feel good when I think about not finishing things; I feel less excited . . . but . . . oh, I know why I feel kind of happy and excited now. It's because I just finished the project I was working on in O.T. My feelings have changed. I'm feeling proud of myself. The doctor said I should describe my feelings. I'm feeling proud that I finished a project instead of leaving it undone like I usually do. This way of seeing what my feelings are and paying attention to them does help me get to know myself better. |

## Scene 3

| | |
|---|---|
| *Narrator:* | Now we are going to see some other times that Jane took note of what she was feeling and paid attention to it. Jane practices the |

step-by-step method the doctor taught her every day because it helped her get to know herself better. You will now see two more times when Jane used this method while she was sitting alone on the ward.

*Jane:*  I am going to try to concentrate on my feelings. First I have to relax. (stretches). Now I am going to close my eyes and see if I can describe what I am feeling. (30 sec) My main feeling is that I am feeling heavy and sad. I'll pay attention to that feeling. (30 sec) The doctor said I should pick a problem that has to do with that feeling. Well, it's a problem that I don't feel like doing anything . . . not getting out of bed in the morning, not going to meals, not talking to anyone. I just feel heavy . . . like I have no get up and go. I'll concentrate on the problem and my feeling. The doctor said to notice if the feeling changes. (30 sec) I don't think it has changed this time. I just feel more and more depressed and sad. He said to describe my feelings. (10 sec) Right now I feel like crying. I'm very unhappy.

*Doctor:*  (Walking by and stopping to chat with Jane) How are you doing, Jane? Are you using the method I taught you to see what your main feeling is and to pay attention to it?

*Jane:*  Yes, Doctor. I just did it before—right before you came over to say hello. But I found out that I am feeling sad and unhappy. I feel like crying. Do you think it does any good to feel sad?

*Doctor:*  Jane, it sounds as if you are saying that you know yourself better than you did before. Now you know how you are feeling and that is a very important thing. I think you are doing very well even though you are feeling sad right now. You know what you are feeling and can pay attention to your feeling and that's what counts. Keep up the good work.

## Scene 4

*Narrator:*  Here is another time that Jane used the doctor's method to see what her main feeling was and to pay attention to it.

*Jane:*  First, I have to relax. (Stretches) Now I'm going to close my eyes and see what I'm feeling. I feel tight . . . . (clenches fists) I feel all charged up. I feel so angry . . . oooh! I'll do what the doctor said and pay attention to my feeling (30 sec) I just feel soooo mad. I know what problem this has to do with. I'm mad at Sue and Betty . . . I feel like I hate them right now. I can feel the anger in my body. The problem was when they went on pass to the movies without me. I had a pass to go and they knew that I wanted to see the picture. Now, I should notice if the feeling changes (30 sec) Really, I'm feeling hurt now. That's a new feeling I got just now. To describe my new feeling I would say that it hurts my feelings that Sue and Betty would go to the movies without me. The doctor's really right. I know more about myself now. I *am* doing pretty good if I do say so myself!

## Focusing–Experiencing: Tape 2

### *Scene 1*

*Narrator:* This film is about a patient like yourself who came to a hospital like this one, but in another state, for help. Her name is Mary and you will see her in two scenes. In the first scene Mary meets with her doctor. He tells her how to *(1)* see what her main feeling is and *(2)* to pay attention to it. He has her do this by telling her to *(a)* relax, *(b)* to see what her main feeling is, *(c)* to concentrate on it, *(d)* to think of a problem that has to do with that feeling, *(e)* to concentrate on that, *(f)* to notice if the feeling changes, and *(g)* to describe how she feels again. These steps enable Mary to see what her main feeling is and to pay attention to it. This will help her understand herself better and she will feel good about that. In the second scene, Mary goes back to the ward and tries to *(1)* see what her main feeling is and *(2)* pay attention to it by herself— that is, without the doctor's help this time. Watch Mary and listen carefully to the steps she uses. After the film is over, we would like you to try to see what your main feeling is and pay attention to it, in the same way that Mary did. This will help you understand yourself better, and could lead to your getting well faster. But we'll tell you more about how you can try this later. Now watch this. Here is *Scene 1* with Mary and her doctor.

*Doctor:* Hi, Mary.

*Mary:* Hello, Doctor.

*Doctor:* I am going to help you see what your feelings are and pay attention to them. I believe this will help you to get to know yourself better. O.K.?

*Mary:* O.K.

*Doctor:* First, relax. Stretch your arms and legs and then let them drop.

*Mary:* O.K. Doctor, how's that? (Stretches.)

*Doctor:* That's fine. Now close your eyes and try to see what your main feeling is. Try to be aware of your main feeling.

*Mary:* (30 sec) I feel scared. I don't really know why I'm scared . . . I just feel kind of shaky.

*Doctor:* It is good that you know what your main feeling is. Now pay attention to that feeling of shakiness. (Waits 30 sec.) Now pick a problem that has to do with your main feeling.

*Mary:* (10 sec) Well, I'm going bowling tomorrow and that is a problem for me because I don't know how to bowl good. Everyone else will probably do better than me. I'll probably look like a jerk.

*Doctor:*    Good. That sounds like a problem that has to do with your feeling. Now, concentrate on it.

*Mary:*    (30 sec) Well, the more I pay attention to the feeling of shakiness, the more I begin to feel afraid that the others at the bowling alley will make fun of me and I'll feel stupid.

*Doctor:*    Describe your present feeling.

*Mary:*    I'm scared that I'll look stupid at the bowling game tomorrow.

*Doctor:*    That's very good, Mary. You've relaxed, saw what your main feeling was, paid attention to it. Then you picked out a problem that had to do with that feeling, noticed if the feelings you had changed, and described your feelings again. You know more about yourself now. I want you to go back to the ward and practice what you have just done; practice seeing what your main feeling is and paying attention to it. You have done very well.

*Mary:*    O.K.

## Scene 2

*Narrator:*    Mary has done a good job and knows herself a little better. She is now going to do what the doctor said to see what her main feeling is and to pay attention to it. She is going to do this while she is sitting alone in a chair on the ward. Here's Mary.

*Mary:*    I'm going to try to do what the doctor said—to see what my main feeling is and to pay attention to it. First, I have to relax. (stretches) . . . . now I'll close my eyes and see what my main feeling is (30 sec.) I'm pretty restless now; I feel like I want to get going on something . . . like it's hard even to just sit here and do nothing. . . . Let's see, the doctor said to pick out a problem that is important to me. . . . This restlessness makes me think of how I don't care about how I look. That's a problem. I don't usually comb my hair and I'm pretty fat and I'm usually sloppy. The doctor said I should describe my feelings. I'm feeling like I want to be neater and take better care of myself. I think I'm going to make an appointment to get my hair done. This way of seeing what my main feeling is and paying attention to it does help me to get to know myself better.

## Scene 3

*Narrator:*    Now we are going to see some other times that Mary took note of what her main feeling was and paid attention to it. Mary practiced what the doctor had told her: to relax, see what her main feeling was, concentrate on it, pick a problem that had to do with it, concentrate on that, notice if the feeling changes, and describe her new feeling. Mary practiced this method every day because it helped her to get to know herself better and that made her feel good. You will now see two more times when Mary used this method while she was sitting alone on the ward.

*Mary:* I am going to try to concentrate on my feelings. First I have to relax. (Stretches) Now I am going to close my eyes and see if I can describe what my main feeling is. (30 sec) Right now I feel nothing. It's like there's nothing inside me. I'll pay attention to that feeling of emptiness. (30 sec) The doctor said I should pick a problem that has to do with the feeling. I just don't feel anything and I don't do anything. That's a problem. I'll concentrate on it. (30 sec) The doctor said to notice if the feeling changes (30 sec) I don't feel any different. I still feel empty and bored. To describe my feeling now I would say that I feel empty and bored. But I guess it's better that I know how I feel and that I'm paying attention to it than if I just ignored how I feel.

## Scene 4

*Narrator:* Here is another time that Mary used the step-by-step method to see what her main feeling was and to pay attention to it.

*Mary:* First, I have to relax. (Stretches) Now I'm going to close my eyes and see what my main feeling is. I feel like running away . . . like hiding . . . I don't want to look at anybody. I'll do what the doctor said and pay attention to my feeling. (30 sec) I just don't feel like looking at anybody, especially not the people who I sat with at lunch. I know what problem this has to do with. I'm so careless, like when I knocked over the milk at lunch and everyone seemed to see me do it. Now, I should concentrate on that feeling . . . the feeling when I knocked over the milk. (30 sec) My feeling is changing. I know it was an accident but I felt embarrassed . . . but I helped clean it up and it's over now. I feel a little relieved. Like it's over now and I don't have to keep thinking that everyone is still thinking about me spilling the milk. My feeling now is that it was embarrassing to spill the milk, but I don't feel bad any more. Seeing how you feel and paying attention to your main feeling can help you learn more about yourself. It can also make you feel better about yourself.

## Role Taking: Hostility Tape

### Scene 1: Narrator's Introduction

Hello, My name is _____. I am the Director of the _____. We have invited you to this meeting, first of all, to listen to a very important tape recording.

The purpose of this tape is to help you learn some things that may be of great use to you in doing something to solve some of the problems that brought you to this center. This tape has been played to people with problems like yours at many other clinics, and it has been very helpful to a large number of people just like you, so we ask you to pay very close attention.

The first thing you will hear is two actors, playing the parts of a husband and wife, have a pretty strong argument. Although these are actors, what you will hear them fight about comes from real fights that many husbands and wives have really had.

On the second part of the tape you will hear a meeting between the wife and her doctor. You will hear the doctor telling her two things she can do to help her and her husband get along better. Listen very carefully to these two ideas, because they have been of great help to real wives who have actually done what this doctor recommends.

On the third part of the tape, you will hear the wife practicing the two ideas, and on the last part of the tape you'll hear how she used them very successfully when it looked like another fight between herself and her husband was about to get started.

## Scene 2: Fight Scene

*H:** Isn't anybody home in this goddamned house?

*W:†* Hi. Yeah, I'm home.

*H:* Bring me a beer, will ya?

*W:* Could you come get it yourself? I've got things to do here.

*H:* No, I can't come get it myself. I just want a beer. Will you bring it in here; you got two legs.

*W:* Oh, jeez, I got so many things to do. Look, O.K.; uh, Jack, bring your father a beer. The kid'll bring it in to you.

*H:* Where's this kid been? In the swamp? How come he's so filthy? What did you do all day today? The kid's filthy, the house is filthy. . . .

*W:* Uh, now, I was doing the laundry and I was sewing that shirt of yours that you ripped the other day and, uh, I don't know . . . I was busy all day.

*H:* Yeah, like hell you were. This place looks just the same as it did two years ago. You haven't done a goddam thing in this house . . . you haven't cleaned the stupid floor in a month.

*W:* Well, if we live in a shitty dump, it's not all my fault.

*H:* When's dinner gonna be ready?

*W:* Six o'clock—like every day.

*H:* Six o'clock?

*W:* Six o'clock; you know. . .

*H:* You know I get home at 4:30 every day. Christt, why do I have to sit

---

* *H* represents Husband throughout the following tapes.

† *W* represents Wife throughout the following tapes.

around for an hour and a half every day waiting for dinner? Why can't I eat when I come home like other people? Why do I go through all this grief when I get home from work? I go through grief all day trying to bring home the money in this house. I get home and I get grief, too.

W:  Look, you never made it home at 4:30 one day in your life. You stop off at a bar every goddam day on your way home from work. You're never home at 4:30.

H:  That's right, lady.

W:  Even when you're not working you're not home at 4:30.

H:  I go to a goddam bar because that's the only place where people will talk to me like a human being—not in this house.

W:  You don't know how to talk to people like a human being; you never knew how to talk to people like a human being.

H:  Ahh . . . Christ, look at these kids. These kids standing around yapping with their drawers off. Why can't you keep them in clothes?

W:  You think I'm the only one knows how to put a pair of pants on?

H:  Shit! I come home and all I want is a little peace and quiet and a decent meal.

W:  Well, you'll get your food. You always get your food.

H:  Yeah . . . you call that food?

W:  Look, you think you can do better, you can cook. I'll go out to work and you can cook.

H:  That'll be the day. I'd like to see you go out to work. What are you going to do with all these friends you yak to all day? You going to bring them to work with you too?

W:  At least I'd show up at work every day.

H:  Show up at work! Christ, you can't even make dinner once a day.

W:  Look, if you don't like what you get here, go out with your bummy friends.

H:  You know, I think I will. I'll go someplace where I can talk to someone at least.

W:  Good . . . well, good. . . .

H:  Christ, I'll get out of here. . .

W:  Get the hell out of here. . . . Good-bye.

H:  Ah, screw you too. Good-bye. . . . .

W:  Good-bye, good-bye. . . . .

## Scene 3: Training Scene

T:°  Hi, Mrs. Johnson. Come on in and sit down.

W:  Hi.

T:  You sound sort of depressed today, more so than the last time I saw you.

W:  I . . . oh, I don't know. . . . I'm pissed off.

---

° T represents Therapist throughout, as previously noted.

T: You pretty angry?

W: Yeah. My husband's been giving me a lot of shit lately.

T: More so than before?

W: Yeah. He gets worse all the time. He just starts fights over nothing.

T: Over nothing at all? What happened?

W: Yeah, over nothing at all. Well, he came home from work . . . oh, look . . . it was like. . . . This happens all the time. It happened last week. He came home from work and he wanted a glass of beer. He couldn't just go and get a beer for himself. I had to go and get him a beer and he started yelling at me about the children being dirty and then he started telling me I don't do anything but sit on my ass, he says, all day, and talk with my neighbors. And that's not true. I just go over and see one friend —Sally, across the hall; and that's not very often.

T: Does he feel that you should do a lot of things that you don't do?

W: Yeah, he does.

T: And that makes you mad?

W: Yeah, that makes me mad. I work all day; what does he do? You know, he bums around half the time; and then he tells me that I'm sitting around doing nothing.

T: He doesn't work?

W: Yeah, sometimes he works and sometimes he doesn't. It depends on— you know—if they have any stuff in to do then.

T: Now, the other day—when he came home mad and what you're telling me about, was he working that day?

W: Yeah, he worked that day.

T: And you had a pretty good fight?

W: Yeah, we had a good fight.

T: What happened? How did it end up?

W: He slammed out. He slammed the door. I told him to get the hell out of there. I didn't want him around like that. I mean, I don't need that.

T: You didn't want him around like *that*.

W: Yeah, he comes around and he was yelling at me and . . . oh, I don't know. I just took so much . . . oh, I don't know . . . I worked so hard myself that day. I don't need him yelling around the house. He could get lost. He could go to a bar and drink all night and I wouldn't care. Just as long as he gave me the money for the house. I really don't care.

T: You don't want him back?

W: No. No way! I don't need him like that.

T: You don't need him like that, but you need him.

W: Sometimes.

T: You want to break up the marriage?

W: No, I don't want to break up the marriage. I mean . . . like . . . I wouldn't be coming here if I wanted the marriage to break up. I want to do something, but I don't know what to do. It keeps getting worse.

T: Yeah, you want more appreciation.

*W:*  Yeah, I sure do.

*T:*  He doesn't show any appreciation.

*W:*  He sure doesn't. Not at all.

*T:*  He came in just yelling and screaming and you don't know what brought it on.

*W:*  No.

*T:*  I think I'd be mad, too, if I were you. I think I can understand exactly how you feel.

*W:*  Yeah.

*T:*  But I wonder what we can do about it?

*W:*  Boy, I don't know that one!

*T:*  You know, we found that when husbands and wives don't get along, that if they try to understand how the other guy felt, like you try to understand how Hal felt maybe, that, uh, maybe you could learn to get along together.

*W:*  Oh, that man has no feelings.

*T:*  You don't think he has any feelings?

*W:*  No. He doesn't . . . oh, everything rolls off his back . . . nothing . . . he doesn't feel anything.

*T:*  I know how mad you can get and I know how men can get that way, but I really think he has feelings and maybe if we could get you to understand how he feels.

*W:*  If you could really figure out how he feels, you deserve to be a doctor; 'cause I don't know anyone who knows how that man feels; even his own mother doesn't understand him. Well, how do you think it would help me if I understood him?

*T:*  Alright, if you try to understand how Hal feels and you show him that you understand, it's most likely that he's going to act differently, act better toward you, and then he, too, will understand how you feel.

*W:*  Huh?

*T:*  That sounds kind of hard?

*W:*  Well, it sounds alright. But, I don't know exactly what you mean.

*T:*  Well, O.K., let's take an example. You say he came home and started to yell and scream and you couldn't figure out what you were doing wrong. Right?

*W:*  Right, yeah.

*T:*  So, let's go back to when he came in the house.

*W:*  O.K.

*T:*  And you said he was kind of mad and upset when he came in and you started to argue. Alright, instead of doing that, how about if you could try to think of how he felt when he came home; how he got mad; and, what do you think made him get mad?

*W:*  Gee, I don't know; I really don't know.

*T:*  You don't have any idea what goes on in his work all day long? What does he do?

W: Yeah, he works in a factory. He works over in the plant on Vine Street.

T: Oh, yes, that plant on Vine Street. What does he do exactly?

W: He's on the assembly line. You know, guys standing around there and they put the parts together.

T: He's helping other guys?

W: Yeah; he does one of the parts. I don't know which part he does. They put . . . uh . . . you know, they put appliances together.

T: He has to be pretty fast, huh?

W: Well, I don't know; I never saw the place.

T: So, you say, you really don't know what he does and you don't know how he feels.

W: No, I really don't.

T: Do you think things get kind of fast there and he gets nervous?

W: Well, he's nervous; he's a nervous type.

T: He is a nervous type?

W: Yeah, he's nervous. He flies off the handle very easily. He always flies off the handle.

T: Does he ever talk about his boss?

W: He hates his boss.

T: Hates him?

W: Yeah, he hates him.

T: What does he say about him?

W: Ah, that boss . . . he pushes the guys around. None of the guys like him. He tells them what to do and he makes them hurry up and he makes them take short coffee breaks, and he watches what time they punch back in from lunch.

T: He's always on his back?

W: Oh, always on his back.

T: Uh-huh. How does Hal act towards his boss, do you know?

W: Gee, I don't know. I know he hates him; I don't know what he says to him.

T: You haven't any idea what he does when he, uh, when his boss is pushing him?

W: Well, he says he feels like punchin' him in the nose, but I know he doesn't do that.

T: Uh-huh. He feels like it; it sounds like he's real mad and he doesn't have a way to show it, right?

W: You can't punch the boss in the nose!

T: I guess you can't or you'll lose your job.

W: Yeah.

T: So, does this go on all day, do you think? Is he on his back all day long?

W: I don't know. I guess so.

T: Sounds like he's mad from the minute he comes in and he can't ever show it.

W: Yeah, well, he can't do that.

*T:* You know, as we talk, it almost seems to me that you're trying very hard to understand Hal and I think you're doing a real good job. Now, you remember before when we were talking, Mrs. Johnson, and I said there were two important things and one was to try to understand how Hal feels and the other was to show him. Now, as we talk, it's clear to me that you understand how he feels and what do you think you should do to show him that you understand how he feels when he comes home?

*W:* I don't know. I never thought about that.

*T:* Mmh. Mmh. Well, let's go back to where the fight started. What happened when he came in?

*W:* He screamed at me to get him a beer.

*T:* He wanted a beer?

*W:* Yeah. He really did.

*T:* Well, what do you think you could do about that so that he wouldn't scream at you?

*W:* I guess I could have gotten it for him; but I was really busy.

*T:* You were busy getting supper ready.

*W:* I guess I could have gotten it for him. I guess he really was pretty tired.

*T:* Yeah, you could have gotten him the beer and that would have shown him that you understood. How about telling him that you understand?

*W:* You mean that I understand that he is tired . . . from work?

*T:* Yeah, just how he feels . . . how about telling him?

*W:* Well, I guess I could have told him I understood that he had a hard day at work.

*T:* That's very good.

*W:* Well, what if I gave him the beer and he was still angry at me? That could happen.

*T:* He'd still be angry at you?

*W:* Yeah.

*T:* What do you think he'd be angry about?

*W:* Well . . . like money! We always fight about that. He could be angry about that. Like I don't manage it very well.

*T:* Yes. Ah, he gets mad because you don't manage the money very well?

*W:* Well, I guess he gets mad because we don't have a lot of money.

*T:* You don't have enough to go around?

*W:* Yeah, I guess he really feels pretty bad about that.

*T:* That's very good. You understand that he worries about the money too. How could you tell him that you understand that?

*W:* That I understand that he worries about the money?

*T:* Right.

*W:* I guess I could just tell him that.

*T:* Yeah.

*W:* Tell him that I understand that he was worried that we don't have enough money?

*T:* Very good. Tell him that you understand.

W: Do you think that would make a difference?

T: It could make a lot of difference. It might make him feel better and act better.

W: I think I understand, now . . . like tell him I understand his feelings and show him . . . like. . . . I guess I could have said to him . . . like, I knew he felt up tight . . . he really didn't feel happy at all and I could have told him that . . . like, "Do you really feel up tight?" and that I understand. . .

T: That sounds just great. You really do get the point.

### Scene 4: Self-Instruction Scene

C:* Hey, Ma, when are we gonna eat?

W: I'm gettin' supper now. It should be ready pretty soon. Your father should be home in about 10 minutes. Hand me those plates, will ya? And then, would you go find your sister?

C: O.K., Momma. (Hands plates and leaves house.)

W: Those are some really good things that Dr. Harris told me. Maybe tonight would be a good time to try them. Now, let me see . . . there were two parts to what she told me. One part was that I should try to understand what he feels and the other part was that I should tell him that I understand how he feels. Like with this tired stuff when he comes home, if I see that he's tired from working, then I can tell him that I understand he had a hard day at work. And then there was that time that Hal left; he really felt that I didn't understand what he was talking about . . . that I wasn't listening to him and I could have . . . I understand . . . that he felt that way . . . that's the first thing I could have done . . . told him that I understood, but I didn't tell him that and I guess I could have told him that . . . he really felt like I wasn't listening to him, but that I was trying. And then there was that other thing with the kids. I guess I could have done that there, too. When he said the kids were dirty and . . . I guess he really is concerned about how the kids look. I think he really gives a damn about the kids and all I could hear at the time was that he was angry at me. I also guess it's pretty hard for him when he comes home to find the house so noisy . . . everyone running around and everything underfoot. I understand that it's not so nice to come home and relax in a place that's so . . . well, crazy, hectic. I guess I could tell him that. And I guess when we're fighting and he got angry with me, I got angry back at him and that really made him feel worse; like if he was feeling tired and if he was not feeling understood and I got angry, that made him feel less understood and I guess . . . let me see . . . the doctor said I should try to understand what his feelings would be. He was probably feeling that I really don't understand and I really would like to tell him,

---

* C represents Child.

but I was so pissed off I couldn't tell him anything, not then. But after
. . . well, now I understand that maybe after I could have told him that
I understand that my being angry made him feel even worse.

### Scene 5: Peace Scene

**H:** I'm home.

**W:** Hello.

**H:** Hi. Jesus. I want to sit down. What's this stuff doing in my chair. Christ, can't even sit down and get comfortable.

**W:** Oh, I guess you're really tired, huh? I'll take the stuff off.

**H:** O.K.

**C:** Hey, Ma, I found her.

**H:** Where's this kid been? Looks like she's been out playing in the garbage again. What do you do all day? Don't you have anything to do with this kid all day? What . . . what's going on?

**W:** You sound worried about the kids, but. . .

**H:** Yeah. . .

**W:** Well, it's O.K., they've just been out playing in the street with their friends.

**H:** Out on the street? You know they. . .

**W:** I know you're worried, but you don't have to . . . it's O.K.

**H:** I *am* worried. I don't know what goes on when I'm at work.

**W:** I know; you really care a lot about the kids.

**H:** Yeah, I do . . . I do.

**W:** Did you get paid today?

**H:** Yeah, I did . . . here's the money for the food. Take it, will ya. I know it's not much, but take it.

**W:** Oh, I know you don't feel good about us not having much money, but it's O.K., I can manage alright.

**H:** Can you really? It's not a hell of a lot of money for anyone. I know it's not that much. Can you really manage on that?

**W:** Yeah, I know you're worried about that, too; but I've got some good recipes I can make real cheap.

**H:** You know that's probably the nicest thing I heard today. You know, you're the first person that has said something really nice today.

**W:** It's pretty nice having you home today.

### Scene 6: Narrator's Summary

Hello, this Mr. _____ again. The tape you have just heard has tried to show you something which has really worked very well over and over again with many husbands and wives who were not getting along. The wife on the tape learned two things: (1) to try to understand what her husband was feeling; and (2) to try to let him know she understood his feelings.

When she did these two things, not only did no fight happen, but her husband began to treat her better.

Since doing this has actually helped so many husbands and wives, it is something we hope you may want to try. In order to help you use these ideas as best you can, the persons leading your meeting today will help you practice how to do these things with *your* husband, how to use them in *your* marriage.

## Role Taking: Apathy Tape

### Scene 1: Narrator's Introduction

Hello, you will remember that the tape you heard at our last meeting tried to show you that it can really help a husband and wife who are fighting a lot if the wife does two things: *(1)* tries to understand what her husband is feeling; and *(2)* tries to tell him that she understands his feelings.

On the first part of the tape you will hear now, the husband and wife are having a different kind of problem. Instead of fighting a lot, the husband just doesn't seem interested in doing *anything*—working, going out, or doing anything with the children.

On the second part of the tape, you will hear the wife discussing this problem with her doctor, who again shows her why it can help her, her husband, and their marriage if she tries to understand how he feels and lets him know.

On the last parts of the tape, you'll hear the wife practicing these ideas alone, and then trying them with her husband. Like most of the people who actually try this in real life, you'll see that she is successful.

### Scene 2: Apathy Scene

**W:** You gonna be staying home again today?

**H:** Uh-huh. Why is the TV in such bad shape?

**W:** Did you call a guy to fix it?

**H:** Nah. Can't you do something with it?

**W:** No; I don't know how to fix a TV. Maybe if you would go out and get some money, we could call a guy in to do it. It's pretty dangerous to fix a TV by yourself.

**H:** I don't want to hear any of that stuff about money.

**W:** What happened to that job you had last week? I thought you started that new thing with the truck?

**H:** Yeah, I had a job last week, so?

**W:** Well, you had a job last week; why can't you have a job today?

**H:** Because I don't have one today, that's why.

**W:** You know, it just seems like you don't want to do anything.

**H:** That's right. I don't want to do a damn thing—just want to sit here.

**W:** Yeah. Hey, you know, Mary stopped by and told me about the bowling dance. You know the league that I'm in? We're gonna have a dinner dance on Saturday. I wanna go.

*H:* You can go.

*W:* Oh, you're telling me . . . I mean, what's the use of going without your husband? Everyone's gonna have their husband there.

*H:* I don't like those things. All those people; I don't know any of them.

*W:* You know . . . you just don't want to do anything . . . you don't even want to have fun.

*H:* I have some fun when I go out with the guys . . . down at the bar . . . that's fun. I can enjoy myself then.

*W:* Yeah, but there's nothing around here that's any fun. We didn't even take the kids for ice cream this week.

*H:* I . . . they don't need that much ice cream.

*W:* It's not that much . . . it's like things are dead.

*H:* Well, what do you want me to do? There's nothing for me to do around here and whenever I go down to that place to work, they tell me there's nothing available so why bother doing that!

*W:* Well, for crying out loud. Get off your ass and be like other men and go down and get yourself a job. That's what I want you to do.

*H:* Yeah, that's easy for you to say. You don't have to go down there. I can't put up with that down there anymore.

*W:* Yeah, but you want money and you want the TV to work and you want. . . . Oh, I don't know . . . you want, you want, you want, but you don't do.

*H:* I do enough. I mean I don't exactly see you tearing up this house to make things right.

*W:* I can't do it alone.

## Scene 3: Training Scene

*T:* Hello, Mrs. Day. Come on in and sit down.

*W:* Hello.

*T:* How are things going?

*W:* Not so good.

*T:* What's happening?

*W:* My husband. He just doesn't want to do anything these days. He just sits around.

*T:* He just sits around? He's not interested in you or anything?

*W:* Yeah.

*T:* Mmh. Mmmh. Something special happen recently? Or just been happening and happening?

*W:* Like all the time he just sits around the house; he doesn't go to work; he doesn't take the kids anywhere. There was this special thing I wanted to go to with my bowling league and he didn't want to go to that.

*T:* Hmm. Hmm. Is he . . .

W: The TV's broken. He just doesn't do anything.
T: Makes you feel pretty discouraged, huh?
W: Yeah, it does.
T: Mmmh. Mmh.
W: Makes me angry too. 'Cause he wants me to fix the TV. I don't know how to fix the TV.
T: Mmh. Mmh. Not only doesn't he want to do something, he wants you to do it for him.
W: Yeah.
T: What happened with this bowling thing that you mentioned?
W: We didn't go. He wanted to go out with his friends instead. So I had to stay home and my friends went.
T: Well, you know, I can certainly understand how you'd feel both discouraged—you've talked about things like this before—and angry, but I wonder if I could ask you something a little different? What do you think his feelings were when you asked him about the bowling—the bowling dinner?
W: Oh, he could care less. I don't think he really gives a damn.
T: You think he has no feelings about that? Just doesn't want to go and that's it?
W: Yeah, that's right, he just doesn't want to go. (sigh)
T: The same thing about work? What do you think his feelings are?
W: Oh, I think he'd much rather hang out on the corner than go to work.
T: Mmh. Mmh.
W: The guys play pool; sometimes someone pays for his games. He's got it pretty good. But me, at home, I don't have it pretty good. I have to do all the work every day, whether or not he goes to work.
T: Yeah. Yeah.
W: The floors have to be cleaned . . .
T: Yeah. Your work goes on, whatever he does.
W: It does; it does . . .
T: Yeah, I can quite understand how you must feel. I'm just asking you though about how he might feel, for a really very special reason. The reason is that I think if you can understand something about how he feels, and maybe let him know that you understand some of those feelings, that might be of great help, not just to him, but to you also—to your marriage. How does that idea sound?
W: How would that help me with my problems, to understand his feelings?
T: Well, I know it's a little complicated. We've done a lot of this, though, with other wives and husbands just like you—the same kinds of problems you came here with. If you would try to understand Tom's feelings, and let him know that, that would probably make him feel alot better about himself—alot better in the sense of someone's understanding him, and when we've done this kind of thing before, we very often find that the husband starts treating the wife better.

*W:*    I'd like *that.*

*T:*    Mmh. Mmh. Well, let me give you an example.

*W:*    O.K.

*T:*    You mentioned about the work and I know that's a major problem and I certainly understand how you feel. It's important the he get a job—for the house, the kids. Why do you think, other than besides just not giving a damn, he might not be too anxious to go down there, wherever he goes to look for work? What kind of things happen to him when he goes there, for example? What has he told you?

*W:*    Well, sometimes the boss tells him there isn't any work.

*T:*    Well, now, you remember a couple of weeks ago when you told me about something just like this? He did go down there and there were about six other guys there and he said almost all of them were hired? Now, it was just for a couple of days they got hired, but they got hired and he didn't.

*W:*    Yeah, that happens to him alot; like, he's pretty near the bottom of the list.

*T:*    How do you think he feels when something like that happens?

*W:*    I think he feels pretty down about it.

*T:*    I think you're probably right. I think you have a good sense of what he might be feeling in that situation. I think I would feel that way and you might, and I guess he would also.

*W:*    I guess so.

*T:*    I guess what I'm asking you is, what do you think would happen if you told him that? If you said to him, when he told you he didn't feel like going out—if you said to him . . . what? What do you think you'd say to him? Now, you seem to know what he's feeling? How could you tell him that?

*W:*    I should tell him, like, he's feeling bad because he didn't get the job?

*T:*    You said to me, just a minute ago, that he's gone to this office or whatever it is he goes to, to look for a job, and things happen to him there that make him feel like he's at the bottom of the barrel. I wonder what would happen if you said that to him? Maybe not those exact words, but something like it.

*W:*    You mean, like sometimes it feels pretty shitty that he gets left out and everyone else gets hired?

*T:*    Exactly! That's very good. That's really excellent! What do you think would happen if you said something like that?

*W:*    Uh, I don't know. I never said anything like that to him.

*T:*    Yeah; but it's interesting that I really think you have that skill—that ability—to sort of sense what he's feeling. What I'm trying to suggest to you is that if you use that ability to let him know, he'd probably feel better because someone who matters to him would understand, and maybe treat you better.

W: Well, if you think that would work, I would try that.

T: Well, let's try one other example. O.K.?

W: O.K.

T: Now, we talked about the work and you seem to understand his feelings about that. You also mentioned you belong to this bowling club that's having this dinner and I can certainly understand—your friends are there and you want to go to it and he says he doesn't. And sure, your first reaction is he doesn't give a damn.

W: Yeah.

T: But, what other kinds of things might be involved? What's happened some of the other times that he has gone to some sort of bowling club thing or other kinds of social things with your friends?

W: Oh, he just kind of walks away and doesn't talk to people; and he drinks. Maybe he feels left out.

T: Mmh. Mmh! Very good! That's terrific. Well, what do you think you could say to him?

W: Something about that I know that sometimes he feels left out at the bowling dances, but that I would like him to come?

T: That's really excellent, Mrs. Day. I really think you can do that and I really encourage you to try that, at the first opportunity you have with Tom.

W: Can I ask you a question?

T: Yes.

W: Do you think it could be that the same thing happens with the kids? Like we didn't go for ice cream this week and do you think that maybe he feels bad that we don't have a lot of money to spend and that maybe that's why he doesn't take them?

T: I think that's very possible. I really think you're on the right track.

W: Should I tell him that, too?

T: Well, I think if you really think you understand what he's feeling; it doesn't have to be that it's 100% right. If you think that you understand what he's feeling, I'm trying to urge you to reach out to him by trying to let him know what you think he's feeling.

W: Well I know he feels bad that he can't get them, like, big ice cream cones. That even when we go, we have to get them little ones . . . I know he feels bad about that but I'd still like him to go with us, 'cause it's nice to be together.

T: Uh-huh . . . quite so . . . certainly.

W: Maybe I should try telling him that.

T: Fine. Why don't you try it and let's see how it goes. O.K.?

W: O.K. Then, you want me to do two things: you want me to understand how Tom feels; and you want me to tell him that, when I understand. Do you think that's going to make a difference in the way we get along together?

*T:*    There's a very good chance that just that is going to happen.

*W:*    O.K. I'll try it.

*T:*    You do that and we'll see you again soon—next time.

### Scene 4: Self-Instruction Scene

*W:*    Let's see now, Tom went out this morning to look for work and he might not be able to find any, like happened last time, so I guess I should think about what that doctor told me. He said . . . there was two things I was supposed to remember: one was I was supposed to understand how Tom was feeling and the other was to tell him so. Suppose he doesn't find any work? He'll probably feel really down again, like he did last time. So if he comes home and didn't find any work, I'm gonna tell him that I understand that he feels really bad about that . . . that he doesn't get any work and other guys do; and I'm gonna let him know that I understand. And there's also . . . oh, my goodness, I might run into that also . . . that social—that church social! I know it's one of those things that I will want to go to and I don't think he does, 'cause he doesn't know those people and he probably won't want to go. Well, I guess that's his feeling; if he doesn't want to go, you know he feels uncomfortable there. But that doctor said it should work—if I understand his feelings and I tell him I understand his feelings. At least Tom would know that I'm in touch with what's going on with him. So if he doesn't want to go to that social, well, even if he does, I'll say, I know you feel uncomfortable with the people there because they're mostly my friends. I'll tell him that. At least he'll know that I understand.

### Scene 5: Activity Scene

*W:*    Hi. How'd it go today?

*H:*    Aah, nothing, as usual.

*W:*    There was no work?

*H:*    There was work, but I didn't get any.

*W:*    Oh, you must feel really bad about that.

*H:*    I don't feel good about it, that's for sure.

*W:*    Other guys get work?

*H:*    Yeah, they had some jobs down there, but they didn't give me any. Even when I try I don't get any work. What's the use?

*W:*    That's really bad when you go down and other guys get work and you don't. It must make you feel bad after wasting all that time . . .

*H:*    Yeah . . . I don't know . . .

*W:*    . . . and then you don't get anything.

*H:*    It's really . . . it gets to me sometimes . . . I really don't feel like going down there anymore . . . when you go down and you try and you don't get anything . . . ah, it's not worth it.

W:  Well, dinner'll be ready soon, and we can eat.

H:  That's good; I'm hungry.

W:  Oh, listen, there's something else I've been meaning to talk to you about.

H:  What?

W:  You know the church . . . it's going to have a social this coming week-
    end . . . you know everybody's gonna get together, kinda talk and have
    coffee . . .

H:  Oh, one of those things? Didn't they have one just a while back?

W:  Yeah. We didn't go to that one. I know that you sometimes don't like
    those things and you feel uncomfortable not knowing some of the people
    there . . .

H:  Yeah, that's true. They're all your friends; I don't feel good; I can't go
    down there and talk to those people. Most of them are working and they
    can get dressed and stuff . . . I don't have clothes to wear to a social
    . . . and why should I go down . . . you know I really feel strange when
    I go down there.

W:  I can really understand how you feel . . . you don't have the same
    clothes and stuff . . . I just thought maybe you'd like to be with the peo-
    ple.

H:  Ahh . . . I don't know about being with those people . . . like, you
    know 'em . . . I don't know 'em and it's tough for me to sit down and
    talk to people I don't know.

W:  Yeah. I can understand why it would be.

H:  Can you?

W:  I think so.

H:  You want to go to this?

W:  Yeah, I'd really like to.

H:  Well, I don't know, I . . . I . . . I'll think about it. I can't say yes or no;
    there's too many things on my mind . . . I . . . I . . . I'll think about it
    though.

W:  O.K. Why don't you come out and sit down for dinner?

H:  What are we having tonight?

W:  Franks and beans.

H:  Oh. . . . Say, did you see my magazine that I had before that I was read-
    ing?

W:  What one was it?

H:  It was an adventure magazine; you remember the one.

W:  Oh; oh, here it is; is this the one?

H:  Yeah, yeah, I want to finish one of the things; there's a story about hunt-
    ing in here I want to look at after dinner. O.K. Let's go eat. Where are
    the kids?

W:  Well, the kids are going to be a little late because they're getting their
    raffle tickets.

H:  Raffle tickets for what?

W:  Oh, you know, every year when the church has that raffle and they sell all those tickets and give all those prizes and stuff. Oh, by the way, you know the little one, John Scott, he may need a little help.

*H:* What kind of help?

*W:* Well, you know, they have to go around to all the different apartments and sell tickets and they should really have an adult to go with them. Do you think you could do that?

*H:* I don't know. You know . . . like . . . is this the same raffle that they used to have?

*W:* Yeah; yeah.

*H:* Why do they need an adult to go around?

*W:* Well, you know, they go around to . . . uh, you know, strange apartments and stuff. . . .

*H:* When do they have to do it? When is it?

*W:* This coming Tuesday at 8 o'clock at night. I know it's kind of hard for you to get going. You know it might be hard to get out there and do it with him. But I know that you really want to spend time with the kids. I think they really like it when you do. I think it will be good for both of you.

*H:* Yeah, you're probably right. I never thought about it like that—getting just to do something like that. . . .

*W:* Yeah, you like being with the kids.

*H:* Yeah, I'll do it. So, when Johnny comes home, tell him I'll go out with him next Tuesday, O.K.?

*W:* Great!

*H:* Let's start supper.

### Scene 6: Narrator's Summary

The tape you have just heard shows you that when the wife tried to understand how her husband was feeling and told him what she thought he was feeling, he began to show more interest in doing the things that would help their marriage. He was somewhat more willing to go out with her, and also agreed to begin doing something with one of their children.

What you heard the actors saying comes from real husbands and wives having this problem. In most of the couples who have tried what the wife tried, it actually has helped change the husband into a more active, interested person who is willing to do things. Because this has been so successful, the persons leading your meeting today will help you practice how you can behave like the actress with *your* husband.

### Role Taking: Affection Tape

### Scene 1: Narrator's Introduction

Hello, this is Mr. _____ speaking again. Our meeting today will once again start with listening to a tape recording about a wife and husband having problems which may be very similar to your problems. On the first part of the tape you will hear the wife describing these troubles to her doctor. The doctor realizes that a main part of the problem is that the wife and the husband are not understanding each other's feelings. So you will hear the doctor encourage the wife to try to tune in better on how her husband feels, and encourage her to tell him what she thinks he feels.

On the next part of the tape you will hear the wife practicing doing this, and on the last part of the tape you will hear her try it with her husband. As you will hear, when she does let him know she is trying to understand his feelings, he begins to really try to understand *her* feelings, and they begin to get along much better.

### Scene 2: *Training Scene*

T: Hello, Mrs. Jones. Come on in and sit down. How are you today?
W: Alright. Pretty good, I guess.
T: Uh-huh. Let's see . . . last time we met we were talking about the union picnic. Did you and Harry go to the picnic?
W: Yeah, we both went.
T: How did that work out?
W: Oh, it was alright, I guess.
T: You don't sound very convinced.
W: I don't think Harry had his heart in it.
T: I'm not sure what you mean.
W: It was like he went, but he wasn't really there.
T: Uh-huh.
W: I mean he did things with the guys—he played football and stuff—but, as far as I was concerned, well, I could have just gone with anybody.
T: So, he was there and he had a more or less good time, but he really wasn't there with you?
W: That's exactly it.
T: Uh-huh. What would you have liked him to have done that he didn't?
W: Oh, he didn't pay any attention to me. Like, ah, my friends' husbands would come over every once in a while and see how they were doing. He just didn't. He didn't seem to care very much about me.
T: Uh-huh. You mentioned things like that before. Remember once there was something at your church; he went with you, but he was sort of off on his own.
W: Uh-huh.
T: And there were one or two other times like that. It seems to be a pretty common sort of way that he treats you, or gets along with you.
W: Yeah, it's more like he's a roommate than he's my husband. We don't really have . . . when it comes to being close, or together, you know like it used to be when we were first in love. It's just not like that.
T: Yeah. He's more like a roommate, which means I guess that this sort of separateness is true around the house also.

W:    Oh, yeah. It's terrible around the house. He has his chair, he comes home and reads the paper, watches his television shows. He wouldn't even know I was around. He doesn't know I'm around at all!

T:    Uh-huh. Sounds like you sort of live alone together.

W:    That's right. We do.

T:    Is he . . . let's take the last month or so . . . is he affectionate at all with you? Do you have sex together, kiss, things like that?

W:    Sometimes we have sex together, but we don't kiss very much at all. He's just not interested in being affectionate.

T:    That must be tough on you.

W:    It really is. I feel very unwanted.

T:    I can really understand how you feel, Mrs. Jones . . . unwanted, unhappy. Would you say that it wasn't that way around the time you got married? I recall that was just a few years ago. What do you think has made the difference, what do you think has happened in those three or four years? How did this sort of thing start changing . . . what was different?

W:    Gee, I don't know.

T:    Well, in the beginning, there was more affection?

W:    Yeah.

T:    Was there, for example, alot more sharing of things, decisions about the house, alot more concern about his feelings for you and your feelings for him? You know what I mean?

W:    Yeah, there was a lot more of that. He was very thoughtful when we first got married.

T:    Uh-huh. And you too, I guess, huh?

W:    Yeah, that's true.

T:    And what happened after, let's say, a year or two? You started sort of drifting apart?

W:    Yeah, like we split things up and he started going out looking for work —and doing his job; and I take care of my end of it.

T:    I see. So, instead of, for example, things around the house or things with your kid being things that would be decided together, he had his part of it and you had your part of it, and you went your separate ways?

W:    Yeah, we did; like, even when we did things with the kid . . . ah . . . he takes the kid someplace sometimes and sometimes I take him someplace. We don't even do that together.

T:    Uh-huh. Yeah. You know, Mrs. Jones, most of the time when there's some problem between a husband and a wife, it's usually true that both the husband is contributing to the problem and the wife is contributing. You've described today how he doesn't tune in on your feelings and he doesn't show affection. I certainly understand how that makes you feel. Is it possible that, starting the year after you got married, let's say, you started doing some of the same things to him—not responding to his feelings, not being a part of him, any of that going on do you think?

W:  Well, there's really no use trying to respond to his feelings because he never responds to mine. I just stopped 'cause there's no use. Like trying to get water out of a stone.

T:  Uh-huh. What you're saying is it doesn't pay to try to break into this—it doesn't pay to try to understand what he's feeling, because he won't come back to try to understand what you feel?

W:  That's right.

T:  How do you know that?

W:  Well, it's been like that for a long time.

T:  Are you saying that you have tried for a while now to figure out what he's feeling, to do something about that—let him know that for example?

W:  No, I haven't done that.

T:  Uh-huh.

W:  Why should I take that chance?

T:  Why is it a chance, Mrs. Jones?

W:  Well, suppose I was, uh . . . understanding of his feelings, like you say and then he didn't change . . . he didn't care about that, or he just went back to reading his paper.

T:  Well, I think it's possible that that could happen. You could try something like we just mentioned and it wouldn't help. But very often we've found if one member of the marriage—the husband or the wife—tries to understand how the other person is feeling and lets him know, the other person starts doing the same thing.

W:  I'd like that.

T:  Uh-huh. What I'm saying, Mrs. Jones, is that both at this center and at other centers, is that . . . it has been found that if the wife tries to understand what the husband is feeling and lets him know that, it is very often helpful to him, to her, and to their marriage. I wonder if we can try to follow that idea? Maybe that's something you can try out. Does it seem to make a little better sense to you now?

W:  A little. I'm not really sure exactly what you're saying yet.

T:  Well, let's try to come up with an example. What would be an example of something you and your husband used to do together when you first got married that you hardly ever do now—that you enjoyed? What would be an example of that?

W:  Well, we used to go to the movies together.

T:  Uh-huh. You used to go to the movies regularly or pretty regularly?

W:  Pretty much . . . it used to be on the weekend . . . mostly every weekend. Yeah.

T:  And you don't do that much any more?

W:  No, he don't . . . no, he just don't seem interested, so sometimes I just go with my friends during the week.

T:  Uh-huh. Now, he doesn't seem interested and you want to go to the movies, so you do that with your friends. Is it possible that that makes him feel . . . what do you think that makes him feel? Let me ask you that another way. Do you think he may have a reaction to that . . . a feeling about that?

*W:* I guess he wants to see some of the movies . . . maybe . . . I don't know.

*T:* Well, you know, you're saying in some ways he's not interested and you want to see the movies and it sort of makes you feel left out. I can certainly understand that. I guess I'm asking you, is it possible if you go to the movies with your girl friend, especially if it's something he wants to see, if he feels left out?

*W:* I guess it's possible. I never thought of him feeling like that.

*T:* Well, I guess I'm wondering with you now, if it makes sense, the next time something like that happens—the next time you've gone to a movie that maybe he wants to see—to say to him something about feeling like that. Try showing him that you might understand that feeling of his. Do you think something like that makes sense?

*W:* Umh . . .

*T:* Well, let me ask you this. Let me ask you this. If he said that to you . . .

*W:* Yeah . . .

*T:* If he said to you, 'Hey, Honey, I know that you wanted to go to the movies with me this weekend and I'm gonna arrange it so that we can do that.' How do you think that would make you feel?

*W:* Terrific. I would like that.

*T:* And I think that to increase the chances that he will do things like that with you, you will have to start doing things like that with him, showing that you understand his feelings.

*W:* Showing him that I understand that he feels left out if I go to the movies without asking him if he wants to go?

*T:* Right! Exactly!

*W:* Huh!

*T:* Let's see if we can look at another example, 'cause I really think that you're getting the idea, Mrs. Jones. You talked a little bit today, and other times we've met, about how sex is with you and your husband. Sort of sounds like it's mechanical . . . like two robots who have sex but who really don't feel close. And you said you felt very badly about that.

*W:* Yeah.

*T:* How do you think he feels, when it comes to sex between the two of you?

*W:* Well, I don't know that he very much cares; he seem to act as if it's O.K., but it used to be different.

*T:* Uh-huh.

*W:* But I don't know. He doesn't talk to me about it.

*T:* How is it different than before?

*W:* Oh, well, there was a lot of love there . . . it wasn't like . . . just sex . . . there was a lot of feeling and closeness.

*T:* And now the feeling isn't there?

*W:* No, not at all.

*T:* You once said, when you were describing this sort of thing to me, that you didn't feel he wanted you . . . you felt unwanted. Is that the feeling you still have?

*W:* Yeah.

*T:* Yeah.

*W:* He doesn't really want me . . . just wants me and the sex . . . he's not really interested in me as a person.

*T:* Uh-huh. And when you're having sex together, he behaves in ways that keep making you feel unwanted.

*W:* Yeah, it's like even where you're supposed to get really close, we don't.

*T:* Do you think that maybe when you're having sex together, you behave in ways that might make him feel unwanted? He sort of turns you off, you're saying. Does that sort of, in some ways, make him feel you're turning him off?

*W:* I guess he doesn't feel I'm very interesting. I guess I don't act interested, 'cause I always expect it'll be bad.

*T:* Uh-huh.

*W:* It's like, I guess I lost my interest, too, in trying to be close.

*T:* Uh-huh. It's always hard to figure out where the thing started and I really doubt sometimes whether it's important to figure that out, but what you're saying now, at least as far as your behavior is concerned, is that you do behave, when you're having sex together, in ways that don't help him feel close, too. Not only does he do that to you, huh?

*W:* Yeah. I guess that's true.

*T:* Well, now, we've been talking about this idea of you trying to figure out what he's feeling and I think you've done a very good job of that, talking about how maybe he feels unwanted also. What do you think would happen if you let him know that, if you said to him something like that?

*W:* Said to him something like I understand that he feels unwanted?

*T:* Yeah.

*W:* But that I really do want him?

*T:* Yeah, uh-huh. If he said something like this to you, how do you think it would make you feel?

*W:* You mean if he said to me that he understands that I feel unwanted, but that he really wants me?

*T:* Yeah.

*W:* Oh that would be really great!

*T:* Right. And I'm thinking that maybe it really makes great sense for you to get the ball rolling by saying something like that to him.

*W:* Well?

*T:* Do you think it's something that's worth a try? It's something that's really helped a lot of other people just like you.

*W:* Well? Yeah, I think that sounds like a pretty good idea, and I'm gonna give that a try.

## Scene 4: Self-Instruction Scene

W:  Let's see now; I'm supposed to try to understand how Harry's feeling—and tell him that. I wonder if I can do that in the situations I talked about with the doctor? Let's see, what did he say? He said—well we have that problem with the movies where we both feel, like—left out—like, I think he's not interested in going to see the movies I want to see, with me; and he thinks I'm just interested in going with my girl friends and we both feel left out; I'm going to do something about that. I'm going to let him know that I understand his feelings about that—about being left out and I'm going to tell this to him. I understand that he feels left out when I go to the movies with my girl friends. And then there's that thing about sex. I guess in a way, we both feel left out there, too. It's like he feels unwanted and I feel unwanted and I'm going to try to do something about that, too. I'm gonna let him know that I understand that he feels unwanted, even though I really do want him. I guess someone's really got to start things going and now that I really understand that if I tell him I understand how he's feeling, that'll help, so I'll do that. Then he felt left out with the kids, too; about that playground business. I never thought that when I took Jimmy to the playground that maybe Harry would want to come. I bet he feels left out about that, too. We used to go together; it used to be fun. Maybe I ought to let him know that I understand that he might like to come along. I think I'll give those things a try. I'll try to understand how he's feeling and let him know that.

## Scene 5: Affection Scene

H:  Hi. I'm home.
W:  Hi. How're you doing?
H:  Oh, pretty good. Where're the kids?
W:  They're out playing.
H:  How're they doing today?
W:  Oh, they're O.K. Jimmy fell off his bike before, but he's O.K.
H:  He didn't get hurt, did he?
W:  No, not much.
H:  That's good. Did anything else happen around the house?
W:  Mmh . . . there was something that I didn't to today.
H:  You didn't do? That you were supposed to do?
W:  Well, you know how sometimes I go to the movies with Selma?
H:  Yeah.
W:  Well, I was thinking about doing that today.
H:  How come you didn't go?
W:  Well, I got to thinking, that maybe . . . well, maybe you felt left out when I go to the movies with her.
H:  No . . . I . . . uh . . .

W: Well, I don't want to do that if you feel like that, so I told her that I wasn't going to go with her, that maybe I was going to go with you.

H: I guess I do feel like that when you go with other people to the movies. We used to do that together alot.

W: Yeah, we did and it was nice then, when we went together.

H: Huh! So, will we go to the movies together?

W: Yeah, that would be nice. Can we do that?

H: I'd like to do that.

W: Good, let's do that.

H: That was a good meal!

W: Good! I'm glad you liked it.

H: Who's gonna be watching the kid tonight while we're at the movies?

W: Mrs. Wilson's gonna sit, I think—keep an eye on him.

H: Good. Is he ready for bed yet?

W: Yep; in his p.j.'s—all ready.

H: That's good. Can we go pretty soon? 'cause the show's gonna start in like 15 or 20 minutes.

W: Heah. And, hey, I was just thinking. You know you said the movies we used to go to together, how it was really nice, we used to do things together?

H: Yeah?

W: We used to take Jimmy to the playground together and that was kind of fun.

H: Yeah, I remember that. It was.

W: Remember you went on the sliding board one time with him?

H: Yeah; fell off too!

W: I was wondering, I don't know, maybe you feel a little left out when I go with him and you never come—like, it's not like we're a family.

II: I kind of get that feeling from you, like you want to go alone with him —you didn't ask me to go along—just you and he went to the park all the time.

W: Well, I'd really like you to come and I know Jimmy would, too.

H: Do you think so?

W: Oh, yeah. I know he would.

H: Cause I miss playing with him on the weekend—that's the only time I have to play with him. When do you wanna go?

W: Maybe tomorrow, if it's a nice day.

H: That'd be good . . . I'd like . . . that'd be good! Let's do that.

W: O.K. Let me get rid of these dishes and then we can get going.

H: That was a pretty good movie wasn't it?

W: Yeah, it was. It was really romantic.

H: Yeah, it was nice just going together, I guess. We haven't done that in a long time.

W: Oh, yeah, I think that was real nice.

H: I wonder how the boy's doing?

W: Oh, shhh, shh, Jim's asleep.

H: We should thank Mrs. Wilson tomorrow for taking care of him.

W: Yeah, she's really good about that. Would you like some coffee? Should I put a pot on?

H: Yeah, that would be nice; why don't you do that? When you finish putting the pot on, why don't you come over here and sit on the couch next to me, O.K.?

W: Oh, yeah, that's nice.

H: You know, it feels different—going to the movies together again, for a change; it's a lot nicer than when you go with your girl friends while I'm at work.

W: Yeah. That's really true. You know, there's something else, you know . . . that I think maybe hasn't been so good—that maybe could be nicer.

H: What's that?

W: Well, it has to do with sex.

H: Yeah?

W: It's like . . . sometimes I get the feeling that you think I don't want you . . . you think that I'm not interested.

H: Yeah. I get that feeling sometimes. It's like when we make love, it's very coarse; it's like, maybe, you don't have any feelings for me.

W: Yeah, it's like two robots, almost—very mechanical. You know, uh, I know that it makes you feel like I don't want you, but that's not true at all. I really do.

H: I guess you do, but, it's hard for me to know that sometimes. I don't know . . . I don't think I ever heard you say that to me.

W: Well, that's really how I feel. I mean, I don't want you to feel that I don't want you, 'cause I do.

H: That's, uh . . . that's really nice. It makes me feel good to hear that. How do you feel right now?

W: I feel very affectionate.

H: Let's go into the other room.

W: O.K.

### Scene 6: Narrator's Summary

So, once again you have heard a wife do two things to help herself and her marriage: (1) try to understand her husband's feelings; and (2) try to tell him what it is she understands. On this tape, and on the other tapes, when the wife did this the husband became more understanding of what the wife was feeling, and they began to get along much better.

Although the wives, husbands, and doctors you have heard on the tapes were actors, what they have said comes from real wives and husbands having problems. The advice the doctor gave each time has been told to hundreds of real husbands and wives, and has been of great help to a very large number of them.

I want to encourage you to try doing this with *your* husband, and to help you we now want to spend the rest of this meeting practicing doing the kinds of things the wife on the tape showed us.

## Role-Taking Study: Direct Test* and Generalization Test

### *Instructions*

We are now going to play a tape recording on which you will hear an actor playing the part of a husband saying things to his wife. As you listen to the tape, pretend that he is *your* husband, and that he is saying the things to you. After *each* thing he says, please tell me what you would actually say to him if *your* husband said it to you.

1. No, I can't come get it myself! I just want a beer. Will you bring it here, you've got two legs!
2. Where's this kid been? In the swamp? How come he's so filthy? What did you do all day? The kid is filthy, the house is filthy. . .
3. You know I get home at 4:30 every day. Christ, why do I have to sit around an hour and a half every day waiting for dinner! Why can't I eat when I come home like other people? Why do I go through all this grief when I get home from work?
4. I want to sit down. What's this stuff doing in my chair? Christ, can't even sit down and get comfortable!
5. Yeah, I got paid. Here's the money for the food. Take it, will ya. I know it's not much, but take it.
6. That's right. I don't want to fix the TV, I don't want to look for a job, I don't want to do a damn thing. I just want to sit here.
7. There was work at the place, but I didn't get any.
8. It really gets to me sometimes. I really don't feel like going down there any more. When you go down and you try and you don't get any work . . . ah, it's not worth it.
9. They're all your friends. I can't go down there and talk to those people. Most of them are working, and they can get dressed up and stuff. . . . I don't have clothes to wear to a social. Why should I go, you know I really feel strange when I go down there.
10. I guess I do feel left out like that when you go to the movies with your friends. We used to do that together alot.
11. I kind of got that feeling from you. Like you wanted to go with Jimmy

---

* Direct Test: items 1–12; Generalization Test: items 13–21.

alone to the playground. You didn't ask me to go along, even though he's my son, too. Just you and he go to the park all the time.

12. Yeah, it was nice just going together to the movies. We haven't done that in a long time.

13. Suppose your husband is offered a job in another state which would increase his pay. He wants the job, but you don't want to move because you'd leave all your friends. One day when talking about this job, he gets very angry and says to you: "Damn it, I'm going to take the job and that's that. If you don't like moving, it's just too bad!" What would you tell him?

14. Suppose your new baby wakes up several times each night. You are tired because you get up at night and also care for the baby during the day while your husband works. You feel he should take turns at getting up at night, but when you ask him to take a turn, he says: "No, I'm no nurse, that's for you to do. So just do it!" What would you tell him?

15. Suppose one morning you agree to prepare your husband's favorite dish for supper, but in the afternoon you take a nap and don't have time to make his favorite dish. He comes home, sees that you haven't cooked it, and says: "You really are lazy. I bet you slept all day!" What would you tell him?

16. Suppose you convince your husband to go to a party. After you are at the party for a short while, although you are having a good time, he says to you: "I'm bored. Let's go home." What would you tell him?

17. Suppose one day your husband tells you that he still loves you, but also that he is attracted to another woman whom you both know. He says to you: "I don't love her, but I sure feel attracted to her." What would you tell him?

18. Suppose you feel that your child isn't doing as well as he could in school. You feel he might do better if your husband helped him with his lessons some of the time. But when you ask your husband to help him, he says: "If the boy doesn't understand something, he should ask his teacher, not bother me about it." What would you say to your husband?

19. Suppose you have been asked to join a bowling club that husbands and wives join as couples. You want to, but when you ask your husband, he says: "I don't want to. It's just too much trouble to join a club, too much bother to bowl every week." What would you say to your husband?

20. Suppose your husband spent so much time doing extra work on his job that you felt that he wasn't home often enough, and that he was spending very little time with you. When you tell him how you feel, he says: "I just do what the boss wants. He says he needs people overtime, so I work overtime." What would you tell your husband?

21. Suppose you tell your husband he is not making your sexual life enjoyable. He says: "What are you complaining about? Are you saying I'm not manly enough for you?" What would you tell him?

## Role Induction—Reward to Model

### Instructions for Listening to Tapes

More and more, it has been found that people have been helped by talking over their problems in therapy. It has also been found that listening to an example of an interview, before going into the interview, gives people a better idea of what goes on in a clinic. It seems to help them feel more comfortable in their own interview.

A tape of an actual first interview that took place in an out-of-town clinic such as this one will be played. You might like to know that both the interviewer and the patient have agreed to let us use this tape.

Before you hear the tape, you might like to know something about the people you will hear. The interviewer (I) is a psychologist who has had much experience in working with alcoholics in clinics like this one. The patient (P) is in his early 30s. Before coming to the clinic, he was just about at the end of his rope. His boss told him he would lose his job if he kept drinking. His wife was threatening to leave him and to take the children with her. He was using most of his pay for drink and was over his head in debts. He had lost most of his friends.

After this first interview, he decided to go into therapy and to work hard at it. He has made much improvement. Knowing that he was trying, his boss held his job open for him, and he's working steadily now. His wife was willing to stick it out with him if he stayed in treatment. They're still together. According to him, he's staying dry. He no longer needs treatment.

Please try to listen to what the interviewer and the patient are saying. Try to think of yourself as that patient and how you would feel in the same place.

I: Hello.

P: Hello—hi (shy and dejected).

I: Please have a seat—anywhere is O.K.

P: Yeah—(dejected)—sure.

I: Now, I'd like to ask you some questions about yourself. Try to answer them as best you can. Could you tell me what *you* see as the causes of your drinking problem?

P: (Hostile) Hell—if I knew what the causes was—I wouldn't be here, would I? I mean—hell—I don't know (annoyed). (Thoughtful) What—what is the causes—hell—ya get lonely—ya get tired—ya spend your time workin'—'n what else? So I drink—that's all—I'm drinkin' all the time. (Slowly and thoughtfully)—but, I gotta stop.

I: How long have you had a drinking problem?

P: Yah—I didn't call it a problem (dejected). I've been drinkin' for years. Uh (thoughtful) when I was 29 or 30—I started drinkin' heavy. I guess —soon after I was married. Let's see—I was 23 when I was married. I was drinkin' before. (Hostile) I've been drinkin' heavy ever since.

*I:*  About 10 years, then. What brings you to the clinic about your drinking problem at *this* time?

*P:*  Yah—everything's fallin' apart. (Ready to cry) The whole thing's fallin' apart! (Dejected) I gotta get out o' this mess.

*I:*  How has your family reacted to your drinking?

*P:*  Well—(sarcastic)—how's my family reacted to my drinkin'. My wife's gonna leave me—and she's takin' the kids (hostile)—*that's* how my family's reacted.

*I:*  How has your drinking affected your work?

*P:*  Yah—(dejected)—my boss is gonna *throw* me out, too.—I was damn sure I lost it last week—I thought I lost it—ya know—he came—he said, "Listen! ya' don't get here—you're here two days—you're here three days a week—you're not here at all—ya do a good job when you're here—but you're not here—because ya drink and I *know* it. So you're *out!!* Straighten up and fly right. This is your last chance." (Dejected, annoyed, hostile) He tole me before—well, anyhow, and then—then—the wife got onto it. (Annoyed) Then the whole thing really started!

*I:*  How has it affected other parts of your life?

*P:*  (Long pause)—(Depressed)—Yah—what other parts of my life—money? Yeah—money, money, money—another part of my life—yeah. O.K. —ah—ah—lousy! I'd—well—I have debts. I—ah—every pay check I get, I owe twice what it's worth—ya know—I—uh—I cash the—check! —I go to the bar!—I celebrate!—I go home—I haven't got much money! I always gave what—(pause)—I had to the wife but—uh—yeah'll—that don't work any more—uh—anyhow, debts—yeah'll—I don't know it's changed anything else—It's—uh—I had a lot of friends once. (Cocky and defensive) I got plenty of friends now—they're different friends, that's all—ya get older, ya get different friends—I don't need—uh—they don't—they don't mean anything to me now.

*I:*  Now, could you try to tell me how you feel about yourself?

*P:*  (Sarcastic, sassy) *Now—could—I—try—to—tell—you—how—I—feel—about— myself!* Well!—(slowly) well—I feel like hell about myself, lady (hostile)— if that's what you want to know. (Depressed) I—I gotta stop this stuff. I'm not gettin' anywhere—I'm losin everything I want—(on verge of tears)— I—got nothin'.

*I:*  Most people get angry. Could you tell me the kinds of things that get you angry?

*P:*  What—the—the kinds of things that get to me?—Yeah—Right! That's what you want to know? Somebody diggin' at me—leanin' over me— breathin' down my neck—(mimicky and sassy). You're not doin' that right—Do some'n else! Get here on time! Do this, do this—Nobody ta help ya—that's what gets me angry. And home—the kids—my God, the noise—four of 'em—they're O.K.—they're good kids, right? But, yack and scream and yell—gimme this, gimme that. Kids ain't got no respect nowadays—and everybody on the job—(hostile)—they push ya—my

God!—a bunch of crooks!—and the wife—she yells—all she does is yell —ya can't do anything right! (Depressed) They're at ya every damn minute.

I: What do you do when you're angry?

P: (Short laugh, chuckles softly, hostile) I thought I tole ya that! I drink! I get mad (sarcastic, evasive). People get mad, ya know!—I'm not the only guy that ever beat anybody up.—It goes on all the time—read it in the newspapers—see it on television.—Ya get tied up—things go in circles—Ya get mad—Ya beat up on somebody—that's what ya do. (Depressed) I don't have any more fights at work than the next guy. (Chuckles) The reason I don't is I'm not there. (Deliberate) I get that way—I get out—I get under the bar. (Hostile and sassy) Sometimes I blow my stack! Sometimes I sock a guy—well, (ashamedly) I don't hit a woman, much—well, I hit the wife but I don't hit 'em at work, much. (Chuckles) Ya can't, boy! (chuckles)—but—ya know—I—I yell. I can't hit—so I yell!

I: Well—now—could you tell me about the kinds of things that get you anxious or fearful?

P: (Annoyed) I tole ya—people get at ya'—get to ya'. (Thoughtfully) Anxious—that's different from mad?—Yeah—I 'spose—Ya feel alone— alone —even when you're with people—nobody's talkin' to ya—not to ya! And it—I don't know—well—ya don't drink? O.K.—but—gee, I've been in some lousy accidents—I get scared sometimes (anxious)—what I'm gonna do—what's gonna happen—where do I get from here?—Ya got no money—ya lie a lot—I mean, I lie a lot—ya have ta—(depressed).— You're stuck with this stuff—I don't know—I've always been kinda scared—of—of meetin' people—they—I—don't know how I seem to them. (Confiding) I wanna be a good guy, ya know—and I come on—oh —sometimes the only thing I can think of is ta buy a lot of drinks—me —I drink two for everybody else's one—and I make a damn fool of myself—I've always been that way—I—I get all tensed up when I meet people—I wanna make a good impression and—I—I always make the wrong kind. I just feel like I don't do anything right—that's the way it is—a failure—a lousy husband—a lousy father—a lousy man.

I: What do you do about the things that get you anxious or fearful?

P: (Annoyed) I thought I tole ya! Oh—well—sure—I do other things sometimes—ya know—we go out sometimes.—It isn't always the same. (Demanding) What am I supposed to do—play golf? (Sarcastic)—yeah, golf—I can't pay the rent—so I should play golf? (Sassy) So—well, some days I just don't go to work—I just stay in bed. (Confiding)—I figure—O.K.—go to work, I'm gonna knock somebody down—I'll get fired —so I stay home and sleep a while. O.K. The wife—she works part-time —she comes in. She says—you're not goin' to work?—She starts puttin' me down. It gets to me—I get mad—she knows it—I say I'm gonna go to work—I know I can't work—I'm gonna blow—so I go down to the bar—what else!—I drink—everything's a mess—so I'm stupid! (Hostile) But, this is the way I do things—I have a drink.

I:    Now, could you tell me about your parents? What were they like?

P:    My—my parents—(Annoyed) They haven't got anything to do with this! (Sighs) Well—I don't want anything to happen to 'em—they're O.K.—I guess. (Inquiringly, dependent)—What do ya want me to say? —how I feel about 'em? Something like that? (Confidingly) Ta tell ya the truth—I don't feel much of anything for 'em.—I don't want anything ta go wrong—I'd try ta do anything I could for 'em—but—I never—they didn't seem to care anything about me, really. Maybe it wasn't that—I never thought they cared anything for each other—ta tell ya the truth— they're kinda (sassy and definite)—*everything was kinda formal and neat and nice*—and ya gotta do this and ya gotta do that—it was what everybody else thought—the aunts—the grandparents—(wistfully) it was never anything ta do with me—never what I thought—my mother kinda ran the roost, I guess—she's a good woman, I 'spose.—My father was sorta —well—he was there—he brought home the bacon—but—he—uh—never stood up for me—or anything—or anybody.—I got out o' there soon as I could—I couldn't stick around.—It wasn't 'cause they did anything ta me—ya know—nothin' like that—they didn't drink.—They didn't beat me up—they didn't do nothin' wrong—they're good people—but it left me sorta—I don't wanna be with 'em much—I never did.—I'd just as soon send 'em a Christmas present and forget it.—They're cold—always been like that—and I—I—don't feel anything about them either.

I:    Tell me—if you had your choice, in what way would your parents be different?

P:    (Long pause)—(Thoughtfully) Ya mean if I could go back and be a kid again. (Pause)—I don't know—it's the kind of feeling—it didn't matter what ya did as long as ya did the right things—If ya felt something—ya weren't 'sposed ta talk about it. It was cold—nobody had any fun—I don't think (slowly)—they even loved me—or each other—and I—uh —I don't think I love them—maybe, if we could start over—lovin' each other—oh—what's the use—ya can't start over—is that right?

I:    I have asked you a number of questions today and you have told me about your problems. They are certainly very real problems which seem to be responsible for your feeling anxious, fearful, angry, and unhappy. These feelings are affecting how you do your day's work, how you get along with the important people in your life, how you handle your problems, and other parts of your life. Feeling this way, things may sometimes seem very confused and confusing.

P:    That's just how it is with me. But—what—can I do?

I:    I would suggest that you return here for therapy.

P:    What do ya mean ther—therapy? What goes on there?

I:    Well, for one thing, if you decide you want to do this, one of our staff members will be your therapist. You will come here regularly. You and your therapist will talk with each other, but you will do most of the talking.

P: Ya mean I'll talk—uh—somebody and me—uh—we'll just talk—and—uh—and that'll change things for me?

I: Yes, you will talk with your therapist who will mostly listen, and then try to help you to understand things about yourself. You, on your part, will have to think about things and practice them in your daily life. You will learn to understand what your real feelings and thoughts are—and how to handle them.

P: If I learn ta understand myself better, I'll—uh—I'll—uh—handle my feelings better? I'll—uh—do things different. Then—I'll—uh—feel better?

I: Yes! That's it! You've got the idea. You will understand why you have troubles with your family, friends, and job. This will help you to change the faulty ways of your behavior. You will be able to change, for the better, those things in your life that are making you unhappy now.

P: Then that person—what'd ya call it?—a thera—uh—a therapist—won't tell me what ta do ta change my life? Won't give me advice—right?

I: That's right. If that's all it took was advice, you probably wouldn't be here now. Unfortunately, when people give advice, it is usually something that will work for themselves but not for the person with the problem. So the therapist can't give you the answer, but can help you to *figure out* what you want to do so you can find out for *yourself* how to solve your problems, how to find the answer that is best for *you*, and how to make better decisions.

P: Then—uh—it'll be up ta me—I'll have ta do most of it. Yeah—I see what ya mean.

I: Very good. You learn quickly. The more freely you talk and the more you express your feelings and thoughts, the more quickly you will learn how to understand them, as well as your actions and behavior. There may be times when it will be hard. You may feel discouraged. Maybe, you will even be angry at your therapist. At times, you may think he's the greatest and, at other times, that he's a complete idiot.

P: I didn't tell ya before—uh—yeah—sometimes I—uh—I like a person one minute, then—uh—I hate their guts the next minute.

I: Yes, people do have mixed feelings. At such times, you may want to stay away from your appointment. But, this is when it is very important to come and talk about your reasons for these feelings. By working this out together, you learn ways to handle other situations in your every day life.

P: Yeah—it's beginnin' ta make sense—maybe there's hope for me—yet.

I: Good. But don't expect to get better all at once. It took your whole life for you to be as you are now, so it will take time to change.

P: (Breaking in) Yeah—change—it's gotta change. I gotta—I gotta make it change.

*I:* And you can! Progress may seem slow. There will be ups and downs but keeping at it is most important. Everyone—

*P:* (Interrupts) Yeah—I noticed that—I got mine—big ones—and this treatment—ya call it therapy—that'll get rid of my problems.

*I:* Therapy won't take away your problems. You, like everyone else, will have problems all your life.

*P:* Then—what's the use of coming here?

*I:* In therapy, you will learn how *you* can handle them better, how *you* can make more satisfying decisions, and how *you* can have control over the things that happen to you.

*P:* So—I'll always have problems—but—uh—but—I see what ya mean—I won't mess up on things like I do now—I'll—uh—learn ta do better about 'em. That'll be—uh—that'll be hard, won't it?

*I:* You won't have to do it alone. You and your therapist, together, will work toward this.

*P:* Yeah—I see what ya mean. I'm beginnin' ta feel—ta feel better—I—uh—I won't be alone.

*I:* That's right. You'll have someone to work with you.

*P:* It feels—yeah—it feels good to know what treatment's gonna be like. But, hey—what about some pills ta help me when I get nervous—or—uh—mad.

*I:* That will be up to you and your therapist to decide. If it's necessary, it can be arranged at that time.

*P:* I'm glad I—uh—yeah, glad I came.

*I:* Good.

*P:* Yeah—I see whatcha mean—ups and downs, huh?—Yeah—ya make me see—maybe I can change.

*I:* Sure—it's hard work, but *you* can do it.

*P:* I'm beginnin' ta believe it—yeah—yeah—beginnin' ta believe it.

*I:* That's great—you'll make it.

*P:* I'll—yeah—I'll sure try—I gotta.

*I:* Good. Should we make your next appointment?

*P:* Sure! Just this once, I feel better. Sure—sure—I want it.

## No Role Induction—Reward to Model

### *Instructions for Listening to Tapes*

More and more, it has been found that people have been helped by talking over their problems in therapy. It has also been found that listening to an example of an interview, before going into the interview, gives people a better idea of what goes on in a clinic. It seems to help them feel more comfortable in their own interview.

A tape of an actual first interview that took place in an out-of-town clinic such as this one will be played. You might like to know that both the interviewer and the patient have agreed to let us use this tape.

Before you hear the tape, you might like to know something about the people you will hear. The interviewer (I) is a psychologist who has had much experience in working with alcoholics in clinics like this one. The patient (P) is in his early 30s. Before coming to the clinic, he was just about at the end of his rope. His boss told him he would lose his job if he kept drinking. His wife was threatening to leave him and to take the children with her. He was using most of his pay for drink and was over his head in debts. He had lost most of his friends.

After this first interview, he decided to go into therapy and to work hard at it. He has made much improvement. Knowing that he was trying, his boss held his job open for him, and he's working steadily now. His wife was willing to stick it out with him if he stayed in treatment. They're still together. According to him, he's staying dry. He no longer needs treatment.

Please try to listen to what the interviewer and the patient are saying. Try to think of yourself as that patient and how you would feel in the same place.

I: Hello.
P: Hello—hi (shy and dejected).
I: Please have a seat—anywhere is O.K.
P: Yeah—(dejected)—sure.
I: Now, I'd like to ask you some questions about yourself. Try to answer them as best you can. Could you tell me what *you* see as the causes of your drinking problem?
P: (Hostile) Hell—if I knew what the causes was—I wouldn't be here, would I? I mean—hell—I don't know (annoyed). (Thoughtful) What—what is the causes—hell—ya get lonely—ya get tired—ya spend your time workin'—'n what else? So I drink—that's all—I'm drinkin' all the time. (Slowly and thoughtfully)—but, I gotta stop.
I: How long have you had a drinking problem?
P: Yah—I didn't call it a problem—(dejected)—I've been drinkin' for years. Uh—(Thoughtful) when I was 29 or 30—I started drinkin' heavy. I guess—soon after I was married. Let's see—I was 23 when I was married. I was drinkin' before. (Hostile) I've been drinkin' heavy ever since.
I: About 10 years, then. What brings you to the clinic about your drinking problem at *this* time?
P: Yah—everything's fallin' apart. (Ready to cry) The whole thing's fallin' apart! (Dejected) I gotta get out o' this mess.
I: How has your family reacted to your drinking?
P: Well—(sarcastic)—how's my family reacted to my drinkin'. My wife's gonna leave me—and she's takin' the kids. (Hostile)—*That's* how my family's reacted.
I: How has your drinking affected your work?
P: Yah—(dejected)—my boss is gonna *throw* me out, too.—I was damn

sure I lost it last week—I thought I lost it—ya know—he came—he said, "Listen! ya don't get here—you're here two days—you're here three days a week—you're not here at all—ya do a good job when you're here—but you're not here—because ya drink and I *know* it. So you're *out!!* Straighten up and fly right. This is your last chance." (Dejected, annoyed, hostile)—He tole me before—well, anyhow and then—then—the wife got onto it. (Annoyed) Then the whole thing really started!

I:      How has it affected other parts of your life?

P:      (Long pause)—(Depressed)—Yah—what other parts of my life—money? Yeah—money, money, money—another part of my life—yeah. O.K. —ah—ah—lousy! I'd—well—I have debts. I—ah—every pay check I get, I owe twice what it's worth—ya know—I—uh—I cash the—check! —I go to the bar!—I celebrate!—I go home—I haven't got much money! I always gave what—(pause)—I had to the wife but—uh—yeah'll—that don't work any more—uh—anyhow, debts—yeah'll—I don't know it's changed anything else—It's—uh—I had a lot of friends once—(cocky and defensive) I got plenty of friends now—they're different friends, that's all—ya get older, ya get different friends—I don't need—uh—they don't—they don't mean anything to me now.

I:      Now, could you try to tell me how you feel about yourself?

P:      (Sarcastic, sassy) *Now—could—I—try—to—tell—you—how—I—feel—about —myself!* Well!—(slowly) well—I feel like hell about myself, lady (hostile)—if that's what you want to know. (Depressed)—I—I gotta stop this stuff. I'm not gettin' anywhere—I'm losin' everything I want— (on verge of tears)—I—got nothin'.

I:      Most people get angry. Could you tell me the kinds of things that get you angry?

P:      What—the—the kinds of things that get to me?—Yeah—Right! That's what you want to know? Somebody diggin' at me—leanin' over me— breathin' down my neck—(mimicky and sassy). You're not doin' that right—Do somep'n else! Get here on time! Do this, do this—Nobody ta help ya—That's what gets me angry. And home—the kids—my God, the noise—four of 'em—they're O.K.—they're good kids, right? But, yack and scream and yell—gimme this, gimme that. Kids ain't got no respect nowadays—and everybody on the job—(hostile)—they push ya—my God!—a bunch of crooks! And the wife—she yells—all she does is yell —ya can't do anything right! (Depressed) They're at ya every damn minute.

I:      What do you do when you're angry?

P:      (Short laugh, chuckles softly, hostile) I thought I tole ya that! I drink! I get mad. (Sarcastic, evasive) People get mad, ya know!—I'm not the only guy that ever beat anybody up.—It goes on all the time—read it in the newspapers—see it on television.—Ya get tied up—things go in cir- cles—Ya get mad—Ya beat up on somebody—that's what ya do. (De- pressed) I don't have any more fights at work than the next guy. (Chuckles) The reason I don't is I'm not there. (Deliberate) I get that way—I get out—I get under the bar. (Hostile and sassy) Sometimes I blow my stack! Sometimes I sock a guy—well, (ashamedly) I don't hit a woman, much—well, I hit the wife but I don't hit 'em at work, much. (chuckles) Ya can't, boy! (Chuckles)—But—ya know—I—I yell. I can't hit—so I yell!

I: Well—now—could you tell me about the kinds of things that get you anxious or fearful?

P: (Annoyed) I tole ya—people get at ya—get to ya. (Thoughtfully) Anxious—that's different from mad?—Yeah—I 'spose—Ya feel alone— alone even when you're with people—nobody's talkin' to ya—not *to* ya! And it—I don't know—well—ya don't drink? O.K.—but—gee, I've been in some lousy accidents—I get scared sometimes. (Anxious)—What I'm gonna do—what's gonna happen—where do I get from here?—Ya got no money—ya lie a lot—I mean, I lie a lot—ya have ta (depressed).— You're stuck with this stuff—I don't know—I've always been kinda scared—of—of meetin' people—I—they—I—I—don't know how I seem to them. (Confiding) I wanna be a good guy, ya know—and I come on —oh—sometimes the only thing I can think of is ta buy a lot of drinks —me—I drink two for everybody else's one—and I make a damn fool of myself—I've always been that way—I—I get all tensed up when I meet people—I wanna make a good impression and—I—I always make the wrong kind. I just feel like I don't do anything right—that's the way it is —a failure—a lousy husband—a lousy father—a lousy man.

I: What do you do about the things that get you anxious or fearful?

P: (Annoyed) I thought I tole ya! Oh—well—sure—I do other things sometimes—ya know—we go out sometimes.—It isn't always the same. (Demanding) What am I supposed to do—play golf? (Sarcastic)— yeah, golf—I can't pay the rent—so I should play golf? (Sassy) So— well, some days I just don't go to work—I just stay in bed—(confiding) —I figure—O.K.—go to work, I'm gonna knock somebody down—I'll get fired—so I stay home and sleep a while. O.K. The wife—she works part-time—she comes in. She says—you're not goin' to work?—She starts puttin' me down. It gets to me—I get mad—she knows it—I say I'm gonna go to work—I know I can't work—I'm gonna blow—so I go down to the bar—what else!—I drink—everything's a mess—so I'm stupid! (Hostile) But, this is the way I do things—I have a drink.

I: Now, could you tell me about your parents? What were they like?

P: My—my parents. (annoyed) They haven't got any thing to do with this! (Sighs) Well—I don't want anything to happen to 'em—they're O.K.—I guess. (Inquiringly, dependent)—What do ya want me to say? —How I feel about 'em? Something like that? (Confidingly) Ta tell ya the truth —I don't feel much of anything for 'em.—I don't want anything ta go wrong—I'd try ta do anything I could for 'em—but—I never—they didn't seem to care anything about me, really. Maybe it wasn't that—I

never thought they cared anything for each other—ta tell ya the truth—
They're kinda—(sassy and definite) *everything was kinda formal and
neat and nice*—and ya gotta do this and ya gotta do that—it was what
everybody else thought—the aunts—the grandparents—(wistfully) it
was never anything ta do with me—never what I thought.—My mother
kinda ran the roost, I guess—she's a good woman, I 'spose.—My father
was sorta—well—he was there—he brought home the bacon—but—he
—uh—never stood up for me—or anything—or anybody.—I got out
o'there soon as I could—I couldn't stick around—It wasn't 'cause
they did anything ta me—ya know—nothin' like that—they didn't drink.
—They didn't beat me up—they didn't do nothin' wrong—they're good
people—but it left me sorta—I don't wanna be with 'em much—I never
did—I'd just as soon send 'em a Christmas present and forget it—.
They're cold—always been like that—and I—I—don't feel anything
about them either.

I:   Tell me—if you had your choice, in what way would your parents be different?

P:   (Long pause)—(Thoughtfully) Ya mean if I could go back and be a kid
again.—(Pause)—I don't know—it's the kind of feeling—it didn't matter what ya did as long as ya did the right things.—If ya felt something
—ya weren't 'sposed ta talk about it. It was cold—nobody had any fun
—I don't think (slowly)—they even loved me—or each other—and I—
uh—I don't think I love them—maybe, if we could start over—lovin'
each other—oh—what's the use—ya can't start over—is that right?

I:   I have asked you a number of questions today and you have told me
about your problems. I would suggest your return here for therapy.

P:   What do ya mean ther—therapy? What goes on there?

I:   One of our staff members will be your therapist. You will come regularly
and you will talk with each other.

P:   Ya mean I'll—uh—talk—uh—somebody and me—uh—we'll just talk—
and—uh—that'll change things for me.

I:   Yes. That's it. You will learn how to handle yourself better.

P:   If I learn ta handle myself better—I'll—uh—then—I'll feel better?

I:   Yes. That's it.

P:   Then that person—what'd ya call it?—a thera—therapist—won't tell me
what ta do ta change my life?

I:   That's right.

P:   We'll—uh—talk—and—I'll—I'll—uh—feel better?

I:   Very good. You learn quickly.

P:   I didn't tell ya before—uh—sometimes I—uh—I like a person one minute—then—yeah—then I hate their guts the next minute.

I:   Yes, people do have mixed feelings.

P:   Yeah—it's beginnin' ta make sense—maybe there's hope for me—yet.

I:   Good. It will take time to change.

P: Yeah—change—it's gotta change. I gotta—I gotta make it change.

I: And it can!

P: I got problems—big ones—and this treatment—ya call it therapy—that'll get rid of my problems.

I: Therapy won't take away your problems.

P: Then—what's the use of coming here?

I: You and your therapist will work on your problems.

P: So—I'll always have problems but—uh—but—I see what ya mean—I—uh—won't mess up on things like I do now—I'll do better about 'em. That'll be—uh—that'll be hard, won't it.

I: Yes, that's right. But, you'll work with your therapist on them.

P: Yeah—I see what ya mean. I'm beginnin' ta feel—ta feel better—I—uh —I won't be alone.

I: That's right.

P: Yeah—it feels—uh—yeah, I feel better already. But, hey—what about some pills ta help me when I get nervous—or—uh—mad.

I: You can talk that over with your therapist.

P: I'm glad I—uh—yeah, glad I came.

I: Good.

P: Yeah—maybe I can change.

I: Sure—*you* can do it.

P: I'm beginnin' ta believe it—yeah—yeah—beginnin' ta believe it.

I: That's great—you'll make it.

P: I'll—yeah—I'll sure try—I gotta.

I: Good. Should we make your next appointment?

P: Sure! Just this once, I feel better. Sure—sure—I want it.

## Role Induction—No Reward to Model

### Instructions for Listening to Tapes

More and more, it has been found that people have been helped by talking over their problems in therapy. It has also been found that listening to an example of an interview, before going into the interview, gives people a better idea of what goes on in a clinic. It seems to help them feel more comfortable in their own interview.

A tape of an actual first interview that took place in an out-of-town clinic such as this one will be played. You might like to know that both the interviewer and the patient have agreed to let us use this tape.

Before you hear the tape, you might like to know something about the people you will hear. The interviewer (I) is a psychologist who has had much experience in working with alcoholics in clinics like this one. The patient (P) is in his early 30s. Before coming to the clinic, he was just about at the end of his rope. His boss told him he would lose his job if he kept drinking. His wife was threatening to leave him and to take the children with her. He was using most of his pay for drink and was over his head in debts. He had lost most of his friends.

After this first interview, he decided to go into therapy and to work hard at it. He has made much improvement. Knowing that he was trying, his boss held his job open for him, and he's working steady now. His wife was willing to stick it out with him if he stayed in treatment. They're still together. According to him, he's staying dry. He no longer needs treatment.

Please try to listen to what the interviewer and the patient are saying. Try to think of yourself as that patient and how you would feel in the same place.

I:   Hello.

P:   Hello–hi (shy and dejected).

I:   Please have a seat–anywhere is O.K.

P:   Yeah–(dejected)–sure.

I:   Now, I'd like to ask you some questions about yourself. Try to answer them as best you can. Could you tell me what *you* see as the causes of your drinking problem?

P:   (Hostile) Hell–if I knew what the causes was–I wouldn't be here, would I? I mean–hell–I don't know (annoyed). (Thoughtful) What– what is the causes–hell–ya get lonely–ya get tired–ya spend your time workin'–'n what else? So I drink–that's all–I'm drinkin' all the time. (Slowly and thoughtfully)–but, I gotta stop.

I:   How long have you had a drinking problem?

P:   Yah–I didn't call it a problem (dejected).–I've been drinkin' for years. Uh–(thoughtful) when I was 29 or 30–I started drinkin' heavy. I guess–soon after I was married. Let's see–I was 23 when I was married. I was drinkin' before. (Hostile) I've been drinkin' heavy ever since.

I:   About 10 years, then. What brings you to the clinic about your drinking problem at *this* time?

P:   Yah–everything's fallin' apart! (Ready to cry). The whole thing's fallin' apart! (Dejected) I gotta get out o' this mess.

I:   How has your family reacted to your drinking?

P:   Well–(sarcastic)–how's my family reacted to my drinkin'. My wife's gonna leave me–and she's takin' the kids–(Hostile)–*that's* how my family's reacted.

I:   How has your drinking affected your work?

P:   Yah–(dejected)–my boss is gonna *throw* me out, too.–I was damn sure I lost it last week–I thought I lost it–ya know–he came–he said, "Listen! ya don't get here–you're here two days–you're here three days a week–you're not here at all–ya do a good job when you're here–but you're not here–because ya drink and I *know* it. So you're *out!!* Straighten up and fly right. This is your last chance." (Dejected, annoyed, hostile)–He tole me before–well, anyhow and then–then–the wife got onto it. (Annoyed) Then thes whole thing really started!

I:   How has it affected other parts of your life?

*P:*  (Long pause)—(Depressed)—Yah—what other parts of my life—money? Yeah—money, money, money—another part of my life—Yeah. O.K. —ah—ah—lousy! I'd—well—I have debts. I—ah—every pay check I get, I owe twice what it's worth—ya know—I—uh—I cash the—check! —I go to the bar!—I celebrate!—I go home—I haven't got much money! I always gave what—(pause)—I had to the wife but—uh—yeah'll—that don't work any more—uh—anyhow, debts—yeah'll—I don't know it's changed anything else—It's—uh—I had a lot of friends once—(cocky and defensive) I got plenty of friends now—they're different friends, that'll all—ya get older, ya get different friends—I don't need—uh—they don't—they don't mean anything to me now.

*I:*  Now, could you try to tell me how you feel about yourself?

*P:*  (Sarcastic, sassy) *Now—could—I—try—to—tell—you—how—I—feel—about —myself!* Well!—(slowly) well—I feel like hell about myself, lady (hostile)—if that's what you want to know. (Depressed)—I—I gotta stop this stuff. I'm not gettin' anywhere—I'm losin' everything I want —(on verge of tears)—I—got nothin'.

*I:*  Most people get angry. Could you tell me the kinds of things that get you angry?

*P:*  What—the—the kinds of things that get to me?—Yeah—Right! That's what you want to know? Somebody diggin' at me—leanin' over me— breathin' down my neck—(Mimicky and sassy). You're not doin' that right—Do somep'n else! Get here on time! Do this, do this—Nobody ta help ya—That's what gets me angry. And home—the kids—my God, the noise—four of 'em—they're O.K.—they're good kids, right? But, yack and scream and yell—gimme this, gimme that. Kids ain't got no respect nowadays—and everybody on the job—(hostile)—they push ya—my God!—a bunch of crooks!—And the wife—she yells—all she does is yell —ya can't do anything right! (depressed) They're at ya every damn minute.

*I:*  What do you do when you're angry?

*P:*  (Short laugh, chuckles softly, hostile) I thought I tole ya that! I drink! I get mad (sarcastic, evasive). People get mad, ya know!—I'm not the only guy that ever beat anybody up.—It goes on all the time—read it in the newspapers—see it on television.—Ya get tied up—things go in circles—ya get mad—ya beat up on somebody—that's what ya do. (depressed)—I don't have any more fights at work than the next guy. (Chuckles) The reason I don't is I'm not there. (Deliberate) I get that way—I get out—I get under the bar. (Hostile, sassy) Sometimes I blow my stack! Sometimes I sock a guy—well, (ashamedly) I don't hit a woman, much—well, I hit the wife but I don't hit 'em at work, much. (Chuckles) Ya can't, boy! (Chuckles)—But—ya know—I—I yell. I can't hit—so I yell!

*I:*  Well—now—could you tell me about the kinds of things that get you anxious or fearful?

*P:*  (Annoyed) I tole ya—people get at ya—get to ya. (Thoughtfully) Anx-

ious—that's different from mad?—yeah—I 'spose—ya feel alone—alone
—even when you're with people—nobody's talkin to ya—not *to* ya! And
it—I don't know—well—ya don't drink? O.K.—but—gee, I've been in
some lousy accidents—I get scared sometimes—(Anxious)—what I'm
gonna do—what's gonna happen—where do I get from here?—Ya got
no money—ya lie a lot—I mean, I lie a lot—ya have ta—(depressed)—
You're stuck with this stuff—I don't know—I've always been kinda
scared—of—of meetin' people—they—I—don't know how I seem to
them. (Confiding) I wanna be a good guy, ya know—and I come on—oh
—sometimes the only thing I can think of is ta buy a lot of drinks—me
—I drink two for everybody else's one—and I make a damn fool of myself—I've always been that way—I—I get all tensed up when I meet people—I wanna make a good impression and—I—I always make the
wrong kind. I just feel like I don't do anything right—that's the way it is
—a failure—a lousy husband—a lousy father—a lousy man.

I:   What do you do about the things that get you anxious or fearful?
P:   (Annoyed) I thought I tole ya! Oh—well—sure—I do other things
     sometimes—ya know—we go out sometimes.—It isn't always the same.
     (Demanding) What am I supposed to do—play golf? (Sarcastic)—
     Yeah, golf—I can't pay the rent—so I should play golf? (Sassy) So—
     well, some days I just don't go to work—I just stay in bed—(Confiding)
     —I figure—O.K.—go to work, I'm gonna knock somebody down—I'll
     get fired—so I stay home and sleep a while. O.K. The wife—she works
     part-time—she comes in. She says—you're not goin' to work?—She
     starts puttin' me down. It gets to me—I get mad—she knows it—I say
     I'm gonna go to work—I know I can't work—I'm gonna blow—so I go
     down to the bar—what else!—I drink—everything's a mess—so I'm stu-
     pid! (Hostile) But, this is the way I do things—I have a drink.
I:   Now, could you tell me about your parents? What were they like?
P:   My—my parents—(Annoyed) They haven't got any thing to do with
     this!—(Sighs) Well—I don't want anything to happen to 'em—they're
     O.K.—I guess—(Inquiringly, dependent) What do ya want me to say?
     —How I feel about 'em? Something like that? (Confidingly) Ta tell ya
     the truth—I don't feel much of anything for 'em.—I don't want anything
     ta go wrong—I'd try ta do anything I could for 'em—but—I never—they
     didn't seem to care anything about me, really. Maybe it wasn't that—I
     never thought they cared anything for each other—ta tell ya the truth—
     They're kinda—(Sassy and definite) *everything was kinda formal and
     neat and nice* and ya gotta do this and ya gotta do that—it was what ev-
     erybody else thought—the aunts—the grandparents—(wistfully)—it was
     never anything ta do with me—never what I thought.—My mother kinda
     ran the roost, I guess—she's a good woman, I 'spose.—My father was
     sorta—well—he was there—he brought home the bacon—but—he—uh
     —never stood up for me—or anything—or anybody.—I got out o' there
     soon as I could—I couldn't stick around—It wasn't 'cause they did any-

thing ta me—ya know—nothin' like that—they didn't drink—they didn't beat me up—they didn't do nothin' wrong—they're good people—but it left me sorta—I don't wanna' be with 'em much—I never did—I'd just as soon send 'em a Christmas present and forget it. They're cold—always been like that—and I—I—don't feel anything about them either.

I: Tell me—if you had your choice, in what way would your parents be different?

P: (Long pause)—(Thoughtfully) Ya mean if I could go back and be a kid again.—(Pause)—I don't know—it's the kind of feeling—it didn't matter what ya did as long as ya did the right things—if ya felt something—ya weren't 'sposed ta talk about it. It was cold—nobody had any fun—I don't think (slowly)—they even loved me—or each other—and I—uh—I don't think I love them—maybe, if we could start over—lovin' each other—oh—what's the use—ya can't start over—is that right?

I: I have asked you a number of questions today and you have told me about your problems. They are certainly very real problems which seem to be responsible for your feeling anxious, fearful, angry, and unhappy. These feelings are affecting how you do your day's work, how you get along with the important people in your life, how you handle your problems, and other parts of your life. Feeling this way, things may sometimes seem very confused and confusing.

P: That's just how it is with me. But—what—can I do?

I: I would suggest that you return here for therapy.

P: What do ya mean ther—therapy? What goes on there?

I: Well, for one thing, if you decide you want to do this, one of our staff members will be your therapist. You will come here regularly. You and your therapist will talk with each other, but you will do most of the talking.

P: Ya mean I'll talk—uh—somebody and me—uh—we'll just talk—and—uh—and that'll change things for me?

I: You will talk with your therapist who will mostly listen, and then try to help you to understand things about yourself. You, on your part, will have to think about things and practice them in your daily life. You will learn to understand what your real feelings and thoughts are—and how to handle them.

P: If I learn ta understand myself better, I'll—uh—do things different.

I: You will understand why you have troubles with your family, friends and job. This will help you to change the faulty ways of your behavior. You will be able to change, for the better, those things in your life that are making you unhappy now.

P: Then that person—what'd ya call it?—a thera—uh—a therapist—won't tell me what ta do ta change my life? Won't give me advice?

I: If that's all it took was advice, you probably wouldn't be here now. Unfortunately, when people give advice, it is usually something that will work for themselves but not for the person with the problem. So the therapist can't give you the answer, but can help you to *figure out* what you want to do so you can find out for *yourself* how to solve your problems, how to find the answer that is best for *you,* and how to make better decisions.

*P:* Then—uh—it'll be up ta me—I'll have ta do most of it.

*I:* The more freely you talk and the more you express your feelings and thoughts, the more quickly you will learn how to understand them, as well as your actions and behavior. There may be times that it will be hard. You may feel discouraged. Maybe, you will even be angry at your therapist. At times, you may think he's the greatest and, at other times, that he's a complete idiot.

*P:* I didn't tell ya before—uh—yeah—sometimes I—uh—I like a person one minute, then—uh—I hate their guts the next minute.

*I:* People do have mixed feelings. At such times, you may want to stay away from your appointment. But, this is when it is very important to come and talk about your reasons for these feelings. By working this out together, you learn ways to handle other situations in your every day life.

*P:* Yeah—yeah.

*I:* But don't expect to get better all at once. It took your whole life for you to be as you are now, so it will take time to change.

*P:* (Breaking in) Yeah—change—it's gotta change.

*I:* Progress may seem slow. There will be ups and downs but keeping at it is most important. Everyone has problems, but—

*P:* (Interrupts) I got mine—big ones.

*I:* Therapy won't take away your problems. You, like everyone else, will have problems all your life.

*P:* Then—what's the use of coming here?

*I:* In therapy, you will learn how *you* can handle them better, how *you* can make more satisfying decisions, and how *you* can have control over the things that happen to you.

*P:* So—I'll always have problems—I'll have ta learn ta do better about 'em. That'll be—uh—hard—won't it?

*I:* You won't have to do it alone. You and your therapist, together, will work toward this.

*P:* Yeah—so that's it.

*I:* You'll have someone to work with you.

*P:* Hey—what about some pills ta help me when I get nervous—or—uh—mad.

*I:* That will be up to you and your therapist to decide. If it's necessary, it can be arranged at that time.

*P:* Yeah—but it sounds hard.

*I:* It's hard work.

*P:* Yeah—'spose I give it a try.

*I:* Should we make your next appointment?

*P:* O.K.—yeah—O.K.

### No Role Induction—No Reward to Model

*Instructions for Listening to Tapes*

More and more, it has been found that people have been helped by talking over their problems in therapy. It has also been found that listening to an example of an interview, before going into the interview, gives people a better idea of what goes on in a clinic. It seems to help them feel more comfortable in their own interview.

A tape of an actual first interview that took place in an out-of-town clinic such as this one will be played. You might like to know that both the interviewer and the patient have agreed to let us use this tape.

Before you hear the tape, you might like to know something about the people you will hear. The interviewer (*I*) is a psychologist who has had much experience in working with alcoholics in clinics like this one. The patient (*P*) is in his early 30s. Before coming to the clinic, he was just about at the end of his rope. His boss told him he would lose his job if he kept drinking. His wife was threatening to leave him and to take the children with her. He was using most of his pay for drink and was over his head in debts. He had lost most of his friends.

After this first interview, he decided to go into therapy and to work hard at it. He has made much improvement. Knowing that he was trying, his boss held his job open for him, and he's working steadily now. His wife was willing to stick it out with him if he stayed in treatment. They're still together. According to him, he's staying dry. He no longer needs treatment.

Please try to listen to what the interviewer and the patient are saying. Try to think of yourself as that patient and how you would feel in the same place.

*I:*     Hello.

*P:*     Hello—hi (shy and dejected).

*I:*     Please have a seat—anywhere is O.K.

*P:*     Yeah—(dejected)—sure.

*I:*     Now, I'd like to ask you some questions about yourself. Try to answer them as best you can. Could you tell me what *you* see as the causes of your drinking problem?

*P:*     (Hostile) Hell—if I knew what the causes was—I wouldn't be here, would I? I mean—hell—I don't know (annoyed). (Thoughtful) What—what is the causes—hell—ya get lonely—ya get tired—ya spend your time workin'—'n what else? So I drink—that's all—I'm drinkin' all the time. (Slowly and thoughtfully)—but, I gotta stop.

*I:*     How long have you had a drinking problem?

*P:*     Yah—I didn't call it a problem—(dejected) I've been drinkin' for years. Uh—(thoughtful) when I was 29 or 30—I started drinkin' heavy. I guess—soon after I was married. Let's see—I was 23 when I was married. I was drinkin' before. (Hostile) I've been drinkin' heavy ever since.

*I:*  About 10 years, then. What brings you to the clinic about your drinking problem at *this* time?

*P:*  Yah—everything's fallin' apart. (Ready to cry) The whole thing's fallin' apart! (Dejected) I gotta get out o' this mess.

*I:*  How has your family reacted to your drinking?

*P:*  Well—(sarcastic)—how's my family reacted to my drinkin'. My wife's gonna leave me—and she's takin' the kids.—(Hostile) *That's* how my family's reacted.

*I:*  How has your drinking affected your work?

*P:*  Yah—(dejected)—my boss is gonna *throw* me out, too.—I was damn sure I lost it last week—I thought I lost it—ya know—he came—he said, "Listen! ya don't get here—you're here two days—you're here three days a week—you're not here at all—ya do a good job when you're here—but you're not here—because ya drink and I *know* it. So you're *out!!* Straighten up and fly right. This is your last chance." (Dejected, annoyed, hostile)—He tole me before—well, anyhow and then—then—the wife got onto it. (Annoyed) Then the whole thing really started!

*I:*  How has it affected other parts of your life?

*P:*  (Long pause)—(Depressed)—Yah—what other parts of my life—money? Yeah—money, money, money—another part of my life—yeah. O.K. —ah—ah—lousy! I'd—well—I have debts. I—ah—every pay check I get, I owe twice what it's worth—ya know—I—uh—I cash the—check! —I go to the bar!—I celebrate!—I go home—I haven't got much money! I always gave what—(pause)—I had to the wife but—uh—yeah'll—that don't work any more—uh—anyhow, debts—yeah'll—I dont' know it's changed anything else—It's—uh—I had a lot of friends once—(cockey and defensive) I got plenty of friends now—they're different friends, that's all—ya get older, ya get different friends—I don't need—uh—they don't—they don't mean anything to me now.

*I:*  Now, could you try to tell me how you feel about yourself?

*P:*  (Sarcastic, sassy) *Now—could—I—try—to—tell—you—how—I—feel—about —myself!* Well!—(slowly) well—I feel like hell about myself, lady (hostile)—if that's what you want to know. (Depressed)—I—I gotta stop this stuff. I'm not gettin' anywhere—I'm losin' everything I want— (on verge of tears)—I—got nothin'.

*I:*  Most people get angry. Could you tell me the kinds of things that get you angry?

*P:*  What—the—the kinds of things that get to me? Yeah—Right! That's what you want to know? Somebody diggin' at me—leanin' over me— breathin' down my neck. (Mimicky and sassy) You're not doin' that right—Do somep'n else! Get here on time! Do this, do this—Nobody ta help ya—that's what gets me angry. And home—the kids—my God, the noise—four of 'em—they're O.K.—they're good kids, right? But, yack and scream and yell—gimme this, gimme that. Kids ain't got no respect nowadays—and everybody on the job—(hostile)—they push ya—my

God!—a bunch of crooks!—And the wife—she yells—all she does is yell
—ya can't do anything right! (depressed) They're at ya every damn minute.

I:    What do you do when you're angry?

P:    (Short laugh, chuckles softly, hostile) I thought I tole ya that! I drink! I
get mad. (Sarcastic, evasive) People get mad, ya know!—I'm not the
only guy that ever beat anybody up.—It goes on all the time—read it in
the newspapers—see it on television.—Ya get tied up—things go in circles—ya get mad—ya beat up on somebody—that's what ya do. (Depressed)—I don't have any more fights at work than the next guy.
(Chuckles) The reason I don't is I'm not there. (Deliberate) I get that
way—I get out—I get under the bar. (Hostile and sassy) Sometimes I
blow my stack! Sometimes I sock a guy—well, (ashamedly) I don't hit a
woman, much—well, I hit the wife but I don't hit 'em at work, much.
(Chuckles) Ya can't, boy! (chuckles)—But—ya know—I—I yell. I
can't hit—so I yell!

I:    Well—now—could you tell me about the kinds of things that get you
anxious or fearful?

P:    (Annoyed) I tole ya—people get at ya—get to ya. (Thoughtfully) Anxious—
that's different from mad?—Yeah—I 'spose—Ya feel alone—alone—even
when you're with people—nobody's talkin' to ya—not *to* ya! And it—I
don't know—well—ya don't drink? O.K.—but—gee, I've been in some
lousy accidents—I get scared sometimes—(anxious)—what I'm gonna
do—what's gonna happen—where do I get from here?—Ya got no money—ya lie a lot—I mean, I lie a lot—ya have ta—(depressed)—You're
stuck with this stuff—I don't know—I've always been kinda scared—of
—of meetin' people—they—I—I don't know how I seem to them. (Confiding) I wanna be a good guy, ya know—and I come on—oh—sometimes the only thing I can think of is ta buy a lot of drinks—me—I drink
two for everybody else's one—and I make a damn fool of myself—I've
always been that way—I—I get all tensed up when I meet people—I
wanna make a good impression and—I—I always make the wrong kind.
I just feel like I don't do anything right—that's the way it is—a failure
—a lousy husband—a lousy father—a lousy man.

I:    What do you do about the things that get you anxious or fearful?

P:    (Annoyed) I thought I tole ya! Oh—well—sure—I do other things
sometimes—ya know—we go out sometimes.—It isn't always the same.
(Demanding) What am I supposed to do—play golf? (Sarcastic)—
Yeah, golf—I can't pay the rent—so I should play golf? (Sassy) So—
well, some days I just don't go to work—I just stay in bed—(Confiding)
—I figure—O.K.—go to work, I'm gonna knock somebody down—I'll
get fired—so I stay home and sleep a while. O.K. The wife—she works
part-time—she comes in. She says—you're not goin' to work? She starts
puttin' me down. It gets to me—I get mad—she knows it—I say I'm gonna go to work—I know I can't work—I'm gonna blow—so I go down to

the bar—what else!—I drink—everything's a mess—so I'm stupid! (Hostile) But, this is the way I do things—I have a drink.

I:  Now, could you tell me about your parents? What were they like?

P:  My—my parents—(Annoyed) They haven't got anything to do with this!—(Sighs) Well—I don't want anything to happen to 'em—they're O.K.—I guess—(Inquiringly, dependent) What do ya want me to say? —How I feel about 'em? Something like that? (Confidingly) Ta tell ya the truth—I don't feel much of anything for 'em.—I don't want anything ta go wrong—I'd try ta do anything I could for 'em—but—I never—they didn't seem to care anything about me, really. Maybe it wasn't that—I never thought they cared anything for each other—ta tell ya the truth— They're kinda—(Sassy and definite)*everything was kinda' formal and neat and nice*—and ya gotta do this and ya gotta do that—it was what everybody else thought—the aunts—the grandparents—(wistfully) it was never anything ta do with me—never what I though.—My mother kinda ran the roost, I guess—she's a good woman, I 'spose.—My father was sorta—well—he was there—he brought home the bacon—but—he —uh—never stood up for me—or anything—or anybody.—I got out o' there soon as I could—I couldn't stick around.—It wasn't 'cause they did anything ta me—ya know—nothin' like that—they didn't drink—they didn't beat me up—they didn't do nothin' wrong—they're good people —but it left me sorta—I don't wanna' be with 'em much—I never did— I'd just as soon send 'em a Christmas present and forget it—. They're cold—always been like that—and I—I—don't feel anything about them either.

I:  Tell me—if you had your choice, in what way would your parents be different?

P:  (Long pause)—(Thoughtfully) Ya mean if I could go back and be a kid again.—(Pause)—I don't know—it's the kind of feeling—it didn't matter what ya did as long as ya did the right things—If ya felt something —ya weren't 'sposed ta talk about it. It was cold—nobody had any fun —I don't think (slowly)—they even loved me—or each other—and I— uh—I don't think I love them—maybe, if we could start over—lovin' each other—oh—what's the use—ya can't start over—is that right?

I:  I have asked you a number of questions today and you have told me about your problems. I would suggest that you return here for therapy.

P:  What do ya mean ther—therapy? What goes on there?

I:  One of our staff members will be your therapist. You will come regularly and you will talk with each other.

P:  Ya mean I'll—uh—talk—uh—somebody and me—uh—we'll just talk— and—uh—that'll change things for me.

I:  You will learn how to handle yourself better.

P:  I'll—uh—learn ta handle myself better.

I:  Mhmm.

P:   Then that person—what'd ya call it?—a thera—therapist—won't tell me what ta do ta change my life?

I:   No—the therapist doesn't give advice.

P:   We'll—uh—talk—things over.

I:   Uh-huh.

P:   I didn't tell ya before—uh—sometimes I—uh—I like a person one minute—then—yeah—then I hate their guts the next minute.

I:   People do have mixed feelings.

P:   They—uh—really do?

I:   Mhmm.

P:   Yeah—it's gotta change.

I:   Mhmm.

P:   I got problems—big ones—and this treatment—ya call it therapy—that'll get rid of my problems.

I:   Therapy won't take away your problems.

P:   Then—what's the use of coming here?

I:   You and your therapist will work on your problems.

P:   So—I'll always have problems but—uh—I'll work on 'em with the—uh—therapist.

I:   Mhmm—you'll work with your therapist.

P:   Yeah—uh—we'll work together.

I:   Mhmm.

P:   Hey—what about some pills ta help me when I get nervous—or—uh—mad.

I:   You can talk that over with your therapist.

P:   Yeah—talk it over with my—uh—therapist.

I:   Mhmm.

P:   I gotta do somethin'—I gotta.

I:   Should we make your next appointment.

P:   Sure—gotta do somethin'—gotta.

# PARAPROFESSIONAL
# SKILL-ENHANCEMENT INVESTIGATIONS

### High Attraction–Low Attraction–No Attraction

*T\*:* Since this is our first interview, I'll be asking you about a number of different areas of your life. Why don't we start off by your telling me about your family?

*P†:* My family. Well, you know sometimes—sometimes I think my family could do—just as well without me. You know. Like I'm a—a useless sort of object that sort of sits around the house. When I—come home from work it's like—like there's nothing there.

*T:* You don't feel that your family looks forward to your coming home at night?

*P:* Sometimes it—sometimes it seems that they don't even know when I'm home. Kids'll be running around and—my wife—well sometimes the way she acts it would be better if I just stayed out. Some of the things that she gets into—MMMMMMMM.

*T:* **(Attraction insert)**

*High:* I'm not clear why your wife would act that way. I find you a rather easy person to talk with. . . . What kind of things does your wife get into?
*Low:* I think I understand a little why your wife acts that way. I find it somewhat hard to talk with you myself. . . . What kind of things does your wife get into?
*No:* No insert.

---

\* *T* represents Therapist throughout as previously noted.
† P represents Patient throughout as previously noted.

P:  —I don't know. She's always yelling and screaming—wants me to do things when I come inside—always telling me I have this to do and that to do. She doesn't realize I just wanna come home and I wanna relax a little bit. Nah—I don't know how she can push me all the time—do this —do that—all the time.

T:  Sounds like marriage has been a lot of trouble for you.

P:  —Yeah. Yeah—really it—it was different before. When we first got married it was—it was nice. We went out and saw different people, did—did some things together. Got along pretty good too. Didn't have all this that's going on now.

T:  **(Attraction insert)**

*High:* From our meeting so far, I'm finding it rather easy to get along with you too. . . . I guess things aren't going very well with your wife now.

*Low:* From our meeting so far, I'm finding it somewhat difficult to get along with you, too. . . . I guess things aren't going very well with your wife now.

*No:* No insert.

P:  No—my wife changed. She got—she got different.—Things started—you know—she started not to care about things. We couldn't go out as much. Then—then the babies came and then—wow—feeding them and taking care of them and doing all those things. Never had any time to do the things that we used to do together.—You know, it's usually hard for me to talk about things like this, but it's easy talking to you. Like—you know when I'd come home from work—my wife—she'd be running around the house after the kids—and when I'd come in the door I'd get ignored you know. No one says hello—no one asks you how you are.

T:  —Somehow all this seemed to happen around the time the children came?

P:  It—seems that way. Before we had the kids we didn't have these problems. Now it—it's just not the same.

*Other voice:*  **What would you say? (1)**

T:  What about your parents; did your father—drink?

P:  Oh yeah. He—could down them with the best of them. My old lady will tell you that. Yeah he really knew how to drink. Used to get into some terrible fights with my old lady though. Boy—he'd come home have a little too much in him—she'd really let him have it. I'd have to—pull the pillow up over my head so I wouldn't hear the noise. Couldn't get to sleep.

T:  Your mother was very hard on your father then.

P:  Yeah. She really used to get mad at him. You know for drinking and all that. She used to yell at him. Get on his back all the time. Really be nasty to him. Maybe that's one of the reasons why he's six feet under right now.

T:      Sort of like the same thing your wife is doing to you?

P:      Yeah. You're right. You really hit the nail on the head. You really understand what's going on. There's a lot of things about the two that are kind of the same. I think she's trying to do the same thing to me that my mother did to my father.—Yell and fight—the yelling and carrying on. They'll both do it. Scream at you—and call you a drunk. Telling me I can't take on any responsibility. Always yelling about something. Money. Why don't you have more of it? Why can't we buy this? Why can't we buy that? I'm working—as hard as I can—and she does—she doesn't realize that. She thinks all I have to do is work—all the time. She thinks it's—it's easy for me to—to work every day.—Always pushing me. I don't like to be pushed. I get—I'll get things done. But I have to work—at my own pace, otherwise—it just doesn't matter if I work or not, if I can't work at my own pace.

T:      **(Attraction insert)**

*High:* You seem to be really trying to make your marriage work. I respect people who really try like that. . . . It sounds like your wife and you just—don't do things the same way.

*Low:* You don't seem to be really trying to see her side of it. I find it hard to respect people who don't at least try to do that. . . . It sounds like your wife and you just—don't do things the same.

*No:* No insert.

P:      Yeah. She's in her own world.—She doesn't care about anything that I do—or say. She doesn't care about me or anyone else. Sometimes I just feel like getting up and leaving. There's nothing there any more.

T:      You'd like to just go away?

P:      Mmhmm.

T:      Have you ever done this?

P:      —Not for any long time. Used to—get away for a couple of days by myself. But I always ended up coming back because I had no one else to go to.

T:      **(Attraction insert)**

*High:* Well, now when you feel like that you can come see me. . . . You don't like being alone.

*Low:* When you feel like that, I don't want you to count on coming to see me. . . . You don't like being alone.

*No:* No insert.

P:      Oh—it's hard when you're alone. It's—I have no place to go. Haven't any friends or—or close family. Except for my—my wife and kids. You know I–the way they treat me I know they don't want me. At least though like when I'm home I have a roof over my head. I know I can sleep–I don't have to be wandering around in the streets for something to do. Someone to feed me.

### Other voice: What would you say? (2)

T: —Uh tell me, uh–how long have you been drinking?

P: Oh, I don't know, quite a few years I guess. I think–I can't figure out the exact time.–It just happens you know you–you don't really know when you start when you–start drinking–there's no big change in your life. You know I–I really don't drink that much I–have a few drinks now and then but–not that many.

T: You don't think you are an alcoholic, then?

P: What's an alcoholic? Probably every guy I know drinks more than I do. My wife thinks I drink a lot, though–she's–boy, you talk to her and you'd think I was the biggest bum on skid row. My wife doesn't understand me the way you do. I wish everyone was like you. They don't realize that every so often I want to relax a little bit–I–I–I can't take all the pressures of–my job and all that–and I–I feel a lot better when I–I–drink–have a few.

T: **(Attraction insert)**

*High:* You seem to have tried to figure out the reasons you drink. I find it easier to work with people who try to figure out the reasons behind their problems. . . . Uh–about how much do you drink?

*Low:* You don't seem to have tried to figure out the reasons you drink. I find it easier to work with people who try to figure out the reasons behind their problems. . . . Uh–about how much do you drink?

*No:* No insert.

P: Oh it depends–on what's going on. Maybe I'll have a couple of drinks during the day and then go home and have one or two. You know–just to relax.

T: Do you drink in the morning?

P: Not all the time. Maybe–you know–when–when I really feel bad in the morning–you know–I'll get up and before I go to work I'll have a drink.

T: A drink helps you start the morning off right?

P: Yeah. Sometimes I don't feel–good at all. Like–like my stomach for instance–like–I throw up alot sometimes, uh I remember some mornings–I'll be shaving in front of the mirror and I'll just double over with pain. My stomach'll be so tight. It's really kind of painful. I don't know –what's it from but–it feels like my stomach is real tight inside. I–I usually just sit down for awhile–and try to relax. Sometimes I'll–I'll have a quick drink you know that might help sometimes. To relax me and help my stomach a little bit—calm me down. Otherwise it's—it's just hell to go through all that pain.

T:     **(Attraction insert)**

*High:* You seem to be trying hard to deal with these problems. I find it difficult to work with patients who don't try hard. . . . It sounds like it's pretty rough for you.
*Low:* You don't seem to be trying hard to deal with these problems. I find it difficult to work with patients who don't try hard. . . . It sounds like it's pretty rough for you.
*No:* No insert.

P:     It's a helluva way to get up in the morning. Stomach's bothering me—it's tight. Back is stiff—getting up like that I really don't feel like going to work. Wish I could just lie in bed—for a little longer—and take it easy for the day. Take the day off. Don't go to work. It's hard—to work when you're feeling miserable like that. But—wife comes in and says get the hell out of bed—who do you think you are? You've got mouths to feed. Go out and get to work. You get in to work and you tell your boss you haven't been feeling well. Hmmm. He doesn't understand either. The—they just want to see you there—whether you're dead on your feet or not. They just want to see you show up and do your job. They don't care what you're feeling like.

## Other voice:     *What would you say? (3)*

T:     Umm—how about—how about your sex life with your wife? What's that like now?
P:     Hmmm. There isn't any. I mean it's—it's gone—it's—it's not there any more. The only time I can get aroused any more is when I had a couple of drinks and as soon as I start drinking well you can forget about getting close to my wife. She doesn't want to have anything to do with me then. So—we just don't do it any more. There's nothing there between us any more anyway.
T:     Sometimes it just seems hopeless?
P:     Yeah. No hope—it's—I just—sometimes I just can't talk to my wife.—I can't say a word to her—about anything. She doesn't listen—she doesn't understand. She just doesn't care. I'll go in and I'll tell her I'm not feeling well. Oh—that—you know when I feel bad and I feel pressured and all tense inside—she doesn't understand that. She has some idea in her mind that she wants to get something done—she wants it done right now and she won't be satisfied until it's all completed and over with. If she says she wants something done right now, you'd better move right now, otherwise it's constant nagging all the time. Pushing.—Always wants me to—to do something else. Who could live with a wife like that? You know what I mean?

T: **(Attraction insert)**

*High*: Yes, it really sounds like a lot more pressure than anyone deserves. . . . It sounds like it's pretty hard for you home.

*Low*: Yes, but don't you feel that a lot of the pressure she puts on you you deserve? . . . It sounds like it's pretty hard for you home.

*No*: No insert.

P: It sure is.

T: And yet—it's also hard to leave.

P: —Sigh—yeah. I wish I could do something about it though. I—I just can't take any more of this.

T: How would you like things to be?

P: I guess I'd like things to be kind of peaceful and quiet. So I can get things done without being pushed into it. I'd like to be around people that—that knew the way I feel, the problems I've had and—and who could understand them. You know—they'd understand sometimes I feel sick—I can't work like I should. A lot of pressure sometimes—I can't handle that. If things were like that it would be different. People just don't care any more—they don't care about anything—care about other people. But you seem to care about me. You remind me of an aunt I had that I liked alot. But other people just don't care—especially about me. I wish things were different.

T: Ummm—if you could have things the way—you want them—uh, would you want to be married and have a family?

P: Probably.

T: **(Attraction insert)**

*High:* I'm not surprised to hear that. It seems to me that you would work very hard to handle that kind of responsibility. . . . It's kind of nice to have a family to go—to go home to.

*Low:* I'm surprised to hear that. I'm not sure how hard you work at handling that kind of responsibility. . . . It's kind of nice to have a family to go—to go home to.

*No:* No insert.

P: Yeah. It's nice to have a home and be—be in it and feel as if you belonged in it. That you're welcome there. Lately—my house is like a strange land. Seems that all they want from me is the money. "Is this the week you get paid, Dad?" My wife comes in with the bills in her hand and says, "These are due this month." We'll never get our head above water. They don't care about anything else. As long as I bring that check in.

*Other voice: What would you say? (4)*

T: Why do you think you're here in the hospital?

P: My wife's the reason why I'm here—in more ways than one. She's the one that got me in here. She's the one that nags me all the time. Makes me feel so bad—when I'm outside. She doesn't realize when I take a couple of drinks it's so I can handle things a little better. No—she thinks when I—I take a couple of drinks that I'm running away from things—I'm avoiding my responsibilities, as she puts it.

*T:*    Sort of like you're not being a man?

*P:*    Yeah. I think that's the way she wants me sometimes. To feel like that.

*T:*    **(Attraction insert)**

*High:* I don't think you should feel like that. You don't seem to be trying to avoid your responsibilities when you're talking to me. I work best with patients who accept their responsibilities in therapy. . . . I guess you feel that even though you're the one that's here—this problem isn't all yours. *Low:* Maybe in some ways you should feel like that. It seems to me that at times you're trying to avoid your responsibilities even when you're talking to me. I work best with patients who accept their responsibilities in therapy. . . . I guess you feel that even though you're the one that's here—this problem isn't all yours.

*No:* No insert.

*P:*    —That's right. I wish someone would take a look at my wife. And some of the other people I come in contact with. Like my boss—the people at work—they're all the same. Telling me what to do—how to do it—when to do it—how fast I should do it. All the time. It's getting so I—I—I can't lead my own life any more.

*T:*    Seems to me as though you're—you're upset with quite a few people. I mean even a little angry with some of them.

*P:*    Who wouldn't be angry with—with people like that? Like you know every time—I meet someone and they tell me—you can be doing a better job or why didn't you do this—what kind of things do they expect from a person? I'm no superman—I just—do the work I'm supposed to do. Or try to do it any way. You seem to understand that. I wish everyone else understood me like you do. I really like you. But you know what everyone else remembers—they remember the day you didn't show up for work or the days that you didn't do the job right. Or how you messed this thing up. That's all they remember—they never remember the good things that you do. My wife—she's the same way. She never tells me what I'm doing right. It's always the things that I've been doing wrong that I get word from her. It's easy for her to pick out those things—things I do wrong. Who wouldn't get angry?

*T:*    **(Attraction insert)**

*High:* Perhaps you may have a right to get angry. It's hard for me to see why she picks on you like that. . . . Have you ever gotten angry at your wife? Have you ever shown you were angry?

*Low:* Perhaps you have no right to get angry. To some extent I can see why she picks on you like that. . . . Have you ever gotten angry at your wife? Have you ever shown you were angry?

*No:* No insert.

**P:** Yeah—a couple of times I did, but she said if I got any angrier or did anything to her she'd call the cops.

**T:** —What about your boss? Have you ever—gotten angry at him?

**P:** Are you kidding? If I ever mouthed off to him I'd—be canned on the spot. And then I'd really be in some fine state. I'd get it twice as bad from home then. I mean without a job. It's the only thing that's keeping me there now. No—I still have my job. I don't like it but I'm there.

## *Other voice: What would you say? (5)*

**T:** I noticed on your record that this is your second hospitalization. What happened the first time around when you came here?

**P:** Mmm—first time I was here it was really a waste of time. —I got out of the hospital and—things were all right for awhile. But then, my wife started up again—she started to nag and pressure started to build again and things started to go wrong at work. Kids started to act up. Began to feel bad at night—not getting any sleep. The only way I could relax was to have a drink. So I'd have a drink and—then a couple more. And the whole thing starts all over again.—If it wasn't for those other things, though, my boss, my wife, I don't think I'd be here, now. I wouldn't have to.

**T:** But the way things work out—it seems as if you—end up right back where you started.

**P:** Oh, yeah. Each time, though—I came—here—I got away from those people. But I'd sure like things to be different. You know . . . better, less problems.

## **T:** (Attraction insert)

*High:* It seems to me that you're really trying. In fact, I feel you're trying alot more than most patients I've seen for therapy. . . . I guess it's sort of like a vacation here.

*Low:* I'm not so sure you're really trying. In fact, I sort of feel you're trying a lot less than most other patients I've seen. . . . I guess it's sort of like a vacation here.

*No:* No insert.

**P:** A little bit. See there's no one around here telling me what I have to do or don't do. No one telling me I have to get out—and go to work in the morning. Here there is someone like you who I can talk to. Someone who understands me and helps me. I really like talking to you. I feel very safe here with you. And I don't have to get up and go to work for 8 hours all day—put up with a boss that's constantly on my back—riding me—telling me that I'm not doing my job just exactly the way he wants it done. I don't have to put up with any of that when I'm here.

*T:*  Mm—but don't we have many rules here, many things you must do?

*P:*  Yeah but—those rules are for everybody. Everybody has to do it and everybody does it, but when I'm not in the hospital—when I'm home—now everybody has to take my wife every day. Her nagging, her—stuff that she hands out every night and things.

*T:*  **(Attraction insert)**

*High:* Well, you won't get that from me. I'm really glad that you were assigned to me. . . . So it's mainly the rules that your wife sets up that, um —present the most problems for you.

*Low:* Well, maybe you deserve to be nagged at times. . . . So it's mainly the rules that your wife sets up that, um—present the most problems for you.

*No:* No insert.

*P:*  She's the one that does it the most.

*T:*  Sounds as though she's pretty tough on you.

*P:*  Hmm. You could say that. She can really get to you sometimes. Yelling at you. Telling you what to do. Telling you what not to do. Constantly saying you're not good enough, you're useless. You're not making enough money. You're a bum. You drink too much. What's a guy supposed to do with a wife like that?

*Other voice:*     ***What would you say? (6)***

*Other voice:*

This ends the part of the therapy session we are playing to you. In the space on your answer sheet that is numbered 7, please write down what you would say as your last comment to end the therapy session. You will have 30 seconds from now (30 sec.). Please turn to the next page of your booklet and read the instructions.

### High Self-Disclosure

*T:*  Since this is our first interview, I'll be asking you about a number of different areas of your life. Why don't we start off by your telling me about your family?

*P:*  My family. Well, you know sometimes, sometimes I think my family could do—just as well without me. You know. Like I'm a—a useless sort of object that sort of sits around the house. When I—come home from work it's like—like there's nothing there.

T: You don't feel that your family looks forward to your coming home at night?

P: Sometimes it—sometimes it seems that they don't even know when I'm home. Kids'll be running around and—my wife well sometimes the way she acts it would be better if I just stayed out. Some of the things she gets into—MMMMMMMM.

*Other voice:* ***What would you say? (1)***

T: What kinds of things does your wife get into?

P: —I don't know. She's always yelling and screaming—wants me to do things when I come inside—always telling me I have this to do and that to do. She doesn't realize I just wanna come home and I wanna relax a little bit. Nah. I don't know how she can push me all the time—do this —do that—all the time. It wasn't always like that—it was different before. When we first got married it was—it was nice. We went out and saw different people, did—did some things together. Got along pretty good too. Didn't have all this that's going on now.

*Other voice:* ***What would you say? (2)***

T: I guess things aren't going very well with your wife now.

P: No—my wife changed. She got—she got different. Things started—you know—she started not to care about things. We couldn't go out as much. Then—then the babies came and then—wow—feeding them and taking care of them and doing all those things. Never had any time to do the things that we used to do together. You know, it's hard for me to talk about things like this, but it's—well—you know when I'd come home from work—my wife—she'd be running around the house after the kids —and when I'd come in the door I'd get ignored you know. No one asks you how you are.

T: —Somehow all this seemed to happen around the time the children came.

P: It—seems that way. Before we had the kids we didn't have these problems. Now it—it's just not the same.

*Other voice:* ***What would you say? (3)***

T: What about your parents; did your father—drink?

P: Oh yeah. He—could down them with the best of them. My old lady will tell you that. Yeah he really knew how to drink. Used to get into some terrible fights with my old lady, though. Boy—he'd come home and have a little too much in him—she'd really let him have it. I'd have to—pull the pillow up over my head so I wouldn't hear the noise. Couldn't get to sleep. Yeah, she really used to get mad at him. You know for drinking and all that. She used to yell at him. Get on his back all the time. Really be nasty to him. Maybe that's one of the reasons why he's six feet under right now.

T:  Sort of like the same thing your wife is doing to you?

P:  Yeah, there's a lot of things about the two that are kind of the same. I think she's trying to do the same thing to me that my mother did to my father. Yell and fight—the yelling and carrying on. They'll both do it. Scream at you—and call you a drunk. Telling me I can't take on any responsibility. Always yelling about something. Money. Why don't you have more of it? Why can't we buy this? Why can't we buy that? I'm working—as hard as I can—and she does—she doesn't realize that. She thinks all I have to do is work—all the time. She thinks it's—it's easy for me to—to work every day.—Always pushing me. I don't like to be pushed. I get—I'll get things done. But I have to work—at my own pace, otherwise—it just doesn't matter if I work or not if I can't work at my own pace.

### Other voice:    What would you say? (4)

T:  I know what you mean, I have to work at my own pace too, and sometimes there are problems when two people operate at a different pace. It seems like it might be that way for you and your wife.

P:  That's it—you're right, you really understand. She's in her own world— she doesn't care about anything that I do—or say. She doesn't care about me or anyone else. Sometimes I just feel like getting up and leaving. There's nothing there any more.

T:  You'd like to just go away?

P:  Mmhmmm.

T:  Have you ever done this?

P:  Not for any long time. Used to—get away for a couple of days by myself. But I always ended up coming back because I had no one else to go to.

T:  I often dislike being alone, do you?

P:  Oh—it's hard when you're alone. It's—I have no place to go. Haven't any friends or—or close family. Except for my—my wife and kids. You know I—the way they treat me I know they don't want me. At least though like when I'm home I have a roof over my head. I know I can sleep—I don't have to be wandering around in the streets for something to do. Someone to feed me.

### Other voice:    What would you say? (5)

T:  —Uh tell me uh—how long have you been drinking?

P:  Oh I don't know, quite a few years I guess. I think—I can't figure out the exact time. It just happens you know you don't really know when you start when you start drinking—there's no big change in your life. You know I—I really don't drink that much—I have a few drinks now and then, but—not that many.

T: Sounds like drinking began socially for you, sort of the way smoking did for me, but for a long time I didn't consider myself a smoker. Do you think you're an alcoholic now?

P: What's an alcoholic? Probably every guy I know drinks more than I do. My wife thinks I drink alot though—she's—boy, you talk to her and you'd think I was the biggest bum on skid row. My wife doesn't understand me the way you do. I wish everyone was like you. They don't realize that every so often I want to relax a little bit—I—I—I can't take all the pressures of my job and all that—and I—I feel a lot better when I—I drink—have a few.

T: You seem to drink because you feel it helps you relax, I used to overeat and smoke for that reason until one day I realized I was eating and smoking a great deal more than I really wanted to. By the way, about how much do you drink?

P: Oh it depends—on what's going on. Maybe I'll have a couple of drinks during the day and then go home and have one or two. You know—just to relax.

T: Very often, I used to reach for a cigarette when I first got up in the morning. Do you drink in the morning?

P: Not all the time. Maybe—you know—when I really feel bad in the morning—you know—I'll get up and before I go to work I'll have a drink.

### Other voice: What would you say? (6)

T: A drink helps you start the morning off right?

P: Sometimes I don't feel—good at all. Like—like my stomach for instance —like I throw up a lot sometimes uh I remember some mornings—I'll be shaving in front of the mirror and I'll just double over with pain. My stomach'll be so tight. It's really kind of painful. I don't know—what it's from but—it feels like my stomach is real tight inside. I—I usually just sit down for awhile—and try to relax. Sometimes I'll—I'll have a quick drink you know that might help sometimes. To relax me and help my stomach a little bit—calm me down. Otherwise it's just hell to go through all that pain.

T: It sounds like it's pretty rough for you, especially in the morning. I guess I can understand what you're saying because, although I've not been as uncomfortable as you seem to be, I rarely wake up full of energy and alert, and mornings are often difficult for me also. I guess you find it pretty tough to face the day.

P: Boy you really understand what I'm talking about, it's a helluva way to get up in the morning. Stomach's bothering me—it's tight. Back is stiff

—getting up like that I really don't feel like going to work. Wish I could just lie in bed for a little longer—and take it easy for the day. Take the day off. Don't go to work. It's hard to work when you're feeling miserable like that.

T: I know what you mean. I've occasionally had that impulse myself, but usually something gets me going. How do you manage to overcome this?

P: I have no choice. The wife comes in and says get the hell out of bed—who do you think you are? You've got mouths to feed. Go out and work . . .

T: You must find it difficult to work if you're feeling so ill.

P: You bet! You get into work and you tell your boss you haven't been feeling well. Hmmm. He doesn't understand either. The—they just want to see you there—whether you're dead on your feet or not. They just want to see you show up and do your job. They don't care what you're feeling like.

T: So after you've made a tremendous effort to get there you feel that you're not appreciated. When I feel that I've made a special effort and come to work in spite of some problem, I sometimes wish it were recognized. It sounds like you might feel the same way.

P: I sure do, that's exactly the way I feel, you really hit the nail on the head. Instead the boss says you sure look awful today, too much night life. Come on get with it, there's work to do, what do ya think this is—some country club?

### Other voice: What would you say? (7)

T: Umm—how about your sex life with your wife? What's that like now?

P: There isn't any. I mean it's gone—it's—it's not there any more. The only time I can get aroused any more is when I had a couple of drinks and as soon as I start drinking well you can forget about getting close to my wife. She doesn't have anything to do with me then. So—we just don't do it any more. There's nothing there between us anyway.

T: You sound as if you sometimes feel that the situation is hopeless. I felt that way once, I had a friend who was very close to me and then due to a misunderstanding the relationship became impossible for a while. But, we managed to straighten things out. At first I thought we'd never be close again. This seems to be what you're saying with regard to your wife.

P: Yeah. No hope—it's—I just—sometimes I just can't say a word to her—about anything. She doesn't listen—she doesn't understand. She just doesn't care. I'll go in and I'll tell her I'm not feeling well. Oh, that, you know when I feel bad and I feel pressured and all tense inside—she doesn't understand that. She has some idea in her mind that she wants to get something done—she wants it done right now and she won't be satisfied until it's all completed and over with. If she says she wants something done right now and you'd better move right now otherwise it's constant nagging all the time. Pushing—always wants me to—to do something else. Who could live with a wife like that? You know what I mean?

T:  It sounds like it's pretty hard for you at home. Your description of your wife reminds me of a supervisor I once had in my first hospital job. When she got an idea, it had to be carried out on the spot. I hated that situation, but there were good things about the job also, so I couldn't bring myself to leave. I bet you would find it hard to leave also.

P:  (Sigh)—yeah. I wish I could do something about it, though. I—I just can't take any more of this.

T:  You seem to want very much to change the situation. In dealing with both the friend and the supervisor I mentioned before, I had to decide how I would like things to be in order that I might be happy. How would you like things to be?

P:  I guess I'd like things to be kind of peaceful and quiet. So I can get things done without being pushed into it. I'd like to be around people that—that knew the way I feel, the problems I've had and—and who could understand them. You know—they'd understand sometimes I feel sick—I can't work like I should. A lot of pressure sometimes—I can't handle that. If things were like that it would be different. People just don't care anymore—they don't care about anything—care about other people. But you seem to care about me. You remind me of an aunt I had that I liked alot. But other people just don't care—especially about me. I wish things were different.

T:  Ummm. If you could have things the way—you want them—uh, would you want to be married and have a family?

P:  Probably.

T:  It's kind of nice to have a family to go home to, people who love and accept you, knowing your strengths and weaknesses, I always believed that. I guess you do, too.

P:  Yeah. It's nice to have a home and be—be in it and feel as if you belonged in it. That you're welcome there. Lately—my home is like a strange land. Seems that all they want from me is the money. "Is this the week you get paid, Dad?" My wife comes in with the bills in her hand and and says, "These are due this month." We'll never get our heads above water. They don't care about anything else. As long as I bring that check in.

**Other voice:  What would you say? (8)**

T:  Why do you think you're here in the hospital?

P:  My wife's the reason why I'm here—in more ways than one. She's the one that got me in here. She's the one that nags me all the time. Makes me feel so bad—when I'm outside. She doesn't realize when I take a couple of drinks it's so I can handle things a little better. No—she thinks when I—I take a couple of drinks that I'm running away from things—I'm avoiding my responsibilities as she puts it.

T:  I guess in some ways you feel that drinking helps you meet the responsibilities that your wife feels you are avoiding. It isn't true now, but in the past when I felt I was under pressure I used to eat a great deal, I used to be very fat. My sister criticized me terribly for this and I always felt that she didn't understand. I was so angry that I ate even more. Are you affected in this way?

P:  I sure am. Boy, it's nice to know you went through something like this, too. You really know what I'm talking about. It's amazing how well you understand. My wife gets me so mad I get into the car and I go down to the tavern and I drink and drink sometimes. I don't care if they have to pour me into bed—she gets me so mad!

T:  I guess you feel that even though you're the one that's here—this problem isn't all yours, just as I felt that my sister was partly responsible for my being so fat.

P:  That's exactly it! I wish someone would take a look at my wife. And some of the other people I come into contact with. Like my boss, the people at work—they're all the same. Telling me what to do—how to do it—when to do it—how fast I should do it. All the time. It's getting so I —I—I can't lead my own life any more.

### Other voice:  *What would you say? (9)*

T:  Seems to me as though you're upset with quite a few people. I mean really angry with some of them.

P:  Who wouldn't be angry with—with people like that? Like you know every time—I meet someone and they tell me—you can be doing a better job, or why didn't you do it this way—what kind of things do they expect from a person? I'm no superman—I just—do the work I'm supposed to do. Or try to do it anyway. You seem to understand that. I wish everyone else would understand me like you do. I really like you. But you know what everyone else remembers—they remember the day you didn't show up for work or the days that you didn't do the job right. Or how you messed this thing up. That's all they remember—they never remember the good things that you do. My wife—she's the same way. She never tells me what I'm doing right. It's always the things that I've been doing wrong that I get word from her. It's easy for her to pick out those things—things I do wrong. Who wouldn't get angry?

T:  You are really furious with them aren't you? Like I was with my sister, but I couldn't let her know that at first because I felt she would retaliate. Have you ever been able to show your wife how angry you really are?

P:  Yeah—a couple of times I did, but she said if I got any angrier or did anything to her she'd call the cops.

T:  I once got so aggravated I yelled at my supervisor. What about your boss? Have you ever—gotten angry with him?

P:  Are you kidding? If I ever mouthed off to him I'd be canned on the spot. And then I'd really be in some fine state. I'd get it twice as bad from home then. I mean without a job. It's the only thing that's keeping me there now. No—I still have my job. I don't like it, but I'm there.

### Other voice:    What would you say? (10)

T:  I noticed on your record that this is your second hospitalization. What happened the first time around when you came here?

P:  Mmm—first time I was here it was really a waste of time. I got out of the hospital and—things were all right for awhile. But then, my wife started up again—she started to nag, and pressure started to build up and things started to go wrong at work. Kids started to act up. Began to feel bad at night—not getting any sleep. The only way I could relax was to have a drink. So I'd have a drink and—then a couple more. And the whole thing starts all over again. If it wasn't for these other things, though, my boss, my wife, I don't think I'd be here, now. I wouldn't have to be.

T:  But the way things work out—it seems as if you—end up right back where you started.

P:  Oh, yeah. Each time though—I came here—I got away from those people. But I'd sure like things to be different. You know . . . better, less problems.

T:  Like I once wished less problems with the friend I told you about, and my sister, and the supervisor. I guess it's sort of like a vacation here.

P:  A little bit. See there's no one around here telling me what I have to do or don't do. No one telling me I have to get out—and go to work in the morning. Here there is someone like you who I can talk to. Someone who understands me and helps me. I really like talking to you. I feel very safe here with you. And I don't have to get up and go to work for 8 hours all day—put up with a boss that's constantly on my back—riding me—telling me that I'm not doing my job just exactly the way he wants it done. I don't have to put up with any of that when I'm here.

T:  Mm—but don't we have many rules here, many rules that you must obey?

P:  Yeah but—those rules are for everybody. Everybody has to do it, and everybody does it, but when I'm not in the hospital—when I'm home—not everybody has to take my wife everyday. Her nagging, her—stuff that she hands out every night and things.

T:  Seems that you feel as I did when I had to deal with my sister, she was just too much to cope with for me for a long time, and I couldn't even begin to know how to deal with her. I guess you feel that your wife is so strong that nobody could cope with her.

P:   Right, she's just too much.

T:   Well, as I've told you, I've had similar feelings in my life in the past—a sister to whom I couldn't express anger, very much like what you feel in the situation with your wife; a supervisor who was unreasonably demanding, almost like your boss. I have had difficulty with smoking and eating, while a little different from your drinking, similar in many ways; and I have also experienced the desire to get away from all of these problems, an escape like you have found here. But at one point in my life, I found that there were choices that could be made, that I could alter the situation in many ways in spite of the criticism and the nagging.

P:   In my whole life nobody has ever listened and understood me the way you do. You really know how it is. You've even had experiences like mine. It's amazing. They're always yelling at you. Telling you what to do. Telling you what not to do. Constantly saying you're not good enough, you're useless. You're not making enough money. You're a bum. You drink too much. What's a guy supposed to do with a wife like that?

**Other voice:     *What would you say? (11)***
**Other voice:**

This ends the part of the therapy session we are playing to you. In the space on your answer sheet that is numbered 12 please write down what you would say as your last comment to end the therapy session. You will have 1 minute from now (1 min). Please turn to the next page of your booklet and read the instructions.

### Low Self-Disclosure

T:   Since this is our first interview, I'll be asking you about a number of different areas of your life. Why don't we start off by your telling me about your family?

P:   My family. Well, you know sometimes—sometimes I think my family could do—just as well without me. You know. Like I'm a—a useless sort of object that sort of sits around the house. When I—come home from work it's like—like there's nothing there.

T:   You don't feel that your family looks forward to your coming home at night?

P:   Sometimes it—sometimes it seems that they don't even know when I'm home. Kids'll be running around and—my wife—well sometimes the way she acts it would be better if I just stayed out. Some of the things that she gets into—MMMMMMMM.

**Other voice:     *What would you say? (1)***

T:   What kind of things does your wife get into?

P:   —I don't know. She always yelling and screaming—wants me to do things when I come inside—always telling me I have this to do and that to do. She doesn't realize I just wanna come home and I wanna relax a little bit. Nah—I don't know how she can push me all the time—do this —do that—all the time.

T: Sounds like—marriage has been a lot of trouble for you.

P: —Yeah. Yeah—really it—it was different before. When we first got married it was—it was nice. We went out and saw different people, did—did some things together. Got along pretty good, too. Didn't have all this that's going on now.

### Other voice: What would you say? (2)

T: I guess things aren't going very well with your wife now.

P: No—my wife changed. She got—she got different. Things started—you know—she started not to care about things. We couldn't go out as much. Then—then the babies came and then—wow—feeding them and taking care of them and doing all those things. Never had any time to do the things that we used to do together. You know, it's usually hard for me to talk about things like this, but it's, well,—you know when I'd come home from work—my wife—she'd be running around the house after the kids —and when I'd come in the door I'd get ignored, you know. No one says hello—no one asks you how you are—

T: —Somehow all this seemed to happen around the time the children came?

P: It—seems that way. Before we had the kids—we didn't have these problems. Now it—it's just not the same.

### Other voice: What would you say? (3)

T: What about your parents; did your father—drink?

P: Oh yeah. He—could down them with the best of them. My old lady will tell you that. Yeah he really knew how to drink. Used to get into some terrible—fights with my old lady, though. Boy—he'd come home have a little too much in him—she'd really let him have it. I'd have to—pull the pillow up over my head so I wouldn't hear the noise. Couldn't get to sleep.

T: Your mother was very hard on your father then.

P: Yeah. She really used to get mad at him. You know for drinking and all that. She used to yell at him. Get on his back all the time. Really be nasty to him. Maybe that's one of the reasons why he's six feet under right now.

T: Sort of like the same thing your wife is doing to you?

P: Yeah. There's a lot of things about the two that are kind of the same. I think she's trying to do the same thing to me that my mother did to my father.—Yell and fight—the yelling and carrying on. They'll both do it. Scream at you—and call you a drunk. Telling me I can't take on any responsibility. Always yelling about some things. Money. Why don't you have more of it? Why can't we buy this? Why can't we buy that? I'm working—as hard as I can—and she does—she doesn't realize that. She thinks all I have to do is work—all the time. She thinks it's—it's easy for me to—to work every day.—Always pushing me. I don't like to be pushed. I get—I'll get things done. But I have to work—at my own pace otherwise—it just doesn't matter if I work or not if I can't work at my own pace.

### Other voice:   What would you say? (4)

T:    It sounds like your wife and you just—don't do things the same way.
P:    That's it you're right. You really understand. She's in her own world. She doesn't care about anything that I do—or say. She doesn't care about me or anyone else. Sometimes I just feel like getting up and leaving. There's nothing there any more.
T:    You'd like to just go away?
P:    Mmhmm.
T:    Have you ever done this?
P:    —Not for any long time. Used to—get away for a couple of days by myself. But I always ended up coming back because I had no one else to go to.
T:    You don't like being alone.
P:    Oh—it's hard when you're alone. It's—I have no place to go. Haven't any friends or—or close family. Except for my—my wife and kids. You know I—the way they treat me I know they don't want me. At least, though—like when I'm home I have a roof over my head. I know I can sleep—I don't have to be wandering around in the streets for something to do. Someone to feed me.

### Other voice:   What would you say? (5)

T:    —Uh tell me uh—how long have you been drinking?
P:    Oh, I don't know, quite a few years I guess. I think—I can't figure out the exact time.—It just happens you know you—you don't really know when you start when you—start drinking—there's no big change in your life. You know I—I really don't drink that much. I—have a few drinks now and then but—not that many.
T:    You don't think you are an alcoholic, then?
P:    What's an alcoholic? Probably every guy I know drinks more than I do. My wife thinks I drink a lot, though—she's—boy, you talk to her and you'd think I was the biggest bum on skid row. My wife doesn't understand me the way you do. I wish everyone was like you. They don't realize that every so often I want to relax a little bit—I—I—I can't take all the pressures of—my job and all that—and I—I feel a lot better when I —I—drink—have a few.

*T:*  —Uh—about how much do you drink?

*P:*  Oh it depends—on what's going on. Maybe I'll have a couple of drinks during the day and then go home and have one or two. You know—just to relax.

*T:*  Do you drink in the morning?

*P:*  Not all the time. Maybe—you know—when—when I really feel bad in the morning—you know—I'll get up and before I go to work I'll have a drink.

***Other voice:    What would you say? (6)***

*T:*  A drink helps you start the morning off right?

*P:*  Yeah, sometimes I don't feel—good at all. Like—like my stomach for instance—like—I throw up a lot sometimes, uh, I remember some mornings—I'll be shaving in front of the mirror and I'll just double over with pain. My stomach'll be so tight. It's really kind of painful. I don't know—what's it from, but—it feels like my stomach is real tight inside. I—I usually just sit down for awhile—and try to relax. Sometimes I'll—I'll have a quick drink you know that might help sometimes. To relax me and help my stomach a little bit—calm me down. Otherwise it's—it's just hell to go through all that pain.

*T:*  It sounds like it's pretty rough for you.

*P:*  Boy, you really understand what I'm talking about, it's a helluva way to get up in the morning. Stomach's bothering me—it's tight. Back is stiff —getting up like that I really don't feel like going to work. Wish I could just lie in bed—for a little longer—and take it easy for the day. Take the day off. Don't go to work. It's hard—to work when you're feeling miserable like that. But—wife comes in and says get the hell out of bed—who do you think you are? You've got—mouths to feed. Go out and get to work. You get into work and you tell your boss you haven't been feeling well. Hmmm. He doesn't understand either. The—they just want to see you there—whether you're dead on your feet or not. They just want to see you show up and do your job. They don't care what you're feeling like.

***Other voice:    What would you say? (7)***

*T:*  Umm—how about—how about your sex life with your wife? What's that like now?

*P:*  Hmmm. There isn't any. I mean it's—it's gone—it's—it's not there any more. The only time I can get aroused any more is when I had a couple of drinks and as soon as I start drinking, well, you can forget about getting close to my wife. She doesn't want to have anything to do with me then. So—we just don't do it any more. There's nothing there between us any more, anyway.

*T:*  Sometimes it just seems hopeless?

*P:*      Yeah. No hope—it's—I just—sometimes I just can't talk to my wife. You really know how I feel, I can talk to you. I can't say a word to her —about anything. She doesn't listen—she doesn't understand. She just doesn't care. I'll go in and I'll tell her I'm not feeling well. Oh—that— you know when I feel bad and I feel pressured and all tense inside—she doesn't understand that. She has some idea in her mind that she wants to get something done—she wants it done right now and she won't be satisfied until it's all completed and over with. If she says she wants something done right now you'd better move right now otherwise it's constant nagging all the time. Pushing.—Always wants me to—to do something else. Who could live with a wife like that? You know what I mean?

*T:*      It sounds like it's pretty hard for you home.

*P:*      It sure is.

*T:*      And yet—it's also hard to leave.

*P:*      (Sigh)—yeah. I wish I could do something about it, though. I—I just can't take any more of this.

*T:*      How would you like things to be?

*P:*      I guess I'd like things to be kind of peaceful and quiet. So I can get things done without being pushed into it. I'd like to be around people that—that knew the way I feel, the problems I've had and—and who could understand them. You know—they'd understand sometimes I feel sick—I can't work like I should. A lot of pressure sometimes—I can't handle that. If things were like that it would be different. People just don't care any more—they don't care about anything—care about other people. But you seem to care about me. You remind me of an aunt I had that I liked alot. But other people just don't care—especially about me. I wish things were different.

*T:*      Ummm—if you could have things the way—you want them—uh would you want to be married and have a family?

*P:*      Probably.

*T:*      It's kind of nice to have a family to go—to go home to.

*P:*      Yeah. It's nice to have a home and be—be in it and feel as if you belonged in it. That you're welcome there. Lately—my house is like a strange land. Seems that all they want from me is the money. "Is this the week you get paid, Dad?" My wife comes in with the bills in her hand and and says, "These are due this month." We'll never get our heads above water. They don't care about anything else. As long as I bring that check in.

**Other voice:**    *What would you say? (8)*

*T:*      Why do you think you're here in the hospital?

*P:*      My wife's the reason why I'm here—in more ways than one. She's the one that got me in here. She's the one that nags me all the time. Makes me feel so bad—when I'm outside. She doesn't realize when I take a couple of drinks it's so I can handle things a little better. No—she thinks

when I—I take a couple of drinks that I'm running away from things—
I'm avoiding my responsibilities as she puts it.

T:  Sort of like you're not being a man?

P:  Yeah. I think that's the way she wants me sometimes—to feel like that.

T:  I guess you feel that even though you're the one that's here—this problem isn't all yours.

P:  That's exactly it, you really get the picture. I wish someone would take a look at my wife. And some of the other people I come in contact with. Like my boss—the people at work—they're all the same. Telling me what to do. How to do it—when to do it—how fast I should do it. All the time. It's getting so I—I—I can't lead my own life any more.

## Other voice: *What would you say? (9)*

T:  Seems to me as though you're—you're upset with quite a few people. I mean really angry with some of them.

P:  Who wouldn't be angry with—with people like that? Like you know every time—I meet someone and they tell me—you can be doing a better job, or why didn't you do this—what kind of things do they expect from a person? I'm no superman—I just—do the work I'm supposed to do. Or try to do it anyway. You seem to understand that. I wish everyone else understood me like you do. I really like you. But you know what everyone else remembers—they remember the day you didn't show up for work or the days that you didn't do the job right. Or how you messed this thing up. That's all they remember—they never remember the good things that you do. My wife—she's the same way. She never tells me what I'm doing right. It's always the things that I've been doing wrong that I get word from her. It's easy for her to pick out those things—things I do wrong. Who wouldn't get angry?

T:  Have you ever gotten angry at your wife? Have you ever shown you were angry?

P:  Yeah—a couple of times I did, but she said if I got any angrier or did anything to her she'd call the cops.

T:  —What about your boss? Have you ever—gotten angry at him?

P:  Are you kidding? If I ever mouthed off to him I'd—be canned on the spot. And then I'd really be in some fine states. I'd get it twice as bad from home then. I mean without a job. It's the only things that's keeping me there now. No—I still have my job. I don't like it but I'm there.

## Other voice: *What would you say? (10)*

T:  I noticed on your record that this is your second hospitalization. What happened the first time around when you came here?

P:  Mmm—first time I was here it was really a waste of time. —I got out of the hospital and—things were all right for awhile. But then, my wife started up again—she started to nag, and pressure started to build again and things started to go wrong at work. Kids started to act up. Began to feel bad at night—not getting any sleep. The only way I could relax was to have a drink. So I'd have a drink and—then a couple more. And the whole thing starts all over again. If it wasn't for those other things, though, my boss, my wife, I don't think I'd be here, now. I wouldn't have to.

T:   But the way things work out—it seems as if you—end up right back where you started.

P:   Oh, yeah. Each time though—I came here—I got away from those people. But I'd sure like things to be different. You know . . . better, less problems.

T:   I guess it's sort of like a vacation here.

P:   A little bit. See, there's no one around here telling me what I have to do or don't do. No one telling me I have to get out—and go to work in the morning. Here there is someone like you who I can talk to. Someone who understands me and helps me. I really like talking to you. I feel very safe here with you. And I don't have to get up and go to work for 8 hours all day—put up with a boss that's constantly on my back—riding me—telling me that I'm not doing my job just exactly the way he wants it done. I don't have to put up with any of that when I'm here.

T:   Mm—but don't we have many rules here, many things you must do?

P:   Yeah, but—those rules are for everybody. Everybody has to do it and everybody does it, but when I'm not in the hospital—when I'm home—not everybody has to take my wife every day. Her nagging, her stuff that she hands out every night and things.

T:   So it's mainly the rules that your wife sets up that, um—present the most problems for you.

P:   She's the one that does it the most.

T:   Sounds as though she's pretty tough on you.

P:   Hmm. You could say that. She can really get to you sometimes. In my whole life, nobody has ever listened and understood the way you do. They're always yelling at you. Telling you what to do. Telling you what not to do. Constantly saying you're not good enough, you're useless. You're not making enough money. You're a bum. You drink too much. What's a guy supposed to do with a wife like that?

**Other voice:     What would you say? (11)**
**Other voice:**

This ends the part of the therapy session we are playing to you. In the space on your answer sheet which is numbered 12, please write down what you would say as your last comment to end the therapy session. You will have one minute from now (1 min). Please turn to the next page on your booklet and read the instructions.

### High Empathy

*T:* Since this is our first interview, why don't we start off by your telling me why you've decided to come for help at this time.

*P:* Well—things are pretty bad for me right now. It seems like—uh—the world's kind of coming down around my ears. All the problems are pretty much tied up together and—uh—and I'm so confused—uh—I'm, I'm not sure I can even straighten things out enough to talk about them sensibly.

*Other voice:* *What would you say? (1)*

*T:* You say you've spent time in the hospital?

*P:* Yeah. Things were really bothering me. Finally I just couldn't take it any longer—I left home, didn't show up on the job—eventually ended up in the hospital. It wasn't really my fault.

*Other voice:* *What would you say? (2)*

*T:* Are you worried now that the same thing might happen again?

*P:* Um, hmm . . . I'm feeling shut off again—like the doors are closed and I can't get to anybody. Uh—doesn't do any good to try any more—'cause it's no use. Probably no use to—uh—to try to talk to you either (sigh), but I haven't tried this before—maybe you're someone who can understand me—nobody else can or even tries.

*Other voice:* *What would you say? (3)*

*T:* Perhaps we can talk about some of the things that bother you.

*P:* I guess that would be a good idea—(long pause). Yeah, but that's tough. I just can't organize my thoughts. I—I can't really say how it feels. I just know I—I've got to do something—talk to—somebody.

*Other voice:* *What would you say? (4)*

*P:* My family. Well, you know sometimes—sometimes I think my family could do—just as well without me. You know. Like I'm a—a useless sort of object that sort of sits around the house. When I—come home from work it's like—like there's nothing there.

*T:* Your family doesn't seem to look forward to your coming home at night. You feel as though they don't really care about you.

*P:* Sometimes it—sometimes it seems that they don't even know when I'm home. Kids'll be running around and—my wife—well sometimes the way she acts it would be better if I just stayed out. Some of the things that she gets into—hmm. . .

*T:*  She lights into you the minute you step in tired from work. Like she doesn't appreciate you and this hurts you.

*P:*  Yeah—She's always yelling and screaming—wants me to do things when I come inside—always telling me I have this to do and that to do. She doesn't realize I just wanna come home and I wanna relax a little bit. Nah—I don't know how she can push me all the time—do this—do that —all the time.

*T:*  Sounds like marriage has been alot of trouble for you—worse than before?

*P:*  —Yeah. Yeah—really it—it was different before. When we first got married it was—it was nice. We went out and saw different people, did—did some things together. Got along pretty good, too. Didn't have all this that's going on now.

*T:*  Those days were better, but now?

*P:*  Now—my wife changed. She got—she got different.—Things started— you know—she started not to care about things. We couldn't go out as much. Then—then the babies came and then—wow—feeding them and taking care of them and doing all those things. Never had any time to do the things we used to do together.—You know, it's usually hard for me to talk about things like this, but it's easy talking to you. Like—you know, when I'd come home from work—my wife—she'd be running around the house after the kids—and when I'd come in the door I'd get ignored, you know. No one says hello—no one asks you how you are.

*T:*  You feel that the babies were more important to your wife than you.

*P:*  It—seems that way. Before we had the kids we didn't have these problems. Now it—it's just not the same. Now it seems like I'm either ignored or it's nag, nag, nag—all the time.

### *Other voice:  What would you say? (5)*

*P:*  Take my father for instance. He could down them with the best of them. My old lady will tell you that. Yeah, he really knew how to drink. Used to get into some terrible fights with my old lady though. Boy—he'd come home with a little too much in him—she'd really let him have it. I'd have to—pull the pillow up over my head so I wouldn't hear the noise. Couldn't get to sleep.

*T:*  Your mother was very hard on your father, then. Kinda upsetting to a young kid to hear all that fighting.

*P:*  Yeah. She really used to get mad at him. You know for drinking and all that. She used to yell at him. Get on his back all the time. Really be nasty to him. Maybe that's one of the reasons why he's six feet under right now.

*T:*  Sort of like the same thing your wife is doing to you?

*P:*  Yeah. You're right. You really hit the nail on the head. You really understand what's going on. There's a lot of things about the two that are kind of the same. I think she's trying to do the same thing to me that my mother did to my father.—Yell and fight—and call you a drunk. Telling me I can't take on any responsibility. Always yelling about something. Money. Why don't you have more of it? Why can't we buy this? Why can't we buy that? I'm working—as hard as I can—and she does—she doesn't realize that. She thinks all I have to do is work—all the time. She thinks it's—it's easy for me to—to work every day.—Always pushing me. I don't like to be pushed. I get—I'll get things done. But I have to work—at my own pace, otherwise—it just doesn't matter if I work or not if I can't work at my own pace.

T:  She just sees you as someone to bring home the dough—like she doesn't really care about you.

P:  Yeah—she's in her own world. She doesn't care about anything that I do —or say. She doesn't care about me or anyone else. Sometimes I just feel like getting up and leaving. There's nothing there any more.

T:  You just want to go—get out—leave all the problems behind.

P:  Um, hmm.

T:  It's probably always been easier to leave problems behind.

P:  Um, hmm. Used to—get away for a couple of days by myself. But I always ended up coming back because I had no one else to go to.

T:  Getting away didn't really solve the problems, though.—You felt kinda lost without your wife and family, huh?

P:  Oh—it's hard when you're alone. It's—I have no place to go. Haven't any friends or—or close family. Except for my—my wife and kids. You know I—the way they treat me I know they don't want me. At least though when I'm home I have a roof over my head. I know I can sleep —I don't have to be wandering around in the streets for something to do. Someone to feed me.

### Other voice:   What would you say? (6)

P:  Well—I've been drinking quite a few years I guess. I think—I can't figure out the exact time.—It just happens you know you—you don't really know when you start when you—start drinking—there's no big change in your life. You know I—I really don't drink that much I—have a few drinks now and then—but not that many.

T:  You don't think that drinking's the big problem.

P:  Probably every guy I know drinks more than I do. My wife thinks I drink alot though—she's—boy, you talk to her and you'd think I was the biggest bum on skid row. My wife doesn't understand me the way you do.

T:  Sounds like she nags you about drinking as well as money.

P:  You do—do understand.—She doesn't realize that every so often I just want to relax a little bit—I—I—I can't take all the pressures of—my job and all that—and I—I feel alot better when I—I—drink—have a few.

*T:* Getting away by drinking is easier than leaving home.

*P:* Yeah—it seems to help me handle what I have to. Maybe I'll have a couple of drinks during the day to help me get by, then I'll go home and have one or two. You know—just to relax. Sometimes when I really feel bad in the morning before I go to work I'll have a drink.

*T:* A drink helps you start the morning off right—kinda like you can face the day better.

*P:* Yeah. Sometimes I don't feel up to working. Like—like my stomach for instance—like—I throw up alot sometimes—uh—I remember some mornings—I'll be shaving in front of the mirror and I'll just double over with pain. My stomach'll be so tight. It's really kind of painful. I don't know what it's from—but it feels like my stomach is real tight inside. I —I usually just sit down for awhile—and try to relax. Sometimes I'll— I'll have a quick drink you know that might help sometimes. To relax me and help my stomach a little bit—calm me down. Otherwise it's—it's just hell to go through all that pain.

*T:* Yeah—I'd agree that's a pretty rough way to start the day. Be nice if you could just get back into bed.

*P:* It's a helluva way to get up in the morning. Stomach's bothering me—it's tight. Back is stiff—getting up like that I really don't feel like going to work. I've often thought about just lying in bed—take it easy for the day. Take the day off. Don't go to work. It's hard—to work when you're feeling miserable like that. But—wife comes in says get the hell out of bed —who do you think you are? You've got mouths to feed. Go out and get to work. You get in to work and you tell your boss you haven't been feeling well. Hmm. He desn't give a damn either. The—they just want to see you show up and do your job. They don't care what you're feeling like.

### Other voice:  What would you say? (7)

*P:* The thing that bothers me most though—is my wife not caring.

*T:* Everything you had together is gone now—doing things, talking, closeness, sex. . .

*P:* Yeah—it's gone—it's—it's not there any more. The only time I can get aroused any more is when I had a couple of drinks and as soon as I start drinking—well you can forget about getting close to my wife. She doesn't want to have anything to do with me then. So—we just don't do it any more. There's nothing there between us any more anyway.

*T:* No sense in trying to get close to her—she just pushes you away. Sometimes it just seems hopeless?

*P:* Yeah. No hope--it's—I just—sometimes I just can't even talk to my wife.—I can't say a word to her—about anything. She doesn't listen—she doesn't understand. She just doesn't care. I'll go in and I'll tell her I'm not feeling well. Oh—that—you know when I feel bad and I feel pressured and all tense inside—she doesn't understand that. She has some idea in her mind that she wants to get something done—she wants it done right now and she won't be satisfied until it's all completed and over with. If she says she wants something done right now you'd better move right now—otherwise it's constant nagging all the time. Pushing—always wants me to do something else. Who could live with a wife like that? You know what I mean?

T: Um, hmm. When you most need her with you she seems to be against you. That's pretty hard to take.

P: It sure is.

T: And yet—it's also hard to leave. That's a real bind, huh?

P: (Sigh)—yeah. I wish I could do something about it though. I—I just can't take any more of this.

T: You'd like to straighten the whole mess. You probably often think about how you'd like things to be.

P: I guess I'd like things to be kind of peaceful and quiet. So I can get things done without being pushed into it. I'd like to be around people that—that know the way I feel, the problems I've had and—and who could understand them. You know—they'd understand sometimes I feel sick—I can't work like I should. A lot of pressure sometimes—I can't handle that. If things were like that it would be different. People just don't care any more—they don't care about anything—care about other people. But you seem to care about me. You remind me of an uncle I had that I liked a lot. But other people just don't care—especially about me. I wish things were different.

T: You wish going home were something to look forward to—like home is a place to feel needed and wanted.

P: Yeah. It's nice to have a home and be—be in it and feel as if you belonged in it. That you're welcome there. Lately—my house is like a strange land. Seems that all they want from me is the money. "Is this the week you get paid, Dad?" My wife comes in with the bills in her hands and says, "These are due this month." We'll never get our heads above water. They don't care about anything else. As long as I bring that check in.

### Other voice:    What would you say? (8)

P: The kids too—they're getting to be like her, nagging me all the time. The only reason they—they care about me coming home is for me to hand them over some money. And the way they go through money—they don't need money, but their mother says, "Get it from your father."

T: They don't seem to appreciate how hard you have to work for your money. I guess there are ways in which you resent that pretty strongly.

P: You'd think by now they'd realize that I have to work 45–50 hours some weeks, just to make ends meet.—Record albums, clothes, movies, toys, bubble gum, and who knows what else.—Like my son—he's got more shirts than I do. You know, I haven't bought a new jacket in 3 years.

*T:* Sounds like you feel cheated—after all, you give, but what do you get?

*P:* Yeah—nothing. They don't even talk to me.

*T:* Sometimes you'd like them to come to you—maybe—just to talk.

*P:* Yeah.—I'd really like to know about school, their friends, stuff like that. You know, the things a father's interested in. My oldest son—he's on the football team, but he doesn't even invite me to the games. He doesn't even care if I show up. I don't understand it.

*T:* It hurts your feelings when he doesn't invite you to the game. It must hurt you very deeply when he doesn't let you be part of his life.

*P:* Um, hmm. I feel bad when I'm left out of things. We used to all do things together—like go fishing alot.

*T:* Sounds like a good time for talking—on fishing trips. You felt closer to your kids then, huh?

*P:* There were some good times then, ah—but the kids grew up to be just like their mother. Now I can hardly talk to them. I can hardly talk to anyone. But it's pretty easy to talk to you. I'm saying things that I haven't thought about for years.—Sometimes I feel like my kids are strangers—as though I don't even know them.

*T:* You feel all alone in your family, as though no one needs you—except for the paycheck.

*P:* That's all I am to them—a paycheck once every two weeks. But I don't know what else to do—I've tried my hardest to be a good father and a good husband, but I never can satisfy them. If I do this, it's wrong—if I do the opposite—that's wrong, too. There's nothing more I can do.

### Other voice: *What would you say? (9)*

*P:* My wife's the reason why I'm here—in more ways than one. She's the one that got me here. She's the one that nags me all the time—makes me feel so bad. She doesn't realize that when I take a couple of drinks it's so I can handle things a little better. No—she thinks when I—I take a couple of drinks that I'm running away from things—I'm avoiding my responsibilities as she puts it.

*T:* Sort of like you're not being a man.

*P:* Yeah. She makes me feel that way sometimes.

*T:* You feel she tries to make you more of her kind of a man by nagging. But it doesn't work that way.

*P:* Nah—just makes me feel worse having it thrown up in my face.

*T:* I guess you feel that even though you're the one that's here—this problem isn't all yours.

*P:* That's right. I wish someone would take a look at my wife. And some of the other people I come in contact with. Like my boss—the people at work—they're all the same. Telling me what to do—and how to do it. It's getting so I—I—I can't lead my own life any more.

*T:* Seems to me as though you're upset with quite a few people. I mean even a little angry with some of them.

*P:* Who wouldn't be angry with—with people like that? Like you know every time I meet someone and they tell me—you can be doing a better job or why didn't you do this—what kind of things do they expect from a person? I'm no superman—I just—do the work I'm supposed to do. Or try to do it, anyway. You seem to understand that. I wish everybody understood me like you do. I really like you. But you know what everyone else remembers—they remember the day you didn't show up for work or the days that you didn't do the job right. Or how you messed this thing up. That's all they remember—they never remember the good things you do. My wife—she's the same way. She never tells me what I'm doing right. It's always the things that I've been doing wrong that I get word from her. It's easy for her to pick out those things—things I do wrong. Who wouldn't get angry?

*T:* It sounds like sometimes you really want to tell her off—let her know how you feel.

*P:* Yeah—a couple of times I did, but she said if I got any angrier or did anything to her she'd call the cops.

*T:* You're afraid to get angry 'cause of what might happen.

*P:* It's that way with other people, too. My boss—if I ever mouthed off to him I'd—be canned on the spot. And then I'd really be in some fine state. I'd get it twice as bad from home then. I mean without a job. It's the only thing that's keeping me there now. No—I still have my job. I don't like it, but I'm there.

### Other voice: What would you say? (10)

*P:* After I got out of the hospital that time—things were all right for awhile. But then, my wife started up again—she started to nag, and pressure started to build up again and things started to go wrong at work. Kids started to act up. Began to feel bad at night—not getting any sleep. The only way I could relax was to have a drink. And the whole thing starts all over again.—If it wasn't for those other things, though, my boss, my wife, I don't think I'd be here now. I wouldn't have to.

*T:* You feel if everybody'd just get off your back things would be O.K. But the way things work out—it seems as if you—end up right back where you started.

*P:* Oh, yeah—I don't think things'll ever stay straightened out—if they ever get that way.—In the hospital though—I got away from those people.

*T:* It was sort of like a vacation in the hospital.

*P:* A little bit. See, there was no one around telling me what I had to do or not do. No one telling me I had to get out—and go to work in the morning. I didn't have to get up and go to work for 8 hours all day—put up with a boss constantly on my back—telling me that I wasn't doing my job just exactly the way he wanted it done. I didn't have to put up with any of that in the hospital.

*T:*    Sounds like in some ways you'd kind of like to rest like that again—to get a little peace and quiet.

*P:*    Yeah.—I guess maybe that's true. But it was kinda lonely there, too—and boring. I—I guess that's why I'm coming to you now, instead. If I can have someone like you to talk to . . . you seem to understand me and help me. I really like talking to you. (Pause) You know in the hospital there were rules—but for everybody. Everybody had to do it and everybody did it. But at home—wow—not everybody has to take my wife everyday. Her nagging, her—stuff that she hands out every night and things.

*T:*    Rules are O.K. if—if they have meaning and—don't single you out—but from your wife—well, they seem to be more like impossible demands than meaningful rules.

*P:*    That's the difference—demands, not simple rules!

*T:*    Perhaps the demands seem more like accusations—like you're not doing what you should, or not being what you should.

*P:*    Um, hmm. She can really get to you sometimes. Yelling at you. Telling you what to do. Telling you what not to do. Constantly saying you're not good enough. You're a bum. You drink too much. What's a guy supposed to do with a wife like that?

### Other voice:    *What would you say? (11)*

*P:*    You know I've been doing a lot of talking—things I haven't thought about for years. But—I wonder—where's it all gonna get me? I mean—a lot of the stuff I talked about just—just sounds like complaining. You know—my wife's on my back, my kids don't talk to me, my boss rides me—what am I going to get out of this?

*T:*    Kind of hard to see how talking can help.

*P:*    Yeah.—I sometimes wonder if anything can help. But I guess if anything can, this'll be it. Something's got to. I don't want to end up out on the streets again like the last time when things got so bad. And I'm afraid if I don't do something now I'll get myself into deep trouble, do something that I'll really regret later—you know, like clobber my wife or kids, lose the job, and watch the bank take the house and the car. I've really got to do something now—I can't wait much longer.

*T:*    You feel you're headed for worse times if things don't change. You'd like some answers now.

*P:*    Yeah.—That's what I'd like—I tell you what's wrong, you tell me what to do.—But I guess it's not that simple, is it?—There's probably no formula that helps everybody.

*T:*  Sure would be nice to have a simple answer, but I guess you're feeling that—that this isn't a simple thing to work out.

*P:*  No—it isn't. I guess each person has to work hard on his own problems. I guess when I first walked in here I couldn't see how you could help me—but now—I really think you can. I guess I've got to start to do a lot of serious thinking. But I don't know—every time I try to work on any change at all, she yells—or nags—you can't win with that woman.

*T:*  You'd really like to make some changes, but you're afraid they might fail.—Another failure would be just too hard to handle.

*P:*  Yeah.—But I guess it's up to me to try something. In a lot of ways I guess I'm a pretty difficult guy to live with too. I don't go out of my way to make things any better. Instead of spending time with my wife and kids, I just sleep or watch TV. And when I feel really lousy, I don't want to have to talk to anyone.

*T:*  You're feeling now that maybe what you do is as much a part of the problems as what your wife does.

*P:*  Um, hmm. And I guess talking about it will help me to see what some of those things are. You know—make me think—and—and figure out some ways to change.

**Other voice:**  *What would you say?*  *(12)*

## Low Empathy

*T:*  Since this is our first interview, why don't we start off by your telling me why you've decided to come for help at this time.

*P:*  Well—things are pretty bad for me right now. It seems like—uh—the world's kind of coming down around my ears. All the problems are pretty much tied up together and—uh—and I'm so confused—uh—I'm, I'm not sure I can even straighten things out enough to talk about them sensibly.

**Other voice:**  *What would you say?*  *(1)*

*T:*  You say you've spent time in the hospital?

*P:*  Yeah. Things were really bothering me. Finally I just couldn't take it any longer—I left home, didn't show up on the job—eventually ended up in the hospital. It wasn't really my fault.

**Other voice:**  *What would you say?*  *(2)*

*T:*  Are you worried now that the same thing might happen again?

*P:*  Um, hmm . . . I'm feeling shut off again—like the doors are closed and

I can't get to anybody. Uh—doesn't do any good to try any more—cause it's no use. Probably no use to—uh—to try to talk to you either, (sigh) but I haven't tried this before—maybe you're someone who can understand me—nobody else can or even tries.

### Other voice:    What would you say? (3)

T:     Perhaps we can talk about some of the things that bother you.
P:     I guess that would be a good idea—(long pause). Yeah, but that's tough. I just can't organize my thoughts. I—I can't really say how it feels. I just know I—I've got to do something—talk to—somebody.

### Other voice:    What would you say? (4)

P:     My family. Well, you know sometimes—sometimes I think my family could do—just as well without me. You know—like I'm a useless sort of object that just sort of sits around the house. When I—come home from work it's like—like there's nothing there.
T:     I don't understand.
P:     Sometimes it—sometimes it seems that they don't even know when I'm home. Kids'll be running around and—my wife—well sometimes the way she acts it would be better if I just stayed out. Some of the things she gets into—hmm. . . .
T:     You mean she gets into a lot of trouble.
P:     Yeah.—She's always yelling and screaming—wants me to do things when I come inside—always telling me I have this to do and that to do. She doesn't realize I just wanna come home and I wanna relax a bit. Nah—I don't know how she can push me all the time—do this—do that—all the time.
T:     You must really cause her a lot of trouble.
P:     Yeah—yeah. It was really different before. When we first got married it was—it was nice. We went out and saw different people, did—did some things together. Got along pretty good, too. Didn't have all this that's going on now.
T:     Things might be better now if you hadn't changed.
P:     No—my wife changed. She got—she got different.—Things started—you know—she started not to care about things. We couldn't go out as much. Then—then the babies came and then—wow—feeding them and taking care of them and doing all those things. Never had any time to do the things we used to do together.—You know, it's usually hard for me to talk about things like this, but it's easy talking to you. Like—you know when I'd come home from work—my wife—she'd be running around the house after the kids—and when I'd come in the door I'd get ignored you know. No one says hello—no one asks you how you are.
T:     Seems like your wife has her hands full with the kids without having to worry about you, too.

*P:* It—seems that way. Before we had the kids we didn't have these problems. Now it—it's just not the same. Now it seems like I'm either ignored or it's nag, nag, nag—all the time.

### Other voice:  *What would you say? (5)*

*P:* Take my father, for instance. He could down drinks with the best of them. My old lady will tell you that. Yeah, he really knew how to drink. Used to get into some terrible fights with my old lady though. Boy—he'd come home with a little too much in him—she'd really let him have it. I'd have to—pull the pillow up over my head so I wouldn't hear the noise. Couldn't get to sleep.

*T:* Sounds like you're following in your father's footsteps.

*P:* Yeah.—She really used to get mad at him. You know, for drinking and all that. She used to yell at him. On his back all the time. Really be nasty to him. Maybe that's one of the reasons he's six feet under right now.

*T:* Your mother used to yell at him—so what's that matter now?

*P:* I think my wife's trying to do the same thing to me that my mother did to my father. There's a lot of things about the two that are kind of the same.—Yell and fight—the yelling and carrying on. They'll both do it. Scream at you and call you a drunk. Telling me I can't take on any responsibility. (Pause) You know, you really understand what's going on. You seem to know how I feel.—But my wife—always yelling about something. Money. Why don't you have more of it? Why can't we buy this? Why can't we buy that? I'm working—as hard as I can—and she does—she doesn't realize that. She thinks all I have to do is work—all the time. She thinks it's—it's easy for me to—to work every day.—Always pushing me—I don't like to be pushed. I get—I'll get things done. But I have to work—at my own pace otherwise—it just doesn't matter if I work or not if I can't work at my own pace.

*T:* Couldn't you try to speed up a little? Try her way? Uh—(pause)—She's in her own world.—She doesn't care about anything that I do—or say. She doesn't care about me or anyone else. Sometimes I just feel like getting up and leaving. There's nothing there any more.

*T:* Why don't you just go away—it might help.

*P:* Um, hmm.

*T:* Have you ever done this?

*P:* Um, hmm. Used to—get away for a couple of days by myself. But I always ended up coming back because I had no one else to go to.

*T:* There must be someone you could visit. Everyone has at least one friend.

*P:* Oh—it's hard when you're alone. It's—I have no place to go. Haven't any friends or close family. Except for my—my wife and kids. You know I—the way they treat me I know they don't want me. At least though like when I'm home I have a roof over my head. I know I can sleep—I don't have to be wandering around in the streets for something to do. Someone to feed me.

### Other voice:    What would you say? (6)

P:   Well—I've been drinking quite a few years, I guess. I think—I can't figure out the exact time.—It just happens you know you—you don't really
know when you start when you—start drinking—there's no big change in
your life. You know I—I really don't drink that much I—have a few
drinks now and then but—but not that many.

T:   You don't remember when you started drinking? Seems to me you'd notice something's different.

P:   Probably every guy I know drinks more than I do. My wife thinks I
drink a lot, though—she's—boy, you talk to her and you'd think I was
the biggest bum on skid row. My wife doesn't understand me the way
you do.

T:   Hmmm.

P:   You do—do understand.—She doesn't realize that every so often I want
to relax a little bit. I—I—I can't take all the pressures of my job and all
that—and I— feel a lot better when I—I drink—have a few.

T:   You don't seem to have tried to figure out the reasons why you drink.
Uh—about how much do you drink?

P:   Maybe I'll have a couple of drinks during the day to help me get by, then
I'll go home and have one or two. You know—just to relax. It seems to
help me handle what I have to. Sometimes when I really feel bad in the
morning before I go to work I'll have a drink.

T:   You know, it's not a good idea to drink before breakfast.

P:   Yeah.—But sometimes I don't feel up to working. Like—like my stomach for instance—like—I throw up alot sometimes—uh—I remember
some mornings—I'll be shaving in front of the mirror and I'll just double
over with pain. My stomach'll be so tight. It's really kind of painful. I
don't know what it's from but—it feels like my stomach is real tight inside. I—I usually just sit down for a while—and try to relax. Sometimes
I'll—I'll have a quick drink you know that might help sometimes. To relax me and help my stomach a little bit—calm me down. Otherwise it's
—it's just hell to go through all that pain.

T:   You think a drink's going to help your stomach? That's probably what's
giving you all the pain.

P:   It's a helluva way to get up in the morning. Stomach's bothering me—
it's tight. Back is stiff—getting up like that I really don't feel like going to
work. I've often thought about just lying in bed—take it easy for the day.
Take the day off. Don't go to work. It's hard—to work when you're feeling miserable like that. But—wife comes in and says get the hell out of
bed—who do you think you are? You've got mouths to feed. Go out and
get to work. You get in to work and tell your boss you haven't been feeling well. Hmmm. He doesn't give a damn either. The—they just want to
see you show up and do your job. They don't care what you're feeling
like.

## Other voice:  *What would you say? (7)*

P:  The thing that bothers me most though—is my wife not caring.

T:  Not caring about what?

P:  About me. I mean it's gone—it's—it's not there any more. The only time I can get aroused any more is when I had a couple of drinks and as soon as I start drinking—well you can forget about getting close to my wife. She doesn't want anything to do with me then. So—we just don't do it any more. There's nothing there between us any more anyway.

T:  You ought not to drink when you want to have sex with your wife.

P:  Yeah.—No hope—it's—I just—sometimes I just can't even talk to my wife.—I can't say a word to her about anything. She doesn't listen—she doesn't understand. She just doesn't care. I'll go in and I'll tell her I'm not feeling well. Oh—that—you know when I feel bad and I feel pressured and all tense inside—she doesn't understand that. She has some idea in her mind that she wants to get something done—she wants it done right now and she won't be satisfied until it's all completed and over with. If she says she wants something done right now you'd better move right now—otherwise it's constant nagging all the time. Pushing—always wants me to—to do something else. Who could live with a wife like that? You know what I mean?

T:  No, I don't understand. It can't be that bad.

P:  It sure is.

T:  Oh.

P:  (Sigh) Yeah. I wish I could do something about it, though. I—I just can't take any more of this.

T:  I don't think you're trying hard enough.

P:  I guess I'd like things to be kind of peaceful and quiet. So I can get things done without being pushed into it. I'd like to be around people that—that knew the way I feel, the problems I've had—and who could understand them. You know—they'd understand sometimes I feel sick— I can't work like I should. A lot of pressure sometimes—I can't handle that. If things were like that it would be different. People just don't care any more—they don't care about anything—care about other people. But you seem to care about me. You remind me of an uncle I had that I liked alot. But other people just don't care, especially about me. I wish things were different.

T:  You'd get bored if it were peaceful and quiet.

P:  Yeah. But it's nice to have a home and be—be in it and feel as if you belonged in it. That you're welcome there. Lately—my house is like a strange land. Seems that all they want from me is the money. "Is this the week that you get paid, Dad?" My wife comes in with the bills in her hands and says, "These are due this month." We'll never get our heads above water. They don't care about anything else. As long as I bring that check in.

### Other voice:    What would you say? (8)

P:  The kids, too—they're getting to be like her, nagging me all the time. The only reason they—they care about me coming home is for me to hand over some money. And the way they go through money—they don't need money, but their mother says, 'Get it from your father.'

T:  Of course they need money, all kids need money.

P:  You'd think by now they'd realize that I have to work 45–50 hours some weeks, just to make ends meet.—Record albums, clothes, movies, toys, bubble gum, and who knows what else.—Like my son—he's got more shirts than I do. You know, I haven't bought a new jacket in 3 years.

T:  Yeah, but you're forgetting, you don't outgrow your clothes like he does.

P:  Yeah. But they don't even talk to me.

T:  Do you talk to them?

P:  Yeah.—I'd really like to know about school, their friends, stuff like that. You know, the things a father's interested in. My oldest son—he's on the football team, but he doesn't even invite me to the games. He doesn't even care if I show up. I don't understand it.

T:  Do you like football?

P:  Um, hmm.—I feel bad when I'm left out of things. We used to all do things together—like go fishing alot.

T:  If you feel left out, you ought to try to do things with them again.

P:  There were some good times then, ah—but the kids grew up to be just like their mother. Now I can hardly talk to them. I can hardly talk to anyone. But it's pretty easy to talk to you. I'm saying things that I haven't thought about for years.—Sometimes I feel like my kids are strangers—as though I don't even know them.

T:  Well, then you really *ought* to do something about it.

P:  But all I am to them is a paycheck—a paycheck once every two weeks. But I don't know what else to do—I've tried my hardest to be a good father and a good husband, but I never can satisfy them. If I do this, it's wrong—if I do the opposite—that's wrong, too. There's nothing more I can do.

### Other voice:    What would you say? (9)

P:  My wife's the reason why I'm here—in more ways than one. She's the one that got me here. She's the one that nags me all the time. Makes me feel so bad. She doesn't realize when I take a couple of drinks it's so I can handle things a little better. No—she thinks when I—I take a couple of drinks that I'm running away from things—I'm avoiding responsibilities as she puts it.

T:  I don't see how taking a couple of drinks helps anyone handle anything better.

P:  Yeah.—She makes me feel like I'm not a man, sometimes.

T:  How's that?

P: Well, she throws it up in my face that I avoid responsibilities.

T: Sounds that way.

P: Well—what about my wife? I wish someone would take a look at her and some of the other people I come in contact with. Like my boss—the people at work—they're all the same. Telling me what to do—how to do it—when to do it—how fast I should do it. It's getting so I–I–I can't lead my own life any more.

T: I'm sure they're not all the same—you just see them that way.

P: Who wouldn't be angry with people like that? Like, you know, every time—I meet someone and they tell me—you can be doing a better job, or why didn't you do this—what kind of things do they expect from a person? I'm no superman—I just—do the work I'm supposed to do. Or try to do it, anyway. You seem to understand that. I wish everybody understood me like you do. I really like you. But you know what everyone else remembers—they remember the day you didn't show up for work or the days that you didn't do the job right. Or how you messed this thing up. That's all they remember—they never remember the good things you do. My wife—she's the same way. She never tells me what I'm doing right. It's always the things that I've been doing wrong that I get word from her. It's easy for her to pick out those things—things I do wrong. Who wouldn't get angry?

T: Have you ever gotten angry with your wife?

P: Yeah—a couple of times I did, but she said if I got any angrier or did anything to her she'd call the cops.

T: What about your boss?

P: Are you kidding? If I ever mouthed off to him I'd—be canned on the spot. And then I'd really be in some fine state. I'd get it twice as bad from home then. I mean without a job. It's the only thing that's keeping me there now. No—I still have my job. I don't like it, but I'm there.

### Other voice: *What would you say? (10)*

P: After I got out of the hospital that time—things were all right for awhile. But then my wife started up again—she started to nag, and pressure started to build up again, and things started to go wrong at work. Kids started to act up. Began to feel bad at night—not getting any sleep. The only way I could relax was to have a drink. So I'd have a drink and—then a couple more. And the whole thing starts all over again.—If it wasn't for those other things though, my boss, my wife, I don't think I'd be here now. I wouldn't have to.

T: They told you to come here.

P: —I don't think things'll ever stay straightened out—if they ever get that way.—In the hospital though—I got away from those people.

T: I don't understand.

P: Well, see there was no one there telling me what I had to do or not to do.

No one telling me I had to get out—and go to work in the morning. I didn't have to get up and go to work for 8 hours all day—put up with a boss constantly on my back—telling me that I wasn't doing my job just exactly the way he wanted it done. I didn't have to put up with any of that in the hospital.

T: Yeah, but they do tell you what to do in the hospital.

P: Yeah, I guess maybe that's true. But it was kinda lonely there too—and boring. I—I guess that's why I'm coming to you now instead. If I can have someone like you to talk to. . . . You seem to understand me and help me. I really like talking to you. (Pause) You know in the hospital there were rules—but for everybody. Everybody had to do it and everybody did it. But at home—wow—not everybody has to take my wife every day. Her nagging her—stuff that she hands out every night and things.

T: Yeah, but rules are rules—doesn't matter who they come from.

P: But there *is* a difference—her's are demands, not simple rules.

T: Are you sure?

P: Um, hmm. She can really get to you sometimes. Yelling at you. Telling you what to do. Telling you what not to do. Constantly saying you're not good enough, you're useless. You're not making enough money. You're a bum. You drink too much. What's a guy supposed to do with a wife like that?

### Other voice: *What would you say?* (11)

P: You know I've been doing a lot of talking—things I haven't thought about for years. But I wonder—where's it all gonna get me? I mean—a lot of the stuff I talked about just—just sounds like complaining. You know—my wife's on my back, my kids don't talk to me, my boss rides me. . . . What am I going to get out of this?

T: Well—if you keep on complaining, you're not going to get very much out of it.

P: Yeah.—I sometimes wonder if anything can help. But I guess if anything can, this'll be it. Something's got to. I don't want to end up out on the streets again like last time when things got so bad. And I'm afraid if I don't do something now I'll get myself into deep trouble, do something that I'll really regret later—you know, like clobber my wife or kids, lose the job, and watch the bank take the house and car. I've really got to do something now—I can't wait much longer.

T: You've got to help yourself.

P: Yeah, I should—but I'd like to just tell you what's wrong, you tell me what to do.—But I guess it's not that simple, is it? There's probably no formula that helps everybody.

T: Huh—impossible.

Well, I guess each person has to work hard on his own problems. I guess when I first walked in here I couldn't see how you could help me—but now—I really think you can. I guess I've got to start to do a lot of serious thinking. But I don't know—every time I try to work on any change at all, she yells—or nags—you can't win with that woman.

*T:* You seem to be competing with your wife.

*P:* Hmm.—But I guess it's up to me to try something. In alot of ways I guess I'm a pretty difficult guy to live with, too. I don't go out of my way to make things any better. Instead of spending time with my wife and kids, I just sleep or watch TV. And when I feel really lousy, I don't want to have to talk to anyone.

*T:* You should spend less time sleeping and watching TV.

Um, hmm.—And I guess talking about it will help me to see what some of those things are. You know, make me think—and—and figure out some ways to change.

***Other voice:  What would you say? (12)***

## Hospital Training Questionnaire: Form A

Listed below you will find statements or descriptions of events which may occur between patients and nurses in a psychiatric hospital. Please read each statement carefully and then, in the space provided after each statement, please write in what you think *you would actually say* to the patient if he made the statement to you, or if you saw the event occur. Assume that each statement is made by a different patient. Please write as clearly as you can and do not spend a lot of time on any given item, just write in the first response that you think you would actually say.

Your answers to this questionnaire will be used for your training. They will be kept in strictest confidence and will not be seen by any employee of this hospital.

1. *N\**:  Here is your medicine, Mr. _____.
   *P†:*  I don't want it. People here are always telling me to do this, do that, do the other thing. I'll take the medicine when *I* want to.
   *N:*  So it's not so much the medicine itself, but you feel you're bossed around all the time. You're tired of people giving you orders.
2.        (Patient is observed to be physically hurting himself.)
   *N:*  You must be feeling terribly angry at yourself.
3. *P:*  I don't want to get out of bed. I just want to sleep some more.
   *N:*  You must be feeling very tired. *(or)* Sometimes people don't feel like getting up when there isn't much to get up for.

---

\* *N* represents Nurse.
† P represents Patient.

4. *P:*     I don't see why Mary can go out of the hospital this weekend and I'm not allowed to.

     *N:*     You feel kind of strongly that you're being treated unfairly.

5.       (Patient on sugar-free diet is seen putting sugar in his coffee.)

     *N:*     It's really kind of hard to eat *only* what's on the diet.

6. *P:*     I don't feel like eating.

     *N:*     Sometimes the food just doesn't seem worth eating. *(or)* Sometimes who we're eating with has alot to do with whether we feel like eating.

7. *N:*     I see you sure have alot of towels there.

     *P:*     Yes, about 30. I like to have them. Can you get me more?

     *N:*     It really makes you feel good to have that many.

8. *P:*     I can't leave the hospital, I'm still sick. What will I do when I get home?

     *N:*     You just don't feel ready to go yet, and wonder if you're up to being home.

9. *P:*     I don't know why they keep giving me this medicine. I've taken it for weeks and I don't feel any better. I've told this to Dr. _____ twice already.

     *N:*     Not only doesn't the medicine seem to work, but the doctor doesn't seem interested in doing anything about it.

10. *P:*     I was in the hospital before. Things were really bothering me. Finally, I just couldn't take it any more. I left home, didn't show up at work, and somehow ended up in the hospital.

     *N:*     Things just piled up and up, from bad to worse, and you wound up here.

11. *P:*     Sometimes I think my family could do just as well without me. It's like I almost don't exist as far as they're concerned. They almost never come to see me.

     *N:*     You'd really like them to visit, but they don't really seem to care about you.

12. *P:*     My wife yelled and screamed at me an awful lot. Always telling me what to do. Like when I'd come home from work and wanted to relax a bit, she would push, push, push.

     *N:*     She really put a lot of pressure on you. It sounds like marriage wasn't much fun for you.

13. *P:*     My father and mother used to get into terrible fights. He'd come home and they'd really go at it. I'd have to pull the pillow over my head so I wouldn't hear the noise.

     *N:*     It sounds like something that would really be upsetting, especially to a child.

14. *P:*     When my boss wanted something done, he wanted it done right then —and wasn't satisfied until it was finished. He would push me all the time, and push hard. Who can work for a boss like that? You know what I mean?

N:  Sounds pretty hard to take. Day after day, all that pressure.

15. P:  I'd really like to know about their school, their friends, things like that. You know, the things a father is interested in. My youngest son, he's on a football team, but he never invited me to a game. He never cared if I was there or not. I don't understand it.

N:  It must hurt very deeply when he doesn't let you be a part of his life.

16. P:  Fred, Bill, and three or four other patients are always watching me, picking on me, making things hard for me. How can I get them to stop?

N:  You're sort of upset with quite a few people, even a little angry with them.

17. P:  I've been here for years, and what's it done for me? Things are the same, nothing's changed much. I don't think it ever will.

N:  You really feel discouraged. Not much has happened, and it doesn't seem like much will.

18. P:  But Miss _____, she was the nurse here up to last week, would always let me smoke in here whenever I felt like it.

N:  You feel I'm being unfair, that I changed the rules on you.

19. P:  I don't like talking to the psychologist. He's OK, but I've been asked *all* the questions many times already.

N:  You're just good and tired of going through the whole procedure.

20. P:  It's just not fair that I have to stay on the ward because of last week-end. My husband was nasty. He made me very nervous. It wasn't my fault. Can't I please go off the ward?

N:  You feel the trouble at home was really your husband's fault, and now you're being punished for it.

N:  It seems that there are other patients here who cause more trouble then me yet they get to have separate rooms. Why can't I have one?

N:  You really feel you deserve a separate room, and that some patients who already have them deserve it less than you.

22. P:  I can't stand her any more. She never shuts up, talk, talk, talk. She talks more than any other patient here. I don't want to sit near her or be near her.

N:  She's really very annoying to you. You'd like to have nothing to do with her.

23.  (Patient crying, but says nothing.)

N:  You're really feeling very badly—sad and alone.

24.  (Patient observed engaged in an intense, but autistic, "conversation" with imaginary voices.)

N:  You seem to be involved in some very important talk.

25. P:  Are you sure you are giving me the right medicine? I feel worse than before.

N:  You're feeling pretty badly, and wonder if it might be my fault.

26. P:  (male) You're very pretty. Do nurses ever go out for dinner or something with patients?

N: You're feeling warmly to me, and would like to get to know me better.

27. P: Why do I have to do that work? I don't get paid for it, and I'm supposed to be here in the hospital to rest, not work!

N: You feel kind of angry. Patients are supposed to take it easy here, not work.

28. P: All I know is that the blue pill helped me a lot the last time I felt this way. Why can't you let me have one now?

N: You sort of feel I'm keeping something from you that would really make you feel better, and you can't understand why.

29. P: I can understand why he did it. I've run away from the hospital twice myself. Sometimes you feel you just have to get away from here.

N: At times it seems impossible to stay here one more day, you simply must leave.

30. P: I don't need an X ray, I don't want an X ray, and I won't go for an X ray!

N: You're really *very* strongly against going.

Date: _____

Name: _____

## Rule-Making, Mild Disapproval, Praise

### Scene 1: Narrator's Introduction

Dr.°: Hi, I'm Dr. Schneiman from Syracuse University. Recently I've been employed as a consultant by the nearby school districts to help them with their teachers-aide training program. As a matter of fact, the film you're about to see was made for one of those specific training programs. What we try to do in this film, today, is to portray a problem that's pretty common to most people who work as teachers-aides or teachers-assistants, and that is—individually tutoring a child who is unwilling to be tutored. The first thing you'll see in the movie is—you'll see the problem itself. The next scene will show the teachers-aide coming to me for help, and hopefully I give it to her. During that scene, I'd like you to be aware of three very important things that I tell her to do. As a matter of fact, you might find them so valuable that you, yourself, would like to do these three things with the kids that you work with in your schools.

After we have the advice giving session, the teachers-aide goes back and tries these techniques, and we'll let you decide whether or not they're successful. So, this short film will start right now.

---

° *Dr.* represents Doctor.

## Scene 2: *Problem Presentation*

*TA\*:*  Patrick, what's the matter?

*S†:*  Nothing.

*TA:*  Patrick, what is it? Why are you standing over there by the window? Patrick, will you answer me, please? Patrick, we have to get on with the lesson. Now come and sit down. *Patrick,* will you please come and sit down here!! Now let's see what book you've brought here, Patrick. Hmm, *Conquest of Space.* That's a new one, huh, you ought to like that. Alright, Patrick, suppose you read to me.

*S:*  Our . . . in space. . .

*TA:*  Patrick, you don't know that word? That word, Patrick, is *neighbor.* Now, Patrick, you know what . . . Patrick, will you please pay attention while I'm talking to you! *Our neighbor in space.* Now, Patrick, you know that a neighbor is someone who lives nearby, or . . . *Patrick,* will you please pay attention to me when I'm talking to you!!! Pull your chair closer here and listen to me!!!! Now, look here; our neighbor in space. . . . Suppose we read a little bit. "From earliest times, man has turned his eyes upward in the night to gaze at our nearest neighbor in space with wonderment and awe. The moon . . . (pause) the moon, for that is indeed" . . . Patrick! will you please stop banging with your pencil. "The moon, for that is indeed what it is, has a very" . . . Patrick, will you please stop banging with your pencil when I'm trying to read to you!! (Sigh!) "The moon, for that is indeed what it is, has at various times been regarded as a mysterious object or form, and God" . . . Patrick!!! what is the matter with you?!! Ever since you came in that door, you've been nothing but trouble. You've been so destructive, and you haven't gotten a thing done. I give up. You'd better go right back to your own room. Patrick, take your book! And go back now!!!!

## Scene 3: *Skill Instruction*

*Dr.:*  Well, Carol, how did it go yesterday?

*TA:*  Ahh . . . I'm afraid I really made a mess of things. I was . . . it seems like I did everything wrong. You know, I'm supposed to tutor this boy, Patrick. . .

*Dr.:*  Yeah, yeah. . .

*TA:*  Well, I just don't know what was the matter, but right from the very beginning I sensed something was wrong. I came into the room and he was standing over by the window looking out. He looked rather dejected and so forth, and so I asked him what was the matter and he didn't answer me, or . . . nothing . . .that kind of thing, you know. . . .

*Dr.:*  Yeah. . .

---

\* TA represents Teachers-Aide.

† S represents Student.

*TA:*  I tried to draw him out; tried to be nice with him and patient and I said, "Now Patrick, come on and sit down and we'll start to read." And frankly, he really got me very annoyed and, finally, after many tries, I hate to admit it, but I grabbed his arm and I pushed him down into the chair. Now, I know it wasn't the right thing to do; I was upset and he was upset, and, of course, I was sorry I did it. Well, anyway I tried to make it up to him by showing an interest in his book, which was something a boy would like to read—about the moon or something like that. So I opened it up and suggested that he start reading to me. So, then, well, the next thing was he couldn't read all the words. . . . I think he got stuck on one word—*neighbor*—something like that. So I proceeded to try to explain to him what it meant. I told him what it was. I started the explanation, and I looked over and here he was daydreaming— looking off into the distance, you know, and I just didn't know what it was with him. So I told him—please pay attention while we're talking, and so forth. I went on again and still couldn't get his interest no matter how hard I tried. Finally I pulled his chair up and said, "Patrick, now you look and watch what we're reading." Again, I know it wasn't right, but I just didn't know what to do. Well, then . . . and this is the worst of all, I started to read to him because he wouldn't read; I really couldn't draw him out that way. So I started to read to him; I thought maybe I could get his attention and then he started tap, tap, tapping on the desk with his pencil. . . .

*Dr.:*  Hmm; it must have been very irritating.

*TA:*  Well, at first, I just . . . I just didn't pay any attention, I went on reading. Then he started again . . . tap, tap. So, I said, "Please, Patrick, not while I'm reading. Don't tap your pencil while I'm reading." So I continued, and he continued, and it seemed to get louder and louder and I got louder and the first thing you know I really lost my temper and I banged the book together and I said, "What are you doing; what's the matter with you; you've been so distracting"; I just . . . you know, bawl him out for everything that had gone wrong since he had come into the room . . . he hadn't paid attention . . . and finally, I just didn't know what to do and I ended up by handing him the book and sending him back to his room, and then, . . . oh, I don't know . . . it's just . . . it just went so badly.

*Dr.:*  Yeah, you sound like it was really pretty upsetting to you.

*TA:*  It was. I felt terrible; and I know Patrick did too. You know, I wished I could have called him back, but then it was too late, I couldn't have done anything.

*Dr.:*  Well, it really does sound like you had a pretty tough time.

*TA:*  I did . . . and, well, this is why I wanted to see you today. Because I really need some help. I hope you can give me some suggestions.

*Dr.:*  Well, you know, I hope I can. Patrick is a difficult boy. There's no doubt about that. Umh . . . well, I think there are a number of things that you might want to try, Carol. One thing that I think would be very good to start with is to, before you even get in the room, is to make a rule . . . if I remember, you told me he went right to the window. . .

*TA:*    That's right, Doctor, he did.

*Dr.:*    O.K. Make a rule. Tell Patrick that when you're in reading you sit at your desk. Alright, now, that's a rule. That is something that he knows he is supposed to do. You've already told him before he's gotten into the situation, right? So, you tell him—when we're in reading, we sit at our desks. Alright; that's a rule.

*TA:*    Uh-huh.

*Dr.:*    Now, probably what's going to happen, knowing Patrick, is: he's not going to obey that.

*TA:*    Yeah; and then what?

*Dr.:*    O.K. Let him do whatever he does. If he goes and stands by the window and starts pouting and business like that, don't pay any attention to that. Don't ask him why or how he's doing; you see, by paying attention to that, you just might be reinforcing the very behavior you don't want him to do. The only thing you have to do is just say to him, two things. This is what we call targeting. After you give the rule, you target for the child who doesn't obey the rule. And the target is two parts. The first part is, you tell him what you don't like. You say, "Patrick, I don't like you standing up during reading." That's the first part. Now the second part is you tell him what you like. You tell him what you what him to do, and that is, "I want you to sit down next to me." So, the target goes, "Patrick, I don't like you standing by the window. I would like it if yo usat down next to me."

*TA:*    Oh, I see; that is very specific, isn't it, Doctor?

*Dr.:*    Very specific, right. And then you don't say a word to him. You just sit there and relax. And don't worry about a thing. Chances are it may take a few minutes at the most, or maybe a few seconds, and he'll see that you're not going to react to his nonsense any more; he'll probably come and sit down. Now, once he does what you want him to do, and that is sitting down, you've got to let him know that you're happy about that. Now this is the third part. This is praise. Now, you can praise the child either verbally or physically. By that I mean if Patrick sits down next to you after you've targeted his behavior, you can say to him, "That's very good"; "That makes me very happy"; or you can pat him on the arm . . . something like that. It depends on what he likes. What does he like? Does he like to be touched?

*TA:*    Well, I guess it depends on his mood. He's a boy and he doesn't want to get too cozy, but I think a little pat or . . . I think I could get away with a little, if he's in the right mood.

*Dr.:*    Alright; then if you feel a bit uncomfortable about touching him, why don't you just say something nice to him. O.K.?

*TA:*    Yes.

*Dr.:*     Alright, well, now, that was the first thing that went on. Kids are going to keep testing you.

*TA:*     Mmh . . . yeah.

*Dr.:*     So, you've got to be kind of consistent in the use of those three rules, not three rules, but three steps.

*TA:*     Yes.

*Dr.:*     Rule—make a rule that's specific. Target the behavior—which means that you tell them what you don't like and you tell them what you want them to do. And the third step is you praise the child when he does what you want him to do. O.K.? Now, let's see, he did some other disturbing things in that last session?

*TA:*     Well, yes, he . . . well, then when I tried to explain a word to him, you know, he was, well, looking out of the window, daydreaming, and then the final thing that really, you know, made me blow my top was the banging on the desk with the pencil.

*Dr.:*     Fine. Let's take a look at that for a minute. Daydreaming, distracted . . . he's not attending to the task at hand. And that's what you want him to do. So, you give him a rule; when you catch him daydreaming —now you don't have to be angry, you don't have to be upset. In a very nice, calm voice you tell him, "Patrick, when we read, we pay attention to our book." That's the rule. Now, he may not do it. He'll probably look out the window again. Then you target on that. You say, "Patrick, I don't want you looking out the window. I would like it if you read your book." Alright? And if he does that, then what do you do?

*TA:*     Well, then I show him praise—either by word or by a gesture of some sort.

*Dr.:*     Right.

*TA:*     I see, Doctor . . . yeah, that sounds good.

*Dr.:*     Right, O.K., now let's try the third one. The third one is this tapping. Now, I think he does that just to get your goat.

*TA:*     So do I, and he surely succeeded.

*Dr.:*     Yeah. O.K., well, I think the secret here, to your success is not to let him get to you . . . alright? And one way to do that is, again, to make a rule. And that is, "During reading we don't do anything else. We read along." So, now he knows the tapping is against the rule. But, he'll probably keep tapping. Now you have to target him. And you tell him, "Patrick, I don't like you tapping your pencil; I want you to read along with me."

*TA:*     I see.

*Dr.:*     Alright? And when he starts to read along with you, that's when you praise him. But, since you're reading together you'll probably want to touch him. I don't know if you want to rough up his hair . . . or pat him on the arm or some such thing. . . .

*TA:*     Yeah, yeah . . . I see.

*Dr.:*     O.K.? So, let's just go over those three steps one more time because I think they're really important. They are: Give the child a rule. . . . Target a behavior you don't like . . . and offer an alternative. And then, give the child praise either verbally or physically, when he does what you ask him to do.

TA: I see . . . three things . . . three steps . . . yes.

Alright? So, why don't you do this. You're going to see him tomorrow. Why don't you try those three things tomorrow and I'll see you the day after. Alright? And all I can wish you is . . . good Luck!

TA: Thank you, Doctor. I'll need it.

### Scene 4: Skill Rehearsal

TA: Oh, dear, only 10 more minutes until I have to tutor Patrick again. Oh, I'm not looking forward to that after what happened the other day. Well, there's no avoiding it. The doctor did give me some good suggestions. I better think those through before I go in. Let me see . . . there were three steps. The first one is to establish a rule. Tell Patrick what the rule is for the specific incident . . . specific situation. The second one is targeting. That is, tell him what I don't like and then tell him what I do like. And then, number three, if he does as he is told, I praise him. I can either do it by word or by patting him or by a little gesture of some sort. Let me think now. I better be more specific. When I come into the room I better tell Patrick the rule right away . . . that when we are reading together, he is to come and sit down at the desk. Now, if he doesn't do that and stands over at the window, I won't pay any attention to him. I will be very calm; I'll be very patient. Then if he doesn't come right away, I'll tell him that I don't like him standing there at the window and that he should come and sit down. I might have to be patient again, but I'm not going to let it fluster me. Then, if he does come and sit next to me so we can get started, I'll show him that I'm pleased. I'll praise him in some way. Yes . . . now, if that works in that one incident, then it certainly ought to work with everything. I think I've got that.

### Scene 5: Skill Implementation

TA: Patrick, there's one thing I want to tell you before we sit down. And that is, we have a rule during reading. That is, we both sit at the desk together. O.K.?

S: O.K.

TA: Patrick, I don't like it when you stand over there by the window. I would like you to come and sit down next to me . . . (Long silence).

TA: Now before we start to read, Patrick, I want you to understand that there's a rule when we read that you must pay attention. Alright?

S: Yeah.

*TA:* O.K. Now, suppose you start here.

*S:* Our nei——in space.

*TA:* Alright, Patrick, that word is *neighbor*. Patrick, I don't like it when you look out the window. I would like you to look at the book. . . . Alright, neighbor is someone who lives nearby or out in space. It can be pretty far away now. I guess it's someone we're interested in. Anyone can be a neighbor. O.K.? Understand?

*S:* Yeah.

*TA:* Alright, that's very good Patrick. Now, Patrick, there's one rule . . . when I'm reading, I want you to pay attention. Alright?

*S:* Yeah.

*TA:* "From earliest times man has turned his eyes upward in the night to gaze at our nearest neighbor in space in wonderment." (tapping noise begins) Patrick, I don't like it when you tap your pencil. I would like you to read to me now.

*S:* "As seen from our own planet today, it is more often viewed merely as a beautiful sight, a celestial lamp in the night sky."

*TA:* Well, that was very good, Patrick! I think it's alot more fun this way, don't you?

*S:* Yeah.

## Scene 6: Social Reinforcement

*Dr.:* (knock on door) Come in!

*TA:* Doctor, I'm so excited, I just had to come in and talk with you a minute.

*Dr.:* Sure, Carol.

*TA:* You know, Patrick; I told you about him the other day. Well, I had a session with him yesterday and it went beautifully. After he was such a little monster and I couldn't do anything with him, I used your three steps and I am so thrilled. I used giving him the rule, and I used targeting, and I used giving him praise. And, honestly, I had him eating out of my hand. I am just delighted. I can't thank you enough.

*Dr.:* Don't thank me! I'm just very proud of you. You were able to dig up some techniques that were new to you, and you applied them, and you deserve the credit, Carol. I just think it's great! The one thing about the use of rules and targeting and praise is that you can use these things with all kinds of children. You just don't have to use them with kids who are bad. I mean you can praise kids who are doing good things right now.

*TA:* Well, yes. I never thought of that, Doctor.

*Dr.:* So, well, really what I think you've learned is a technique that you'll be able to use an awful lot in your daily work.

*TA:* Oh, I'm sure I will. And I do thank you so much again.

*Dr.:* Well, I'm glad it worked out so well for you.

*TA:* I am, too.

# REFERENCES

Abrahamson, S. Our status system and scholastic rewards. *Journal of Educational Sociology,* 1952, **25**, 441–450.

Adams, P. L., & McDonald, N. F. Clinical cooling out of poor people. *American Journal of Orthopsychiatry,* 1968, 38, 457–463.

Adamson, J. D., & Schmale, A. H. Object loss, giving up, and the onset of psychiatric disease. *Psychosomatic Medicine,* 1965, **27**, 557–576.

Albert, G. Identification therapy. *Psychotherapy: Theory, Research, and Practice,* 1968, **5**, 104–107.

Alexander, J. F. The therapist as a model—and as himself. *Psychotherapy: Theory, Research and Practice,* 1967, 4, 164–165.

Anastasi, A. *Differential psychology.* New York: Macmillan, 1958.

Appleby, L., Scher, J. M., & Cumming, J. *Chronic schizophrenia.* Glencoe, Ill.: Free Press, 1960.

Arieti, S. *Interpretation of schizophrenia.* New York: Bruner, 1955.

Aronfreed, J. The concept of internalization. In D. Goslin & D. Glass (Eds.), *Handbook of socialization theory and research.* Chicago: Rand McNally, 1970.

Artiss, K. L. *Milieu therapy in schizophrenia.* New York: Grune & Stratton, 1962.

Asch, S. E. Forming impressions of personality. *Journal of Abnormal and Social Psychology,* 1946, **41**, 258–290.

Asch, S. E. Effects of group pressure upon the modification and distortion of judgments. In H. Guetzkow (Ed.), *Groups, leadership and men.* Pittsburgh: Carnegie Press, 1951. Pp. 76–89.

Ashby, J. D., Ford, D. H., Guerney, B. G., Jr., & Guerney, L. Effects on clients of a reflective and a leading type of psychotherapy. *Psychological Monographs,* 1957, **71**, 1–32.

Atthowe, J. M., & Krasner, L. A preliminary report on the application of contingent reinforcement procedures (token economy) on a "chronic" psychiatric ward. *Journal of Abnormal Psychology,* 1968, **73**, 37–43.

Atwater, S. K. Proactive inhibition and associative facilitation as affected by degree of prior learning. *Journal of Experimental Psychology,* 1953, **46**, 400–404.

387

Ausubel, D. P. *The psychology of meaningful verbal behavior.* New York: Grune & Stratton, 1963.

Ayllon, T., & Azrin, N. H. The measurement and reinforcement of behavior of psychotics. *Journal for the Experimental Analysis of Behavior,* 1965, **8,** 357–383.

Ayllon, T., & Azrin, N. H. *The token economy: A motivational system for therapy and rehabilitation.* New York: Appleton, 1968.

Bailey, K. G., & Sowder, W. G., Jr., Audiotape and videotape self-confrontation in psychotherapy. *Psychological Bulletin,* 1970, **74,** 127–137.

Bandura, A. *Principles of behavior modification.* New York: Holt, 1969.

Bandura, A., Blanchard, E. B., & Ritter, B. The relative efficacy of desensitization and modeling approaches for inducing behavioral, affective and attitudinal changes. *Journal of Personality and Social Psychology,* 1969, **13,** 173–199.

Bandura, A., Grusec, J. E., & Menlove, F. L. Vicarious extinction of avoidance behavior. *Journal of Personality and Social Psychology,* 1967, **5,** 16–23.

Bandura, A., & Huston, A. C. Identification as a process of incidental learning. *Journal of Abnormal and Social Psychology,* 1961, **63,** 311–318.

Bandura, A., & Kupers, C. J. The transmission of patterns of self-reinforcement through modeling. *Journal of Abnormal and Social Psychology,* 1964, **69,** 1–9

Bandura, A., & McDonald, F. J. The influence of social reinforcement and the behavior of models in shaping children's moral judgments. *Journal of Abnormal and Social Psychology,* 1963, **67,** 274–281.

Bandura, A., & Menlove, F. L. Factors determining vicarious extinction of avoidance behavior through symbolic modeling. *Journal of Personality and Social Psychology,* 1968, **8,** 99–108.

Bandura, A., Ross, D., & Ross, S. A. Imitation of file-mediated aggressive models. *Journal of Abnormal and Social Psychology,* 1963, **66,** 3–11 (a)

Bandura, A., Ross, D., & Ross, S. A. A comparative test of the status envy, social power, and secondary reinforcement theories of identicatory learning. *Journal of Abnormal and Social Psychology,* 1963, **67,** 527–534 (b)

Baratz, J. C. Teaching reading in an urban Negro school system. In F. Williams (Ed.), *Language and poverty.* Chicago: Markham, 1970. Pp. 11–24.

Barrett-Lennard, G. T. Dimensions of the client's experience of his therapist associated with personality change. *Genetic Psychology Monographs,* 1962, **76,** No. 43.

Baum, O. E., & Felzer, S. B. Activity in initial interviews with lower class patients. *Archives of General Psychiatry,* 1964, **10,** 345–353.

Baum, O. E., Felzer, S. B., D'zmura, F. L., & Shumaker, E. Psychotherapy, dropouts and lower socioeconomic patients. *American Journal of Orthopsychiatry,* 1966, **36,** 629–635.

Bayley, N., & Schaefer, E. S. Relationships between socioeconomic variables and the behavior of mothers toward young children. *Journal of General Psychology,* 1960, **96,** 61–77.

Beal, A. Biased therapists: The effects of prior exposure to case history material on the therapists' attitudes and behavior toward patients. Unpublished doctoral dissertation, Syracuse University, 1969.

Beck, J. C., Kanto, D., & Gelineau, V. A. Follow-up study of chronic psychotic patients "treated" by college case-aide volunteers. *American Journal of Psychiatry,* 1963, **120,** 269–271.

Becker, H. S. Social class variations in the teacher-pupil relationship. *Journal of Educational Sociology,* 1952, **25,** 451–465. (a)

Becker, H. S. The career of the Chicago public school teacher. *American Journal of Sociology*, 1952, **57**, 470–477. (b)

Becker, W. C., Madsen, C. H., Jr., Arnold, C. R., & Thomas, D. R. The contingent use of teacher attention and praise in reducing classroom behavior problems. *Journal of Special Education*, 1967, **1**, 287–307.

Beilin, H. Effects of set upon impression formation. Presented at American Psychological Association, Chicago, 1960.

Beldoch, M. Sensitivity to expression of emotional meaning in three modes of communication. In J. R. Davitz (Ed.), *The communication of emotional meaning*. New York: McGraw-Hill, 1964. Pp. 31–42.

Bell, D. *Work and its discontents: The cult of efficiency in America*. Boston: Beacon Press, 1956.

Ben, D. Mood change in lower-class alcoholic outpatients as a function of role induction and reward to model. Unpublished doctoral dissertation, Syracuse University, 1973.

Bennett, W. J., Jr., & Falk, R. F. *New careers and urban schools*. New York: Holt, 1970.

Benschoter, R. A. Use of videotape to provide individual instruction in techniques of psychotherapy. *Journal of Medical Education*, 1965, **40**, 1159.

Bereiter, C., & Engelmann, S. *Teaching disadvantaged children in the preschool*. Englewood Cliffs, N. J.: Prentice-Hall, 1966.

Berger, M. M. Confrontation through videotape. In M. M. Berger (Ed.), *Videotape techniques in psychiatric training and treatment*. New York: Brunner Mazel, 1970. Pp. 18–36.

Berger, S. M. Incidental learning through vicarious reinforcement. *Psychological Reports*, 1961, **9**, 477–491.

Bergin, A. E., & Solomon, S. Personality and performance correlates of empathic understanding in psychotherapy. Presented at American Psychological Association, Philadelphia, September, 1963.

Berliner, D. C. Aptitude-treatment interactions in two studies of learning from lecture instruction. Berkeley, Calif: Far West Laboratory for Educational Research and Development, 1971.

Bernal, M. E. Behavioral feedback in the modification of brat behaviors. *Journal of Nervous and Mental Disease*, 1969, **148**, 375–385.

Bernard, V. W. Psychoanalysis and members of minority groups. *Journal of American Psychoanalytic Association*, 1953, **1**, 256–267.

Bernstein, B. A public language: Some sociological determinants of linguistic form. *British Journal of Sociology*, 1959, **10**, 311–326.

Bernstein, B. Aspects of languages in the genesis of the social process. *Journal of Child Psychology and Psychiatry*, 1961, **1**, 313–324. (a)

Bernstein, B. Social structure, language and learning. *Educational Research*, 1961, **3**, 163–176. (b)

Bernstein, B. Social class and linguistic development: A theory of social learning. In A. Halsey, J. Floud & C. A. Anderson (Eds.), *Education, economy and society*. New York: Free Press, 1961. Pp. 288–314. (c)

Bernstein, B. Linguistic codes, hesitation phenomena and intelligence. *Language and Speech*, 1962, **5**, 31–46.

Bernstein, B. Social class, speech systems and psychotherapy. *British Journal of Sociology*, 1964, **15**, 54–64.

Bernstein, B. A socio-linguistic approach to social learning. In J. Gould (Ed.), *Social science survey*. London: Social Science Survey, 1965.

Bertrand, A. L. School attendance and attainment: Function and dysfunction of school and family social systems. *Social Forces*, 1962, **40**, 228–233.

Binder, A., McConnell, D., & Sjoholm, N. A. Verbal conditioning as a function of experimenter characteristics. *Journal of Abnormal and Social Psychology*, 1957, **55**, 309–314.

Blackburn, J. R. The efficacy of modeled self-disclosure on subject's response in an interview situation. Unpublished doctoral dissertation, University of Arkansas, 1970.

Blake, R. R., & Brehm, J. W. The use of tape recorders to simulate a group atmosphere. *Journal of Abnormal and Social Psychology*, 1954, **49**, 311–313.

Blake, R. R., & Mouton, J. S. Conformity, resistance and conversion. In J. A. Berg & B. M. Bass (Eds.), *Conformity and deviation*. New York: Harper, 1961. Pp. 1–37.

Blane, H. T., & Meyers, W. R. Social class and establishment of treatment relations by alcoholics. *Journal of Clinical Psychology*, 1964, **20**, 287–290.

Blood, R. O., & Wolfe, D. M. *Husbands and wives: The dynamics of married living.* Glencoe, Ill.: Free Press, 1960.

Bloom, B. L., & Arkoff, A. Role playing in acute and chronic schizophrenics. *Journal of Consulting Psychology*, 1961, **25**, 24–28.

Bloombaum, M., Yamamoto, J., & James, L. Cultural stereotyping among psychotherapists. *Journal of Consulting and Clinical Psychology*, 1968, **32**, 99.

Bodian, C. Socioeconomic indications from census tract data related to rates of mental illness. Bureau of Census, United States Department of Commerce, Washington, D. C., 1963.

Boek, W. E., Sussman, M., & Yankauer, A. Social class and child care practices. *Marriage and Family Living*, 1958, **20**, 326–333.

Bordin, E. S. Ambiguity as a therapeutic variable. *Journal of Consulting Psychology*, 1955, **19**, 9–15. (a)

Bordin, E. S. The implications of client expectations for the counseling process. *Journal of Counseling Psychology*, 1955, **2**, 17–21. (b)

Borgatta, E. F. An analysis of three levels of response: An approach to some relationships among dimensions of personality. *Sociometry*, 1951, **14**, 267–316.

Borghi, J. H. Premature termination of psychotherapy and patient-therapist expectations. *American Journal of Psychotherapy*, 1965, **22**, 460–473.

Bowman, G. W., & Klopf, G. J. *New careers and roles in the American school.* New York: Bank Street College of Education, 1968.

Bradburn, M. M., & Caplovitz, D. *Reports on happiness: A pilot study of behavior related to mental health.* Chicago: Aldine, 1965.

Braginsky, B. M., Grosse, M., & Ring, K. Controlling outcomes through impression-management: An experimental study of the manipulative tactics of mental patients. *Journal of Consulting Psychology*, 1966, **30**, 295–300.

Brandis, W., & Henderson, D. *Social class, language and communication.* London: Routledge & Kegan, 1970.

Brill, N. L., & Storrow, H. A. Social class and psychiatric treatment. *Archives of General Psychiatry*, 1960, **3**, 340–344.

Brody, E. B. Status and role influence on initial interview behavior in psychiatric patients. In S. Lessee (Ed.), *An evaluation of the results of the psychotherapies.* Springfield: Thomas, 1968. Pp. 269–279.

Brody, H. A. The effect of three modeling procedures on the frequency of self-referent affect statements. *Dissertation Abstracts*, 1968, **29**, 767B.

Broen, W. *Schizophrenia*. New York: Academic Press, 1968.

Bronfenbrenner, U. Socialization and social class through time and space. In E. E. Maccoby, T. M. Newcomb & E. L. Hartley (Eds.), *Readings in social psychology*. New York: Holt, 1958. Pp. 400–425.

Brooke, E. E., Buri, J., Byrne, E. A., & Hudson, M. C. Economic factors, parental attitudes and school attendance. *Social Work*, 1962, 7, 103–108.

Brown, F. A comparative study of the influence of race and locale upon emotional stability of children. *Journal of Genetic Psychology*, 1936, 49, 325–342.

Brown, G. W., & Birley, J. L. Crisis and life changes and the onset of schizophrenia. *Journal of Health and Social Behavior*, 1969, 9, 203–214.

Brown, R. *Words and things*. New York: Free Press, 1958.

Browne, S. E. Short psychotherapy with passive patients. *British Journal of Psychiatry*, 1964, 110, 233–239.

Brunelle, P. Exploring skills of family life at school: Sociodrama with a fourth grade group. *Group Psychotherapy*, 1954, 6, 227–255.

Bryan, J. H., & Test, M. Models and helping: Naturalistic studies in aiding behavior. *Journal of Personality and Social Psychology*, 1967, 6, 400–407.

Buckley, N. K., & Walker, H. M. *Modifying classroom behavior*. Champaign, Ill.: Research Press Co., 1970.

Budner, S. Intolerance of ambiguity as a personality variable. *Journal of Personality*, 1962, 30, 29–50.

Buell, P., Dunn, J., & Breslow, L. The occupational social class risks of cancer mortality in man. *Journal of Chronic Disease*, 1960, 12, 600–621.

Buerkle, J. V., & Badgley, R. F. Couple role-taking: The Yale marital interaction battery. *Marriage and Family Living*, 1959, 21, 53–58.

Bugental, J. F. *The search for authenticity*. New York: Holt, 1965.

Burchinal, L., Gardner, B., & Hawkes, G. R. Children's personality adjustment and the socioeconomic status of their families. *Journal of General Psychology*, 1958, 92, 149–159.

Burrs, V., & Kapche, R. Modeling of social behavior in chronic hospital patients. Unpublished manuscript. California State College, Long Beach, California, 1969.

Byrne, D. *The attraction paradigm*. New York: Academic Press, 1971.

Byrne, D., Clore, G. L., Jr., & Worchel, P. Effect of economic similarity-dissimilarity on interpersonal attraction. *Journal of Personality and Social Psychology*, 1966, 4, 220–224.

Cadman, W. H., Misbach, L., & Brown, D. V. An assessment of round-table psychotherapy. *Psychological Monographs*, 1954, 68, Whole No. 384.

Callantine, M. F., & Warren, J. M. Learning sets in human concept formation. *Psychological Reports*, 1955, 1, 363–367.

Cameron, N. Experimental analysis of schizophrenic thinking. In J. S. Kasanin (Ed.), *Language and thought in schizophrenia*. Berkeley: Univ. of California Press, 1944. Pp. 50–63.

Campbell, D. T. Conformity in psychology's theories of acquired behavioral dispositions. In I. A. Berg & B. M. Bass (Eds.), *Conformity and deviation*. New York: Harper, 1961. Pp. 101–142.

Cantor, J. H. Amount of pretraining as a factor in stimulus pre-differentiation and performance set. *Journal of Experimental Psychology*, 1955, 50, 180–184.

Carkhuff, R. R. *Helping and human relations*. New York: Holt, 1969.

Carkuff, R. R., & Pierce, R. Differential effects of the therapist, race and social class upon patient depth of self-exploration in initial clinical interview. *Journal of Consulting Psychology,* 1967, **31**, 632–634.

Carroll, J. B. *Language and thought.* Englewood cliffs, N. J.: Prentice-Hall, 1964.

Carson, R. C. A and B therapist "types": A possible critical variable in psychotherapy. *Journal of Nervous and Mental Disease,* 1967, **144**, 47–54.

Casey, R. L., Masuda, M., & Holmes, T. H. Quantitative study of recall of life events. *Journal of Psychosomatic Medicine,* 1967, **11**, 239–247.

Centers, R., & Cantril, H. Income satisfaction and income aspiration. *Journal of Abnormal and Social Psychology,* 1946, **41**, 64–69.

Chance, E. *Families in treatment.* New York: Basic Books, 1959.

Chapin, F. S. The relationship of housing to mental health. World Health Organization, June, 1961. Mimeographed.

Chesler, M., & Fox, R. *Role playing methods in the classroom.* Chicago: Science Research Associates, 1966.

Chessick, R. D. *How psychotherapy heals: The process of intensive psychotherapy.* New York: Science House, 1969.

Chilman, C. S. *Growing up poor.* Washington, D. C.: United States Department of Health, Education and Welfare, 1970.

Chilman, C. S., & Sussman, M. Poverty in the United States in the mid-sixties. *Journal of Marriage and the Family,* 1964, **26**, 391–395.

Chittenden, G. E. An experimental study in measuring and modifying assertive behavior in young children. *Monographs of the Society for Research in Child Development,* 1942, **7**, (1, Serial #31).

Clark, F. W., Evans, D. R., & Hamerlynck, L. A. (Eds.) *Implementing behavioral programs for schools and clinics.* Champaign, Ill.: Research Press Co., 1972.

Clark, R. E. Psychosis, income and occupational prestige. *American Journal of Sociology,* 1948, **49**, 433–440. (a)

Clark, R. E. The relationship of schizophrenia to occupational income and occupational prestige. *American Sociological Review,* 1948, **13**, 325–330. (b)

Clausen, J. A., & Kohn, M. L. Relation of schizophrenia to the social structure of a small city. In B. Pasamanick (Ed.), *Epidemiology of mental disorder.* Washington, D. C.: American Association for the Advancement of Science, 1959. Pp. 69–86.

Clayton, P., Desmaris, L., & Winokur, G. A study of normal bereavement. *American Journal of Psychiatry,* 1968, **125**, 168–178.

Clemes, S. R., & D'Andrea, V. J. Patients anxiety as a function of expectation and degree of initial interview anxiety. *Journal of Consulting Psychology,* 1965, **29**, 397–404.

Clements, P. W., Roberts, P. V., & Lantz, C. E. Social models and token reinforcement in the treatment of shy, withdrawn boys. *Proceedings of the 78th Annual Convention.* American Psychological Association, 1970. Pp. 515.

Cohen, A. K., & Hodges, H. Characteristics of the lower blue-collar class. *Social Problems,* 1962, **10**, 303–334.

Cohen, B. D., Kalish, H. I., Thurston, J. R., & Cohen, E. Experimental manipulation of verbal behavior. *Journal of Experimental Psychology,* 1954, **47**, 106–110.

Cole, N. J., Branch, C. H., & Allison, R. B. Some relationships between social class and the practice of dynamic psychotherapy. *American Journal of Psychiatry,* 1962, **118**, 1004–1012.

Coleman, H. A. The relationship of socioeconomic status to the performance of high school students. *Journal of Experimental Education*, 1940, **9**, 61–63.

Coleman, J. C., & Hewett, F. M. Open-door therapy: A new approach to the treatment of underachieving adolescent boys who resist needed psychotherapy. *Journal of Clinical Psychology*, 1962, **18**, 28–33.

Cook, L. A. An experimental sociographic study of a stratified tenth grade class. *American Sociological Review*, 1945, **10**, 250–261.

Cornelison, F. S., & Arsenian, J. A study of the responses of psychotic patients to photographic self-image experience. *Psychiatric Quarterly*, 1960, **34**, 1–8.

Corsini, R. J. *Role playing in psychotherapy: A manual*. Chicago: Aldine, 1966.

Coster, J. K. Attitudes toward school of high school pupils from three income levels. *Journal of Educational Psychology*, 1958, **49**, 61–66.

Crafts, L. W. Transfer as related to number of common elements. *Journal of General Psychology*, 1935, **13**, 147–158.

Crandell, J. E. Self-perception and interpersonal attraction as related to tolerance-intolerance of ambiguity. *Journal of Personality*, 1969, **37**, 127–140.

Creer, T. L., & Miklich, D. R. The application of a self-modeling procedure to modify inappropriate behavior: A preliminary report. *Behavior Research and Therapy*, 1970, **8**, 91–92.

Crutchfield, R. S. Conformity and character. *American Psychologist*, 1955, **10**, 191–195.

Culbertson, F. M. Modification of an emotionally held attitude through role playing. *Journal of Abnormal and Social Psychology*, 1957, **54**, 230–233.

Cumming, J., & Cumming, E. *Ego and milieu*. New York: Atherton, 1962.

Dain, N. *Concepts of insanity in the United States, 1789–1865*. New Brunswick, N. J.: Rutgers University Press, 1964.

Daniels, D., & Kuldau, J. Marginal man, the tether of tradition and intentional social system therapy. *Community Mental Health Journal*, 1967, **3**, 13–20.

Davidoff, L. L. Schizophrenic patients in psychotherapy: The effects of degree of information and compatibility expectations on behavior in the interview setting. Unpublished doctoral dissertation, Syracuse University, 1969.

Davis, A. Language and social class perspectives. In B. Goldstein (Ed.), *Low income youth in urban areas*. New York: Holt, 1967. Pp. 140–151.

Davis, A., & Dollard, J. *Children of bondage*. Washington: American Council on Education, 1948.

Davis, A., & Havighurst, R. J. Social class and color differences in child rearing. In C. Kluckholm, H. A. Murray & D. M. Schneider (Eds.), *Personality in nature, society and culture*. New York: Knopf, 1954. Pp. 308–320.

Davis, K. Mental hygiene and the class structure. *Psychiatry*, 1938, **1**, 55–65.

Davitz, J. R. *The communication of emotional meaning*. New York: McGraw-Hill, 1964.

Davitz, J. R., & Mattis, S. The communication of emotional meaning by metaphor. In J. R. Davitz (Ed.), *The communication of emotional meaning*. New York: McGraw-Hill, 1964. Pp. 157–176.

Day, E. J. The development of language in twins. *Child Development*, 1932, **3**, 298–316.

Dean, D. G. Alienation: Its meaning and measurement. *American Sociological Review*, 1961, **26**, 753–758.

DeCharms, R., & Rosenbaum, M. E. The problem of vicarious experience. In D. Wilner (Ed.), *Decisions, values and groups*. New York: Pergamon, 1960. Pp. 267–277.

Deese, J. *The psychology of learning*. New York: McGraw-Hill, 1958.

Deutsch, M. Trust, trustworthiness, and the F scale. *Journal of Abnormal and Social Psychology*, 1960, 61, 138–140.

Deutsch, M. P. The disadvantaged child and the learning process. In A. H. Passon (Ed.), *Education in depressed areas*. New York: Columbia Univ. Press, 1963. Pp. 163–179.

Dibner, A. S. Ambiguity and anxiety. *Journal of Abnormal and Social Psychology*, 1958, 56, 165–174.

Diebold, R., Jr. A survey of psycholinguistic research, 1954–1964. In C. E. Osgood & T. A. Sebeck (Eds.), *Psycholinguistics*. Bloomington: Indiana Univ. Press, 1965. Pp. 205–291.

Dittman, A. T., Parloff, M. B., & Boomer, D. S. Facial and bodily expression: A study of receptivity of emotional cues. *Psychiatry*, 1965, 28, 239–244.

Divesta, F. J., & Bossart, P. The effects of sets induced by labeling on the modification of attitudes. *Journal of Personality*, 1958, 26, 379–387.

Dohrenwend, B. P. Social status stress and psychological symptoms. *American Journal of Public Health*, 1967, 57, 625–632.

Dohrenwend, B. P., & Dohrenwend, B. S. The problem of validity in field studies of psychological disorder. *Journal of Abnormal Psychology*, 1965, 70, 52–69.

Dohrenwend, B. S., & Dohrenwend, B. P. Field studies of social factors in relation to three types of psychological disorder. *Journal of Abnormal Psychology*, 1967, 72, 369–378.

Dolger, L., & Ginandes, J. Children's attitudes toward discipline as related to socioeconomic status. *Journal of Experimental Education*, 1946, 15, 161–165.

Dorfman, E., & Kleiner, R. J. Race of examiner and patient in psychiatric diagnosis and recommendations. *Journal of Consulting Psychology*, 1962, 26, 393.

Dorn, H. F., & Cutler, S. J. Morbidity from cancer in the United States. P.H.S. Public No. 590, Public Health Monograph No. 56. United States Printing Office, Washington, D.C., 1959.

Dotson, F. Patterns of voluntary association among urban working-class families. *American Sociological Review*, 1951, 16, 687–693.

Drag, L. R. Experimenter subject interaction: A situational determinant of differential levels of self-disclosure. Unpublished masters thesis, University of Florida, 1968.

Dublin, J. E. Perception of and reaction to ambiguity by repressors and sensitizers. *Journal of Consulting and Clinical Psychology*, 1968, 32, 198–205.

Duke, M. P., Frankel, A. S., Sipes, M., & Stewart, R. W. The effects of different kinds of models on interview behavior and feelings about an interview situation. Unpublished manuscript. Indiana University, 1965.

Duncan, C. P. Transfer in motor learning as a function of degree of first-task learning and inter-task similarity. *Journal of Experimental Psychology*, 1953, 45, 1–11.

Duncan, C. P. Transfer after training with single versus multiple tasks. *Journal of Experimental Psychology*, 1958, 55, 63–72.

Duncan, C. P. Recent research on human problem solving. *Psychological Bulletin*, 1959, 56, 397–429.

Dunham, H. W. Social class and schizophrenia. *American Journal of Orthopsychiatry*, 1964, 34, 634–642.

Dunham, H. W. *Community and schizophrenia*. Detroit: Wayne State Univ. Press, 1965.

Dunham, H. W., & Weinberg, S. K. *The culture of the state mental hospital*. Detroit: Wayne State Univ. Press, 1960.

Duvall, E. M. Conceptions of parenthood. *American Journal of Sociology,* 1946, **52,** 193–203.

Eells, K., Davis, A., Havighurst, R. J., Herman, V. E., & Tyler, R. *Intelligence and cultural differences.* Chicago: Univ. of Chicago Press, 1951.

Ekman, P., & Friesen, W. V. Nonverbal behavior in psychotherapy research. In J. M. Shlien (Ed.), *Research in psychotherapy.* Vol. 3. Washington, D. C.: American Psychological Association, 1968.

Ekman, P., Friesen, W. V., & Ellsworth, P. *Emotion in the human face.* New York: Pergamon, 1972. Pp. 179–216.

Elliot, T. D. *The juvenile court and the community.* New York: Macmillan, 1914.

Ellis, H. *The transfer of learning.* New York: Macmillan, 1965.

Ellsworth, R. B. The MACC Behavioral adjustment scale: revised 1971. Los Angeles: Western Psychological Services, 1971.

Elms, A. C., & Janis, L. L. Counter norm attitudes induced by consonant versus dissonant conditions in role playing. *Journal of Experimental Research in Personality,* 1965, **1,** 50–60.

Empey, L. T. Social class and occupational aspiration. *American Sociological Review,* 1956, **21,** 703–709.

Epstein, R. Aggression towards outgroups as a function of authoritarianism and imitation of aggressive models. *Journal of Personality and Social Psychology,* 1966, **3,** 574–579.

Ericson, M. C. Child rearing and social status. *American Journal of Sociology,* 1946–1947, **52,** 190–192.

Faris, R. Cultural patterns as affecting personality structure. *American Journal of Sociology,* 1932, **26,** 188.

Faris, R., & Dunham, H. W. *Mental disorders in urban areas.* Chicago: Univ. of Chicago Press, 1939.

Faris, R. E., & Dunham, H. W. *Mental disorders in urban areas: An ecological study of schizophrenia and other psychoses.* Chicago: Univ. of Chicago Press, 1960.

Feldman, S. E., & Rice, J. K. Tolerance for unambiguous feedback. *Journal of Personality and Social Psychology,* 1965, **2,** 341–347.

Ferster, C. B. Classification of behavioral pathology. In L. Krasner & L. P. Ullmann (Eds.), *Research in behavior modification: New developments and implications.* New York: Holt, 1965. Pp. 6–26.

Fikso, A. Vicarious versus participant group psychotherapy of underachievers. Unpublished doctoral dissertation, Illinois Institute of Technology, 1970.

Fishman, J. A., Deutsch, M., Kogan, L., North, R., & Whiteman, M. Guidelines for testing minority group children. *Journal of Social Issues,* 1964, **20,** 129–145.

Flanders, J. P. A review of research on imitative behavior. *Psychological Bulletin,* 1968, **69,** 316–337.

Fontana, A. F., & Klein, E. B. Self-presentation and the schizophrenic "deficit." *Journal of Consulting and Clinical Psychology,* 1968, **32,** 250–256.

Fontana, A. F., Klein, E. B., Lewis, E., & Levine, L. Presentation of self in mental illness. *Journal of Consulting and Clinical Psychology,* 1968, **32,** 110–119.

Ford, D. H., & Urban, H. B. *Systems of psychotherapy: A comparative study.* New York: Wiley, 1963.

Frank, L. K. Society as the patient. *American Journal of Sociology,* 1936, **42,** 333–344.

Frank, L. K. Cultural coercion and individual distortion. *Psychiatry,* 1939, **2,** 11–27.

Franks, C. M. *Behavior therapy: Appraisal and status.* New York: McGraw-Hill, 1969.

Freedman, N., Englehardt, D. M., & Hankoff, L. D. Drop-out from outpatient psychiatric treatment. *Archives of Neurology and Psychiatry,* 1958, **80**, 657–666.

Freeman, T. On the psychopathogy of schizophrenia. *Journal of Mental Science,* 1960, **106**, 925–937.

French, J. R. P., Jr. The social environment and mental health. *Journal of Social Issues,* 1963, **19**, 39–56.

Frenkel-Brunswik, E. Intolerance of ambiguity as an emotional and perceptual personality variable. *Journal of Personality,* 1949, **18**, 108–143.

Friedenberg, W. P. Verbal and nonverbal attraction modeling in an initial therapy interview analogue. Unpublished masters thesis, Syracuse University, 1971.

Friedman, P. H. The effects of modeling and role playing on assertive behavior. Unpublished doctoral dissertation, University of Wisconsin, 1968.

Frumkin, R. M. Occupation and major mental disorders. In A. M. Rose (Ed.), *Mental health and mental disorders.* New York: Norton, 1955. Pp. 136–160.

Fryrear, J. L., & Werner, S. Treatment of a phobia by use of a video-taped modeling procedure: A case study. *Behavior Therapy,* 1970, **1**, 391–394.

Fuson, W. M. Research note: Occupations of functional psychotics. *American Journal of Sociology,* 1943, **43**, 612–613.

Gagne, R. M., & Foster, H. Transfer to a motor skill from practice on a pictured represntation. *Journal of Experimental Psychology,* 1949, **39**, 342–354.

Gagne, R. M., Baker, K. E., & Foster, H. On the relation between similarity and transfer of training in the learning of discriminative motor tasks. *Psychological Review,* 1950, **57**, 67–79.

Galioni, E. F., Adams, F. H., & Tallman, F. F. Intensive treatment of back ward patients: A controlled pilot study. *American Journal of Psychiatry,* 1953, **109**, 576–583.

Garbin, A. P., & Bates, F. L. Occupational prestige and its correlates: A re-examination. *Social Forces,* 1966, **44**, 296–302.

Gardner, E. A., & Babigian, H. B. A longitudinal comparison of psychiatric service to selected socioeconomic areas of Monroe County, New York. *American Journal of Orthopsychiatry,* 1966, **36**, 818–828.

Gardner, G. G. The psychotherapeutic relationship. *Psychological Bulletin,* 1964, **61**, 426–437.

Garfield, J. C., & Weiss, S. L. Effects of the child's social class upon school counselors' decision-making. *American Journal of Orthopsychiatry,* 1971, **41**, 256–257.

Garfield, S. L. New developments in the preparation of counselors. *Community Mental Health Journal,* 1969, **5**, 240–246.

Garner, H. H. A review of confrontation in psychotherapy from hypnosis to the problem-solving technique. In M. M. Berger (Ed.), *Videotape techniques in psychiatric training and treatment.* New York: Brunner Mazel, 1970. Pp. 3–17.

Geer, J., & Turteltaub, A. Fear reduction following observation of a model. *Journal of Personality and Social Psychology,* 1967, **6**, 327–331.

Geertsma, R. H., & Reivich, R. S. Repetitive self observation by videotape playback. *Journal of Nervous and Mental Disease,* 1965, **141**, 29–41.

Gelfand, D. M., & Singer, R. D. Generalization of reinforced personality evaluations: A further investigation. *Journal of Clinical Psychology,* 1968, **24**, 24–26.

Geller, J. D. Some personal and situational determinants of interpersonal trust. Unpublished doctoral dissertation, University of Connecticut, 1966.

Gendlin, E. T. Initiating psychotherapy with "unmotivated" patients. *Psychiatric Quarterly,* 1961, **35**, 134–139. (a)

Gendlin, E. T. Experiencing: A variable in the process of therapeutic change. *American Journal of Psychotherapy*, 1961, 15, 233–245. (b)

Gendlin, E. T. A theory of personality change. In P. Worchel & D. Byrne (Eds.), *Personality change*. New York: Wiley, 1964. Pp. 100–148.

Gendlin, E. T. Focussing. *Psychotherapy: Theory, Research and Practice*, 1969, 6, 4–15.

Gendlin, E. T., & Tomlinson, T. M. Psychotherapy process rating scale: Experiencing scale. Unpublished manuscript, University of Wisconsin, 1961.

Gendlin, E. T., Beebe, J., Cassens, J., Klein, M., & Oberlander, M. Focussing ability in psychotherapy, personality and creativity. In J. M. Shlien, H. F. Hunt, J. D. Matarazzo & C. Savage (Eds.), *Research in psychotherapy*. Vol. 3. Washington, D. C.: American Psychological Association, 1968. Pp. 217–241.

Gerard, D. L., & Houston, L. C. Family setting and the social ecology of schizophrenia. *Psychiatric Quarterly*, 1953, 27, 90–101.

Gerwitz, J. L., Stingle, K. C. The learning of generalized imitation as the basis for identification. *Psychological Review*, 1968, 75, 374–397.

Gittelman, M. Behavior rehearsal as a technique in child treatment. *Journal of Child Psychology and Psychiatry*, 1965, 6, 251–255.

Gladfelter, J. H. Videotape supervision of co-therapists. In M. M. Berger (Ed.), *Videotape techniques in psychiatric training and treatment*. New York: Brunner Mazel, 1970. Pp. 74–82.

Glaser, R. *The nature of reinforcement*. New York: Academic Press, 1971.

Godwin, R. The influence of self-esteem on modeling behavior in a psychotherapy analogue. Unpublished masters thesis, Syracuse University, 1970.

Goldbeck, R. A., Bernstein, B. B., Hillix, W. A., & Marx, M. H. Application of the half-split technique to problem-solving tasks. *Journal of Experimental Psychology*, 1957, 53, 330–338.

Goldberg, A. D. A sequential program for supervising counselors using the interpersonal process recall technique. Unpublished doctoral dissertation, Michigan State University, 1967.

Goldberg, E. M., & Morrison, S. L. Schizophrenia and social class. *British Journal of Psychiatry*, 1963, 109, 785–802.

Goldman, E., & Goldman, S. Sociodrama and psychodrama with urban disadvantaged youth. *Group Psychotherapy*, 1968, 21, 206–210.

Goldstein, A. P. *Therapist-patient expectancies in psychotherapy*. New York: Pergamon, 1962.

Goldstein, A. P. *Psychotherapeutic attraction*. New York: Pergamon, 1971.

Goldstein, A. P., Cohen, R., Blake, G., & Walsh, W. The effects of modeling and social class structuring in paraprofessional psychotherapist training. *Journal of Nervous and Mental Disease*, 1971, 153, 47–56.

Goldstein, A. P., Gassner, S., Greenberg, R., Gustin, A., Land, J., Liberman, B., & Streiner, D. The use of planted patients in group psychotherapy. *American Journal of Psychotherapy*, 1967, 21, 767–773.

Goldstein, A. P., Heller, K., & Sechrest, L. B. *Psychotherapy and the psychology of behavior change*. New York: Wiley, 1966.

Goldstein, A. P., Martens, J., Hubben, J., Van Belle, H. A., Schaaf, W., Wiersema, H., & Goodhart, A. The use of modeling to increase independent behavior. Unpublished manuscript, Syracuse University, 1972.

Goldstein, A. P., & Simonson, N. R. Social psychological approaches to psychotherapy research. In A. Bergan & S. Garfield (Eds.), *Handbook of psychotherapy research*. New York: Wiley, 1971. Pp. 154–195.

Goode, W. J. *After divorce*. Glencoe, Ill.: Free Press, 1956.

Gordon, M. *Social class in American sociology*. New York: McGraw-Hill, 1950.

Gordon, M. *Social change in American sociology*. Durham, N. C.: Duke Univ. Press, 1958.

Goth, W. P. Validation of a criterion of lecture effectiveness. Stanford, Calif.: Stanford University, Office of Education, Report No. SU-SCRDT-RM, 1968.

Gould, R. Some sociological determinants of goal striving. *Journal of Social Psychology*, 1941, 13, 461–473.

Gould, R. E. Dr. Strangeclass: Or how I stopped worrying about the theory and began treating the blue-collar worker. *American Journal of Orthopsychiatry*, 1967, 37, 78–86.

Grambs, R. Paraprofessionals and teacher-aides: An annotated bibliography. Syracuse: Educational Resources Information Center, 1970.

Gray, S., & Klaus, R. A. An experimental preschool program for culturally deprived children. *Child Development*, 1965, 36, 887–898.

Green, H. W. *Persons admitted to the Cleveland State Hospital, 1928–1937*. Cleveland Health Council, 1939.

Grey, A. L. Social class and the psychiatric patient: A study in composite character. In A. L. Grey (Ed.), *Class and personality in society*. New York: Atherton Press, 1969. Pp. 136–160.

Greenberg, E. M. Community conditions and psychoses of the elderly. *American Journal of Psychiatry*, 1954, 110, 888–896.

Groff, P. Dissatisfactions in teaching the culturally deprived child. *Phi Delta Kappan*, 1963, 34, 76.

Grosser, C., Henry, W. E., & Kelly, J. G. *Nonprofessionals in the human services*. San Francisco: Jossey-Bass, 1969.

Gruenberg, P., Liston, E. H., & Wayne, G. J. Intensive supervision of psychotherapy with videotape recording. In M. M. Berger (Ed.), *Videotape techniques in psychiatric training and treatment*. New York: Brunner Mazel, 1970. Pp. 47–54.

Grusec, J. E., & Mischel, W. The model's characteristics as determinants of social learning. *Journal of Personality and Social Psychology*, 1966, 4, 211–215.

Gruver, G. G. College students as therapeutic agents. *Psychological Bulletin*, 1971, 76, 111–127.

Guerney, B. G. *Psychotherapeutic agents: New roles for non-professionals, parents and teachers*. New York: Holt, 1969.

Gurin, P., Gurin, G., Lao, R. C., & Beattie, M. Internal-external control in the motivational dynamics of negro youth. *Journal of Social Issues*, 1969, 25, 29–53.

Gursslin, O. R., Hunt, R. G., & Roach, J. L. Social class and the mental health movement. *Social Problems*, 1959–1960, 7, 210–218.

Gutride, M., Goldstein, A. P., & Hunter, G. F. The use of modeling and role playing to increase social interaction among schizophrenic patients. Unpublished manuscript, Syracuse University, 1972. (a)

Gutride, M., Goldstein, A. P., & Hunter, G. F. Structured learning therapy for increasing social interaction skills. Unpublished manuscript, Syracuse University, 1972. (b)

Haas, K. The middle-class professional and the lower class patient. *Mental Hygiene*, 1965, 47, 408–410.

Haase, W. The role of socioeconomic class in examiner bias. In F. Riessman, J. Cohen & A. Pearl (Eds.), *Mental health of the poor*. New York: Free Press, 1964. Pp. 241–248.

Hadley, E. Military psychiatry—an ecological note. *Psychiatry*, 1944, 7, 379–407.

Hall, R. Inferred Meanings Test, Johns Hopkins Univ., 1969, Unpublished.

Hallowell, I. Culture and mental disorder. *Journal of Abnormal and Social Psychology,* 1934, **29,** 1–9.

Halmos, P. *Solitude and privacy.* London: Routledge & Kegan, 1952.

Hare, E. H. Mental illness and social condition in Bristol. *Journal of Mental Science,* 1956, **102,** 349–357.

Harlow, H. F. The formation of learning sets. *Psychological Review,* 1949, **56,** 51–65.

Harris, P. L. Paraprofessionals, their role and potential in the classroom. Presented at International Reading Association, Atlantic City, 1971.

Harrison, S. I., McDermott, J. F., Wilson, P. T., & Schrager, J. Social class and mental illness in children's choice of treatment. Presented at American Psychiatric Association, Los Angeles, 1944.

Harrow, G. S. The effects of psychodrama group therapy on role behavior of schizophrenic patients. *Group Psychotherapy,* 1951, **3,** 316–320.

Hart, J. T., & Tomlinson, T. M. *New directions in client-centered psychotherapy.* New York: Houghton, 1970.

Harth, R. Changing attitudes toward school, classroom behavior, and reaction to frustration of emotionally disturbed children through role playing. *Exceptional Children,* 1966, **33,** 119–120.

Harvey, O. J., & Beverly, G. D. Some personality correlates of concept change through role playing. *Journal of Abnormal and Social Psychology,* 1961, **63,** 125–130.

Havighurst, R. J., & Janke, L. L. Relation between ability and social status in a midwestern community. *Journal of Educational Psychology,* 1944, **35,** 357–368.

Heider, E. R. Style and accuracy of verbal communications within and between social classes. *Journal of Personality and Social Psychology,* 1971, **18,** 33–47.

Heifitz, M. L. Experimenter effect upon openness of response to the Rotter Incomplete Sentences Blank. Unpublished honors paper, University of Florida, 1967.

Heine, R. W., & Trosman, H. Initial expectations of the doctor-patient interaction as a factor in the continuance of psychotherapy. *Psychiatry,* 1960, **23,** 275–278.

Helfand, I. Role taking in schizophrenia. *Journal of Consulting Psychology,* 1956, **20,** 37–41.

Heller, K. Experimental analogues of psychotherapy. The clinical relevance of laboratory findings of social influence. *Journal of Nervous and Mental Disease,* 1963, **137,** 420–426.

Heller, K. Ambiguity in the interview interaction. In J. M. Shlein, H. F. Hunt, J. D. Matarazzo & C. Savage (Eds.), *Research in psychotherapy.* Vol. 3. Washington, D. C.: American Psychological Association, 1967. Pp. 242–259.

Heller, K., & Goldstein, A. P. Client dependency and therapist expectancy as relationship maintaining variables in psychotherapy. *Journal of Consulting Psychology,* 1961, **25,** 371–375.

Heller, K., Davis, J. D., & Meyers, R. A. The effects of interviewer style in a standardized interview. *Journal of Consulting Psychology,* 1966, **30,** 501–508.

Hendrickson, G., & Schroeder, W. H. Transfer of training in learning to hit a submerged target. *Journal of Educational Psychology,* 1941, **32,** 205–213.

Hendrix, V. L. Comparison of audio-tape and lecture procedures in social science. Unpublished manuscript, Dallas County Junior College, 1968.

Herriott, R. E., & St. John. N. H. *Social class and the urban school.* New York: Wiley, 1966.

Hess, R. D., & Shipman, V. C. Early experience and the socialization of cognitive modes in children. *Child Development,* 1965, **36,** 869–886.

Higgins, W. H., Ivey, A. E., & Uhlemann, M. R. Media therapy: A programmed approach to teaching behavioral skills. Columbia University, 1969. Mimeographed.

Hildum, D. C., & Brown, R. W. Verbal reinforcement and interviewer bias. *Journal of Abnormal and Social Psychology*, 1956, 53, 108–111.

Hill, J. H., Liebert, R. M., & Mott, D. E. W. Vicarious extinction of avoidance behavior through films. *Psychological Reports*, 1968, 22, 192.

Hill, R. J. A comparative study of lecture and discussion methods. White Plains, N. Y.: Fund for Adult Education, 1960.

Hill, T. J. Dating patterns and family position. *Clearing House*, 1955, 29, 552–554.

Himmelsbach, J. T. The influence of conformity pressure on psychotherapeutic attraction. Unpublished masters thesis, Syracuse University, 1970.

Hinkle, L. E., & Wolf, H. G. Health and social environment: Experimental investigations. In A. H. Leighton, K. A. Clausen, & R. N. Wilson (Eds.), *Explorations in social psychiatry*. New York: Basic Books, 1957. Pp. 105–137.

Hingtgen, J. N., Coulter, S. K., & Churchill, D. W. Intensive reinforcement of imitative behavior in mute autistic children. *Archives of General Psychiatry*, 1967, 17, 36–43.

Hodge, R. W. Occupational prestige in the United States, 1925–1963. *American Journal of Sociology*, 1964, 69, 286–302.

Hoehn-Saric, R., Frank, J. D., Imber, S. D., Nash, E. H., Stone, A. R., & Battle, C. C. Systematic preparation of patients for psychotherapy. I. Effects on therapy behavior and outcome. *Journal of Psychiatric Research*, 1964, 2, 267–281.

Hoffeditz, E. L. Family resemblances in personality traits. *Journal of Social Psychology*, 1934, 5, 214–227.

Hoffman, M. L., & Albizu-Miranda, C. Middle-class bias in personality testing. *Journal of Abnormal and Social Psychology*, 1955, 51, 150–152.

Hoijer, H. Cultural implications of some Navaho linquistic categories. *Language*, 1951, 27.

Holland, G. A. *Fundamentals of Psychotherapy*. New York: Holt, 1965.

Hollander, T. G. The effects of role playing on attraction, disclosure and attitude change in a psychotherapy analogue. Unpublished doctoral dissertation, Syracuse University, 1970.

Hollingshead, A. B., Ellis, R. A. & Kirby, E. C. Social mobility and mental illness. *American Sociological Review*, 1954, 19, 577–584.

Hollingshead, A. B., & Redlich, F. C. *Social class and mental illness*. New York: Wiley, 1958.

Holzberg, J. D., Knapp, R. H., & Turner, J. L. College students as companions to the mentally ill. In E. L. Cowen, E. A. Gardner & M. Zax (Eds.), *Emergent approaches to mental health problems*. New York: Appleton, 1967. Pp. 91–109.

Hsu, J. J. Electro-conditioning treatment for alcoholics. *Quarterly Journal for Studies on Alcoholism*, 1965, 26, 449–459.

Hubbell, A. Two person role playing for guidance in social readjustment. *Group Psychotherapy*, 1954, 7, 249–254.

Hyde, R. W. Factors in group motivation in a mental hospital. *Journal of Nervous and Mental Disease*, 1953, 117, 212–225.

Hyde, R. W., & Kingsley, L. V. Studies in medical sociology: 1. The relation of mental disorders to the community socioeconomic level. *New England Journal of Medicine*, 1944, 231, 543–548.

Hymes, D. H. (Ed.) *Language and society. A reader in linguistics and anthropology*. New York: Harper, 1964.

Imber, S., Nash, E. H., Jr., & Stone, A. R. Social class and duration of psychotherapy. *Journal of Clinical Psychology*, 1955, 11, 281–284.

Inkeles, A. Industrial man: The relation of status to experience, perception and value. *American Journal of Sociology*, 1960, **66**, 1–32.

Ivey, A. E. *Microcounseling: Innovations in interviewing training*. Springfield, Ill.: Thomas, 1971.

Jack, L. M. An experimental study of ascendant behavior in preschool children. *University of Iowa Studies in Child Welfare*, 1934, **9**, 7–65.

Jaco, E. G. The social isolation hypothesis and schizophrenia. *American Sociological Review*, 1954, **19**, 567–577.

Jaco, E. G. *The social epidemiology of mental disorder*. New York: Russell Sage Foundation, 1960.

Jacobs, D., Charles, E., Jacobs, T., Weinstein, H., & Mann, D. Preparation for treatment of the disadvantaged patient: Effects on disposition and outcome. *American Journal of Orthopsychiatry*, 1972, **42**, 666–674.

Jacobs, P. A view from the other side: Unemployment as part of identity. In W. G. Bowen & F. H. Harbison (Eds.), *Unemployment in a prosperous economy*. Princeton: Industrial Relations Section, 1965. Pp. 59–71.

Jacobson, G. F., Strickler, M., & Morley, W. Generic and individual approaches to crisis intervention. *American Journal of Public Health*, 1968, **58**, 338–343.

Jaffe, P.—cited as unpublished in: Jourard, S. M. The effects of experimenter self-disclosure on subject's behavior. In C. Speilberger (Ed.), *Current topics in community and clinical psychology*. New York: Academic Press, 1969.

Jaffe, A. J., & Shanas, E. Economic differentials in the probability of insanity. *American Journal of Sociology*, 1939, **44**, 534–539.

James, G. Poverty and public health—new outlooks. *American Journal of Public Health*, 1965, **55**, 1757–1771.

Janis, I. L. *Psychological stress*. New York: Wiley, 1958.

Janis, I. L., & King, B. T. The influence of role playing on opinion change. *Journal of Abnormal and Social Psychology*, 1954, **49**, 211–218.

Janis, I. L., & Mann, L. Effectiveness of emotional role playing in modifying smoking habits and attitudes. *Journal of Experimental Research in Personality*, 1965, **1**, 84–90.

Jensen, A. R. *Social class and verbal learning*. Berkeley: Univ. of California, 1964.

Jensen, A. R. Social class and verbal learning. In J. P. DeCecco (Ed.), *The psychology of language, thought and instruction*. New York: Holt, 1967. Pp. 103–117.

John, V. P. The intellectual development of slum children. Some preliminary findings. *American Journal of Orthopsychiatry*, 1963, **33**, 813–822.

Jones, F. D., & Peters, A. N. An experimental evaluation of group psychotherapy. *Journal of Abnormal and Social Psychology*, 1952, **47**, 345–353.

Jones, M. C. A laboratory study of fear: The case of Peter. In H. J. Eysenck (Ed.), *Behavior therapy and the neuroses*. New York: Pergamon, 1960. Pp. 45–51.

Jones, N. F., & Kahn, M. W. Patient attitudes as related to social class and other variables concerned with hospitalization. *Journal of Counseling Psychology*, 1964, **28**, 403–408.

Jones, N. F., Kahn, M. W., & Wolcott, O. Wearing street clothing by mental hospital personnel. *International Journal of Social Psychiatry*, 1964, **10**, 216–222.

Jourard, S. M. The effects of experimenter's self-disclosure on subject's behavior. In C. Speilberger (Ed.), *Current topics in community and clinical psychology*. New York: Academic Press, 1969. Pp. 109–150.

Jourard, S. M., & Landsman, M. Cognition, cathexis, and the dyadic effect on men's self-disclosing behavior. *Merrill Palmer Quarterly*, 1960, **6**, 178–186.

Jourard, S. M., & Richman, P. Some factors in the self-disclosure inputs of college students. *Merrill Palmer Quarterly*, 1963, **9**, 141–148.

Judd, C. H. Practice and its effects on the perception of illusions. *Psychological Review,* 1902, **9**, 27–39.

Kadushin, C. *Why people go to psychiatrists.* New York: Atherton Press, 1969.

Kagan, N. Television in counselor supervision—educational tool or toy? In M. M. Berger (Ed.), *Videotape techniques in psychiatric training and treatment.* New York: Brunner Mazel, 1970. Pp. 83–92.

Kahl, J. A. *The American class structure.* New York: Holt, 1957.

Kalis, B. L. Crisis theory: Its relevance for community psychology and directions for development. In D. Adelson & B. L. Kalis (Eds.), *Community psychology and mental health.* Scranton, Pa.: Chandler, 1970. Pp. 69–88.

Kanfer, F. H., & Phillips, J. S. *Learning foundations of behavior therapy.* New York: Wiley, 1970.

Kasius, R. V. The social breakdown syndrome in a cohort of long-stay patients in the Dutchess County unit, 1960–1963. In E. M. Gruenberg (Ed.), *Evaluating the effectiveness of community mental health services.* New York: Milbank, 1966.

Kelley, G. A. *The psychology of personal constructs.* New York: Norton, 1955.

Kelley, H. H. Warm-cold variable in first impressions. *Journal of Personality,* 1950, **18**, 431–439.

Kerckhoff, A. C. Early antecedants of role-taking and role-playing ability. *Merrill-Palmer Quarterly,* 1969, 15, 227–247.

Kiesler, D. J. Some myths of psychotherapy research and the search for a paradigm. *Psychological Bulletin,* 1966, **65**, 110–136.

Kiesler, D. J. Patient experiencing and successful outcome in individual psychotherapy of schizophrenics and psychoneurotics. *Journal of Consulting and Clinical Psychology,* 1971, **37**, 370–385.

Kiev, A. *Magic, faith and healing.* New York: Free Press of Glencoe, 1964.

King, B. T., & Janis, I. L. Comparison of the effectiveness of improvised versus non-improvised role playing in producing opinion change. *Human Relations,* 1956, **9**, 177–186.

King, G. F., Armistage, S. G., & Tilton, J. R. A therapeutic approach to schizophrenics of extreme pathology: An operant-interpersonal method. *Journal of Abnormal and Social Psychology,* 1960, **61**, 276–286.

Klatskin, E. H. Shifts in child care practices in three social classes under an infant care program of flexible methodology. *American Journal of Orthopsychiatry,* 1952, **22**, 52–61.

Klee, G. P. An ecological analysis of diagnosed mental illness in Baltimore. Paper presented at American Psychiatric Association, Baltimore, 1966.

Klein, D. C. Some concepts concerning the mental health of the individual. *Journal of Consulting Psychology,* 1960, 24, 288–293.

Klein, M. H., Mathieu, P. L., & Kiesler, D. J. *The experiencing scale: A research and training manual.* Madison, Wisc.: Wisconsin Psychiatric Institute, 1969.

Kleiner, R. J., & Parker, S. Migration and mental illness: A new look. *American Sociological Review,* 1959, 24, 687–690.

Kleiner, R. J., & Parker, S. Goal-striving, social status, and mental disorder: A research review. *American Sociological Review,* 1963, **28**, 169–203.

Kleinsasser, L. D. The reduction of performance anxiety as a function of desensitization, pretherapy vicarious learning, and vicarious learning alone. Unpublished doctoral dissertation, Pennsylvania State University, 1968.

Knapp, P. H. *Expression of the emotions in men.* New York: International Universities Press, 1963.

Koegler, R. R., & Brill, N. I. *Treatment of psychiatric outpatients.* New York: Appleton, 1967.

Kohn, M. L. Social class and parental values. *American Journal of Sociology*, 1959, **44**, 337–35. (a)

Kohn, M. L. Social class and the exercise of parental authority. *American Sociological Review*, 1959, **24**, 352–366. (b)

Kohn, M. L. Social class and parent-child relationships: An interpretation. *American Journal of Sociology*, 1963, **68**, 471–480.

Kohn, M. L. *Class and conformity.* Homewood, Ill.: Dorsey Press, 1969.

Kohn, M. L. Social class and schizophrenia: A critical review. In H. Wechsler, L. Soloman & B. M. Kramer (Eds.), *Social psychology and mental health.* New York: Holt, 1970. Pp. 113–127.

Kohn, M. L., & Clausen, J. A. Social isolation and schizophrenia. *American Sociological Review*, 1955, **20**, 265–273.

Korman, L. Getting to know the experimenter and its effects on Edward's Personal Preference Schedule test performance. Unpublished master's thesis, University of Florida, 1967.

Kotlar, S. L. Middle-class marital role perceptions and marital adjustment. *Sociological and Social Research*, 1965, **49**, 283–293.

Kraft, A. M. The therapeutic community. In S. Arieti (Ed.), *American handbook of psychiatry*, New York: Basic Books, 1966. Vol. 3, Pp. 542–551.

Krasner, L. Studies of the conditioning of verbal behavior. *Psychological Bulletin*, 1958, **55**, 148–170.

Krasner, L. Role taking research and psychotherapy. *Research Report of VA Palo Alto*, 1959, No. 5.

Kraus, P. S. Considerations and problems of ward care for schizophrenic patients. *Psychiatry*, 1954, **17**, 283–292.

Krumboltz, J. D., & Goodwin, D. L. Increasing task-oriented behavior: An experimental evaluation of training teachers in reinforcement techniques. Stanford, Calif.: Stanford University School of Education, 1966.

Krumboltz, J. D., & Schroeder, W. W. Promoting career planning through reinforcement. *Personnel and Guidance Journal*, 1965, **44**, 19–26.

Krumboltz, J. D., Varenhorst, B. B., & Thorensen, C. E. Non-verbal factors in the effectiveness of models in counseling. *Journal of Counseling Psychology*, 1967, **14**, 412–418.

Labov, W. The logic of nonstandard English. In F. Williams (Ed.), *Language and poverty.* Chicago: Markham, 1970. Pp. 153–189.

Lack, D. Z. The effect of a model and instructions on psychotherapist self-disclosure. Unpublished master's thesis, Syracuse University, 1971.

LaFleur, N. K., & Johnson, R. G. Separate effects of social modeling and reinforcement in counseling adolescents. *Journal of Conseling Psychology*, 1972, **19**, 292–295.

Landy, E. *The underground dictionary.* New York: Simon & Schuster, 1971.

Lang, W. J. An exploratory study of the use of role playing with severely retarded children. *American Journal of Mental Deficiency*, 1959, **63**, 784–791.

Langner, T. S., & Michael, S. T. *Life stress and mental health.* Glencoe, Ill.: Free Press, 1963.

Lapouse, R., Monk, M., & Terris, M. The drift hypothesis and socio-economic differentials in schizophrenia. *American Journal of Public Health*, 1956, **46**, 978–986.

Lawton, D. *Social class, language and education*. New York: Schocken Books, 1968.

Lazarsfield, P. F., & Kendall, P. The communication behavior of the average American. In W. L. Schramm (Ed.), *Mass communication*. Urbana: Univ. of Illinois Press, 1966. Pp. 425–437.

Lazarus, A. A. Behavior therapy, incomplete treatment, and symptom substitution. *Journal of Nervous Mental Disease*, 1965, **140**, 80–86.

Lazarus, A. A. Behavior rehearsal vs. non-directive therapy vs. advice in effecting behavior change. *Behavior Research and Therapy*, 1966, **4**, 209–212.

Lee, R. E., & Schneider, R. F. Hypertension and arteriosclerosis in executive and nonexecutive personnel. *Journal of the American Medical Association*, 1958, **167**, 1447–1450.

Lee, S. D., & Temerlin, M. K. Social class, diagnosis and prognosis for psychotherapy. *Psychotherapy: Theory, Research and Practice*, 1970, **7**, 181–185.

Lefcourt, H. M. Internal versus external control of reinforcement: A review. *Psychological Bulletin*, 1966, **65**, 206–220.

Lefkowitz, M. M., Blake, R. R., & Mouton, J. S. Status factors in pedestrian violation of traffic signals. *Journal of Abnormal and Social Psychology*, 1955, **51**, 704–706.

Leighton, A. H. *Psychiatric disorders among the Yoruba*. Ithaca, N. Y.: Cornell Univ. Press, 1963.

Leighton, D. C., & Lambo, T. Psychiatric findings of the Stirling County study. *American Journal of Psychiatry*, 1963, **119**, 1021–1026.

Lemert, E. M. An exploratory study of mental disorder in a rural problem area. *Rural Sociology*, 1948, **13**, 18–60.

Lennard, H. L., & Bernstein, A. *The anatomy of psychotherapy*. New York: Columbia Univ. Press, 1960.

Lerner, B. *Therapy in the ghetto*. Baltimore: Johns Hopkins Press, 1972.

Leshan, L. L. Time orientation and social class. *Journal of Abnormal and Social Psychology*, 1952, **47**, 589–592.

Lesser, G. S., Fifer, G., & Clark, D. H. Mental abilities of children from different social class and cultural groups. *Child Development Monographs*, 1965, **30**, No. 4.

Levine, S., & Scotch, N. A. *Social stress*. Chicago: Aldine, 1970.

Levinger, G., & Breedlove, J. Interpersonal attraction and agreement: A study of marriage partners. *Journal of Personality and Social Psychology*, 1966, **3**, 367–372.

Levit, G., & Jennings, H. *Learning through role playing*. Adult Education Association, 1960.

Levy, D. M. Trends in therapy: III. Release therapy. *American Journal of Orthopsychiatry*, 1939, **9**, 713–737.

Levy, M., & Kahn, M. Interpreter bias on the Rorschach test as a function of patients' socioeconomic status. *Journal of Projective Techniques and Personality Assessment*, 1970, **34**, 106–112.

Liberman, B. The effect of modeling procedures on attraction and disclosure in a psychotherapy analogue. Unpublished doctoral dissertation, Syracuse University, 1970.

Lichtenstein, E., Keutzer, C. S., & Himes, K. H. "Emotional" role playing and changes in smoking attitudes and behavior. *Psychological Reports*, 1969, **25**, 379–387.

Lin, T. Y. Mental disorders in Taiwan, 15 years later. Paper presented on Mental Health in Asia. Honolulu, March 1966.

Lipset, S. M. Value patterns, class and the democratic polity. In R. Bendix & S. M. Lipset (Eds.), *Class, status and power.* New York: Free Press, 1966. Pp. 161–171.

Litvak, S. B. A comparison of two brief group behavior therapy techniques on the reduction of avoidance behavior. *Psychological Record,* 1969, **19**, 329–334.

Locke, B. Problems in interpretation of patterns of first admissions to Ohio State Public Mental Hospitals for patients with schizophrenic reactions. In B. Pasamanick & P. Knapp (Eds.), *Social aspects of psychiatry.* Psychiatric Research Report #10, American Psychiatric Association, 1958. Pp. 172–196.

Lorr, M., & Vestre, N. D. *Psychotic inpatient profile, test and manual.* Los Angeles: Western Psychological Services, 1968.

Lovaas, O. I. A Behavior therapy approach to the treatment of childhood schizophrenia. In J. P. Hill (Ed.), *Minnesota symposia on child psychology.* Minneapolis: Univ. of Minnesota Press, 1967. Pp. 108–159.

Lovaas, O. I., Berberick, J. P., Perloff, B. F., & Schaeffer, B. Acquisition of imitative speech by schizophrenic children. *Science,* 1966, **151**, 705–707.

Lovaas, O. I., Freitag, L., Nelson, K., & Whalen, C. The establishment of imitation and its use for the development of complex behavior in schizophrenic children. *Behavior Research and Therapy,* 1967, **5**, 171–181.

Lystad, M. H. Social mobility among selected groups of schizophrenic patients. *American Sociological Review,* 1957, **22**, 288–292.

Maccoby, E. E., & Wilson, W. C. Identification and observational learning from films. *Journal of Abnormal and Social Psychology,* 1957, **55**, 76–87.

Madsen, C. H., Jr., Becker, W. C., & Thomas, D. R. Rules, praise and ignoring: Elements of elementary classroom control. *Journal of Applied Behavior Analysis,* 1968, **1**, 139–150.

Magaro, P. A. A prescriptive treatment model based upon social class and premorbid adjustment. *Psychotherapy: Theory, Research & Practice,* 1969, **6**, 57–70.

Malzberg, B. *Social and biological aspects of mental disease.* Utica, N. Y.: Utica State Hospital Press, 1940.

Malzberg, B. Mental disease in relation to economic status. *Journal of Nervous and Mental Disease,* 1956, **123**, 257–261.

Mandler, G. Transfer of training as a function of degree of response overlearning. *Journal of Experimental Psychology,* 1954, **47**, 411–417.

Mandler, G., & Heinemann, S. H. Effect of overlearning of a verbal response on transfer of training. *Journal of Experimental Psychology,* 1956, **52**, 39–46.

Mann, J. Vicarious desensitization of test anxiety through observation of videotaped treatment. *Journal of Counseling Psychology,* 1972, **19**, 1–7.

Mann, J., & Rosenthal, T. L. Vicarious and direct counterconditioning of test anxiety through individual and group desensitization. *Behavior Research and Therapy,* 1969, **7**, 359–367.

Mann, J. H. Experimental evaluations of role playing. *Psychological Bulletin,* 1956, **53**, 227–234.

Mann, L. The effects of emotional role playing on desire to modify smoking habits. *Journal of Experimental Social Psychology,* 1967, **3**, 334–348.

Marlatt, G. A., Jacobson, E. A., Johnson, D. L., & Morrice, D. J. Effect of exposure to a model receiving evaluative feedback upon subsequent behavior in an interview. *Journal of Consulting and Clinical Psychology,* 1970, **34**, 104–112.

Marshall, H. R., & Hahn, S. C. Experimental modification of dramatic play. *Journal of Personality and Social Psychology,* 1967, **5**, 119–122.

Masters, J. C. Treatment of "adolescent rebellion" by the reconstrual of stimuli. *Journal of Consulting and Clinical Psychology,* 1970, **35,** 213–216.

Masters, J. C., & Branch, M. N. A comparison of the relative effectiveness of instructions, modeling and reinforcement procedures for inducing behavior change. *Journal of Experimental Psychology,* 1969, **80,** 364–368.

Matarazzo, J. D., & Wiens, A. N. Interviewer influence on durations of interviewee silence. *Journal of Experimental Research in Personality,* 1967, **2,** 56–59.

Matarazzo, J. D., Wiens, A. N., & Saslow, G. Studies in interview speech behavior. In L. Krasner & L. P. Ullmann (Eds.), *Research in behavior modification.* New York: Holt, 1965. Pp. 179–210.

Matheny, K. B., & Oslin, Y. Utilization of paraprofessionals in education and the helping professions. Presented at American Educational Research Association, Minneapolis, 1970.

Mayer, J. E., & Timms, N. Clash in perspective between worker and client. *Social Casework,* 1969, **50,** 32–40.

Mayo, E. Psychiatry and sociology in relation to social disorganization. *American Journal of Sociology,* 1937, **42,** 825–831.

McCarthy, D. M. The language development of the pre-school child. *The Institute of Child Welfare—Monographs,* No. 4, 1930.

McClelland, D. C., Atkinson, J. W., Clark, R. A., & Lowell, E. L. *The achievement motive.* New York: Appleton, 1953.

McDonald, L. *Social class and delinquency.* London: Faber & Faber, 1969.

McDougall, W. *An introduction to social psychology.* London: Methuen, 1908.

McFall, R. M., & Lillesand, D. B. Behavioral rehearsal with modeling and coaching in assertion training. *Journal of Abnormal Psychology,* 1971, **77,** 313–323.

McFall, R. M., & Marston, A. R. An experimental investigation of behavior rehearsal in assertive training. *Journal of Abnormal Psychology,* 1970, **76,** 295–303.

McGhie, A. *Pathology of attention.* Baltimore: Penguin Books, 1969.

McMahon, A. W., & Shore, M. F. Some psychological reactions to working with the poor. *Archives of General Psychiatry,* 1968, **18,** 562–568.

McMahon, J. T. The working class psychiatric patient: A clinical view. In F. Riessman, J. Cohen & A. Pearl (Eds.), *Mental health of the poor.* New York: Free Press, 1964. Pp. 283–302.

McNair, D. M., Callahan, D. M., & Lorr, M. Therapist "type" and patient response to psychotherapy. *Journal of Consulting Psychology,* 1962, **26,** 425–429.

McNair, D. M., & Lorr, M. An analysis of mood in neurotics. *Journal of Abnormal and Social Psychology,* 1964, **69,** 620–626.

Mechanic, D. The influence of mothers on their children's health attitudes and behavior. *Pediatrics,* 1965, **33,** 444–453.

Mehrabian, A. Significance of posture and position in the communication of attitude and status relationships. *Psychological Bulletin,* 1969, **71,** 359–372. (a)

Mehrabian, A. Some referents and measures of nonverbal behavior. *Behavior Research Methods and Instrumentation,* 1969, **1,** 203–207. (b)

Mehrabian, A., & Friar, J. T. Encoding of attitude by a seated communicator via posture, orientation, and distance cues. *Journal of Consulting and Clinical Psychology,* 1969, **33,** 330–336.

Meichenbaum, D. Examination of model characteristics in reducing avoidance behavior. *Journal of Personality and Social Psychology,* 1971, **17,** 298–307. (a)

Meichenbaum, D. Reducing fear by modifying what clients say to themselves: A means of developing stress inoculation. Unpublished manuscript, University of Waterloo, 1971. (b)

Meichenbaum, D. Cognitive modification of test anxious college students. *Journal of Consulting and Clinical Psychology,* in press.

Meichenbaum, D., & Goodman, J. Training impulsive children to talk to themselves: A means of developing self-control. *Journal of Abnormal Psychology,* 1971, **77,** 115–126.

Meichenbaum, D., Gilmore, J., & Fedoravicius, A. Group insight vs. group desensitization in treating speech anxiety. *Journal of Consulting and Clinical Psychology,* 1971, **36,** 410–421.

Meldman, M. J. *Diseases of attention and perception.* New York: Pergamon, 1970.

Merry, J. An experiment in a chronic psychotic ward. *British Journal of Medical Psychology,* 1956, **29,** 287–293.

Merton, R. *Social theory and social structure.* Glencoe, Ill.: Free Press, 1957.

Meyer, E., Spiro, H. R., Slaughter, R., Pollack, I. W., Weingartner, H., & Novey, S. Contractually time-limited psychotherapy in an outpatient psychosomatic clinic. *American Journal of Psychiatry,* 1967, **124,** 57–68.

Meyer, R. J., & Haggerty, R. J. Streptococcal infections in families: Factors altering individual susceptibility. *Pediatrics,* 1962, **29,** 539–549.

Michaels, J. A. High school climates and plans for entering college. *Public Opinion Quarterly,* 1961, **20,** 585–595.

Milby, J. B. Modification of extreme social isolation by contingent social reinforcement. *Journal of Applied Behavior Analysis,* 1970, **3,** 149–152.

Miller, D., & Swanson, G. E. *The changing American parent.* New York: Wiley, 1958.

Miller, D. H. The rehabilitation of chronic open ward neuropsychiatric patients. *Psychiatry,* 1954, **17,** 287–293.

Miller, D. H., & Clancy, J. An approach to the social rehabilitation of chronic psychotic patients. *Psychiatry,* 1952, **15,** 435–443.

Miller, G. A. *Language and communication.* New York: McGraw-Hill, 1951.

Miller, G. A., Heise, G. A., & Lichten, W. The intelligibility of speech as a function of the test material. *Journal of Experimental Psychology,* 1951, **41,** 329–335.

Miller, H. A. The oppression psychoses. In *Race, nations and classes.* Philadelphia: Lippincott, 1924. Pp. 32–38.

Miller, J. G. Information input overload and psychopathology. *American Journal of Psychiatry,* 1960, **116,** 695–704.

Miller, K., & Iscoe, I. The concept of crisis: Current status and mental health implications. *Human Organization,* 1963, **22,** 195–201.

Miller, N. E., & Dollard, J. *Social learning and imitation.* New Haven: Yale Univ. Press, 1941.

Miller, P. M., & Drennen, W. T. Establishment of social reinforcement as an effective modifier of verbal behavior in chronic psychiatric patients. *Journal of Abnormal Psychology,* 1970, **76,** 392–395.

Miller, W. B. Implications of urban lower-class culture for social work. *Social Science Review,* 1959, **33,** 219–236.

Miller, S. M., Mishler, E. G. Social class, mental illness and American psychiatry. In F. Riessman, J. Cohen & A. Pearl (Eds.), *Mental health of the poor.* New York: Free Press, 1964. Pp. 16–36.

Miller, S. M., & Riessman, F. The working class subculture: A new view. In A. L. Grey (Ed.), *Class and personality in society.* New York: Atherton Press, 1969. Pp. 99–117.

Minuchin, S., & Montalvo, B. An approach for diagnosis of the low socioeconomic family. *Psychiatric Research Reports,* 1966, **20,** 163–174.

Mishler, E. G., & Scotch, N. A. Sociocultural factors in the epidemiology of schizophrenia. *Psychiatry,* 1963, **26,** 315–351.

Mitchell, J. V. Identification of items in the California test of personality that differentiate between subjects of high and low socioeconomic status at the 5th and 7th grade levels. *Journal of Educational Research,* 1957, **51,** 241–250.

Mitchell, K. M., & Namenek, T. M. A comparison of therapist and client social class. *Professional Psychology,* 1970, **1,** 225–229.

Moore, F. J., Chernell, E., & West, M. J. Television as a therapeutic tool. *Archives of General Psychiatry,* 1965, **12,** 217–220.

Moos, R. H. *Ward atmosphere scale, test and manual.* Stanford: Stanford University School of Medicine, 1969.

Morgan, C. L. *Habit and instinct.* London: Arnold, 1896.

Mowrer, O. H. Freudianism, behavior therapy and self-disclosure. *Behavior Research and Therapy,* 1963, **11,** 321–337.

Mowrer, O. H. The behavior therapies with special reference to modeling and imitation. *American Journal of Psychotherapy,* 1966, **20,** 429–461.

Murphy, R. J. Stratification and mental illness: Issues and strategies for research. In S. C. Ploz & R. B. Edgerton (Eds.), *Changing perspectives in mental illness.* New York: Holt, 1969. Pp. 313–335.

Mussen, P. H., Conger, J. J., & Kagen, J. *Child development and personality.* New York: Harper, 1963.

Myrick, R. D. Effect of a model on verbal behavior in counseling. *Journal of Counseling Psychology,* 1969, **16,** 185–190.

Navran, L. Communication and adjustment in marriage. *Family Process,* 1967, **6,** 173–184.

Nash, E. H., Hoehn-Saric, R., Battle, C. C., Stone, A. R., Imber, S. D., & Frank, J. D. Systematic preparation of patients for short-term psychotherapy. II. Relation to characteristics of patients, therapists and the psychotherapeutic process. *Journal of Nervous and Mental Disease,* 1965, **140,** 374–383.

Nelson, M. C. Effect of paradigmatic techniques on the psychic economy of borderline patients. *Psychiatry,* 1962, **25,** 119–134.

Neugarten, B. L. Social class and friendships among school children. *American Journal of Sociology,* 1956, **51,** 305–313.

Nichols, H. Role playing in primary grades. *Group Psychotherapy,* 1954, **7,** 238–241.

Nolan, W. J. Occupation and dementia praecox. *New York State Hospital Quarterly,* 1917, **3.**

Nuthman, A. M. Conditioning of a response class on a personality test. *Journal of Abnormal and Social Psychology,* 1957, **54,** 19–23.

Oakes, W. F. Reinforcement of Bales' categories in group discussion. *Psychological Reports,* 1962, **11,** 427–435.

Oakes, W. F., Droge, A. E., & August, B. Reinforcement effects on participation in group discussion. *Psychological Reports,* 1960, **7,** 503–514.

Oakes, W. F., Droge, A. E., & August, B. Reinforcement effects on conclusions reached in group discussion. *Psychological Reports,* 1961, **9,** 27–34.

O'Connell, W. E. Adlerian psychodrama with schizophrenics. *Journal of Individual Psychology,* 1963, **19,** 69–76.

O'Connor, R. D. Modification of symbolic withdrawal through symbolic modeling. *Journal of Applied Behavior Analysis*, 1969, **2**, 15–22.

O'Connor, R. D. Relative efficacy of modeling, shaping, and the combined procedures for modification of social withdrawal. *Journal of Abnormal Psychology*, 1972, **79**, 327–334.

Odegaard, O. Emigration and insanity: A study of mental disease among the Norweigian-born population of Minnesota. *Acta Psychiatrica et Neurologica*, Supp. #4, 1932.

O'Leary, K. D., & O'Leary, S. G. *Classroom management*. New York: Pergamon, 1972.

Olmstead, D. L. Ethnolinguistics so far. In G. L. Prager (Ed.), *Studies of linguistics*. Norman, Okla.: Univ. of Oklahoma, 1950.

Olmstead, J. A. Theory and state of the art of small group methods of instruction. Alexandria, Va.: Human Resources Research Organization, 1970.

Orenstein, R. Effect of teaching patients to focus on their feelings on level of experiencing in a subsequent interview. Unpublished doctoral dissertation, Syracuse University, 1973.

Orne, M. I., & Wender, P. H. Anticipatory socialization for psychotherapy: Method and rationale. *American Journal of Psychiatry*, 1968, **124**, 1202–1212.

Osgood, C. E. The similarity paradox in human learning: A resolution. *Psychological Review*, 1949, **56**, 132–143.

Osgood, C. E. *Method and theory in experimental psychology*. New York: Oxford Univ. Press, 1953.

Otto, H. A. Toward a holistic treatment program. In H. Greenwald (Ed.), *Active psychotherapy*. New York: Atherton Press, 1967. Pp. 145–162.

Overall, B., & Aronson, H. Expectations of psychotherapy in patients of lower socioeconomic class. *American Journal of Orthopsychiatry*, 1963, **33**, 421–430.

Pace, R. E. Situational therapy. *Journal of Personality*, 1957, **25**, 578–588.

Page, M. L. The modification of ascendant behavior in preschool children. *University of Iowa Studies in Child Welfare*, 1935, **12**, 1–69.

Parad, H. J. *Crisis intervention, selected readings*. New York: Family Service Association, 1965.

Parker, S., & Kleiner, R. J. *Mental illness in the urban negro community*. New York: Free Press, 1966.

Parloff, M. B., Iflund, B., & Goldstein, N. Communication of "therapy values" between therapist and schizophrenic patients. *Journal of Nervous and Mental Diseases*, 1960, **130**, 193–199.

Pasamanick, B., & Knoblock, H. Early language behavior in negro children and the testing of intelligence. *Journal of Abnormal and Social Psychology*, 1950, **50**, 401–402.

Pasamanick, B., Roberts, D. W., Lemkau, P. W., & Krueger, D. B. A survey of mental disease in an urban population: Prevalence by race and income. In B. Pasamanick (Ed.), *Epidemiology of mental disorder*. Washington, D. C.: American Association for the Advancement of Sciences, 1959. Pp. 183–191.

Paul, G. L. Chronic mental patient: Current status-future directions. *Psychological Bulletin*, 1969, **71**, 81–94.

Pavenstedt, E. A comparison of the child-rearing environment of upper-lower and very low-lower class families. *American Journal of Orthopsychiatry*, 1963, **35**, 89–98.

Pearlin, L. I., & Kohn, M. L. Social class, occupation, and parental values: A cross-national study. In A. L. Grey (Ed.), *Class and personality in society*. New York: Atherton Press, 1969. Pp. 161–184.

Pell, S., & D'Alonzo, C. A. A three-year study of myocardial infarction in a large employed population. *Journal of the American Medical Association,* 1961, **175,** 463–470.

Pentony, P. Value change in psychotherapy. *Human Relations,* 1966, **19,** 39–46.

Pepinsky, H. B., & Karst, T. O. Convergence, a phenomenon in counseling and psychotherapy. *American Psychologist,* 1964, **19,** 333–338.

Perls, F., Hefferline, R. F., & Goodman, P. *Gestalt therapy: Excitement and growth in the human personality.* New York: Dell Publ., 1951.

Perry, M. A. Didactic instructions for and modeling of empathy. Unpublished doctoral dissertation, Syracuse University, 1970.

Pfautz, H. W. The current literature on social stratification: Critique and bibliography. *American Journal of Sociology,* 1952, **58,** 391–418.

Phillips, E. L. Achievement place: Token reinforcement procedures in a home-style rehabilitation setting for "pre-delinquent" boys. *Journal of Applied Behavior Analysis,* 1968, **1,** 213–223.

Piaget, G. W., & Lazarus, A. A. The use of rehearsal-desensitization. *Psychotherapy: Therory, Research and Practice,* 1969, **6,** 264–266.

Platt, E. S., Krassen, E., & Mausner, B. Individual variation in behavioral change following role playing. *Psychological Reports,* 1969, **24,** 155–170.

Pollack, I. W., Ochberg, F. M., & Meyer, E. Social class and the subjective sense of time. *Archives of General Psychiatry,* 1969, **21,** 1–14.

Prince, R. Psychotherapy and the chronically poor. In J. C. Finney (Ed.), *Culture change, mental health and poverty.* Lexington, Ky.: Univ. of Kentucky Press, 1969. Pp. 20–41.

Queen, S. A. The ecological studies of mental disorder. *American Sociological Review,* 1940, **5,** 201–209.

Rabbie, J. M. Differential preference for companionship under threat. *Journal of Abnormal Social Psychology,* 1963, **67,** 643–648.

Radin, N., & Glasser, P. H. The use of Parental Attitudes Questionnaires with culturally disadvantaged families. *Journal of Marriage and the Family,* 1965, **27,** 373–382.

Rahe, R. H., Meyer, M., Smith, M., Kjaer, G., & Holmes, T. H. Social stress and illness onset. *Journal of Psychosomatic Research,* 1964, **8,** 35–44.

Raines, G. H., & Rehrer, J. H. The operational matrix of psychiatric practice. *American Journal of Psychiatry,* 1955, **111,** 720–733.

Rapaport, L. The state of crisis: Some theoretical considerations. *Social Service Review,* 1962, **36,** 211–217.

Redlich, F. C., Hollingshead, A. B., & Bellis, E. Social class differences in attitudes toward psychiatry. *American Journal of Orthopsychiatry,* 1955, **25,** 60–70.

Rees, T. P., & Glatt, M. M. The organization of a mental hospital on the basis of group participation. *International Journal of Group Psychotherapy,* 1955, **5,** 157–161.

Reimanis, G. Effects of experimental IE modification techniques and home environment variable on IE. Presented at American Psychological Association, Washington, D. C., 1971.

Reiss, A. J., Jr. *Occupations and social status.* Glencoe, Ill.: Free Press, 1961.

Resnick, J.—cited as unpublished in: Jourard, S. M. The effects of experimenter self-disclosure on subject's behavior. In C. Speilberger (Ed.), *Current topics in community and clinical psychology.* New York: Academic Press, 1969.

Rider, R. V., Taback, M., & Knoblock, H. Associations between premature births and socioeconomic status. *American Journal of Public Health,* 1955, **45,** 1022–1028.

Riessman, F. Role-playing and the lower socio-economic group. *Group Psychotherapy,* 1964, **17,** 36–48. (a)

Riessman, F. Are the deprived non-verbal? In F. Riessman, J. Cohen & A. Pearl (Eds.), *Mental health of the poor.* New York: Free Press, 1964. Pp. 188–193. (b)

Riessman, F. Strategies and suggestions for training nonprofessionals. In B. G. Guerney, Jr. (Ed.), *Psychotherapeutic agents.* New York: Holt, 1969. Pp. 152–164.

Riessman, F., & Goldfarb, J. Role playing and the poor. *Group Psychotherapy,* 1964, **17,** 36–48.

Riessman, F., & Miller, S. M. Social class and projective tests. *Journal of Projective Techniques,* 1958, **22,** 432–439.

Riessman, F., Cohen, J., & Pearl, A. *Mental health of the poor.* New York: Free Press, 1964.

Rimm, D. C., & Madeiros, D. C. The role of muscle relaxation in participant modeling. *Behavior Research and Therapy,* 1970, **8,** 127–132.

Rimm, D. C., & Mahoney, M. J. The application of reinforcement and participant modeling procedures in the treatment of snake-phobic behavior. *Behavior Research and Therapy,* 1969, **7,** 369–376.

Risley, T., & Wolf, M. Establishing functional speech in echolalic children. *Behavior Research and Therapy,* 1967, **5,** 73–88.

Ritter, B. Treatment of dissection phobia. Unpublished manuscript, Queens College, 1965.

Ritter, B. Eliminating excessive fears of the environment through contact desensitization. In J. B. Krumboltz & C. E. Thoreson (Eds.), *Behavioral counseling: Cases and techniques.* New York: Holt, 1969. Pp. 168–178. (a)

Ritter, B. Treatment of acrophobia with contact desensitization. *Behavior Research and Therapy,* 1969, **7,** 41–45. (b)

Roach, J. L., & Gursslin, O. R. The lower class, status frustration, and social disorganization. *Social Forces,* 1964–1965, **43,** 501–510.

Rogers, C. R. The necessary and sufficient conditions of therapeutic personality change. *Journal of Consulting Psychology,* 1957, **21,** 95–103.

Rogers, C. R., Gendlin, E. T., Kiesler, D. J., & Truax, C. B. *The therapeutic relationship and its impact: A study of psychotherapy with schizophrenics.* Madison: Univ. of Wisconsin Press, 1967.

Rogler, L. H., & Hollingshead, A. B. *Trapped: Families and schizophrenia.* New York: Wiley, 1965.

Roman, P. M., & Trice, H. M. *Schizophrenia and the poor.* Ithaca, N. Y.: Cornell Univ. Press, 1967.

Rosen, B. C. The achievement syndrome: A psychocultural dimension of social stratification. *American Sociological Review,* 1956, **21,** 203–211.

Rosenbaum, M. E., & Arenson, S. J. Observational learning: Some theory, some variables, some findings. In E. C. Simmel, R. A. Hoppe & G. A. Milton (Eds.), *Social facilitation and imitative behavior.* Boston: Allyn & Bacon, 1968. Pp. 111–134.

Rosenberg, P. An experimental analysis of psychodrama. Unpublished doctoral dissertation, Harvard University, 1952.

Rosenblatt, D., & Suchman, E. A. Blue-collar attitudes and information toward health and illness. In A. B. Shostak & W. Gomberg (Eds.), *Blue collar world.* Englewood Cliffs, N. J.: Prentice-Hall, 1964. Pp. 324–333.

Rosenblith, J. F. Learning by imitation in kindergarten children. *Child Development,* 1959, **30,** 69–80.

Rosenblith, J. F. Imitative color choices in kindergarten children. *Child Development,* 1961, 32, 211–223.

Rosenhan, D., & White, G. M. Observation and rehearsal as determinants of prosocial behavior. *Journal of Personality and Social Psychology,* 1967, 5, 424, 431.

Rosenstock, I. M. Public knowledge, opinion and action concerning three public health issues. *Journal of Health and Human Behavior,* 1966, 7, 91–98.

Rosenthal, D. Changes in some moral values following psychotherapy. *Journal of Consulting Psychology,* 1955, 19, 431–436.

Rosenthal, D., & Frank, J. D. The fate of psychiatric clinic outpatients assigned to psychotherapy. *Journal of Nervous and Mental Diseases,* 1958, 127, 330–343.

Rosenzweig, S. *Rosenzweig picture-frustration study, test and manual.* St. Louis, Author, 1947.

Ross, J. A. Social class and medical care. *Journal of Health and Human Behavior,* 1962, 3, 35–40.

Roth, J., & Peck, R. F. Social class and social mobility factors related to marital adjustment. *American Sociological Review,* 1951, 16, 478–487.

Rothaus, P. Instrumented role playing in psychiatric training laboratory. *Archives of General Psychiatry,* 1964, 11, 400–410.

Rothaus, P., & Morton, R. B. Problem-centered versus mental illness self-descriptions. *Journal of Health and Human Behavior,* 1962, 3, 198–203.

Rotter, J. B. *Social learning and clinical psychology.* Englewood cliffs, N. J.: Prentice-Hall, 1954.

Rotter, J. B. Generalized expectancies for internal versus external control of reinforcement. *Psychological Monographs,* 1966, 80, Whole No. 609.

Rotter, J. B. A new scale for the measurement of interpersonal trust. *Journal of Personality,* 1967, 35, 651–665.

Ruesch, J. *Disturbed communication.* New York: Norton, 1957.

Ruhe, D. S., Gundle, S., Laybourne, P. C., Forman, L. H., & Jacobs, M. Television in the teaching of psychiatry. *Journal of Medical Education,* 1960, 35, 916–927.

Salzinger, K., & Pisoni, S. Reinforcement of verbal affect responses of schizophrenics during the clinical interview. Presented at American Psychological Association, New York, 1957.

Sanders, R., Smith, R. S., & Weinman, B. S. *Chronic psychoses and recovery.* San Francisco: Jossey-Bass, 1967.

Sapir, E. Communication. *Encyclopedia of Social Science,* 1931, 4, 78–81.

Sarason, I. G., & Ganzer, V. J. Social influence techniques in clinical and community psychology. In C. D. Spielberger (Ed.), *Current topics in clinical and community psychology.* New York: Academic Press, 1969. Pp. 1–66.

Schaefer, H. H., & Martin, P. L. Behavioral therapy for "apathy" of hospitalized schizophrenics. *Psychological Reports,* 1966, 19, 1147–1155.

Schaeffer, D. T., & Von Nessen, R. Intervention for disadvantaged girls: Insight for school faculties. *American Journal of Orthopsychiatry,* 1968, 38, 666–671.

Schaffer, L., & Myers, J. K. Psychotherapy and social stratification. *Psychiatry,* 1954, 17, 83–93.

Schatzman, L., & Strauss, A. Social class and modes of communication. *American Journal of Sociology,* 1955, 60, 329–338.

Scheflin, A. E. The significance of posture in communication systems. *Psychiatry,* 1964, 27, 316–331.

Schermerhorn, R. A. Social psychiatry. In A. M. Rose (Ed.), *Mental health and mental disorder.* London: Routledge & Kegan, 1956. Pp. 42–60.

Schmidt, W., Smart, R. G., & Moss, M. K. *Social class and the treatment of alcoholism.* Toronto: Univ. of Toronto Press, 1968.

Schneider, L., & Lysgaard, S. The deferred gratification pattern: A preliminary study. *American Sociological Review,* 1953, **18,** 142–149.

Schneiderman, L. Social class, diagnosis and treatment. *American Journal of Orthopsychiatry,* 1965, **35,** 99–105.

Schneiman, R. An evaluation of structured learning and didactic learning as methods of training behavior modification skills to low and middle socio-economic level teacher-aides. Unpublished doctoral dissertation, Syracuse University, 1972.

Schofield, W. *Psychotherapy, the purchase of friendship.* Englewood Cliffs, N. J.: Prentice-Hall, 1964.

Schorr, A. L. *Slums and social insecurity.* London: Nelson, 1964.

Schorr, A. L. Housing policy and poverty. In P. Townsend (Ed.), *The concept of poverty.* London: Heinemann, 1970. Pp. 113–123.

Schroeder, C. W. Mental disorders in cities. *American Journal of Sociology,* 1942, **48,** 40–47.

Schroeder, H., & Suedfeld, P. *Personality theory and information processing.* New York: Ronald Press, 1970.

Schroeder, H., Driver, M., & Streufert, S. *Human information processing.* New York: Holt, 1965.

Schulberg, H. C., & Sheldon, A. The probability for crisis and strategies for preventive intervention. *Archives of General Psychiatry,* 1968, **18,** 553–558.

Schutz, W. C. *Fundamental interpersonal relations orientation-behavior, test and manual.* Palo Alto: Consulting Psychologists Press, 1967.

Schwartz, A. N., & Hawkins, H. L. Patient models and affect statements in group therapy. Presented at American Psychological Association, Washington, D. C., 1965.

Schwartz, D. T., & Mintz, N. L. Ecology and psychosis among Italians in 27 Boston communities. *Social Problems,* 1963, **10,** 371–374.

Schwartz, M. S. The economic and spatial mobility of paranoid schizophrenics and manic depressives. Unpublished masters thesis, University of Chicago, 1946.

Scott, W. O. Social psychological correlates of mental illness and mental health. *Psychological Bulletin,* 1958, **55,** 72–87.

Sears, R. R., Maccoby, E. E., & Levin, H. *Patterns of child rearing.* New York: Harper, 1957.

Sewell, W. H. Social class and childhood personality. *Sociometry,* 1961, **24,** 340–356.

Sewell, W. H., & Haller, A. O. Factors in the relationship between social status and the personality adjustment of the child. *American Sociological Review,* 1959, **24,** 511–521.

Sexton, P. C. *Education and income.* New York: Viking Press, 1961.

Shader, R. I., Binstock, W. A., Scott, D. Subjective determinants of drug prescription: A study of therapists' attitudes. *Hospital and Community Psychiatry,* 1968, **19,** 384–387.

Shaffer, J. B. Paradigmatic therapy and the low income patient. In M. C. Nelson, B. Nelson, M. H. Sherman & H. S. Strean (Eds.), *Roles and paradigms in therapy.* New York: Grune & Stratton, 1967. Pp. 249–263.

Shapiro, D. A. Empathy, warmth and genuineness in psychotherapy. *British Journal of Social and Clinical Psychology,* 1969, **8,** 350–361.

Sherif, M. *The psychology of social norms.* New York: Harper, 1936.

Sherman, J. S. Use of reinforcement and imitation to reinstate verbal behavior in mute psychotics. *Journal of Abnormal Psychology,* 1965, **70,** 155–164.

Shore, E., & Sechrest, L. Concept attainment as a function of number of positive instances presented. *Journal of Educational Psychology*, 1961, **52**, 303–307.

Shostak, A. B. *Blue-collar life.* New York: Random House, 1969.

Shuy, R. W. The sociolinguists and urban language problems. In F. Williams (Ed.), *Language and poverty.* Chicago: Markham, 1970. Pp. 335–350.

Siegel, N. H., Kahn, R. L., Pollack, M., & Fink, M. Social class, diagnoses and treatment in three psychiatric hospitals. *Social Problems*, 1962, **10**, 191–196.

Sifneos, P. E. A concept of emotional crisis. *Mental Hygiene*, 1960, **45**, 169–179.

Simon, W. B. The outpatient waiting list. *American Journal of Psychotherapy*, 1967, **21**, 54–61.

Slavson, S. R. *Activity group therapy.* (16 mm. sound film.) New York: Columbia Univ. Press, 1950.

Sloane, H. N., Johnston, M. K., & Harris, F. R. Remedial procedures for teaching verbal behavior to speech deficient or defective young children. In H. N. Sloane & B. A. MacAuley (Eds.), *Operant procedures in remedial speech and language training.* Boston: Houghton, 1968. Pp. 77–101.

Sloane, R. B., Cristol, A. J., Pepernik, M. C., & Staples, F. R. Role preparation and expectation of improvement in psychotherapy. *Journal of Nervous and Mental Diseases*, 1970, **150**, 18–26.

Sobel, R., & Ingalls, A. Resistance to treatment: Explorations of the patient's sick role. *American Journal of Psychotherapy*, 1964, **18**, 562–573.

Sorcher, M., & Goldstein, A. P. *Applied learning in supervisor training.* New York: Pergamon Press, in press.

Spiegler, M. D., Liebert, R. M., McMains, M. J., & Fernandez, L. E. Experimental development of a modeling treatment to extinguish persistent avoidance behavior. Unpublished manuscript, Vanderbilt University, 1968.

Spiritas, A. A., & Holmes, D. S. Effects of models on interview responses. *Journal of Counseling Psychology*, 1971, **18**, 217–220.

Springer, N. N. The influence of general social status on the emotional stability of children. *Journal of Genetic Psychology*, 1938, **53**, 321–328.

Srole, L., & Langner, T. Socioeconomic status groups: Their mental health composition. In L. Srole, T. Langner, S. Michael, M. Kapter & T. Rennie, *Mental health in the metropolis: The mid-town Manhattan study.* Vol. 1. New York: McGraw-Hill, 1962. Pp. 210–239.

Stadt, Z. M. Socioeconomic status and dental caries experience of 3,911 five-year old natives of Contra Costa County, California. *Journal of Public Health Dentistry,* 1967, **27**, 2–6.

Staples, F. R., Wilson, F. S., & Walters, R. H. Increasing the verbal responsiveness of chronic schizophrenics. Unpublished manuscript, University of Waterloo, 1963.

Steffy, R., Torney, D., Hart, J., Craw, M., & Martlett, N. An application of learning techniques to the management and rehabilitation of severely regressed, chronically ill patients: Preliminary findings. Presented at the Orthopsychiatric Association, Ottawa, Canada, 1966.

Stein, N., Goldstein, A. P., Driscoll, S., & Sheets, J. Contingency management training through structured learning. Unpublished manuscript, Syracuse University, 1973.

Stendler, B. Sixty years of child training practices. *Journal of Pediatrics*, 1950, **36**, 122–134.

Stendler, C. B. *Children of Brasstown: Their awareness of the symbols of social class.* Urbana, Ill.: Univ. of Illinois Press, 1949.

Stevenson, I. The use of rewards and punishments in psychotherapy. *Comprehensive Psychiatry*, 1962, **3**, 20–28.

Stewart, W. A. Toward a history of American negro dialect. In F. Williams (Ed.), *Language and poverty*. Chicago: Markham, 1970. Pp. 351–379.

Stieper, D. R., & Wiener, D. N. *Dimensions of psychotherapy*. Chicago: Aldine, 1965.

Stodolsky, S. S., & Lesser, G. Learning patterns in the disadvantaged. *Harvard Educational Review*, 1967, **37**, 546–593.

Stoller, F. TV and the patient's self-image. *Frontiers of Hospital Psychiatry*, 1965, **2**, 1–2.

Strean, H. S. Difficulties met in the treatment of adolescents. *Psychoanalysis and Psychoanalytic Review*, 1961, **48**, 69–80.

Streltzer, N. E., & Koch, G. V. Influence of emotional role-playing on smoking habits and attitudes. *Psychological Reports*, 1968, **22**, 817–820.

Strotzka, H. Psychotherapy for the working class patient. *Research publication of the association for research in nervous and mental disorders*, 1969, **47**, 256–266.

Strupp, H. H. *Psychotherapists in action*. New York: Grune & Stratton, 1960.

Strupp, H. H., & Bloxom, A. L. Preparing the lower-class patient for psychotherapy: Development and evaluation of a role induction procedure. Unpublished manuscript, Vanderbuilt University, 1971.

Strupp, H. H., & Jenkins, J. J. The development of six sound motion pictures stimulating psychotherapeutic situations. *Journal of Nervous and Mental Disease*, 1963, **136**, 317–328.

Stuckert, R. P. Role perception and marital satisfaction: A configurational approach. *Marriage and Family Living*, 1963, **25**, 415–419.

Sturm, I. E. The behavioristic aspect of psychodrama. *Group Psychotherapy*, 1965, **18**, 50–64.

Sutton-Simon, K. The effects of two types of modeling and rehearsal procedures upon the adequacy of social behavior of hospitalized schizophrenics. Unpublished doctoral dissertation, Syracuse University, 1973.

Sutton, K. Effects of modeled empathy and structured social class upon level of therapist displayed empathy. Unpublished master's thesis, Syracuse University, 1970.

Szwejda, L. F. Observed differences of total caries experience among white children of various socioeconomic groups. *Journal of Public Health Dentistry*, 1960, **20**, 59–66.

Szwejda, L. F. Dental caries experience by race and socioeconomic level after 11 years fluoridation in Charlotte, North Carolina. *Journal of Public Health Dentistry*, 1962, **22**, 91–98.

Taplin, J. R. Crisis theory: Critique and reformulation. *Community Mental Health Journal*, 1971, **7**, 13–23.

Tarde, G. *The Laws of imitation*. New York: Holt, 1903.

Taylor, A. B. Role perception, empathy and marriage adjustment. *Sociological and Social Research*, 1967, **52**, 22–34.

Temerlin, M. K. Diagnostic bias in community mental health. *Community Mental Health Journal*, 1970, **6**, 110–117.

Templin, M. C. Certain language skills in children. *Institute for Child Welfare Monographs*, No. 26. Minneapolis: Univ. of Minnesota Press, 1957.

Thain, H. R. Diagnosis of maladaptive behavior and prognosis for psychotherapy in relation to social class. Unpublished doctoral dissertation, University of Texas, 1968.

Tharp, R. G. Dimensions of marriage roles. *Marriage and Family Living,* 1963, **25,** 389–404.

Tharp, R. G., & Wetzel, R. J. *Behavior modification in the natural environment.* New York: Academic Press, 1969.

Toby, J. Orientation to education as a factor in the school maladjustment of lower-class children. *Social Forces,* 1957, **35,** 259–266.

Trachtman, J. Socio-economic class bias in Rorschach diagnosis: Contributing psychological attributes of the clinician. *Journal of Projective Techniques and Personality Assessment,* 1971, **35,** 229–240.

Traux, C. B. The process of group psychotherapy: Relationships between hypothesized therapeutic conditions and intrapersonal exploration. *Psychological Monographs,* 1961, **75,** Whole No. 511.

Traux, C. B. Effective ingredients in psychotherapy: An approach to unraveling the patient-therapist interaction. *Journal of Counseling Psychology,* 1963, **10,** 256–263.

Truax, C. B., & Carkhuff, R. R. *Toward effective counseling and psychotherapy.* Chicago: Aldine, 1967.

Traux, C. B., Carkhuff, R. R., & Kodman, F. Relationships between therapist-offered conditions and patient change in group psychotherapy. *Journal of Clinical Psychology,* 1965, **21,** 327–329.

Truax, C. B., Wargo, D. G., Carkhuff, R. R., Kodman, F., Jr., & Noles, E. A. Changes in self-concept during group psychotherapy as a function of alternate sessions and vicarious therapy pretraining in institutionalized mental patients and juvenile delinquents. *Journal of Consulting Psychology,* 1966, **30,** 309–314.

Tuckman, J., & Kleiner, R. J. Discrepancy between aspiration and achievement as a predictor of schizophrenia. *Behavioral Science,* 1962, **7,** 443–447.

Tuma, E., & Livson, N. Family socioeconomic status and adolescent attitudes to authority. *Child Development,* 1960, **31,** 387–399.

Tumin, M. M. Social stratification. *The forms and functions of inequality.* Englewood Cliffs, N. J.: Prentice-Hall, 1967.

Turner, R. H. *The social context of ambition.* San Francisco: Chandler, 1964.

Turner, R. J., Wagonfeld, M. Occupational mobility and schizophrenia: An assessment of the social causation and social selection hypothesis. *American Sociological Review,* 1967, **32,** 104–113.

Ullmann, L. P., & Krasner, L. *A psychological approach to abnormal behavior.* Englewood Cliffs, N. J.: Prentice-Hall, 1969.

Ullmann, L. P., Krasner, L., & Edinger, R. L. Verbal conditioning of common associations in long-term schizophrenic patients. *Behavior Research and Therapy,* 1964, **2,** 15–18.

Ulmer, G. Teaching geometry to cultivate reflective thinking: An experimental study with 1239 high school pupils. *Journal of Experimental Education,* 1939, **8,** 18–25.

Umbarger, C. C., Dalsimer, J. S., Morrison, A. P., & Breggin, P. R. *College students in a mental hospital.* New York: Grune & Stratton, 1962.

Underwood, B. J. Associative transfer in verbal learning as a function of response similarity and degree of first-list learning. *Journal of Experimental Psychology,* 1951, **42,** 44–53.

Underwood, B. J., & Schulz, R. W. *Meaningfulness and verbal behavior.* New York: Lippincott, 1960.

United States National Health Center for Statistics, medical care, health status and family income. Washington. D. C.: United States Government Printing Office, No. 10. 1964.

Verplank, W. S. The control of the content of conversation: Reinforcement of statements of opinion. *Journal of Abnormal and Social Psychology*, 1955, **51**, 668–676.

Vygotsky, L. S. *Thought and language*. Cambridge: MIT Press, 1962.

Walker, A., Rablen, R. A., & Rogers, C. R. Development of a scale to measure process change in psychotherapy. *Journal of Clinical Psychology*, 1960, **16**, 79–85.

Wallin, P., & Waldo, L. C. *Social class backgrounds of 8th grade pupils, social composition of their schools, their academic aspirations and school adjustment*. Washington, D. C.: U. S. Office of Education, 1964.

Walsh, W. G. The effect of conformity pressure on attraction and disclosure in an interview. Unpublished masters thesis, Syracuse University, 1970.

Walsh, W. G. The effects of conformity pressure and modeling on the attraction of hospitalized patients toward an interviewer. Unpublished doctoral dissertation, Syracuse University, 1971.

Walters, R. H., Bowen, N. V., & Parke, R. D. Experimentally induced disinhibition of sexual responses. Unpublished manuscript, University of Waterloo, 1963.

Wanklin, J. M., Flemming, D. F., Buck, C. W., & Hobbs, G. E. Factors influencing the rate of first admissions to mental hospital. *Journal of Nervous and Mental Diseases*, 1955, **121**, 103–116.

Warman, R. E. Comments on T. N. Ewing: Changes during counseling appropriate to client's initial problem. *Journal of Counseling Psychology*, 1964, **11**, 151.

Warner, R. W., & Hansen, J. C. Verbal-reinforcement and model-reinforcement group counseling with alienated students. *Journal of Counseling Psychology*, 1970, **17**, 168–172.

Wechsler, H., & Pugh, T. F. Fit of individual and community characteristics and rates of psychiatric hospitalization. *American Journal of Sociology*, 1967, **73**, 331–338.

Whalen, C. Effects of a model and instructions on group verbal behavior. *Journal of Consulting and Clinical Psychology*, 1969, **3**, 509–521.

Whalen, C., & Henker, B. Play therapy conducted by mentally retarded inpatients. *Psychotherapy: Theory, Research and Practice*, 1971, **8**, 236–245.

White, M. S. Social class, child-rearing practices, and child behavior. *American Sociological Review*, 1957, **22**, 704–712.

Whitehorn, J. C., & Betz, B. J. Further studies of the doctor as a crucial variable in the outcome of treatment with schizophrenic patients. *American Journal of Psychiatry*, 1960, **11**, 215–223.

Whorf, B. L. Science and linguistics. In J. B. Carroll (Ed.), *Language, thought and the school*. Cambridge, Mass.: M.I.T. Press, 1956. Pp. 207–219.

Wiener, M., & Mehrabian, A. *Language within language: Immediacy, a channel in verbal communication*. New York: Appleton, 1968.

Wilder, S. N. The effect of verbal modeling and verbal reinforcement on the frequency of self-referred affect statements. *Dissertation Abstracts*, 1968, **28**, 4304–4305B.

Williams, F. Some preliminaries and prospects. In F. Williams (Ed.), *Language and poverty*. Chicago: Markham, 1970. Pp. 1–10.

Williams, F., & Naremore, R. C. On the functional analysis of social class differences in modes of speech. *Speech Monographs*, 1969, **36**, 77–102.

Williams, W. S. Class differences in the attitudes of psychiatric patients. *Social Problems*, 1956, **4**, 240–244.

Wilner, D. M., Walkley, R. P., Pinkerton, T. C., & Tayback, M. *The housing environment and family life*. Baltimore: Johns Hopkins Press, 1962.

Wilson, A. B. Residential segregation of social classes and aspirations of high school boys. *American Sociological Review*, 1959, **24**, 836–845.

Wilson, F. S., & Walters, R. H. Modification of speech output of near-mute schizophrenics through social-learning procedures. *Behavior Research and Therapy*, 1966, **4**, 59–67.

Winder, A. E., & Hersko, M. The effect of social class on the length and type of psychotherapy in a Veterans Administration Mental Hygiene Clinic. *Journal of Clinical Psychology*, 1955, **11**, 77–79.

Wolf, I., Chafetz, M. E., Blane, H. T., & Hill, M. J. Social factors in the diagnosis of alcoholism. *Quarterly Journal of Studies on Alcoholism*, 1965, **26**, 72–79.

Wolfenstein, M. Trends in infant care. *American Journal of Orthopsychiatry*, 1953, **33**, 120–130.

Wolpe, J., & Lazarus, A. A. *Behavior therapy techniques.* New York: Pergamon, 1966.

Woodrow, H. The effect of type of training upon transference. *Journal of Educational Psychology*, 1927, **18**, 159–172.

Wright, C. R., & Hyman, H. H. Voluntary association memberships of American adults: Evidence from national sample surveys. *American Sociological Review*, 1958, **23**, 284–294.

Yalom, I. D., Houts, P. S., Newell, G., & Rand, K. H. Preparation of patients for group therapy. *Archives of General Psychiatry*, 1967, **17**, 416–427.

Yamamoto, J., & Goin, M. K. On the treatment of the poor. *American Journal of Psychiatry*, 1965, **122**, 267–271.

Yonge, K. A. The use of closed-circuit television for the teaching of psychotherapeutic interviewing to medical students. *Canadian Medical Association Journal*, 1965, **92**, 747–751.

Young, B. F., & Rosenberg, M. Role-playing as a participation technique. *Journal of Social Issues*, 1945, **5**, 42–45.

Young, R. K., & Underwood, B. J. Transfer in verbal materials with dissimilar stimuli and response similarity varied. *Journal of Experimental Psychology*, 1954, **47**, 153–159.

Zdep, S. M., & Oakes, W. F. Reinforcement of leadership behavior in group discussion. *Journal of Experimental Social Psychology*, 1967, **3**, 310–320.

Ziferstein, I. The impact of the socioeconomic order on the psychotherapeutic process in the Soviet Union. In S. Lesse (Ed.), *An evaluation of the results of the psychotherapies.* Springfield, Ill.: Thomas, 1968. Pp. 254–268.

Zuckerman, M., & Lubin, B. *Multiple affect adjective checklist.* San Diego: Educational and Industrial Testing Service, 1965.

# SUBJECT INDEX

419

C
D  7
E  8
F  9
G  0
H  1
I   2
J   3